BEETHOVEN ESSAYS

BEETHOVEN
ESSAYS

Maynard Solomon

HARVARD UNIVERSITY PRESS
CAMBRIDGE, MASSACHUSETTS
LONDON, ENGLAND

Text design by Joyce C. Weston

First Harvard University Press paperback edition, 1990

Library of Congress Cataloging in Publication Data

Solomon, Maynard.
  Beethoven essays / Maynard Solomon.
    p.   cm.
  Bibliography: p.
  Includes indexes.
    1. Beethoven, Ludwig van, 1770–1827.   I. Title.
ML410.B4S65 1988
780'.92'4—dc19   87-34227   CIP   MN
ISBN 0-674-06377-5 (alk. paper) (cloth)
ISBN 0-674-06379-1 (paper)

In memory of
Dora and Benjamin Solomon

Contents

Contents

Preface

THIS book contains virtually all of my more important Beethoven essays, most of which were written during the past ten years. Primarily, these are depth studies of psychological, historical, and creative issues whose implications cannot be fully explored within the confines of a narrative biography. It also includes the complete texts of several detailed "background" papers—Beethoven's birth-year delusion, his nobility pretense, his struggle for the guardianship of his nephew, his religious outlook, his creative periods—which could only be summarized in my biography of Beethoven (1977). "The Posthumous Life of Ludwig Maria van Beethoven," "Recherche de Josephine Deym," and part two of "On Beethoven's Deafness" were written expressly for this volume. Similarly, "Antonie Brentano and Beethoven" has been considerably expanded for this occasion, and all of the previously published papers have been extensively revised and corrected. For those who are diverted by psychoanalytic speculation, I have included several papers that ordinarily would be addressed only to specialists in applied psychoanalysis. Those who cannot abide such speculations are cautioned to avoid Chapters 4, 5, and 6.

The past few years have seen a realignment in my view of Beethoven's relation to Romanticism. In seeking to identify a number of obscure literary extracts which Beethoven had copied into his Tagebuch, I had to immerse myself in some of the esoteric literature of the time, especially those writings—mostly long-forgotten—dealing with Indian philosophy and religion. In the process I discovered numerous points of contact between Beethoven and early German Romanticism, not only in its Orientalist manifestation, but in its search for fundamental guiding principles of creativity, aesthetics, and faith. The pattern is one of parallelism rather than of derivation: Beethoven's devotion to the classical aesthetic and to Enlightenment ideals is not thrown into question. Rather, it is precisely in his constant questing for these ideals that Beethoven redefines Romanticism as a yearning for a felicitous condition unattainable in actuality but momentarily reachable in the sphere of his own music. A preliminary conclusion may be that the widespread view of Beethoven as the culminating composer of the Classical style—a view that downplays Beethoven's radical modernism while emphasizing his derivation from eighteenth-century traditions—is only a limited aspect of a many-sided phenomenon. My study of the Ninth Symphony results in some measure from this investigation of the "overlappings" between Beethoven and Romanticism, stressing the ways in which Beethoven's masterworks—like his life—arise out of a perpetual tension between archaic sources and utopian possibilities.

FOR advice, corrections, new information, and suggestions I am grateful to Joseph Kerman (University of California at Berkeley), Alan Tyson (All Souls College, Oxford University), Sieghard Brandenburg (Director, Beethoven-Archiv Bonn), Lewis Lockwood (Harvard University), Clemens Brenneis (Berlin), Martin Staehelin (University of Göttingen), Robert Winter (University of California at Los Angeles), Peter Riethus (Österreichische Nationalbibliothek), Martella Gutiérrez-Denhoff (Beethoven-Archiv, Bonn), Ingrid Scheib-Rothbart (Goethe House, New York), Aileen Ward (New York University), Richard Taruskin (University of California at Berkeley), William S. Newman (University of North Carolina at Chapel Hill), and Douglas Johnson (Rutgers University). W. M. Senner of Arizona State University kindly checked my translations of Brentano documents in Chapter 12. The transcription of Anton Gräffer's copy of Beethoven's Tagebuch is made by kind permission of Stadtarchiv Iserlohn, whose director is Götz Bettge. Alan Tyson's sure editorial hand guided the preparation of the initial bilingual edition of the Tagebuch; many details of its present thoroughgoing revision were suggested by Sieghard Brandenburg. Grateful acknowledgment is also due to the Bayerische Staatsbibliothek Munich, Beethoven-Archiv, Bibliothèque Nationale, British Library, Columbia University Libraries, Deutsche Staatsbibliothek Berlin, Freies Deutsches

Hochstift (Goethe Museum) Frankfurt, Library of Congress, New York Public Library, New York Society Library, Österreichische Nationalbibliothek, Royal College of Music, Staatsbibliothek Preussischer Kulturbesitz, Stadt- und Universitätsbibliothek Frankfurt, Stadtarchiv Frankfurt, Universitätsbibliothek Bonn, Universitätsbibliothek Heidelberg, Universitätsbibliothek Mainz, Universitätsbibliothek Munich, Universitätsbibliothek Münster, and Yale University Libraries. Also the libraries of Harvard University, Iowa University, State University of New York at Buffalo, Union Theological Seminary, University of California at Los Angeles, University of Chicago, University of Illinois, University of Massachusetts, and University of Virginia. Many thanks to Kate Schmit of Harvard University Press for her care in seeing this book through its final stages.

Three readers of "The Dreams of Beethoven" have, by their letters, reminded me that it was both possible and necessary to carry my investigation of Beethoven's inner life somewhat further: Joseph Kerman, Jonathan C. Petty, and Noel Bradley—all of northern California. Thanks also to Anthony Lunt, London, who wrote to me about Caspar Carl and Ludwig Maria. I shall miss my friend, the late Harry Goldschmidt, whose challenging letters were a perpetual stimulus. Harry Slochower's profoundly elliptical comments have greatly enriched my work, as has his repeated caution that I ought to devote myself more fully to the suprahistorical dimensions of creativity. Finally, thanks to my wife, Eva, for her endless reading and revising.

This reprint edition benefits from numerous small corrections, for most of which I am grateful to Hans-Werner Küthen of the Beethoven-Archiv, Bonn.

MUSIC AND MYTH

1

The Ninth Symphony: A Search for Order

WE MAY begin, as Beethoven did, with hovering open fifths, *pianissimo*, a missing third, a sense of expectancy, soon to be fulfilled by a quickening into life and the forceful emergence of a theme and a definite tonality. The opening of the Ninth Symphony functions, like similar rhetorical gestures in the Seventh Symphony, the Hammerklavier Sonata, and several of the late quartets, to raise a curtain so that the action may begin, or so that we may witness the unveiling of a distant universe.

More than a gesture is involved. There is a sense in which this passage foreshadows *in nuce* the whole of the future action, inasmuch as it represents "an initial ambiguity leading to clarification."[1] At this stage, however, though we know that we have begun, we cannot imagine where Beethoven intends to take us: we do not know what to expect, we do not know how, or even if, the cluster of harmonic, thematic, and rhythmic riddles offered in these measures will be solved. We do not know why this oversized orchestra and these massed choruses and soloists are assembled before us. We may even discover that each step toward clarification discloses a new ambiguity, in a constant interchange of questions and answers.

3

Figure 1. Movt. I, mm. 305–314.

Figure 2. Movt. III, mm. 23–26.

Thus, although we have come to know that the Ninth Symphony is implicit in its opening measures, we cannot predict the Ninth Symphony from them. As the work unfolds, we soon discover that these measures are not merely introductory but are central to the thematic and tonal trajectory of the movement, which, however unique its sound, scoring, and dimensions, turns out to be in one of the sonata forms. Learning this, we are not surprised to hear the opening measures again—varied in key, texture, dynamics, and harmonic detail—at the counterstatement of the opening (mm. 35–50), or again at the recapitulation, *fortissimo* (fig. 1). However, those coming to the Ninth Symphony for the first time are wholly unprepared for the reappearance of the hovering fifths in the first section of the finale, which passes in review themes from each of the prior movements before getting on to its own business. And only a few listeners might sense that in the Adagio Beethoven has rehearsed that reappearance by an allusion to this passage—just the barest hint of it—by the violins, in the transition leading from the Adagio molto to the second theme, Andante (fig. 2).

Like the critical inspection of themes that opens the finale, this is a reminiscence, a reference backward, which engages the memory and compels us to consider present action in the light of past events. After 1815, a variety of such flashbacks becomes almost an obsessional signature technique for Beethoven: in the Sonata, op. 101, a fleeting echo of the opening theme breaks the yearning mood of the Adagio, and in the Sonata, op. 110, the somberly draped Arioso dolente arises unbidden from the depths of the fugue to deliver its message again, before succumbing to the fugue's inexorable affirmation. *The whole (Dialectical process)*

There are other such retrospective moments in the Ninth Symphony. An aphoristic example, again derived from the opening theme, occurs when the sustained tremolo open fifths give way to the symphony's first melodic gesture—a descending fifth, E to A, on the open strings of the violins. As though to balance the scales, Beethoven opens the recitative of the finale with precisely this same interval, but now moving powerfully upward in the low strings from A to E in a decisive change of direction (fig. 3). Along similar lines, commentators have often observed that a descending fourth is central to the opening action of every movement, and a descending fifth concludes the action of each movement, as well as forming the last notes of the chorus in the Prestissimo of the finale.

Another class of recurrent patterns in the symphony consists primarily of forecasts rather than of reminiscences. The simplest and most literal of these occurs in the finale, after the cellos and basses have found the Adagio wanting, whereupon the winds, over a pedal in the horns, play a four-measure preview of the "Ode to Joy" theme *dolce*. And there is a sense in which the *Schreckensfanfare* ("terror fanfare," as Wagner dubbed it) and instrumental recitative that opens

Figure 3. Movt. IV, Presto I, mm. 9–11.

Figure 4. a. Movt. I, mm. 15–16. b. Movt. IV, Alla Marcia, mm. 187–195.

the finale are to be considered as quite literal harbingers of the second Presto fanfare and vocal recitative.

More often, the cross-references are sufficiently transformed so that their relationship to what has gone before is fairly oblique. For example, the octave swings in the violins and violas, which mark the climax of the crescendo inaugurating the first-movement theme on each of its appearances, reappear *fortissimo*, heavily syncopated, and now played by the full string section, in the Alla Marcia at the moment which heralds the return of the Ode to Joy theme in its most triumphant form (fig. 4).

To similar ends, Beethoven may employ a series of related gestures, such as the highly individual "curtains" that inaugurate not only the first movement but also each of the other movements. Or he may utilize a sequence of passages drawn from "characteristic styles," whose denotative significance is fairly transparent. Such are the military style fanfares that are woven into—or superimposed upon—each of the movements. In the first movement (mm. 150–158, 419–427) the fanfare figuration is wholly structural—a "cadence theme" seamlessly proclaiming, in turn, the end of the exposition and the recapitulation. The rhythmically disjointed octave figures that announce the scherzo may be regarded as a parody fanfare—a musical exemplification of Marx's old saw that history always occurs twice: once as tragedy and again as farce.[2] In the Adagio, the repeated fanfares (mm. 120–123, 130–133) are heard almost offstage, vainly striving to break a mood of deep contemplation; they seem to be an attempt at an arousal, if not a call to action. "Etwas aufgewecktes [Something awakened]," wrote Beethoven on the sketches for the baritone recitative, upon the recall of the Adagio theme.[3] But the fanfare cannot counteract the pull to tragic contemplation (or to dream), and it takes another fanfare finally to accomplish that awakening—the dissonantly frenzied terror fanfare of the finale, now no longer on a tonic arpeggio but on the simultaneously sounded tonics of D minor and B-flat major.

Beethoven was no stranger to the characteristic styles and to their capacities for musical symbolism; titles such as *Sinfonia Pastorale, Sinfonia Eroica, Sonate Pathétique,* and *Quartetto Serioso* are only the most obvious confirmation of his habitual utilization of these styles to suggest denotative ideas.[4] The most extensive such use in the Ninth Symphony is in the trio of the scherzo, which, as has been frequently observed, is composed in an idealized pastoral style, one closely akin to that of the opening of the Sixth Symphony (especially mm. 67–127).[5] A bright, simple eight-measure tune, *alla breve,* is endlessly repeated over flowing strings, sustained horns, pedal effects, and drones reminiscent of peasant instruments.

The refinement of pastoral style for expressive purposes was one of Beethoven's ongoing projects, spanning all of his creative periods. Normally, the style is to be understood as representing an achieved return to Nature, though there are pastoral movements in Beethoven (I am thinking of the finales of the Violin Sonata in G, op. 96, and the String Quartet in F, op. 135) where it carries overtones of Romantic irony—the confession that we can never wholly satisfy our metaphysical desires and thus must settle for more finite satisfactions, the enjoyments of which are inevitably suffused with a sense of loss. Perhaps the trio of the Ninth Symphony fuses the naive and the ironic, telling of Nature recaptured and lost once again. And this may help to explain why subtle suggestions of pastoral style reverberate in the Adagio (mm. 92–94 and 114–118), in passages for winds and horns that inspired Mahler to his own explorations of rusticity penetrated by elegiac sadness.[6]

Many of these forecasts and reminiscences are fairly close to the surface. They were intended to be so, it seems to me, for Beethoven's aim apparently was to encode such patterns into his symphony so that the reasonably aware listener could readily decipher them— could at least sense their presence and respond to their implications. Other procedures show greater subtlety, such as the scale gestures in the endings of every movement (fig. 5a–d).

Endings of this type seem intended to symbolize transcendence over the intransigent materials that preceded them. Lenz com-

a.

b.

c.

d.

e.

mented: "Even his scales must be victorious!"[7] Well, not always: the Adagio concludes on a rising scale in the winds, to which Beethoven has added a contrapuntal descending scale in the first violins. The scale simultaneously rises and falls: are we being asked to consider scalewise contrary motion as a symbol of yearning incompletion? Be that as it may, the conspicuous thematic, textural, and harmonic connections between these passages, to which Lewis Lockwood has called my attention, suggest that they are also intended as binding strands in the symphony's pattern of referential moments, "a series of closing events that relate to one another almost as strikingly as do the 'curtains' that open each of the four movements." Lockwood further observes that the upward rushing triplets in the winds in the final measures of the symphony are not a new idea (as Tovey thought) but an explicit reference to a theme—also in the winds over contrary motion in the strings—that closes the first large section of the scherzo (mm. 139–143; fig. 5e). Thus, Beethoven simultaneously refers back to "an ending theme from within the scherzo and to the basic interval (the pentachord of the D mode) . . . that in a sense underlies many aspects of the whole work."[8]

II

EVEN without further examples, and with due allowance for the probability that some of these interconnecting details may be fortuitous or may simply be conventional formulas, this preliminary survey discloses the presence in the Ninth Symphony of an unprecedentedly complex network of recurrent patterns and cyclic transformations. Each of the events in this network may be likened to a discrete musical image or image-cluster within a grand design. Like revenants in a drama, the reminiscences suggest the residue of past events in the present, while the forecasts—less literal than the reminiscences, in a process of emergence—foreshadow things to come. In them, the principles of development and variation spill over the fermata and double-bar which normally fence off one movement of a sonata cycle from the others. Details originating in an earlier movement are projected onto a later one, and materials which are embryonic, latent with possibilities in their initial incarnations, are

Figure 5 (facing page). a. Movt. I, mm. 543–547. b. Movt. II, mm. 549–559. c. Movt. III, mm. 157–158. d. Movt. IV, Prestissimo, mm. 86–90. e. Movt. II, mm. 139–143.

brought to completion, undergo reversal, or are superseded at the very moment that their implicit meanings have been revealed.

Such connective features in a sonata cycle are often said to strengthen the work's "organic" structure. This is an attractive suggestion. However, such procedures may in fact disrupt the organic flow of the materials and their orderly development. They may well obscure the underlying tonal and harmonic issues, and to the extent that they are "foreign bodies" in a movement, they may compel Beethoven to create mixed forms to accommodate their presence. Ultimately, in seeking to accommodate such disruptive elements within essentially classical designs, Beethoven's structural powers are put to their most extreme test: he succeeds in retaining each of the cross-references both as a functional image and as a part of the formal structure. The references become embedded within the form itself, lending coherence at the same time that they press beyond the merely formal to extramusical denotation.

The precise nature of Beethoven's programmatic intentions will always remain open. Nevertheless, the clear drive toward representation of determinate states in certain of his works is far from tangential to his creative nature. For it is apparent that Beethoven—who delighted in calling himself a *Tondichter*, a "tone poet," and who regarded poets as "the leading teachers of the nation"—quite consciously wanted us to find "meaning" in the symphony's text, design, and tonal symbols.[9] The encoded network of imagery—the foreshadowings, the reminiscences, the pastoral episodes, the heraldic calls to action, the terror fanfare, the review of the themes, the Ode to Joy itself, and each of Schiller's powerful images—are only "moments" in the total design. They do not spell out a literal narrative, but they vibrate with an implied significance that overflows the musical scenario, lending a sense of extramusical narrativity to otherwise untranslatable events. The totality of these resonating signposts suggests the outline of a narrative in minimal form, which is nonetheless sufficient to set in motion within each listener a process of imaginative probing for the potentialities of the entire design.

One model of Beethoven's intentionality in the Ninth Symphony was offered in the late nineteenth century by the literary scholar and Wagner devotee Heinrich von Stein. Perhaps under Wagner's influence, Stein proposed that, in their perfection and sublimity, Beethoven's last symphonies portray the "idyllic" state that Schiller had proposed to be the goal of the modern poet.[10] Schiller's was the most influential form of the scenario of alienation and reconciliation that dominated aesthetic and philosophical thought in the post-Enlightenment era. In his essay "Naive and Sentimental Poetry" (1795–1796), of which "The Idyll" is the closing section, Schiller pictured a primal Golden Age, where humanity once dwelt "in a state of pure nature . . . like a harmonious whole." Ruptured by the onset of civilization, this "*sensuous* harmony which was in him disappears, and henceforth he can only manifest himself as a *moral unity*, that is, as aspiring to unity. The harmony that existed as a fact in the former state, the harmony of feeling and thought, only exists now in an *ideal* state."[11] The role of the modern (termed by Schiller the "sentimental") artist is thus imaginatively to represent the possibility of a renewed harmony to heal the wounds inflicted by mankind's alienation from Nature. This attempt to recapture the idyllic condition that existed "before the dawn of civilization" takes a utopian form. We cannot go backward to our biological or historical beginnings, as the pastoral poet desires, for this would place "*behind* us the end *toward which it ought to lead us.*" In Schiller's famous phrase, the task of the artist is therefore to lead us, "who no longer can return to Arcadia, forward to Elysium."[12]

Stein's glancing remark entered the Beethoven literature by way of a richly speculative monograph on the Ninth Symphony by Otto Baensch, who, somewhat reluctantly, combined this suggestion with Lenz's earlier one that the first movement outlined a narrative of Creation and the cycle as a whole a "symphonic cosmogony." After noting certain similarities between the scenarios of Haydn's *Creation* and the Ninth Symphony, Baensch asserted that Beethoven "starts with a portrait of Chaos . . . and he crowns the Symphony with the drama of the close of man's history, in the . . . Elysian state of civilization."[13] This line of interpretation was accepted by Romain Rolland and augmented by Harry Goldschmidt, who took the pastoral-style trio of the second movement as an explicit musical metaphor for Arcadia.[14] The implication is that the Ninth Symphony is intended as a musical analogue of a mythic narrative, a cosmic history, told by an evangelist-narrator recalling the span of universal experience.

Schiller's scenario is, of course, but a special case of other mythic patterns: the spiral journey from Arcadia to Elysium is also that of Paradise lost and regained, and of all utopian recoveries of a mourned

Golden Age. Beethoven's utilization of Schiller's myth-drenched poem potentially activates not only the more universal mythic design to which it belongs but also its numberless correlatives in literature, folklore, theology, and philosophy.

Nor is there any reason to suppose that Beethoven intended to limit his narrative to a musical translation of Schiller's parable. The story of the journey from Arcadia to Elysium may have already been implicitly merged with another narrative, one that traces the route from Lenz's Creation (or to remain within Greek mythological terms, from Chaos-Night as the source of all being) to Cataclysm, to the end of history. For the symphony does not open in Arcadian innocence; its first measures sound a coming into existence, a stirring, an awakening to life. Furthermore, there is here a twin orbit—an historical one that takes place within the order of chronological time, and, concurrently, a vertical, spatial route from the underworld (for the Romans tell us that Elysium lies next to Hades) to the earth (Arcadia's location in the Peloponnese), to the starry heavens, and beyond to the place of the deity.[15]

These concentric myths are so fundamental in their shape that a host of related myths may be subsumed in the scheme. Cosmogonic narrative is an organizing structure, offering models for social existence. It is also an extended metaphor for the individual's road in life, his expulsion, exile, and return to a transfigured home. Abrams sees this mythic journey "as a fall from unity into division and into a conflict of contraries which in turn compel the movement back towards a higher integration."[16] And Slochower stresses that such mythic transcendence is active and ongoing: "the harmony attained carries within itself the earlier moments of dissidence and contains the seeds of a renewed conflict."[17] On a less cosmic scale, the alienation-reconciliation myths have the power to touch the deepest familial and fraternal yearnings, while the Creation myths echo with issues attendant upon birth, ancestry, and death.

Among the Romantics, for whom exile was felt to be the primary human condition, it is precisely "homesickness" (*Heimweh*) and "yearning" (*Sehnsucht*) which keep alive the potential to return. "Where are we going, then?" asked Novalis: "Always homeward." The distant goal is Blake's "Sweet golden clime / Where the traveller's journey is done," and it is Bunyan's high mountainside with its promise of refreshment in "the pleasant beams of the sun." Here, the goal is Schiller's and Beethoven's Elysium, where brothers find release from struggle as well as the protection of a benevolent deity and the nourishment of an eternally young goddess of joy.

Beneath the literary, mythic, and psychological levels, the symphony's shape mirrors the ordered shapes of nature itself: the turning of the seasons, the ceaseless interchange between life and death, the movement of the heavenly spheres, the rhythms of biological existence and natural phenomena.[18] And this reminds us of the difficulties of trying to endow music with denotative meaning. To give only one example: it is surely plausible, particularly in view of the symphony's frankly apocalyptic *telos,* for the Romantic commentators to claim that Beethoven's opening measures suggest chaos striving for lucid formation and therefore may be taken as an image of universal origins. But all we can really say is that the opening expresses a sense of emergence or of crystallization, which, though it may be taken to represent Creation, can also symbolize birth, the transition from darkness into light, the awakening from dream, the occurrence of a thought. The nebula of possibilities precludes any attempt at delimitation. The scenario of the Ninth Symphony is a nuclear design, standing for an infinity of related designs.

But this merely confirms once again the inexhaustibility of the symbol: the Ninth Symphony is a symbol whose referents cannot be completely known and whose full effects will never be experienced. And there is no need to mourn the loss, for, as Eco explained, to decode a symbol is to render it mute.[19] In uncovering the mythic substratum of Beethoven's Ninth Symphony, we uncover a fragment of his intentionality; in refusing to accept the mythic design as the ultimate or sole meaning of the symphony, we remain true to the nature of music, whose meanings are beyond translation—and beyond intentionality. "The composer reveals the inner nature of the world," wrote Schopenhauer, "and expresses the deepest wisdom in a language which his reason does not understand."[20] Nevertheless, intentionality cannot be wholly annihilated. And so we return, for what it may be worth, to one aspect of Beethoven's apparent intentions, to try to learn more about how his symbol found its form.

III

WOVEN into the Ninth Symphony's system of forecasts and reminiscences are several overarching patterns to which Beethoven has given the shape of quests. The symphony as a whole is an extended metaphor of a quest for Elysium. The geography of this odyssey is retrospectively mapped by the review and rejection of the opening themes of the earlier movements; the contours of Elysium are described in Schiller's text, and the arrival is heralded by the Ode to Joy theme. However, that joyous unveiling may itself be viewed as the climax of another teleological pattern, which we may term a *thematic* quest—a succession of themes and thematic fragments which, by their prefiguration of the Ode to Joy melody, suggest that it was intended to be the culmination of a series of melodies aspiring to achieve an ultimate, lapidary form.

This notion seems to have originated with Richard Wagner in 1851, when he observed that the Ode to Joy melody was complete in Beethoven's mind *"from the beginning"*; Beethoven, he maintained, "shattered it into its component parts" at the outset, and only in the course of the symphony did he finally "set his full melody before us as a finished whole."[21] Wagner's Russian disciple, Alexander Serov, was the first seriously to elaborate on this procedure, which he described as the "transformation of a *single* idea through a 'chain of metamorphoses,' without departing from the main image" of the theme. He held that the symphony is a series of moments within a "great monothematic plan" by which Beethoven unfolds the Ode to Joy as a symbol of Elysium. "In both the opening Allegro and the scherzo, there are not only flashes of major taken verbatim from the theme of the [Ode to Joy], but even the developments in the minor are built on it."[22]

Of course, reliance on this sort of tune detection can be fairly risky, for it is not difficult to discover what one wishes to find, especially with a melody constructed of such commonplace elements. But it seemed clear enough to Wagner and Serov from the pervasiveness of the pattern that it was an intentional design. If they are correct, each of the precursors of the Ode to Joy theme is a separate idea rather than a literal anticipation. They are linked by the similarity of their melodic shapes, which move upward and downward in stepwise patterns. Most of them begin on a degree of the scale different from the Joy theme, and all present rhythmic variants of the ascending and descending progressions (fig. 6). These may be seen as the Ode to Joy in a state of becoming, as melody yearning for a condition that has yet to be defined. However, what Serov had in mind was no doubt even more literal: the rhythmically disguised presence, in the introduction to the second subject (mm. 76–77), of

Figure 6. a. Movt. I, mm. 74–79. b. Movt. I, mm. 108–110.

Figure 7. a. Movt. II, mm. 93–100. b. Movt. II, mm. 117–127. c. Movt. II, mm. 210–212.

the actual sequence of notes that make up the opening bars of the theme.

The scherzo is bursting with fragments of the Ode to Joy melody (fig. 7). But the trio contains the most fulfilled of these "premature variants" of the theme. Here the thematic journey finds a temporary resting place in a glowing Arcadian moment within which may be glimpsed the sublimated kernel of the Joy theme (fig. 8). In contrast

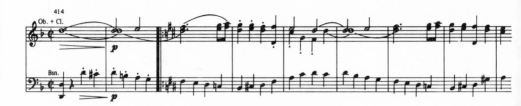

Figure 8. Movt. II, mm. 414–422.

Figure 9. Movt. III, mm. 8–11.

Figure 10. Movt. III, mm. 127–128.

to this tonic-centered folklike tune, several of these thematic materials embody the common configuration of so many of Beethoven's
"*Sehnsucht*" melodies—an upward striving that is ultimately defeated and returns to a point of unrest or disequilibrium. The Adagio's
themes are especially contoured in this "yearning" pattern (fig. 9).
The second phrase of the opening theme (m. 10) contains in the
strings a subtle forecast of the characteristic turning figure of the Joy
melody, followed by an upward chromatic movement through a C
sharp, almost as though reaching out for D major. Later, during a
free variation on the Adagio theme in the Coda, occurs an almost
literal statement of the opening strain of the Ode to Joy (fig. 10). A
counterpoint to the main melody is heard in the flutes and oboes, in
B-flat major, with altered rhythmic values but virtually unchanged
melodic line, like a somnambulistic previsioning of the theme.

We now know that Wagner was correct in surmising that the melody of the Ode to Joy was fully formed by the time that Beethoven worked on the earlier movements, for Robert Winter and Sieghard Brandenburg have shown that the Artaria 201 sketchbook, which contains the melody and presents a layout of the symphony essentially corresponding to its final shape, was written as early as October 1822.[23] That Beethoven intended to suggest a process of thematic quest and discovery also seems to find confirmation in his sketches for the finale's vocal recitative. Rejecting the Adagio theme, he writes: "Also not this; it is too tender; *we must seek* something more animated."[24] And upon the arrival of the Joy theme he writes: "This is it. Ha! *It is now discovered,*" words that would have been equally appropriate to the discovery of any sacred object of a quest-romance.[25]

It follows that these themes and melodic fragments are to be regarded as subliminal foreshadowings or anticipatory variations of the Ode to Joy, with at least one veiled but virtually literal version of the melody encoded into each of the first three movements. Each stage except the last is unfulfilled, thereby impelling the symphony toward its eventual consummation in a melody characterized by legato movement, stepwise motion, the avoidance of chromaticism or dissonance, and, above all, by a smooth, gratifying, and predictable orbit around the tonic center, which is touched upon ten times in the course of its first sixteen measures. Inevitably, the internal dynamic of Beethoven's procedure is not exhausted by a view that regards each theme merely as a step toward discovery of the Ode to Joy. For just as each fragment is an augury of that melody, it is equally a referent of the other themes in the sequence, both retrospectively and prospectively. The introduction to the second subject of the first movement forecasts the trio of the scherzo as well as the Ode to Joy. The trio supersedes pathetic striving and is in turn superseded by the Adagio's inwardness, with its own momentary backward glances to the pastoral style.

Nor are the earlier moments in Beethoven's thematic quest forgotten in the choral jubilation. In the Alla Marcia, as a preparation for the climactic *fortissimo* return of the chorus on the words "Freude schöner Götterfunken [Joy, divine spark of the gods]," is a passage containing three fragments of the Ode to Joy theme (mm. 199–212). The first, a sequence of three notes, D sharp–E–F sharp, a clear reference to the theme, rises to the dominant of B major. But Beethoven then modulates to the minor, presenting a second rising sequence

D–E–F sharp, which sounds the same notes as the opening of the scherzo's pastoral-style trio. The effect is of a distant recall of the Arcadian moment, but now darkly colored by the B-minor tonality to suggest that this major-key experience can no longer be regained, at least not in its original form. The third sequence repeats the first, but with an urgency of signification and sense of irresistible momentum owing to its having now emerged from its descent to the minor as well as from the memory of an unrecapturable innocence.

The Ninth Symphony's thematic quest does not end with the finding of the Ode to Joy. Thereafter the melody becomes the point of departure for an immense number of transformations, implying that even this theme is not an ultimate place of simple tranquility. In its initial incarnation, the theme is pitched at human scale; but with each succeeding variation it begins its separation from the earthly and in the later variations cuts loose altogether from its human moorings to engage other, indefinable levels of experience. The march variation is to be seen as only the first way-station on a journey into exoticism which reaches a climax in the ecstatic medievalism of the Andante maestoso, where, at the words, "Seid umschlungen, Millionen [Be embraced, ye multitudes]," a new melody in an archaic style makes its appearance, sharply disrupting the melodic and tonal patterns of the movement. But in the subsequent Allegro energico the "new" melody turns out to have been an implicit component of, indeed a countermelody to, the Ode to Joy, as though to illuminate the exotic underside of Beethoven's *Humanitätsmelodie*.

IV

THE Ninth Symphony is usually said to represent the victory of D major over D minor. In Leo Treitler's trenchant formulation, the "sense of a drive to move out of the one and into the other" is "one of the main narrative lines of the work as a whole."[26] Looked at from a slightly different standpoint, the symphony's tonal trajectory encompasses a quest for D major, wherein almost every allusion to potential transcendence appears to be inscribed in that key, or, to invert the thought, every allusion to D major compels us to consider it as a symbol of potential transcendence. In the scenario, each D-major passage implies a momentary arrival point—but no permanent haven—in the ongoing journey toward the D-major Joy theme.

The issue had been raised in the opening measures of the symphony with the catastrophic plunge into D minor, an event that, Beethoven noted in a sketchbook, "reminds us of our despair."[27] This event might be nullified only by a full transformation into the tonic major; and such a transformation occurs at the onset of the recapitulation, where the introduction returns *fortissimo* on what appears to be a D-major chord, with the F sharp in the bass instruments (fig. 1). There is, of course, more than one way to interpret a chord, and, as is notorious in Beethoven, things are often not what they appear to be at first glance. Schenker showed that the chord may be read as an inversion of the dominant of G minor.[28] The effect is to offer an apparent D-major moment which is ironically subverted by its G-minor implication. In any event, the F sharp is insufficient to offset the negative inner core of this theme, which soon yields to D minor and then moves on to B flat, another of the symphony's tonal centers.[29] Two further D-major passages in the recapitulation are filled with pathos but have little chance of prevailing against more powerful, less fragmented forces.

It is only in the coda that a D-major passage proves capable of withstanding the pull to the minor long enough to serve as an image of possible transcendence. The strings suddenly form a soft tapestry against which the horns in D, in full major tonic, develop the utopian implications of the second phrase of the first theme. One by one the winds add their commentary in a rising pattern of sighing phrases, thus to affirm the superlative character of the moment, which endures for a brief eight measures until, at last, it slips back into the tonic minor (fig. 11).

Like the first harbingers of the Ode to Joy melody, the early D-major episodes of the symphony may be held to represent a striving toward an as-yet-undefined condition. And this is true of the swift glimpse of D major in the scherzo's recapitulation of the second subject (mm. 330–338), a blazing eight-measure segment that reverts to the minor mode almost before one can grasp its implications. Only in the trio do we at last discover a defined state, that of the Arcadian-Edenic, symbolized, we have seen, by pastoral-style, tonic-centered melody, and, of course, by the key of D major as well. Indeed, this is the first extended, self-enclosed section of the symphony with a D-major signature.

With the return of the scherzo, the earthly paradise is again lost, along with its characteristic tonality. In the Adagio, this Arcadian experience is briefly recalled several times as an unrecoverable wisp

Figure 11. Movt. I, mm. 469–476.

of memory emerging from the depths of inwardness. However, the slow movement has its own window on Eden—the second theme, Andante, in D major, with an elegiac aching for the tonic, which it finally touches, only to fall away of its own weight to the F sharp with which it began (fig. 12). Kerman hears the Andante as "an echo of the D-major horn theme in the coda of the first movement"—as another strand in the web of interrelationships which Beethoven has designed.[30]

The finale reaches D major eagerly, but hesitantly, with the first intimation of the Ode to Joy (mm. 77–80); but even the confident D-major arrival of the full theme itself is a consummation too much desired to be so easily achieved or permanently retained. A second exposition, with chorus, is required for that purpose. And even so, the tonic major will have to undergo numerous vicissitudes before its supremacy is at last granted in the *prestissimo* closing measures of the symphony. This is an unsurpassable affirmation of the tonic, apparently aiming to suppress all further doubts or uncertainties and to bring the tonal quest to a resounding close.

One might speculate that by omitting the third and fifth degrees of the scale in the crashing octaves of the final chord, Beethoven intends to offer a new tonal ambiguity, perhaps thereby to suggest that

D minor has not been altogether exorcised. More likely, the closing unison is intended to override all contradictions between major and minor by reaching the substratum of the underlying D mode. For Beethoven, such a unison on the tonic offers the most radical possible simplication of the issues, the irrefutable reply to—and completion of—the hovering fifths with which he began. Beethoven's ultimate destination thus contains a reminiscence, by way of maximum contrast, of the opening *pianissimo* gesture of the Allegro ma non troppo. And in a spectacular stroke, the final *fortissimo* measures revert to the triplet figure with which the symphony began, suddenly revealing this rhythmic pattern to have been one of the motivating forces of the entire work. By these means, and by allusions to prior scale passages, to descending and ascending fifths and octaves, the closing measures of the symphony spiral back, in a dizzying instant of simultaneous recollection, to the chorus's final "Freude, schöner Götterfunken," to the opening notes of the cello-baritone recitative, to the closing measures of each movement, to the triplet passages of the scherzo, Adagio, and Alla Marcia, to the original D-minor theme, and even to the initial movement of equivocality. The effect is of a temporal compression so extreme that it appears as a drive not merely for unity—"Alle Menschen werden Brüder"—but for unbounded fusion—"Diesen Kuß der ganzen Welt!"

V

To summarize: a multiplicity of drives converges in the Ninth Symphony's finale—for a visionary D major to overcome the

Figure 12. Movt. III, mm. 25–33.

power of D minor; for a theme adequate to represent "Joy, divine spark of the Gods"; for Elysium, with its promise of brotherhood, reconciliation, and eternal life; for a recovery of the Classical ideal of humanity united with Nature. And more: for a deity who transcends any particularizations of religious creed; for a fusion of Christian and pagan beliefs, a marriage of Faust and Helen. All of this resonates in the stanzas Beethoven selected from Schiller's poem. The Ninth Symphony may also be taken as an emblem of the idealism of Beethoven's youth, when he was enflamed by what he called the "fever of the Revolution" (*Revolutionsfieber*).[31] This by virtue of its Classicism, its renovation of a heroic style steeped in the celebratory festivals of the French Revolution, and its doubling back to Schiller's politically radical, quasi-Masonic text of the mid-1780s. In an era of reaction, the Ninth Symphony represents homesickness for the Enlightenment (*Aufklärung*) as an historical model of a Golden Age. The Ode to Joy revives the naive dream of benevolent (and equally important to Beethoven, aesthetically enlightened) kings and princes, presiding over a harmony of national and class interests during a moment of shared beliefs in progress, fraternity, and social justice.

From this point of view, the Ninth Symphony is Beethoven's *À la recherche du temps perdu*—that, at least, is one way of reading his backward glances to Schiller, to France, to the Enlightenment, and to Classicism; of explaining his revival of a project dating back to 1792; and of understanding why he fashioned the Joy theme out of a dancelike pastoral tune that he had already used three times, the first as early as 1794. An Elysium still to come is modeled on a legendary dream-history out of the accumulated desires of a composer's lifetime.

I stress Beethoven's futuristic orientation in the Ninth Symphony. Whatever his yearning for the past, he does not seek pure restoration. His purpose is to create a cosmos that has never before existed; he wants to discover his own Ninth Symphony. His unprecedentedly complex use of text, scenarios, programmatic indications, characteristic styles, musical symbolism, and the web of forecasts, reminiscences, and other denotational devices is the hallmark of a profoundly modernist perspective.

To come to this point quickly: in some of his most "Beethovenian" sonata-style instrumental works, a range of novel, extreme states of being were heard expressed for the first time in music—

states that had previously been approximated, if at all, only in certain discursive forms of dramatic vocal music. We encounter a wide spectrum of such extreme states in the Ninth Symphony, touching upon such issues as creation, aggression, immensity, the ecstatic, the celestial, or if one were to attempt to find a single term to encompass them all, the transcendental. It is not that prior composers of instrumental music had lacked depth of passion or had failed to write music of the deepest emotional substance. But Beethoven strove to represent states of being that essentially were regarded as off limits by his predecessors. For example, writing to his father in 1781, Mozart expressed this typical attitude as a matter of course, in a tone very like that of Hamlet in his instructions to the players: "Passions, whether violent or not, must never be expressed to the point of exciting disgust, and music, even in the most terrible situations, must never offend the ear, but must please the listener, or in other words must never cease to be music."[32] And this is in conformity with the functions of music in the salons, theaters, churches, and courts of Europe—to instruct, to give pleasure, to reinforce faith, to arouse the passions only to soothe them, to probe but not to disrupt.

Beethoven's music sought to disrupt. This new quality was first understood, or at least articulated, by Hoffmann in his 1810 review of the Fifth Symphony in the *Allgemeine musikalische Zeitung.* "Beethoven's music opens the floodgates of fear, of terror, of horror, of pain, and arouses that yearning for the infinite which is the essence of Romanticism," wrote Hoffmann.[33] And although he claimed that Beethoven's music represents the immeasurable, he did so within a framework that we, too, may find workable, for he went on to demonstrate the connectedness of Beethoven's symphonic form. Taking cognizance of the widespread contemporary allegations of Beethoven's immoderation, bizarrerie, and infringements of the Classical models, he nonetheless insisted that Beethoven "can be placed directly alongside Haydn and Mozart with regard to his self-possession [*Besonnenheit*]." By this idiosyncratic term, which Hoffmann adapted from Jean Paul's *School for Aesthetics,* he signified the composure, serenity, and reflectiveness that are the qualities of an achieved Classicism.[34]

In his earlier years, Beethoven had invented (or adapted from other composers) numerous propulsive techniques with which to represent energy in motion and relentless striving. Concurrently, he devised a syntax that aimed to create, postpone, modulate, and fulfill cathartic expectations by a variety of innovative formal procedures. We may want to designate this dynamic vocabulary and syntax of the middle-period sonata cycles as a "heroic" characteristic style, and it served as such for subsequent nineteenth-century music. Overlapping with the development of this style and culminating in the last works is the emergence of several other characteristic styles, intended to represent a range of transcendent states—states attainable, it seems, only through the compounding of unceasing striving by eternal longing.

The Romantic idea of such restless longing is, of course, central to Beethoven's aesthetic. He wrote to Christine Gerhardi as early as 1797 about the need "to strive toward the inaccessible goal which art and nature have set us," and he remarked to Wegeler in 1801 that "every day brings me nearer to the goal which I feel but cannot describe"; similarly, to a young admirer in 1812 he confessed that the artist "sees unfortunately that art has no boundaries; he feels dimly how remote he is from his goal."[35] For Beethoven, as for his contemporaries, the drive for personal realization was the subjective aspect of a transcendental longing as well. Such longing, wrote Fichte in 1794, is "the impulse toward something entirely unknown that reveals itself only in a sense of need, in a feeling of dissatisfaction or emptiness."[36] To revert to Schiller's framework (but now in Nietzsche's paraphrase), Nature and the Ideal have become "objects of grief," in which the "former is felt to be lost, and the latter to be beyond reach." Fortunately, however, "both may become objects of joy when they are represented as actual."[37] The Ninth Symphony's representation of this grief and this joy is sculpted out of unprecedented materials sufficient to portray, if not to solve, this dilemma.

To create a vocabulary that represents extremes of despair and bliss, and their gradations, became Beethoven's project in the Ninth Symphony and other works of his final decade (in his hubris, he would not accept that, strictly speaking, neither the invisible nor the infinite can be represented).[38] For this undertaking he developed a wide variety of procedures, including harmonic and rhythmic motion slowed to the edge of motionlessness, clouded harmonic progressions, passages in indeterminate keys, nebulous and nocturnal effects, multivalent tonal trajectories, enormously extended time spans, highly idiosyncratic fugue styles, and a supremely ornamented variation style that implies the infinite possibilities latent in even the simplest musical materials.[39] Sometimes, though he was wont to disavow the practice in theory, he used a more literal kind of symbolism.[40] On a leaf of sketches to "Ueber Sternen muss er wohnen [Beyond the stars he surely dwells]," he wrote, "The height of the stars [can be pictured] more by way of the instruments."[41] In *Calm Sea and Prosperous Voyage*, op. 112, the words "Tiefe Stille [deep calm]" are represented by a long, sustained *pianissimo* chord, and the words "der ungeheuren Weite [immense distance]" are described by an upward leap of an octave and a fourth in the soprano and a downward plunge of an octave in the bass. Other representations of the boundless are the astonishing consecutive repetition of a single high A twenty-seven times in the Arioso dolente of op. 110 and the use of patently circular shapes—symbols of infinity—in the Allegretto of the Seventh Symphony and the song cycle *An die ferne Geliebte*.

Beethoven's modernist contribution, then, was to symbolize extreme states by means of a host of new musical images and image clusters that we may collectively designate as authentic characteristic styles, prototypical styles which have yet to be named, let alone fully analyzed. This disruptive new content forced a reshaping of sonata structure in the direction of extreme organicist integration of highly dissociative materials. To the other Ninth Symphony quests, therefore, can be added a quest for style and a quest for form. And at the root of the symphony's many questing patterns is a single impulse: to discover a principle of order in the face of chaotic and hostile energy.

Of course, all art seeks simplification of the perplexities of experience. "Really, universally, relations stop nowhere," observed Henry James, "and the exquisite problem of the artist is eternally but to draw, by a geometry of his own, the circle, within which they shall happily appear to do so."[42] In Poulet's words, the work of art "creates a cloister in whose shelter reality can be isolated, contemplated and represented, without running the risk of melting into the universal multiplicity of phenomena."[43] There is this difference, however: Beethoven limits chaos not by avoiding but by *picturing* it, thereby circumscribing its jurisdiction. ("We gain power over worldly things by naming them," writes Wackenroder, to which Cassirer adds, "knowledge of the name gives him who knows it mastery even over the being and will of the god.")[44]

Beethoven's is a risky Classicism, which introduces the original and the bizarre (i.e. the modern) in the service of a higher conception of the Classic, one that does not remain content to imitate a preexistent model of harmony. He casts suspicion on all such models, with their implications of complacency. He rejects everything that can readily be completed, for he seeks *das Unendliche*—the "unending."[45] Disruption, disorientation, and dissociation are essential to his project. The late works alter, or dispense with, easy conceptions of order, symmetry, and decorum. Ultimately, of course, his new forms may be even more coherent than those of his predecessors, but their coherence bears the impress of a journey through the reaches of chaos.

In some sense, Beethoven's aesthetic exemplifies the early Romantic dual program: to shatter the apparent order of experience and to transcend chaos through form. Novalis urged that "in every poem chaos must shimmer through the regular veil of orderliness."[46] Friedrich Schlegel insisted that "understanding and caprice must be chaoticized in poetry."[47] Their aim, of course, was, by a process of estrangement, to reach an underlying reality. In Shelley's words, "poetry lifts the veil from the hidden beauty of the world, and makes familiar objects appear as if they were not familiar."[48] The early Romantics thereby wished also to repudiate the dilute rationality of the post-Enlightenment, to enlarge the claims of intuition and of the productive imagination. Schubert became quite emotional about this issue in a diary entry of 1824: "O imagination! Man's greatest treasure, inexhaustible source at which both Art and Learning come to drink! O remain with us . . . so that we may be safeguarded from so-called Enlightenment, that hideous skeleton without blood or flesh."[49]

Unlike the main exponents of German literary Romanticism, whose works so often splintered into oracular aphorism or into truncated structures, Beethoven achieved what Schiller had thought in principle to be impossible—to map the infinite without losing hold of the center. Repeatedly Beethoven gave rein to chaos without being overwhelmed, in the widest spectrum of forms and with a limitless imagery of the seemingly unsymbolizable. Thus, in the last instance, he transcended the existential states of yearning and imperfection, creating a series of individual universes which are at the same time perfected and dynamically open.

VI

BEETHOVEN'S life, too, embodies a precarious search for order. Perhaps this is why the Ninth Symphony—beyond its mythic universality, beneath its congruence with certain conventions of contemporaneous thought—appears to touch upon so many of its composer's inner preoccupations. Of course we can never know the ways in which the Ninth Symphony was carved out of Beethoven's own experience. But the objects of his desire seem to be quite on the surface here: the reconstruction of a splintered family, recapture of an idyllic past, achievement of a loving brotherhood, attainment of an extended moment of pure joy, and eternal life. No small order. The objects of his fears—more obscure, even opaque—are equally at hand. To Beethoven, chaos is not merely the riot of disorganized sense impressions that constitute the flux of perception, nor is it simply a convenient mythological category to serve as pretext for a mythopoeic symphony. It is these, of course, but it is also the totality of those tendencies within his personality that require the imposition of order: the libidinal drives toward forbidden objects; the egoistic and authoritarian components of his character, constantly at war with his innate altruism; the eruptions of irrationality, countered by a grandiose complexity of aesthetic structure; a variety of terrors, known and unknown—of illegitimacy, passivity, deprivation, punishment, and death. And the yearning for chaos itself—the ultimate sign for the loss of boundaries. An exterminating *Sehnsucht* is transcended by its own symbolization.

Ever fearful of death (except, it seems, at the very end), prone on occasion to suicide, and preoccupied not only with immortality but also with mortality, Beethoven in his last years came to know that the comedy would not last much longer. "I often despair and would like to die," he wrote to Zmeskall as he entered his last decade. "For I can foresee no end to all my infirmities. God have mercy upon me, I consider myself as good as lost . . . Thank God that I shall soon have finished playing my part."[50] His body knew it was dying, particularly after an attack of jaundice in 1821, the first clear symptom of the illness that eventually took his life. In the face of physical decline and of the emotional chaos that had undermined his psychological integrity for a decade, Beethoven's creativity may have served to ward off death, to stimulate the will to continue—to provide an imaginative counterbalance to the forces of disintegration. The *Missa solemnis* has the implication of a double question to the deity: Am I merely mortal? Is there hope for eternal life? "Even if you don't believe in it [religion], you will be glorified . . . You will arise with me from the dead—because you must," writes his friend Karl Peters assuringly in the conversation book for April 1823.[51]

Even a frivolous canon, composed as a gift to his physician in 1825, tells the story of his fears, his helplessness, and his faith in music as a countervailing force against death. "Doctor, bar the door to Death! Music too will help in my hour of need."[52] For Beethoven, music, whatever else it represented, was also a form of protective magic, in whose efficacy he placed his full trust. "Apollo and the Muses are not yet going to let me be handed over to Death," he wrote to Schotts Söhne during the creative surge that bridged the Ninth Symphony and the late quartets, "for I still owe them so much; and before my departure for the Elysian fields [the reference to Elysium is not fortuitous] I must leave behind me what the Eternal spirit has infused into my soul and bids me complete."[53] The *Heiliger Dankgesang* of the A-minor Quartet, op. 132, fuses gratitude—to music, to the Godhead—for continued life with the foretaste of supernal beauty beyond life itself.[54] The nullification of death through its transfiguration into bliss is a covert program of the Ninth Symphony. Beneath his frequent protestations of adherence to Reason, Beethoven was far from immune to Romanticism's longing for the twilight.

In some way, the Ninth Symphony may be read as a succession of flights from the Night-Side, as a search for alternative refuges from an inner or outer annihilating agency. Each refuge is not only impermanent but also somehow suffused with a sense of potential dissolution, thus compelling the pilgrimage onward. The catastrophic implications of the first movement are unmistakable, thrown into even higher relief by the fleeting moments of yearning encoded into the fabric of inexorable pursuit. The sense of flight spills over into the scherzo, but now parodistically transformed from tragedy into farce. The trio flees into the primitive, to Nature, to childhood, to the communal, to the Arcadian Golden Age. But Death dwells in Arcadia, its presence there marked by manifold symbols of decay and all-devouring time. "Whenever, in a beautiful landscape," wrote the poet Jacobi, "I encounter a tomb with the inscription *Auch Ich war in Arkadien* ["I, too, was in Arcadia"], I point it out to my friends;

we stop a moment, press each other's hands, and proceed."[55] Arcadia is "the retrospective vision of an unsurpassable happiness, enjoyed in the past, unattainable ever after, yet enduringly alive in the memory," wrote Panofsky: "a bygone happiness ended by death."[56]

Of the Adagio Beethoven wrote, "This is too tender."[57] Evidently at that moment, and in this work, he found insufficient the modalities of beauty, sensuousness, and perfection, which he may have seen as leading to passivity and, beyond passivity, to the termination of life. At least, this is one implication of Beethoven's comment, which has a parallel in Schiller's caveat that the beautiful, in contrast to the sublime, achieves a reconciliation of man with the sensuous world of objects, thereby disabling activity. Schiller prefers the sublime, which "opens to us a road to overstep the limits of the world of sense, in which the feeling of the beautiful would forever imprison us."[58]

> He whose eyes have gazed upon beauty,
> Is already delivered over to death.   (Platen)

A Paterian equation of beauty with death is not required to understand Beethoven's need at last to emerge from the realm of the Sirens. It was enough that he had permitted himself, in luxuriant and reverent detail, to partake of these forbidden delights before yielding them up at last.

Of course Beethoven knew that the Adagio was the necessary precondition of the Ode to Joy. As early as the *Eroica* Symphony, he had learned that every resurrection requires a funeral; here he demonstrates that every awakening presupposes a sleep—a turning inward from which to gather strength for action.

The symphony's triumphant, final refuge is in Elysium, where those shades of the fortunate dead favored by the gods escape the plains of Asphodel and discover "the Elysian plain / Beyond death's gloomy portal."[59] In the *Eroica* Symphony, *Egmont, Coriolanus,* and *Christus am Oelberge,* the death of the hero is explicit. In the Ninth Symphony his death is implicit, the transition is miraculously accomplished, and he is neither mourned nor exalted as an individual, but merged through transfiguration into the community of heroes:

> Brothers, run your course,
> joyfully, like a hero to the victory!

Death and resurrection—a pairing central to the Romantic outlook—here occur simultaneously rather than successively.[60] In Elysium, death is no longer chaotic and destructive but affirmative, loving, and transcendent. "Here, crowned at last, love never knows decay."[61]

In Elysium, Beethoven may at last have found his warrant of immortality. The Ode to Joy melody appears to herald a personal as well as a universal resurrection. For though the images of this Utopia belong to us all, the underlying impulse contains a unique—if unrecoverable—biographical nucleus. In that resurrection, Beethoven may have unconsciously expected to find answers to several long-standing riddles. Seizing upon an ambiguity in the reports of his birth year and aware of other rumors that he was the illegitimate son of King Friedrich Wilhelm II, Beethoven had long been in search of his origins, seeking to discover both how and when he came into being, seeking reconciliation with the memory of his real parents even as he sought noble and royal surrogates for them. His longing for an ideal father merges with the symphony's quest for a divine father. He dedicates this masterwork to King Friedrich Wilhelm III, the son of his rumored father. In it he celebrates the principle of fraternity; indeed, he succeeds in creating the most universal paradigm of fraternity in world culture. Yet there is uncertainty, even in Elysium. Beethoven-Schiller would not fix either time or tense for us: "Alle Menschen werden Brüder [All men become brothers]." The tense is neither past, present, nor even quite future, but a process tense, implying what will happen "if." Slochower suggests that, "Poetically, it is a *prayer* for brotherhood."[62] Fraternity remains upon the horizon of possibility.

Nor is the search for an ideal father quite concluded. The deity may be tacitly present in the "Creation" scenario of the opening and explicitly present in the text of the finale; he presides over both ends of the temporal spectrum. But while present, he is not yet discovered. "Seek him beyond the stars! Beyond the stars he surely dwells"—and Beethoven's music supplies a heart-rending question mark (fig. 13). The chorus's measured rhythmic unison disintegrates on the word "muß," which is sounded successively by the basses, the tenors and altos, and finally by the sopranos, as though by repeated emphasis to query what they dare not acknowledge in reality, that the multitudes have been embracing before an absent deity, *Deus absconditus.*

Despite the resounding affirmations that try to erase the memory of this moment of the Andante Maestoso, Beethoven has led us to

Figure 13. Movt. IV, Andante Maestoso, mm. 25–32.

understand that the question indeed remains alive. In the Messianic myth the world is redeemed, and its redemption coincides with the end of history. But Beethoven is no mere translator of old stories; whatever his models, he invented a new mythology at the dawn of our age. We may add Beethoven to Northrop Frye's short list of mythmakers: "Those who have really changed the modern world— Rousseau, Freud, Marx—are those who have changed its mythology, and whatever is beneficent in their influence has to do with giving man increased power over his own vision."[63]

In Beethoven's re-creation of myth, history is kept open—as quest for the unreachable, for the as-yet-undiscovered, for the vision of an ultimate felicity. He refuses to accept that history is closed at either its source or its goal, for a perfected order would signal the termination of life and of striving. In the Ninth Symphony, the condition of joy is elusive, even in Elysium. The search continues for a hidden God, a distant beloved, brotherhood. And Creation can begin again merely by the omission of a major or minor third.

THE INTERIOR
DIMENSION

2

Beethoven's Birth Year

"I LIVED for a while without knowing how old I was," Beethoven wrote to Wegeler on 2 May 1810.[1] In fact, for many years of his life, especially in his last two decades, Beethoven believed that he had been born in December 1772 rather than in December 1770. Thayer claims that the incorrect birth year, 1772, is the one that is "given in all the old biographical notices, and which corresponds to the dates affixed to many of his first works, and indeed to nearly all allusions to his age in the early years."[2] Beethoven's father is blamed for the alleged discrepancy. Some biographers accuse him of deliberate falsification. Thayer finds the "conclusion irresistible" that the boy's age was "purposely falsified" by his father in order to promote his possibilities as a *Wunderkind* along the lines of the Mozart children. "There is, unfortunately," Thayer notes, "nothing known of Johann van Beethoven's character which renders such a trick improbable."[3] Schiedermair, whose approach is more lenient, gives Johann the benefit of the doubt, stressing the widespread laxity in keeping family records at that time and wondering whether the alcoholic father might not have simply made a mistake: "It is more obvious and natural to assume that father Johann even as early as 1778 no longer knew precisely the birth year of his son."[4] In either case, there is no disagreement as to the existence of a two-year discrepancy during the Bonn period, and Beethoven's false beliefs about his age are universally attributed either to the father's falsification of his age or to errors on the first editions or autographs of his earliest works.

Thayer is not accurate, however, in stating that all the old biographical notices gave 1772 as Beethoven's birth year or in asserting that 1772 corresponded to the dates of many of his first works. Nor can it be shown that Johann van Beethoven ever deducted two years from his son's age. Close scrutiny reveals not a single confirmable instance of a discrepancy exceeding one year during the Bonn period and only one biographical notice with a 1772 birth year. There is a consistent pattern of deductions of one year, which leads to the conclusion that Beethoven, his family, and his associates all believed during those years that he had been born in December 1771. The deduction of two (and on occasion even more than two) years was made by Beethoven himself, and this evidently took place only at some time after his arrival in Vienna.

On 26 March 1778, Johann presented Ludwig at a concert in Cologne and listed him in the promotional announcement as being "his little son of six years."[5] Beethoven was then a few months past seven. It is therefore clear that Johann—deliberately or by miscalculation—deducted one year. The documentary evidence contains no further reference connecting Johann with the subject of the birth year.

There are other documents showing an understatement of Beethoven's age during this period. On 14 October 1783, Beethoven submitted a dedicatory letter to Elector Maximilian Friedrich, accompanying his dedication of the three Sonatas for Pianoforte, WoO 47 (for abbreviations, see p. 299, below), in which he writes: "I have now reached my eleventh year . . . Eleven years old." The title page of the sonatas reads, "Ludwig van Beethoven, age eleven years," and the publisher announced the works in Cramer's Magazine of 14 October 1783 as compositions "of a young genius of 11 years."[6] Here again, only one year has been deducted, since Beethoven was then twelve. Because of the unquestioned assumption that there was a two-year discrepancy during the Bonn period, many scholars have made simple arithmetical errors regarding this dedication and other documents of the period, and these errors have perpetuated the myth of the two-year differential.[7] Thayer, although his generalizations are incorrect, commits no such arithmetical errors, and he notes that "at first, the falsification rarely extends beyond one year."[8]

Other works that tend to confirm a consistent pattern of one-year deductions are the Variations on a March by Dressler, WoO 63 ("composed . . . by a young amateur Louis van Beethoven aged ten"), published in 1782 or at the latest in early 1783, and the song "Schilderung eines Mädchens," WoO 107 ("11 years old"), published in 1783. When a work composed in these years bears a notation on the score as to Beethoven's age but is published only many years later, there is clearly some difficulty in dating it. Such are the Fugue in D major for Organ, WoO 31 ("at the age of 11 years"), the Concerto in E-flat major for Pianoforte and Orchestra, WoO 4 ("composed by Louis van Beethoven, aged twelve"), the Minuet for Pianoforte in E-flat major, WoO 82 (a copy seen by Nottebohm, now lost, stated "at the age of 13"), and the Prelude for Pianoforte in F minor, WoO 55 (again, according to Nottebohm, "at the age of 15 years").[9] Some Beethoven scholars have dated these works by circular reasoning, using an assumed birthday of December 1772 as the point of departure and adding the designated number of years. In 1868 Nottebohm arrived at an incorrect date of 1780 for the Variations on a March by Dressler via the same method, but using the date of December 1770 as his reference point.[10] Kinsky dates these works by analogy to the Electoral Sonatas, thereby arriving at a one-year difference even though he assumes a two-year deduction from Beethoven's age in this period.

As for the older biographical notices, the first in print is Christian Gottlob Neefe's report of 2 March 1783:

> Louis van Beethoven, son of the tenor singer mentioned, a boy of eleven years and of the most promising talent. He plays the clavier very skillfully and with power, reads at sight very well, and . . . he plays chiefly *The Well-Tempered Clavier* of Sebastian Bach, which Herr Neefe put into his hands . . . So far as his duties permitted, Herr Neefe has also given him instruction in thorough-bass. He is now training him in composition and for his encouragement has had nine variations for the pianoforte [WoO 63] . . . engraved at Mannheim. This youthful genius is deserving of help to enable him to travel. He would surely become a second Wolfgang Amadeus Mozart were he to continue as he has begun.[11]

It is evident that Neefe, here and in connection with Beethoven's earliest publications, consistently believed his pupil to have been one year younger than his actual age.

Another early biographical notice is that of Carl Ludwig Junker, published on 23 November 1791: "I heard also one of the greatest of pianists—the dear, good Bethofen, some compositions by whom appeared in the Speier *Blumenlese* in 1783, written in his eleventh year . . . Three sonatas for pianoforte by him were also printed around that time by Bossler's publishing house."[12] Junker provides no new information on this subject. The ambiguity of the phrase "in his eleventh year" (rather than "at the age of eleven") should not lead to the assumption that he believed Beethoven to have been born in 1772.

A significant reference, in the *Allgemeine musikalische Zeitung* in 1799, refers to "the worthy pianist Beethoven, who in his thirteenth year had already published sonatas of his own."[13] If "in his thirteenth year" is taken to mean that Beethoven was twelve, then this is a correct statement of his age by someone who was probably a fellow Rhinelander. The comment is particularly significant in view of the words "completed by Beethoven, aged eleven" appearing on the title page of the Sonatas, WoO 47.

Only one notice published before 1800 specifies a 1772 birth year, and it appears to have been widely copied by early nineteenth-century dictionary and encyclopedia authors. This is Ernst Ludwig Gerber's biographical note of 1790: "Beethoven (Louis van). Son of a tenor in the Electoral Court at Bonn; born there 1772, a student of Neefe; in his 11th year he was already playing Sebastian Bach's *Well-Tempered Clavier*. Also in the same year he had already published at Speier and Mannheim his earliest attempts at composition—9 Variations on a March, 3 Clavier Sonatas and several Lieder."[14] This notice derives primarily from Neefe's of 2 March 1783. Gerber's errors are easily attributable to hasty research and to the same simple arithmetical error that has plagued so many biographers and scholars—the miscalculation which stems from overlooking the month in which Beethoven was born. In this case, Gerber probably deducted eleven (the age given on Beethoven's first publications) from 1783 (the year of the first publications) and thereby arrived at a birth year of 1772. I am not aware of any early biographical notice which gives both the month and the year of Beethoven's birth.

Apart from Gerber's secondhand entry, at no point during Beethoven's stay in Bonn can it be confirmed that his age was understated by two years. Moreover, his age was in almost every case clearly understated by one year. Those Bonn compositions that bear an age reference may therefore be safely dated by assuming a consistent birth date of December 1771. The notions that Beethoven's father deducted two years from Beethoven's age and that the first publications and biographical notices understate his age by two years may be discarded. Beethoven's persistent belief that he was born in December 1772 (or later) had no documentary basis, and it arose at a time that cannot be fixed with certainty.

T H E first indication of Beethoven's own confusion about his age dates from 1785. In that year he wrote on the autograph of his three Quartets for Piano and Strings, WoO 36: "trois quatuors p[o]ur le clave[c]in, violino, viola e Basso, 1785, compose par luis van Beethoven, agè 13 ans." This would be congruent with the December 1771 birth date, but Thayer notes: "The figure indicating the composer's age was first written '14' and then changed."[15] Fourteen, of course, was his correct age. Perhaps there is some connection between this indecision and an official report to Elector Maximilian Franz in mid-1784 which states Beethoven's age correctly: "Ludwig van Beethoven, age 13, born at Bonn, has served two years, no salary."[16] Clearly the court itself was under no misapprehension about Beethoven's age, and the information in the report may have been brought to the young composer's attention, perhaps by some court official who noted the discrepancy. Whatever the cause, in 1785, far from believing that he was two years younger, Beethoven gives evidence in his own hand that, if anything, he then regarded himself as having been born in either 1770 or 1771 and was undecided about his real age.

In March or April 1787, during a visit to Augsburg, Beethoven apparently mentioned that he was fourteen years old, for that was the recollection of his close friend Anna Maria (Nanette) Streicher (née Stein), who initially met the young composer there on his return trip from Vienna to Bonn. We know this because Beethoven's nephew Karl wrote in a conversation book of 1824: "Frau von Streicher says that she is delighted that at the age of fourteen you saw the instruments made by her father and now see those made by her son."[17]

What appears to be the next reference by Beethoven to his age is written in an account or memorandum book that he began to keep shortly after his arrival in Vienna in late 1792. It contains a startling entry, perhaps jotted down in connection with Beethoven's birthday in late 1793 or at the beginning of the next year: "Courage! My spirit shall triumph over all weaknesses of the body. You have lived twenty-five years; this year must determine the whole man. Nothing must remain undone."[18] Beethoven was then just twenty-three years old. If this diary entry is not a citation from an as-yet-unidentified literary source, at that moment he possibly believed himself to have been two—or even three—years *older* than his actual age. Perhaps his uncertainty about his age was such that he did not know whether he was younger or older than his true age, so that he alternated between extremes of speculation.

This view finds apparent confirmation in Beethoven's Heiligenstadt Testament of 6 October 1802, a last will addressed to his brothers: "Perhaps I shall get better, perhaps not, I am ready.—Forced to become a philosopher already in my 28th year, oh, it is not easy."[19] Whether at this time Beethoven believed that he had been born in 1773 (or later) cannot be known for certain, but it appears so. In any event, he was soon to fix on 1772 as the "real" year of his birth.

IN 1806 Ferdinand Ries, seeking to find out Beethoven's exact date of birth, obtained a copy of his certificate of baptism, dated 17 December 1770, and sent it to Beethoven in Vienna, succeeding only in arousing the composer's anger. The subject remained a matter of friction between them until as late as 1809, when Beethoven wrote to Ries: "Your friends have given you bad advice—But I know all about these friends, for they are the same people to whom you also sent those nice reports from Paris about me—the very same people who enquired *about my age,* about which you were able to provide them with such reliable information—the very same people who have already lowered my good opinion of you on several occasions and have now done so for good."[20] Ries explains the underlying events without specifying who the friends were: "Some friends of Beethoven wanted to know with certitude the day of his birth. With much effort, in 1806, when I was in Bonn, I looked up his baptismal certificate which I finally located and sent to Vienna. Beethoven never wanted to speak about his age."[21]

Despite the heavy irony and anger of Beethoven's reply, his mind was not set at rest concerning the discrepancy between the evidence of the baptismal certificate and his own belief that he was younger. On 2 May 1810, he wrote an urgent letter to Wegeler in Coblenz, asking that he obtain another, "correct" certificate of baptism:

> I ask you to obtain for me *my certificate of baptism* . . . take note of the fact that I had a brother *born before me,* who was also called Ludwig, but with the additional name of "Maria," and who died. In order to determine my true age, you should,

therefore, first find this Ludwig. For I know that other people, by giving out that I am older than I really am, have been responsible for this error—Unfortunately I lived for a while without knowing how old I was—I had a family book but it was lost, Heavens knows how—So please do not be annoyed at my earnestly requesting you to find out all about Ludwig Maria and the present Ludwig, who was born after him—The sooner you send me the certificate of baptism, the greater will be my gratitude.[22]

Wegeler's response was a confirmation of Ries's evidence. He sent Beethoven a copy of his baptismal certificate dated 2 June 1810, duly signed by the "Mayor's office of Bonn," which sets forth 1770 as his birth year. Beethoven still would not accept the document as valid. He wrote the date "1772" on the back of it and added: "The baptismal certificate seems to be incorrect, since there was a Ludwig born before me. A Baumgarten was my sponsor, I believe."[23] Uncertainty lingered, as confirmed by Bettina Brentano's letter to Anton Bihler of 9 July 1810: "He does not know his age himself but believes he is thirty-five."[24]

The subject recurred in later years. Beethoven's Tagebuch (journal) of 1818 has the notation: "Frau Baumgarten concerning the first and second Ludwig."[25] And a conversation book entry from February 1820 reveals Beethoven still speculating about his sponsor's identity, which might serve as a means of proving that he had indeed been born in 1772: "Bongard or Baumgarten must have been the name of the woman who was my godmother."[26] Actually her name was Gertrud Baum, which is clearly set forth in the church register and in the baptismal certificates that he had received first from Ries, then from Wegeler, and now from another well-wisher, Wilhelm Christian Müller.

In a letter to an unknown correspondent dated 22 April 1827, Müller describes his experiences with Beethoven concerning the birth-year question: "We wanted to know from him when his birthday was, in order to celebrate it—actually we wanted to send him a ring. He replied that he didn't know precisely either the day or the year. My daughter wrote to Professor Arndt in Bonn and asked him to obtain and send us a birth certificate from the Church Register. This designated the date as 17 December 1770. Through us he came to know the truth, and we spoke with him about it as recently as 1820, and he jestingly said that he would not have believed that he was such an old bloke."[27] It is nice to learn that Beethoven had reached the point where he could joke about his age, but Müller's evidence did not settle the question either. In the conversation book for 15 December 1823, Beethoven's nephew wrote: "Today is the 15th of December, the day of your birth, but I am not sure whether it is the 15th or 17th, inasmuch as we can not depend on the certificate of baptism and I read it only *once* when I was still with you in January."[28] Beethoven had not yet, nor would he ever wholly, come to terms with the facts set forth so simply on the certificate.

Beethoven manifestly had all the dates available to convince himself of his real birth year: at least three copies of the baptismal certificate; the independent researches of Ries, Wegeler, and the Müllers; the name of his sponsor clearly given as Frau Baum—obviously the "Frau Baumgarten" or "Bongard" he had been seeking; and the fact that the baptismal certificate gives his correct baptismal day. It is improbable that Beethoven imagined he was only one year and four months older than his brother Caspar Carl, who was born in April 1774.[29] And the vivid memories that Beethoven retained of his grandfather (who died on 24 December 1773) would have been impossible if he had been only one year old when the kapellmeister died.

In view of the unmistakable ways in which Beethoven could have tested and confirmed the accuracy of the baptismal certificates, it seems clear that he was unwilling or unable to subject the issue of his birth year to rational consideration. The birth-year delusion can no longer be described as rising from a deliberate falsification by Johann van Beethoven of his son's age. The delusion was Beethoven's own.

When I first encountered this curious fantasy, I surmised that the "missing" years served to veil from memory events or relationships belonging to Beethoven's childhood—perhaps to his very first years. That may well be, but further reflection on this possibility has not yet clarified the issue.

3

The Nobility Pretense

VITAL to an understanding of Beethoven's life in Vienna is the certainty that until 11 December 1818 he encouraged, or at least permitted to pass unchallenged, the assumption that he was of noble birth. On that date he was in the midst of a crucial lawsuit with his sister-in-law Johanna, concerning the guardianship of his nephew, Karl, the son of his deceased brother Caspar Carl. The hearing was being conducted before the Imperial Landrecht of Vienna, which Thayer described as "a tribunal with jurisdiction in litigations and other matters affecting the nobility."[1] The contest between Beethoven and Johanna had no place before the Landrecht, but as Thayer observed, "acting on the assumption that the Dutch 'van,' like the German 'von,' was a badge of noble birth, it had listened to Beethoven's plea and appointed him the sole guardian of his nephew" on 9 January 1816.[2] The mother sued to recover her child, and her appeal was now being heard.

It had been apparent during the initial suit, from which Beethoven emerged victorious, that the Landrecht was heavily prejudiced in his favor, perhaps because of the different status of the two parties to the suit—one a presumed noble (Beethoven), the other a commoner (Johanna van Beethoven)—partly because of his fame, and decisively because of the influence of his highly placed aristocratic friends whom he had undoubtedly persuaded to intervene on his behalf. The outcome of the appeal was thus a foregone conclusion until Beethoven, in what appeared to be a moment of confusion, gratuitously raised the question of his family's nobility. His testimony is preserved in the minutes of the Landrecht.[3]

The court asked Beethoven of his plans for Karl, and he responded: "After half a year he would send him to the Mölker Convict, which he had heard highly commended, or if he were but of noble birth, give him to the Theresianum." The court, hearing the negative reference to Karl's nobility, pursued the question: "Were he and his brother of the nobility, and did he have documents to prove it?" Beethoven admitted that he had no proof, though he tried to imply that he was indeed noble: "'Van' was a Dutch predicate which was not exclusively applied to the nobility; he had neither a diploma nor any other proof of his nobility."

Johanna van Beethoven was then questioned: "Was her husband of noble birth?" Her reply: "So the brothers had said; the documentary proof of nobility was said to be in the possession of the oldest brother, the composer. At the legal hearing on the death of her husband, proofs of nobility had been demanded; she herself had no document bearing on the subject." The Landrecht thereupon dismissed the case from its jurisdiction, in a declaration of 18 December 1818: "It . . . appears from the statement of Ludwig van Beethoven, as the accompanying copy of the court minutes of 11 December of this year shows, that he is unable to prove nobility; hence the matter of guardianship is transferred to the Magistracy."[4]

Thayer thought it "scarcely conceivable that Beethoven should have cherished the thought that possibly he was of noble birth or that he seriously encouraged such a belief among his exalted friends," but the evidence is overwhelmingly against his view.[5] Clearly Beethoven had intended to deceive the court. Furthermore, the lawsuit had already been in progress for almost three years, and no one had come forward to question the deception, a situation which indicated that all of Vienna shared the belief in Beethoven's nobility. The case was a sensational one, involving as it did the attempt of Vienna's greatest composer to take sole possession of his nephew from a still living mother—a case in which charges of immorality and scandal flew freely in such a way as to strike the public fancy and cause it to take sides. Schindler recalled that "all of musical Vienna had taken the liveliest interest" in the lawsuit.[6] Nohl remarked that Johanna van Beethoven had the "sympathy of the public" entirely on her side.[7] If, in the course of these years, no individual raised the question of why the case was being disputed before a court of the nobility, it is quite probable that Beethoven's friends, acquaintances, patrons, and the general public shared the belief of the Landrecht that he was of noble birth. It is therefore also probable that this assumption dated from the earliest days of his introduction into Viennese society by Count Waldstein.[8]

Wegeler was fully aware of his friend's nobility pretense. Writing in 1845, he stated flatly: "Louis van Beethoven passed from time to time for a noble, because people regarded the Dutch particle 'van' as the equivalent of the German 'von.' In Vienna, this lasted three years. Indeed, a lawsuit of Beethoven lasted for this time at the Landrecht, and, this error being discovered, was brought before the Magistracy."[9] Schindler was equally unequivocal: "Had the nobles not believed him to be one of them, neither his genius nor his works of art would have won for him the favored position he had enjoyed in aristocratic circles up to that time . . . The little word 'van' had exercised a magic power."[10] Nohl, who weighed the evidence in 1867 in the second volume of his Beethoven biography, came to the same conclusion as the earlier biographers.[11]

The *van* actually was transformed into the unimpeachable *von* on numerous occasions. For example, the announcements and review of the 29 March 1795 concert refer to "Herr Ludwig von Beethoven."[12] Both the announcement of his appearance at Romberg's 1797 benefit concert and a legal document concerning the Bohemian Landrecht contain the *von*.[13] Goethe used "Herr von Beethoven" in a letter to his wife of 29 July 1812, and the police during the Congress of Vienna filed a secret report on this same "Herr von Beethoven."[14] These examples confirm the ready and widespread acceptance of Beethoven's assumed nobility.

The effect of the Landrecht decision on Beethoven was devastating. Schindler, in the earliest edition of his *Biographie* (1840), wrote that it "drove Beethoven beside himself; for he considered it the grossest insult that he had ever received and as an unjustifiable depreciation and humiliation of the artist—an impression too deep to be ever erased from his mind." He was so "deeply mortified" that he "would have quitted the country."[15]

In this harmless but meaningful pretense Beethoven revealed himself to be a typical Viennese, as he was in so many other respects. A visitor to Vienna in the 1820s commented on the general "fondness for being honored with high sounding forms of address . . . no where is it carried to such an extravagant length as in Vienna . . . It is equally common, and still more absurd, for both sexes to prefix *von* (of), the symbol of nobility, to the surname."[16] The acute modern observer Ilsa Barea noted how ubiquitous "the spurious use of *von* had become . . . in Vienna" by the 1830s, stemming from the emergence of rigid bureaucratic forms in the mid-eighteenth century, which made official or noble titles an economic and psychological necessity: "A sense of social inferiority went with the material insecurity of the middle class; therefore the smallest official title that placed the bearer at a fixed point of the Establishment became a saving grace."[17]

Even after the dismissal of the case from the Landrecht, Beethoven and his attorney, Johann Baptist Bach, found it expedient to use (though with trepidation) a false official title in their presentation of the case to the Magistracy. Beethoven became "Royal Imperial Kapellmeister and Composer," a title that he had also used before the Landrecht as early as 29 November 1815.[18] Schindler, who understood the Viennese better than Thayer, knowingly wrote: "In Austria one had to have some sort of official title if he were to gain anything like respect from the lower courts."[19]

Class lines were not easily crossed in the Vienna of Beethoven's time. An English visitor pointed out in 1806: "There are two classes of society, what is called the first class consisting of the nobles and families of distinction, and ministers and officers of state, and the second made up of the second nobility so called, barons for example, and persons of fortune without titles or family honours. The division is . . . complete."[20] If class barriers were impassable between the hereditary nobility and the nobility of wealth, what could be said of the bars to social access that confronted the remaining classes of Viennese society? After Beethoven's departure from Bonn, where the status of the artist was clearly delineated as a cross between servant and artisan, his position in the social hierarchy became confused and rudderless; he was cut adrift, becoming a *petit bourgeois* whose links to feudal patronage were not altogether severed, a small businessman-artist whose complicated role it was to haggle with publishers, to seek favor with the individual nobles who commissioned many of his works, and to preserve his newly won independence while simultaneously seeking a financial anchor.

Beethoven's brother Caspar Carl also pretended to nobility. His last will, dated 14 November 1815, was filed with the Landrecht; in referring the guardianship case to the Magistracy, the Landrecht took notice of this deception.[21] And as early as 1800 the *Hof-und-Staats-Schematismus*, which listed all court and state employees, had given his name as "Carl v. Beethoven," indicating that the *van* was considered equivalent to the noble *von* by Carl's superiors and that he may already have been passing as a noble.[22] In the case of Caspar Carl, the nobility deception may have had an economic motivation, since it was perhaps helpful to be a member of the nobility in order to obtain a respectable post in public service.[23]

The youngest of the Beethoven brothers, the pharmacist Nikolaus Johann, had an obviously bourgeois occupation, and no pretense would have been necessary for him to advance in his profession. But he was concerned about matters of rank, and he, too, appears to have attempted to pass as a noble.[24] In approximately early 1816 (at the beginning of the guardianship suit) Beethoven wrote a letter of introduction to Baron Ludwig von Türkheim, an official in the Bohemian Chancellery, asking him to assist Nikolaus Johann on "a certain matter." He wrote in a bantering tone: "Do not forget our old friendship; and if you can do something for my brother without overthrowing the Austrian Monarchy, I hope to find you willing."[25] According to Frimmel, tradition had it "that Johann van Beethoven wanted his pretended membership in the Netherlandish nobility confirmed in Austria."[26] It is tempting to speculate that Beethoven was here utilizing Nikolaus Johann for the purpose of testing whether a van Beethoven claim to nobility could be authenticated by Türkheim; if the answer had been affirmative (which it evidently was not), he himself would surely have made similar application or utilized Johann's evidence as confirmation of his own nobility. Beethoven probably lofted this trial balloon immediately after institution of the lawsuit at the Landrecht, thereby hoping to shore up his unsteady claim to nobility. In a related event in early December 1815, a magisterial deputation delivered to Beethoven a certificate conferring upon him the citizenship of Vienna. This conferral was presumably arranged for at Beethoven's instigation, perhaps in connection with the guardianship claim.[27]

Ironically, Beethoven's pretense of nobility made it impossible for him to seek and to obtain a conferral of nobility (such as Goethe, Schiller, Dittersdorf, Sonnenfels, and many others had obtained), which probably could have been arranged for him by one of his powerful aristocratic friends or patrons (certainly by Archduke Rudolph), despite the fact that he was not a favorite of Emperor Franz himself. As Schenk observed, "Ennoblements were fairly frequent in eighteenth-century Austria. Agents who could pull a few strings were employed in the process."[28] "Joseph II made financiers into noblemen by the dozen," noted W. H. Bruford, to which Arthur Loesser added, "Wealth was not the only gateway to aristocracy; talents, too, were rewarded with ennobling recognition: botanists, librarians, physicians, and archaeologists acquired the beneficent 'von' when their achievements were sufficiently noted."[29] This pattern continued in the early nineteenth century. At the height of Beethoven's Viennese popularity, around the time of the Congress of Vienna, the court would surely have been sympathetic to such a request; but this course was foreclosed to Beethoven.

CENTRAL to the nobility pretense is the desire for acceptance by those in command of society: by the leaders and shapers, the royalty and nobility. That Beethoven felt he had to pretend nobility in order to obtain such acceptance is a poignant indication of the depth of his need. He treasured virtually every medal, honor, or other distinction that was awarded him. Thayer noted gently that "Beethoven was not always as indifferent to distinctions of all kinds as he sometimes professed."[30] Ries made the same point: "Although his manner was alike to men, whether of the highest or the lowest conditions, yet he was by no means insensible to the civilities of the former." MacArdle concurred: "Beneath Beethoven's overt disregard for nobility there was a very real deference to titles."[31] And Schindler, though he was present in the later years when Beethoven "frequently lashed unmercifully one or the other of his contemporaries for their 'longing and snapping after ribbons,'" related that Beethoven's receipt on 20 February 1824 of a gold medal weighing twenty-one louis d'or inscribed by the king of France was "the greatest distinction conferred upon the master during his lifetime."[32] Beethoven wrote to his friend Karl Bernard that Louis XVIII's gift showed "that he is a generous King and a man of refined feeling," and he asked Bernard to print the news of the royal distinction in the periodical he edited.[33] Beethoven sent an impression of the medal to Prince Galitzin in Russia and wrote proudly to him: "The medal weighs a half a pound in gold . . ."[34] In a similar vein he wrote to Pilat in July 1823: "I should consider it an honour if you would be kind enough to mention in your so generally esteemed paper my election as foreign member of the Royal Swedish Academy of Music."[35]

Beethoven's letter to Wegeler of 7 December 1826 contains a proud summary of honors that he had received and expresses the hope that he might receive a Royal Order from King Friedrich Wilhelm III, to whom he had just dedicated the Ninth Symphony:

> I will write briefly of my diplomas: I am an honorary member of the Royal Society of Sciences in Sweden, as well as in Amsterdam, and am also an Honorary Freeman of Vienna.—A short time ago a certain Dr. Spiker took my last big symphony with choruses to Berlin; it is dedicated to the King, and I had to write out the dedication in my own hand. Earlier I had sought permission from the Embassy to be allowed to dedicate the work to the King, which he then gave me . . . Something has been said to me in this connection about the Order of the Red Eagle, Second Class [a slight exaggeration: it was Third Class which had been spoken of]. What the outcome will be I do not know, for I have never sought for such marks of honor. But at my present age they could not be unwelcome for several reasons . . . Of the marks of honor which I know give you joy, I can report also that a medal was sent to me from the deceased King of France with the inscription: Donné par le Roi à Monsieur Beethoven, which was accompanied by a very courteous note from the Premier Gentilhomme du Roi, the Duc de Chartres.[36]

That Beethoven's attitude toward honors occasionally turned ambivalent is clear, even without Schindler's probably apocryphal story that in 1823 Beethoven was offered the choice of a royal decoration or fifty ducats for the Prussian court's subscription to the *Missa solemnis;* Beethoven unhesitatingly answered "Fifty ducats," preferring the cash to the ribbon.[37] Schindler took this as "striking proof of how lightly he prized insignia of honor or distinctions in general."[38] However, Schindler knew full well Beethoven's high regard for the symbols of acceptance. In a conversation book of 1824 there is this unctuous speech by Schindler: "Master! Listen! I have something to say, so follow me: How shall the placard be worded [for the Beethoven concert of 7 May 1824] . . . shall I put in Member of the Royal Academy at Stockholm and Amsterdam? Tell me briefly. What a tremendous title!!"[39] It remained for Schuppanzigh to oppose Schindler's suggestion: "I am not in favor of it. Beethoven is *dictator* and *president* of all the academies in the world and sensible people will look upon this title as vanity on his part." Schindler thereupon reversed his field: "My lord is not wrong . . . The name *Beethoven* shines brightest without affix of any kind and when most unassuming; all the world knows who and what you are."[40]

Nor was Beethoven's pride at honors and gifts a product of his late years. Ries related that on Beethoven's departure from Berlin in 1796, following his visit to the court of Friedrich Wilhelm II and his performances there, "he received a gold snuff-box filled with Louis d'ors. Beethoven declared with pride that it was not an ordinary snuff-box, but such a one as it might have been customary to give to an ambassador."[41] A good example of the abashedness with which Beethoven acknowledged his deep desire for tokens of recognition is in his letter of 5 April 1809, to Breitkopf and Härtel, asking that the *Allgemeine musikalische Zeitung* mention that he had been offered the post of chief kappellmeister of the court of Westphalia: "Be sure not to forget to mention the *Chief Kapellmeister* [heavily underlined]. I laugh at such things, but there are *Miserabiles* who know how, after the manner of cooks, to serve up such trimmings."[42]

One of Beethoven's profound wishes was to obtain an imperial post in Vienna. The first references to this desire appear in his correspondence shortly after the turn of the century. He wrote to Wegeler on 29 June 1801 that Prince Lichnowsky "has disbursed for my benefit a fixed sum of 600 gulden, on which I can draw until I obtain a suitable appointment."[43] And in a letter around 18 September 1803 to Hoffmeister and Kühnel he wrote: "I would most willingly give you everything if I could only make my way in the world, but—please remember that all my acquaintances hold appointments and know exactly what they have to live on; but, Heaven help us! what appointment at the Imperial Court could be given to such a *parvum talentum com ego?*"[44]

This yearning for an imperial post was presumably motivated in part by a desire for the feudal security which was slipping from his grasp as he made the transition from feudal status to "freedom," and in part by a desire to emulate the great kapellmeister of his youth—his grandfather. (Inevitably, Beethoven's father had haplessly aspired to the post of kapellmeister.) The link with the nobility pretense is clear, for it, too, is expressive of that simple need for status and recognition which is so marked in Beethoven's personality.

The kapellmeister leitmotif was sounded repeatedly during the next twenty years. In late 1808 Beethoven was actually offered the post of kapellmeister to Napoleon's brother Jérôme, who had just been installed as king of the newly created kingdom of Westphalia. Beethoven was on the verge of accepting this offer and used it as a lever to acquire from Archduke Rudolph and the princes Lobkowitz and Kinsky an annuity which guaranteed lifelong financial support, in return for his promise to make his domicile in Vienna a permanent one. During the course of these negotiations Beethoven drew up the outline of a proposal to be submitted to the noblemen: "His greatest longing and his most ardent wish is to enter the Imperial service at some future time . . . For the time being, however, the title of Imperial Kapellmeister would make him very happy; and if this title could be obtained for him, his permanent residence in Vienna would become even more attractive."[45] Beethoven received the annuity, but not the title that would have made him "very happy." He continued to hope, however, and on 18 March he wrote confidently to his intimate friend Gleichenstein that "the title of Imperial Kapellmeister will also come later." That the desire was deeply rooted is shown touchingly in a Tagebuch entry of 1815: "If possible, bring the ear-trumpets to perfection and then travel. This you owe to yourself, to Mankind and to Him, the Almighty. Only thus can you once again develop everything that has to remain within you—And a small court—a small chapel—in it the hymn written by me, performed for the glory of the Almighty, the Eternal, the Infinite."[46]

At about this same time, the years of the Congress of Vienna, when he was acclaimed as a national patriotic composer, Beethoven was paid homage by the assembled rulers of Europe. "In later years," wrote Schindler, "the great master would recall not without emotion those days in the imperial castle and the palace of the Russian prince and would say with a tinge of pride that he had allowed himself to be courted by the highest rulers of Europe and had comported himself admirably."[47] In the following years, however, the neglect of Beethoven by the court seemed all the more painful in view of the heights of appreciation that had been reached, causing him to complain and fret about the unfeeling and inartistic qualities of the aristocracy and the imperial court.[48]

That Beethoven appropriated to himself the title "Royal Imperial

Kapellmeister and Composer" should be regarded not just as a deception but primarily as the expression of a profound wish. In November 1822, the opportunity arose to make the wish come true: the imperial court composer, Anton Teyber, died, and Beethoven applied for the position in a letter to Count Moritz Dietrichstein around 1 January 1823: "I hear that the post of Imperial and Royal Chamber Music Composer, which Teyber held, is again to be filled, and I gladly apply for it, particularly if, as I fancy, one of the requirements is that I should occasionally provide a composition for the Imperial Court."[49]

The irony of this story is that the depth of Beethoven's desire for an imperial post was matched by his inner certainty that it would not be granted to him. Thus, when his friends at court—Count Lichnowsky, Count Dietrichstein, and Archduke Rudolph—paved the way for the appointment and evidently obtained a verbal commitment that the position would be his if Beethoven would write a Mass for the emperor to show his sincerity and homage (to place him, as Thayer noted, "into the Emperor's good books"), Beethoven did not believe it.[50] The Mass for the emperor was not written—to the disappointment of Beethoven's noble friends. Perhaps Beethoven felt that it was too late for the court to make amends for a generation of neglect. Perhaps he was unwilling to abandon the freedom from patronage within which his creativity had unhampered space to develop. Perhaps he did not wish to invite another rejection by a royal or noble personage, rejections which, in his fear of them, he did so much to bring about. Perhaps, too, there was some inner resistance to obtaining the post which meant so much to him, for this might have meant the attainment of that which his father had vainly desired. These factors may bear upon his failure to write the Mass, his refusal of the post of kapellmeister of Westphalia in 1809, and his rejection of an invitation (possibly to join the Prussian court permanently) from Friedrich Wilhelm II as early as 1796, which Czerny described: "he declined to accept an invitation which the King of Prussia gave him after one of the extemporary performances."[51] Perhaps in the last analysis, Beethoven's desire to be free was in perpetual and irreconcilable conflict with his desire for acceptance and for financial stability.

BEETHOVEN'S acknowledgment of nonnobility before the Landrecht led to dismay, embarrassment, and humiliation, and it was probably a factor in the withdrawal from society that marked his last years. One day in 1820 Peters, his friend and the coguardian of Karl, wrote in a conversation book: "You are as discontented today as I." Beethoven took up the pencil and responded: "The burgher ought to be excluded from the society of higher men, and here I am fallen among them."⁵² However, neither his dramatic exclusion from the nobility nor the exposure of his pretense at aristocratic descent fully dissuaded Beethoven from continuing to believe in his noble origin.

On 19 July 1819, he wrote to Franz Xaver Piuk of the Magistracy about the Landrecht incident: "Despite all the defamatory statements made by the mother and her abettors, no accusation could be brought against me. But the discussion turned on the little word 'van'; and I had sufficient personal pride to declare that I had *never* worried *about my nobility*—And that is how we came to the worshipful Magistracy."⁵³ What Beethoven had told the Landrecht does not coincide with this letter. In neither instance does Beethoven admit nonnobility, only that he cannot (to the Landrecht) or will not (to Piuk) prove it.⁵⁴ In a draft memorandum concerning the lawsuit, Beethoven refers to his nephew's unfortunate "lack of a title of nobility" and adds: "The same can be said too of *myself.*"⁵⁵ The letter to Piuk gives the impression that his nobility was so certain (and his pride so great) that he would not debate it with those who required proof of it. (Actually, Schindler's discredited tale of Beethoven defying the Landrecht with the words, "My nobility is *here* and *here*," pointing to his head and heart, is close to the psychological truth of the matter.) And in a letter to Schindler toward the end of June 1823, Beethoven invented a new form of nobility with the line: "As for the question of 'being noble,' I think I have given sufficient proof to you that I am so on principle."⁵⁶

Beethoven was not shamming in these statements. He knew that he could not prove his nobility, that in a technical sense he had now fallen into the bourgeoisie, which he despised with an aristocrat's disdain for the lowborn and the money-grubbing. He was, however, genuinely unsettled about the facts of the matter. In a conversation book of 1820, he wrote that the court had "learned that my brother was not of the nobility," and added, in a note of puzzlement, "It is singular, so far as I know, that there is a blank here which ought to be filled, for my nature shows that I do not belong with this plebeian M[agistracy]."[57] These lines perhaps link Beethoven's nobility pretense with another crucial component of his biography—the legend of his supposed royal descent, which had found its way into print by 1810 and gained increasing currency during the remainder of his life.[58]

Beethoven's attitude toward the rumor of his royal birth (his "family romance" in Freudian terminology) has rich implications.[59] Its central significance with regard to the nobility pretense is to indicate and confirm Beethoven's belief that he was indeed of noble origin; his nobility pretense was the form whereby he lived out the family romance.

Beethoven spent the first quarter-century of his life in Vienna as an impostor. Imposture, however, generally needs the cooperation of its victims. There is a possibility, then, that the aristocracy was aware of Beethoven's nonnobility and went along with the deception without exposing it. This may be the meaning of an anecdote told by Ries:

> During Prince Louis-Ferdinand's stay at Vienna, an old countess gave a musical soirée for a few friends . . . but, at supper, there was a table laid for the prince and the highest nobility alone, and no cover for Beethoven. He became vexed, uttered some coarse expressions, and took his hat and left the house.
>
> A few days later, Prince Louis gave a dinner party, to which the old countess had also been invited. On sitting down, places were assigned to the countess on one, to Beethoven on the other side of the prince, a distinction which he always talked of with great pleasure.[60]

Were they humoring his pretense? Actually, the so-called hereditary nobility itself possessed no eternal pedigrees of aristocracy. Many of them had been ennobled within recent years or generations. The expulsion and persecution of a large proportion of the hereditary nobility of the Austrian realms in the seventeenth-century Counter Reformation had shattered continuity, and the ranks of the nobility had in many cases been filled from questionable sources— by foreigners and adventurers who had taken the side of the crown and altar. It is therefore possible that segments of the nobility itself suffered from a sense of impostorship, of shared deception, which would have predisposed them to acceptance of Beethoven's claim. On a more poignant level, it is also conceivable that the aristocracy, or portions of it, tolerated the great composer's pretense with a fine combination of tact and secret amusement.

Among the motivations for Beethoven's nobility pretense were: the acting out of the family romance; the appropriation of power through feigned participation in the circles of power; the inner belief that he was indeed noble; the transcendence of his parentage and lowly origins; the quest for a mythical, noble father; and the attempt to create a personality congruent with his creative accomplishments and capabilities. Ernst Bloch understood this curious aspect of Beethoven's personality better than anyone: "Even when the young musician Beethoven suddenly knew or claimed that he was a genius, he was practicing a scurrilous swindle, for he felt himself to be like Ludwig van Beethoven, a person he had not yet become. This piece of presumption, which was not justified by anything at the time, was needed to enable him to become Beethoven, and in the absence of the audacity, indeed brazenness, of such anticipations, nothing great would ever be achieved."[61]

On a simpler level, the pretense may also have arisen from Beethoven's desire to be loved, accepted, and applauded, which came into conflict with the feeling that he was not deserving of being loved for what he was. In conclusion, then, we may recall Cäcilia Fischer's remark to the young Beethoven in Bonn: "How dirty you are looking again—you ought to keep yourself clean!"—and Beethoven's reply: "When I become a lord, no one will take any notice of that."[62] At bottom, Beethoven's nobility pretense may be the materialization and continuation of this youthful daydream.

4

The Dreams of Beethoven

MINDFUL of objections raised to early psychoanalytical writings, Freud once warned that dream interpretation, when conducted "without reference to the dreamer's associations, would in the most favorable case remain a piece of unscientific virtuosity of the most doubtful value."[1] Nevertheless, Freud himself was more than once tempted by the seeming transparency of commonplace dream symbols to ignore his own warnings. Such symbols, he observed on one such occasion, "allow us in certain circumstances to interpret a dream without questioning the dreamer . . . If we are acquainted with the ordinary dream-symbols, and in addition with the dreamer's personality, the circumstances in which he lives and the impressions which preceded the occurrence of the dream, we are often in a position to interpret a dream straightaway—to translate it at sight, as it were."[2] Whether or not such simultaneous prohibitions and consents cancel each other out, the biographer who unearths his subject's dreams inevitably will want to try his own hand at their analysis.

My interpretation of the four dreams that Ludwig van Beethoven recorded in his correspondence provisionally concludes that they are all elaborations of a single "core" dream. This conclusion might have found favor with several of the less conventional early psychoanalysts. Róheim assumed "that there is such a thing as a *basic* dream," a view that derived from Rank's belief that dreams universally express the desire to return to the mother's womb or anxiety at that prospect.[3] Stekel, too, asserted the unity of each person's dreams, seeing them as "like a serial novel, each instalment ending with the subscription 'to be continued.'"[4] And such serial interpretation may well be in line with Freud's suggestion that the analysis of a single dream ultimately touches the entire personality and fantasy life of the dreamer, that every dream is, as Eissler noted, "infinite in its depth of meaning, and the analysis of it can never safely be regarded as having been concluded."[5]

Although dreams are known to be, in Freud's words, "a substitute for an infantile scene modified by being transferred onto a recent experience," they do not merely cast up reflections from a petrified layer of the psyche.[6] Dreams, like masterworks of art, are, in Ricoeur's formulation, "not mere projections of the artist's conflicts, but also the sketch of their solution."[7] The search for common elements in the dreams of Beethoven is, therefore, only a necessary prelude to further exploration of the ways in which the archaic materials that fuel the repeated hallucinatory dream-revivals are constantly altered by the counterpressures of the active ego. Beethoven's dreams mediate between the constant and the mobile patterns in his personality. His dreams make it possible to trace the surfacing of his tenacious birth and family romance fantasies as well as his struggle for their clarification, allowing us not only to follow the elaboration of Beethoven's richly wrought fantasies but also to observe the process by which he ultimately tried to free himself of those self-mystifying delusions.

Clinical confirmation of my speculations about Beethoven's dreams is not possible, and it may be, as Freud warned, that I will have "produced a complete caricature of an interpretation by introducing into an innocent work of art [here, a dream] purposes of which its creator had no notion, and by so doing have shown once more how easy it is to find what one is looking for and what is occupying one's own mind."[8] The test of my interpretations, then, may be whether the dream analysis clarifies any of the otherwise opaque, pathological, and delusory elements in Beethoven's biography. There can be no certainty in such matters, nor is it necessarily desirable to be wholly free of error, to "fix" the meaning of a dream so as to preclude further interpretation. As Beethoven himself liked to say: "We all make mistakes, but each errs in his own way."

The first dream is contained in a letter of 13 June 1807 to Ignaz von Gleichenstein, written from Baden:

Dear Gleichenstein,
    The night before last I had a dream in which you seemed to me to be *in a stable*, where you were so wholly bewitched and

captivated by a pair of magnificent horses that you were oblivious to everything around you.

Your purchase of a hat has been a failure, for yesterday already, as I came out here early in the morning, it got *a rip* in it.
Seeing that it cost too much for us to be so horribly swindled,
you must see that those people take it back and give you another one. In the meantime you may tell those vile *trades-
people* that I am sending it back to you—it is really too vexing—

Yesterday and today I have been very wretched, I still have
a terrible headache—Heaven help me to be rid of it—I have
quite enough with one infirmity—If you can, send me Bahrdt's
translation of Tacitus—More another time. I feel so ill that
I can only write a few lines—Farewell—think of my dream
and of me—

> your faithful
> Beethoven

It is clear from Simrock's letter that we may certainly—expect another favorable reply from Paris—If you think so too,
let my brother know this, so that everything may be copied out
again quickly—Send me the number of your house—
[On the verso] Let me have a reply about the hat.[9]

Baron Ignaz von Gleichenstein (1778–1828) was a native of Freiburg in Breisgau and a secretary in the Imperial War Department in
Vienna. He was a fine cellist, and his musical ability, together with
his Rhenish origin, may have initially attracted Beethoven to him.
Beethoven's surviving intimate correspondence with him begins
with the dream letter, although their friendship dates from around
1804. He was Beethoven's most intimate male friend between 1807
and 1810. He handled many of Beethoven's business affairs during
these years and received in return in 1809 the dedication of the Cello
Sonata, op. 69, with the inscription "Inter lacrymas et luctum." In
becoming Beethoven's agent, Gleichenstein replaced Beethoven's
brother Caspar Carl, who had married and become a father the previous year and who rapidly withdrew from the management of his
brother's affairs. In 1809 Beethoven enlisted Gleichenstein's aid in
helping him to marry: "Now you can help me to look for a wife . . . If
you do find one, however, please form the connection in advance."[10]
Later that year, both of them courted the Malfatti sisters, Gleichenstein successfully and Beethoven unsuccessfully. The strains of their
unacknowledged libidinal ties, as well as Gleichenstein's decision to

marry, led Beethoven to sever the relationship around 1810: "Again and again your friendship only causes me fresh irritation and pain"; "My cold friend, I send you all good wishes—Whatever is wrong with you, you are not really my friend—not by far as much as I am yours."[11]

The second dream appears in a letter of 15 October 1819 to the Archduke Rudolph, written from Mödling:

> Steiner already has Your Imperial Highness' Variations; he will thank you himself for them. As for the title page, it just occurs to me that the Emperor Joseph traveled under the name of a Count von Falkenstein.
>
> As I saw in the *Diarium*, Baumeister has built for himself a home in eternity. Without making the slightest claim as a recommender, I would know someone who would fill this place with Your Imperial Highness to perfect satisfaction.
>
> I am greatly looking forward to being with Y. I. H. [Your Imperial Highness] tomorrow. Last night I dreamed about Y. I. H. Although no music was performed, yet it was a musical dream. But in my waking hours too I think of Y. I. H. The Mass will now soon be finished—May Heaven empty the cornucopia of its blessings daily and hourly upon your illustrious head. As for me I am and shall remain until the last moments of my life
>
> > Your Imperial Highness's most
> > faithful and most obedient servant
> > L. v. Beethoven[12]

Archduke Rudolph (1788–1831), son of Emperor Leopold II, brother of Emperor Franz II, and later cardinal archbishop of Olmütz, was Beethoven's foremost patron after 1808 and the recipient of fifteen dedications (more than twice the number of any other dedicatee), including the *Missa solemnis* and other major works. For many years he was Beethoven's sole piano student and his only composition student. Rudolph worshipped Beethoven, carefully preserving more than one hundred letters and collecting first editions, autographs, and fair copies of his compositions. He was one of three noblemen who granted a lifetime annuity to Beethoven in 1809, on the proviso that Beethoven remain in Vienna. Beethoven, in turn, deeply loved Rudolph, regarding this nephew of Emperor Joseph II as the fairest hope for a return of the Josephinian reform period in Austria, as well as his personal passport to the imperial court. Beethoven reportedly spoke Rudolph's name "with childlike reverence, as he does no other," and his letters to the Archduke are filled with expressions of adoration.[13] Beethoven's numerous negative or ambivalent statements about Rudolph to third persons serve only to preserve the secret of his love for this orphaned and epileptic aristocrat. The essence of their relationship is reached in a passionate letter of 1820, where Beethoven calls Rudolph his Richard Coeur-de-Lion and describes himself as Blondel, faithful minstrel of the warrior-king.[14] Beethoven's attachment to Rudolph perhaps also stemmed from Rudolph's being a nephew of Max Franz, prince elector of Cologne, who was the most powerful authority-figure of Beethoven's adolescence in Bonn. In later years, Rudolph's was the one voice that the deaf Beethoven could understand through his ear trumpets.[15]

The third dream is recorded in a letter of 10 September 1821 to Tobias Haslinger, written from Baden, and addressed, "Very Best One!":

> Yesterday, as I found myself in the carriage on the way to Vienna, I was overcome by sleep, all the more so, since I scarcely ever (on account of the early rising here) have had a proper sleep. While thus slumbering, I dreamed that I was taking a very long journey, as far even as Syria, as far even as India, back again, as far even as Arabia; finally I came, indeed, to Jerusalem. The Holy City prompted thoughts of Holy Scripture, and small wonder that the man Tobias occurred to me, and naturally that our little Tobias and the pertobiasser should enter my mind; now during my dream journey the following Canon came to me:

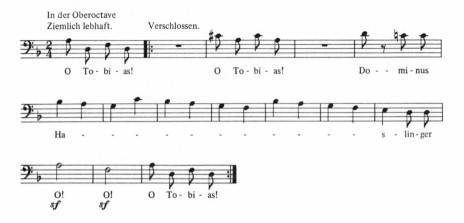

But I had scarcely awakened, when away went the Canon, and nothing of it would come back to my memory. But when, next day, I was on my way hither in the same conveyance (that of a poor Austrian musician), while awake, the dream journey went on, and behold, according to the law of association of ideas, the same Canon came back to me. Now fully awake, I held it fast, as once Menelaus did Proteus, only allowing it just to change itself into three voices:

Farewell. Presently I will send you something on Steiner to show that he has not a stony (*Steinernes*) heart. Farewell, very best of fellows, we ever wish that you will always belie your name of publisher (*Verleger*) and never become embarrassed (*verlegen*) but remain a publisher (*Verleger*) never at a loss (*verlegen*) either in receiving or paying. Sing the epistles of St. Paul every day, go every Sunday to Pater Werner, who will show you the little book by which you may go to heaven in a jiffy. You see my anxiety for the salvation of your soul, and I remain with the greatest pleasure from everlasting to everlasting

> Your most faithful debtor,
> Beethoven[16]

Tobias Haslinger (1787–1842) trained early in life as an instrumentalist, vocalist, and composer, was associated after 1814 with Beethoven's Viennese publisher, S. A. Steiner, and ultimately became sole owner of the firm. Beethoven "conceived an odd and whimsical liking for the young man" and engaged in a zany, merry correspondence with him during his last decade.[17] In a mischievous moment, Beethoven in 1825 wrote a fictional "Romantic Biography of Tobias Haslinger," in which the young man confounds the masters of counterpoint: "Tobias appears as the apprentice of the famous Kapellmeister Fux, who is firm in his saddle—and he is holding the ladder to the latter's *Gradus ad Parnassum*. Then, as he feels inclined to indulge in practical jokes, Tobias by rattling and shaking the ladder makes many a person who has already climbed rather high up, suddenly break his neck and so forth."[18] Beethoven apparently saw Haslinger as an eternal trickster, a Till Eulenspiegel who prevents parental intercourse, unseating the musical "fathers" from their firm place in the "saddle," toppling them from the "ladder," and thereby castrating them (breaking their "necks"). Occasional strains in their relationship were readily dissolved in jest. Beethoven often addressed Haslinger as his "Little Adjutant," while dubbing himself "Generalissimus."

The fourth dream is included in a letter of the summer of 1826 to Karl Holz, written from Vienna:

> The sister of the sister will come today to you. Yesterday she handed me a testimonial "non hai danaro [you have no money]."
> So please advance her the money. At the same time, tell her

that she is to have 100 gulden yearly and 36 kreuzer a week for bread-money. I forgot to say all of this yesterday. Bring with you the remainder of the B-flat quartet.—

I dreamed last night that your parents were begetting you for this world, and how much sweat it cost them to bring such an amazing piece of work into the light of day. I congratulate you on your existence—how? why?! and so forth, the riddles solve themselves—

I will see you here at dinner today—Until then keep well.

> Yours
> Beethoven[19]

Karl Holz (1798–1858) was the last in the long succession of Beethoven's unpaid secretary-factotums, replacing Anton Schindler in that post during 1825–1826. A conductor and music teacher, he was also a violinist in several string quartets that specialized in Beethoven's music and additionally retained a post in the States' Chancellory of Lower Austria. He attended to Beethoven's minutest needs—copying his works, supervising his nephew, hiring his servants, directing his finances—with dedication and an apparent absence of resentment. "When I think of the music of Beethoven," he wrote in a conversation book, "I am happy to be alive."[20] Beethoven thought so highly of Holz that in August 1826 he authorized him to prepare his biography. The name Holz, meaning "wood" in German, became the subject of Beethoven's inveterate addiction to verbal punning. He dubbed Holz "Best Mahogany," "Best Splinter from the Cross of Christ," and "Best lignum crucis." Once Beethoven unkindly observed to Holz that "wood is a neuter noun," adding: "So what a contradiction is the masculine form, and what other consequences may be drawn from *personified wood?*"[21]

In the fall of 1826, Holz determined to marry and retire from Beethoven's service. The composer, though he joked about the matter, could not conceal his sorrow at this abandonment. "Mr. Enamoured," he wrote to Holz, "I bow my knee before the almighty power of love," but added poignantly, "Memento Mori."[22]

FERENCZI wrote, "One feels impelled to relate one's dreams to the very person to whom the content relates."[23] On the surface, there were sharp differences in the class and social status of the four men to whom Beethoven told his dreams. Rudolph was of the imperial family; Gleichenstein was of the lesser nobility; Holz and Haslinger were ordinary citizens.[24] They nevertheless held important traits in common, which assist in explaining how they came to be recipients of Beethoven's dreams. Perhaps a necessary precondition was that all of them were musicians, advocates and performers of Beethoven's music, and therefore had this mode of access to his private, creative world. Furthermore, each man was considerably younger than Beethoven, enabling him to express sublimated homosexual feelings relatively unmixed with the patricidal or submissive attitudes which many older men aroused in him.

Another common factor was that each performed services for Beethoven with regularity and dependability and were sources of income to him. Unlike other, sycophantic members of Beethoven's later entourage, each of these men maintained his discrete identity under the pressure of Beethoven's incorporative tendencies, and Beethoven in turn relied upon their counsel and professionalism in significant matters. In these respects, despite their manifest differences of personality, background, and temperament, they were all idealized male siblings from whom Beethoven could receive the devotion and attention that his younger brothers, Caspar Carl and Nikolaus Johann, were unable to grant for extended periods.

Beethoven's most important patrons, closest friends, and love objects of both sexes were typically not native to Vienna, toward which he held an ambivalent attitude. Gleichenstein stemmed from the Rhineland; Rudolph was born in Florence, although he was brought to Vienna at an early age; Haslinger was born in Zell, in Upper Austria; and Holz presumably was born in or near Linz, where he (like Haslinger) received his early musical education. Although Rudolph may constitute a separate case, it is fair to say that Beethoven's dreams were shared with four younger "brothers" who, like him, were "exiles" in an adopted mother-city.[25]

The first dream, described to Gleichenstein, occurred when Beethoven was thirty-six years old, internationally famous, and at the height of his "heroic style." He was at work on the Fifth and Sixth Symphonies, the Cello Sonata, op. 69, and the Mass in C, op. 86. The most recent of his platonic, idealized love-affairs—with Josephine von Deym—was drawing to a close: her attentions were engaged elsewhere, and shortly thereafter she repeatedly refused Beethoven entrance to her house. During the preceding spring, Beethoven's yearning to join the family circle of Marie Bigot and her husband had been misread by them as an attempted seduction of Marie, leading to a painful rejection. The dream arose, therefore, at a time when Beethoven's heterosexuality was sorely tried and a sense of sexual failure was rising slowly and inexorably to the surface. (It was not, however, a critical period; several further rejections by women and the painful termination of the Immortal Beloved affair of 1812 would take place before a sense of impotence overwhelmed Beethoven and brought his creativity to a temporary halt in 1813.)

It is not surprising, therefore, that the dream's main symbols and associations are of a bisexual character. The hat, which in Freud's view has "a male significance as a rule, but [is] also capable of a female one," here is "ripped," suggesting the onlooker's feelings of anxiety and castration in the presence of a primal scene.[26] The family romance fantasy is present in both of its classic routes—the lowering of the parents (representation by animals; birth in the stable) and the elevation of the parents ("magnificent," noble horses). The horses enact the primal scene, which takes place "in a stable," an overdetermined symbol condensing such linked ideas as the bedroom, birthplace of the Savior, and bowels of the mother, together with allied anal and excremental associations. Mythology and psychoanalysis are in agreement on the bisexual symbolism of the horse. According to Bachofen, it is the sacred animal of the phallic god who represents also the tellurian "image of the generative waters."[27] Abraham noted that the horse embodies "masculine activity and at the same time feminine libido; it is also a symbol of the penis."[28] Jones discovered in a variety of myths the coexistence of the mare and the phallic horse, concluding that "this illustrates the remarkable interchangeability of the sexes in this whole group of myths."[29] Jones also stressed the unconscious association—confirmed by primitive myths—between animals and ancestors, the animal in dreams and myths denoting "the action of the incest complex."[30] In Beethoven's dream, the presence of "a pair" of horses apparently designates a married couple, though the libidinal attachment to Gleichenstein may here, too, have found its outlet in wish-fulfilling homosexual imagery. The vivid birth-content of the dream tends, in my opinion, to make this aspect a subordinate one.

A profound silence mingled with a sense of (phallic) awe links the Gleichenstein dream to the Archduke Rudolph dream. In the former, Gleichenstein is so completely "bewitched and captivated" that he is "oblivious to everything around" him. Not a word is uttered. At the close of the letter Beethoven makes a rare veiled reference to his advancing deafness ("I have quite enough with one infirmity"), which may be interpreted as a denial of the terrifying sounds within the dream. In the Rudolph dream, music is sounded, yet none is heard ("Although no music was performed, yet it was a musical dream").

The legal contest for the guardianship of Beethoven's nephew was at its most critical stage in the fall of 1819. On 17 September, one month before the dream, the Vienna Magistracy had decreed "that the guardianship should not again be entrusted to Beethoven but to the mother, the natural guardian under the law, with a capable and honest man as coguardian."[31] Beethoven had suffered a serious defeat and now was in process of appealing the decision. By a supreme effort of will, he early in the year began composition of the *Missa solemnis*, with a view to its performance at the installation of the Archduke Rudolph as cardinal and archbishop on 9 March 1820. He managed to complete both the Kyrie and the Gloria during 1819 and was at work on the Credo during the fall. In early June, he wrote to Rudolph: "The day when a High Mass of mine shall be performed at the ceremonies for Y. I. H. will be for me the most beautiful day of my life, and God will inspire me so that my weak powers may contribute to the glorification of this solemn day."[32] When Beethoven related the dream to Rudolph in October, however, it was already apparent that the Mass would not be ready in time. The manifest content of this dream may therefore be paraphrased: "The *Missa solemnis*, which I pledged to have completed for performance at your enthronement, and which is the deepest expression of my love for you, will not be finished in time. I can only dream of fulfilling my promise." Although Beethoven's dream letter asserts, "The Mass will soon be finished," the dream itself confesses that "no music [will be] performed."

The "deafness" of the dream is a clue to its latent content, for silence is the condition not only of unheard music but also of the maternal womb. Simultaneously, as in Gleichenstein's dream, silence is the denial of the nocturnal sounds of parental intercourse. The presence of the omnipotent father looms over the dream, arousing fantasies of father transcendence. Rudolph's elderly companion-secretary and librarian, Joseph Anton von Baumeister (1750–1819), had just died. He had also been Rudolph's tutor since 1792. Beethoven noted in the letter—somewhat callously in view of Rudolph's long association with his chamberlain—that "Baumeister has built for himself a home in eternity" and, without the slightest expression of sympathy or regret, immediately volunteers that he knows of someone "who would fill this place with Your Imperial Highness to perfect satisfaction." In 1789, Beethoven had petitioned the elector of Cologne, in view of his father's alcoholic state, to dispense completely with the services of the elder Beethoven as court musician and to disburse half of his salary directly to Beethoven. Thayer described this petition as "the extraordinary step of placing himself at the head of the family." This patricidal act (however much warranted by real circumstances), which Beethoven's father "begged me not to do" and which undoubtedly burdened the young man with a deep sense of guilt, is now repeated in somewhat different form in respect to Baumeister.[33] In a striking parapraxis, Beethoven may have revealed the unconscious connection between these widely separated events, for the dream letter to Rudolph states that he read Baumeister's obituary in the *Wienerische Diarium*, a Viennese newspaper whose name had been changed to the *Wiener Zeitung* more than thirty years before Beethoven's dream.

These patricidal feelings were, in turn, generated by associations from the preceding paragraph of the dream: "Steiner already has Your Imperial Highness' Variations; . . . As for the title page, it just occurs to me that Emperor Joseph traveled under the name of a Count von Falkenstein." The archduke had written a set of piano variations on a theme by Beethoven, to whom the work was to be dedicated, and Beethoven arranged for its publication. Rudolph planned to use a *nom de plume*, and the name Falkenstein was suggested.[34] In the dream letter, Beethoven recalls that this name was the pseudonym of Emperor Joseph, thereby activating the constellation of Beethoven's family romance and nobility pretense fantasies. The composer's quarter-century nobility pretense had been exposed the previous December, causing Beethoven such mortification that he momentarily contemplated quitting the country.[35] However, he still refused to admit to nonnobility, despite his lack of a patent, and during this period he would not permit his friends to refute the rumor of his royal birth which had just reappeared in the latest edition of the standard German encyclopedia. The realization that Emperor Joseph had also assumed a false identity may have reinforced Beethoven's own conviction that, because of his fantasied royal origin, his pretense was no impostorship. This conviction was reinforced as well by the recollection of Emperor Joseph, whom Beethoven adored and whose death in 1790 had been the subject of the first work—Cantata on the Death of Emperor Joseph II—which had adumbrated Beethoven's heroic style and which had also signaled the end of his subjection to the will of his father.

The next paragraph in the letter, with its *Diarium* parapraxis, reinforces our sense that this dream had been activated by and gave expression to the most archaic strata of Beethoven's mental life. The three paragraphs may therefore be interpreted as follows. The family romance fantasies stir the patricidal drive against the "false" impostor-father. The unconscious quest for the father is launched once again, now reanimated by the suggestion that Emperor Joseph had begotten him. If so, Rudolph is Beethoven's cousin ("brother"). Doubt wars with this belief: Joseph is dead, and he, too, was an impostor. To settle the issue, it is necessary to go back to the very beginning. Thus, the associations turn to the primal scene in which Beethoven's conception had taken place, but the picture is dim, there is no sound, and no visual image can be formed. Sexual intercourse is sublimated (repressed) into "music," but Beethoven cannot identify the "performers"; that is, he cannot see his parents because it is too dark.

The close of the guardianship struggle inaugurated several years of relatively peaceful existence, during which Beethoven achieved an accommodation and partial reconciliation with his sister-in-law, who in 1820 bore an illegitimate child and was now largely beyond his reach. Beethoven's matricidal impulses subsided, perhaps because they no longer had available a ready object to engender them. Simultaneously he had begun to come to terms with the incest fear that was at the root of this drive. His late style, which had been in agonizing process of formation during the previous half-decade, was now fully crystallized and his productivity restored at a supremely high level. In the year of the Haslinger dream, he had finished the Sonata, op. 110, and was in process of completing the C-minor Sonata, op. 111, and the *Missa solemnis*. By a gathering of his recuperative powers, Beethoven was in the midst of consolidating the most unprecedented advance of his creative career. At the same time, prematurely aged and weakened by a decade of inner torment, he was moving inexorably toward death.

The Haslinger dream—the most poetic of Beethoven's dreams—recapitulates Beethoven's life journey and signals that he had embarked upon the final voyage, that he was in motion toward a transfigured Eden. The dream begins in "the carriage" (birth) on the road to Vienna (mother). Freud: "Departure in dreams means dying."[36] The unconscious equivalence of dying and the return to the mother (Ferenczi, Rank) is at work here: "While thus slumbering, I dreamed that I was taking a very long journey." The horses that draw Beethoven's carriage are hidden within the depths of the dream, but they draw him forward on his voyage (linking this dream to the "stable" dream). Hero fantasies emerge; the son is in quest of his origins. First, he must find and conquer his real father on the eternal battleground—the body of the mother (the "road" on which Oedipus slew Laius). He journeys to the most distant and exotic lands: "as far even as Syria, as far even as India, back again, as far even as Arabia." The conquistador here fuses with Don Juan, for distant nations are the embodiment of the (taboo) female. Simultaneously, these lands represent the exotic bisexual religions of the East and Mediterranean, to which Beethoven had been drawn during the prior decade.[37]

The hero comes home in triumph: "finally I reached Jerusalem"— the "Holy City" of Christ, born in "the stable," whose mother, like Beethoven's, bore the name Maria, and who saved a fallen woman named, like Beethoven's mother, Maria Magdalena. The mother-death equation is inescapable, for Christ's triumph is prelude to his crucifixion: the entrance to the Temple leads also to the passion of Golgotha. Beethoven's family romance—here represented by identification with Christ (who never discovered who had begotten him)—is not yet resolved, for though he has almost found his way back to his mother, he has not accepted his father.[38] The family romance blocked the passage to rebirth for, as Rank knew, "besides its conscious ennobling tendency and the unconscious aversion to the father, [the family romance] has the final meaning of canceling one's own birth."[39] The end of the journey draws closer, and the images become clearer. The face of the father will be revealed only after Beethoven has forgiven his mother. Or, perhaps, he will find them both at the same instant of recognition.

It is appropriate that this narrative of a magical journey should be dreamed by a man who suffered from a travel phobia. In adolescence, his only long journey (to Vienna in 1787) had been prematurely terminated by the onset of his mother's final illness and by his father's wheedling insistence that Beethoven return to Bonn. On his return, he developed "asthma, which may, I fear, eventually develop into consumption."[40] (Here, separation anxiety coincides with mother identification, for she had died of tuberculosis.) In 1792, Beethoven left his native city for Vienna; a few weeks after his departure his father died. Beethoven did not return to Bonn at that time or ever again. Each of his Vienna journeys had "resulted" in the death of a parent. In 1796, Beethoven accompanied by his foremost patron and father surrogate, Prince Karl Lichnowsky, toured Prague, Dresden, Leipzig, and Berlin, where he performed for his supposed father, Friedrich Wilhelm II. Thereafter, despite numerous intended journeys—to Italy, Paris, London, and Germany—he never ventured farther than Hungary or the Bohemian spas. In 1817 and again in 1824, Beethoven was invited to London by the Philharmonic Society; on each occasion, he accepted but then could not overcome his travel resistances.

Immediately after the conclusion of the guardianship struggle, Beethoven expressed a desire to return to his birthplace. He wrote to his Bonn publisher-friend, Simrock, on 5 August 1820: "I cherish the hope of being able perhaps to set foot next year on my native soil and to visit my parents' graves."[41] This constitutes the first reference to his mother in the correspondence since 1787 and the first reference to his father since 1793. He wrote again to Simrock in March 1821: "I am still hoping to visit Bonn this summer."[42] But he could not make the journey which would have reunited him with his parents, perhaps because he did not wish to shatter the idealized image of his childhood home, perhaps because this would have meant returning to the locus of his primal and traumatic experiences. Nevertheless, the drive to return "home" retained its force and found its imagined fulfillment in the Haslinger dream—for the "Holy City" is the Bonn infancy-Eden converted into the prospective image of Paradise, which, as Freud wrote, "is no more than a group phantasy of the childhood of the individual."[43]

There is yet another route to the interior of this dream. Driving and traveling are universal symbols of sexual union, and Beethoven's "long journey" is the wish fulfillment of an incompletely realized heterosexuality. It is not far, however, from the polymorphous perverse: Jones notes that such dreams "represent a sexual act, usually conceived of in infantile and often sadistic-masochistic terms."[44] The homosexual component is suggested by references to anxiety and to a cleansing religiosity. Beethoven advises Haslinger to "Sing the Epistles of St. Paul every day," adding: "You see my anxiety for the salvation of your soul."[45] The reference to Menelaus's conquest of Proteus, the old man of the sea, has similar implications: "I held it fast, as once Menelaus did Proteus." However, the oedipal aspects are more decisive. Proteus, lord of the ocean (mother), who could change his shape at will, is the immaterial and multifarious image of the father in union with the mother.[46] The hero-son arrives, perhaps "to prevent the parents from coming together," or to witness and thereby participate in the act of parental intercourse that constituted the moment of his own conception.[47] The patricidal implications may not be overlooked, but the psychological substratum appears to be the desire to strip the veils of mystery from the identity of the father, for in subduing Proteus, Menelaus compelled him to assume his real form and thus was able to recognize him. Held fast, Proteus could be compelled to foretell the future; here, the oracle's insight would clarify the mystery of Beethoven's archaic past.

At twelve, one of Beethoven's first musical settings of a text already revealed his preoccupation with the unknowability of his ancestry. He composed a song, "An einen Säugling" (To a suckling baby), WoO 108, with these words:

> You still do not know whose child you are. You do not know who prepares the swaddling clothes, who it is that warms you and gives you milk. You grow in peace nevertheless. Within a few years, among all those who have cared for you, you will learn to distinguish your mother. Nonetheless there is some occult giver who cares for us all—our thanks go out to him—provides us with food and drink. My dim intelligence does not comprehend this, but after the years have gone by, if I am pious and a believer, even he will be revealed.

As a grown man, Beethoven underscored Telemachus's statement to Athene: "Verily, my mother saith that he is my father; for myself, I know it not: no man knoweth who hath begotten him."[48] Here Telemachus has removed the mask of Odysseus.

The entire content of the dream is recapitulated in the reference to the central personage of the dream—"the man Tobias"—to whose namesake the letter is addressed. Tobias (of the Apocryphal *Book of Tobit*) is sent on a mythic quest by his blind father against the wishes of his mother. Protected by the angel Raphael, he conquers the devouring sea-monster and marries Sara, whose nuptial bed has been the deathbed of seven previous bridegrooms. Laden with wealth, he returns home and cures the blindness of his father, who blesses his son and foretells both the glory and the ruin of Jerusalem. The contours of this mythic pattern are those of Beethoven's dream itself: exile, quest, escape from phallic dangers (Proteus), conquest of the exotic witch-bride (Helen, wife of Menelaus), return to the homeland (Jerusalem, Ithaca, Bonn), reunion with the mother, and ultimately recognition of the father, which permits the hero to take his place among the elders.

Finally, in this dream Beethoven breaks into song: there is lively music, the canon that "came to me" during "my dream journey." Music was performed but not heard in the Rudolph dream; here, it is created, performed, and celebrated. The "creativity" of Beethoven's Haslinger dream may express his joy at the loosening of his bondage to his fantasies, at the imminence of a breakthrough.

Unfortunately, the Holz letter can be dated no more precisely than the summer of 1826. On 29 July Beethoven's nephew, Karl, made an unsuccessful suicide attempt in an act whose multiple determinants included the desire to be reunited with his mother (who had replaced him with another child in the final stages of the guardianship struggle, and whom he had rejected during several of the intervening years) and the need to escape the infantilizing and incorporative embrace of his uncle who, during the antecedent period, had set Holz to spying upon the boy, attempted to separate him from his closest male companion, and tried in every way to prevent him from engaging in sexual activities. Beethoven's reawakened incestuous desire for his brother's widow was projected onto his nephew, where it could be stifled, if not annihilated. This is the last, vain effort of Beethoven's neurosis to resist his drive toward reconciliation with the mother image, a reconciliation that had already been achieved symbolically, perhaps, in the return to the wellsprings of music represented by the Ninth Symphony, *Missa solemnis*, Diabelli Variations, and last sonatas and quartets.

In the final dream Beethoven abandons all recourse to disguise and symbol; he witnesses the primal scene-conception-birth direct and unmediated: "I dreamed last night that your parents were begetting you for this world, and how much sweat it cost them to bring such an amazing piece of work into the light of day." The darkness has lifted, replaced by "the light of day." Only after the long journey of a lifetime can Beethoven freely acknowledge his mother's complicity in the primal scene. Simultaneously, the family romance is at an end: it is no divine God or royal father who had impregnated the mother, but an ordinary human being perspiring freely and humanly in the act of sexual intercourse. This, then, is no "dream," no imagining, but direct perception—"knowledge"—which is why Beethoven forgoes use of the verb *träumen*, "to dream," and substitutes *können*, "to know." The veils of fantasy have lifted, and the "memory" for which Beethoven had striven all his life rises into consciousness. It was "an amazing piece of work," which called for jubilant celebration: "I congratulate you on your *existence*." The terror of the dark ("the stable") is dissolved; the frozen silence ("no music was performed") is broken; mythic ciphers ("the Holy City," "Tobias," "Menelaus-Proteus") are swept aside; and in a flash of insight the questions of "how" and "why" receive their answer, in Beethoven's final sentence: "the riddles solve themselves."

Beethoven had sought, not merely to return to Bonn to achieve reconciliation with the facts of his ancestry, but also to find the origins of his existence. In a letter to Treitschke of 1821, he had hinted that he knew the answer: "Let us begin with the primary original causes of all things, how something came about, wherefore and why it came about *in that particular way and became what it is*, why something *cannot be exactly so!!!* Here, dear friend, we have reached the ticklish point which my delicacy forbids me to reveal to you at once. *All that we can say is:* it cannot be."[49] In the Holz dream, delicacy is abjured, and the oneiric riddle of existence—the Delphic riddle—is posed and deciphered. Birth and rebirth are one. Beethoven has restored the primal triad of infancy: he has no further need to fear, kill, or compete with the father, whom he freely acknowledges, desiring only that he be permitted to share the mother with him.[50]

T HE central desire expressed in all four of Beethoven's dreams is to return to the Bonn infancy-Eden where he and his parents had been harmoniously united (in wish if not in fact). The birth stable, the musicale, the Holy City, and the parental bed are four symbols expressing this underlying "reality." As Freud observed, the dream "endeavours to re-shape the present upon the model of the remote past. For the wish which creates the dream always springs from the period of childhood; and it is continually trying to summon childhood back into reality and to correct the present day by the measure of childhood."[51] However, as Freud knew, the dream is not merely reproductive of actuality; the productive imagination is also at work, reshaping the past in accordance with the semantics of desire, seeking fulfillment of a repressed infantile wish. The constant latent content of the "core" dream rises into Beethoven's consciousness at different stages of his life, making it possible to trace his psychic evolution up to the point at which he can accept the dream without reservation. The image of a desired and "remembered" condition wars with the delusions of illegitimacy and the fantasies of royal or divine birth which had protected Beethoven's ego from the memories of a tragic childhood. Thus, the Gleichenstein dream of 1807 denies the dream by its references to "failure," to the "rip" in the hat, to having been "horribly swindled." Beethoven feels "wretched," and cannot rid himself of his "terrible headache." In 1819 Beethoven tries to renege on the visionary implications of his Rudolph dream by expressing patricidal impulses and impostor fantasies in the lines preceding the dream itself. By 1821, with the explosion of his nobility pretense and the termination of the guardianship struggle, the Haslinger dream is filled with wonder and expectation. Beethoven is ready to take the "very long journey" which will reunite him with his parents, but the dream itself is cloaked in mythic imagery which disguises its real meaning from the dreamer. Only in the Holz dream of 1826 does jubilation mingle with realistic acceptance of his own desires.

ONE riddle remains. Each of Beethoven's dreams constitutes a restoration of the primal triad: Gleichenstein and the pair of horses; Rudolph attending the primal scene-musicale; Beethoven in the Holy City; Holz conceived in parental embrace. On this level, all of the dreams are of the conception and birth of the dreamer. But a fourth character is present in each dream: Beethoven witnesses the triad in the stable, observes Rudolph at the musicale, and sees the conception of Holz, while "little Tobias" is inextricably present within the mythic dream of the return to Jerusalem. Of course, as

Abraham observed, a dream often seems to be like "a play of which the dreamer is a mere onlooker," and often the dreamer "is represented by the actor who plays the leading role."[52] But the dreamer and his characters, who may be splittings of the one, are also multiple and separate (in the same way that the Haslinger dream canon converts one voice into three). The ego is the sum of its introjects, but those introjects may preside over the ego, maintaining their discrete identities. We dream of them and, in our fantasy, they dream of us. Thus, the fourth character, observing the birth of the hero, may be the lost brother Ludwig Maria, who lived for six days in April 1769 and who Beethoven consciously believed was the rightful possessor of the baptismal records that constituted the only evidence of his own birth. Or inasmuch as Beethoven, skeptical that proof of his own separate existence could be established, had unconsciously merged his identity with that of his dead brother in order to share his "power," Beethoven may himself be the observer presiding over the conception and birth of the first-born.

In 1806, on a sketch leaf, Beethoven wrote: "A weeping willow or Acacia-tree upon my brother's grave."[53] Mourning for (and worship of) Ludwig Maria merges with the attempt to bring him back to life. Beethoven's appropriation of his nephew (his brother's first-born son and the only child born to any of the Beethoven brothers) as his own "son" after 1815 may have had as one of its nuclear elements this same desire for the reincarnation of Ludwig Maria. In the summer of 1826, two weeks after Karl's suicide attempt and coincident with the Holz dream, Beethoven again wrote an opaque, seemingly inexplicable sentence: "Upon the death of the dead Beethoven."[54] Its meaning may be: "I now know that Ludwig Maria is dead."

There is a sense in which Ludwig Maria had possessed Beethoven's ego, becoming his good "double" (the angel Raphael), who controlled Beethoven's actions and created his works.[55] Ultimately, the family romance signified Beethoven's belief that he was the "false" son, who could never take the place of his dead brother and therefore must seek new parents. Beethoven's apodictic outcry, "I too am a King!" is not merely the assertion of a desired nobility or the delusory rejection of his humble parents but also, perhaps on the deepest level, the admission of a pathetic longing to have been the first-born, who was mourned but not forgotten by his parents.

The rarely assuaged tragic family circumstances in which Beethoven grew up placed his "Golden Age" not in his earliest childhood but in the period before he was born, immediately after the marriage of his parents in 1767 and up to the birth of their son. "What is marriage?" Beethoven's mother asked her young neighbor Cäcilia Fischer, while her son Ludwig listened: "A little joy, and then a chain of sorrows."[56] The death of Ludwig Maria placed the double bar to the brief happiness of the young married couple. Ludwig van Beethoven, neglected by his parents in his earliest years and surrounded by sadness, marked the beginnings of the catastrophe that inexorably engulfed his family from the date of his own conception and birth. Acting under the sway of the repetition compulsion, Beethoven regularly revisited this traumatic primal scene, constantly reshaping its contours in accordance with the pleasure principle, actively absorbing it into his ego, and ultimately mastering it by demystification—the restoration of the naturalistic content of the perception (or hallucinatory memory) itself.

Beethoven looked back in anguish to a Golden Age which he could not reach except by sharing the identity of his omnipotent older brother. It is Gleichenstein (Ludwig Maria) who is permitted to enter the "bedroom" of the parents; it is Rudolph (Ludwig Maria) who is the true son of an emperor; it is Haslinger (Ludwig Maria) who is "Tobias dominus (Our Lord) Haslinger"; and it is Holz (Ludwig Maria) whom Beethoven, in the first letter written after the onset of his fatal illness, addresses as "Your official Majesty." Beethoven could not erase his brother's priority. All of his delusions and dreams, then, have a single source: they are the expression, denial, and symbolic transcendence of the "knowledge" that he was unloved and unwanted. They are the rectifications of a presumed illegitimacy. They are the heartfelt—and unanswered—cry of a child for his parents' love.

5

The Posthumous Life of Ludwig Maria van Beethoven

BEETHOVEN suffered from a central wounding fantasy—that he was illegitimate, that he was not the son of Johann van Beethoven. Upon this illusory foundation was fashioned an unstable pyramid of interconnected countervailing fantasies—the birth-year delusion, the nobility pretense, the fantasy of being the son of some elevated personage, even the strange belief that he was the "real physical father" of his nephew. These closely related birth and ancestry fantasies elaborated the core delusion while simultaneously denying an unbearable condition, thereby providing partial reparation and surcease. In the recesses of Beethoven's inner world, his woundedness was wished out of existence.

Beethoven never emerged fully victorious from this unending series of struggles. For each momentary triumph created a further doubt, a different kind of pain. The curious dialectic of Beethoven's family romance involved the perpetually flawed attempt to repair his presumed illegitimacy by asserting precisely that which he feared most: that he was not a Beethoven. By his family romance, Beethoven orphaned himself: in fantasy he disposed of his own parents, thereby confirming his worst fears of illegitimacy. And with the passing of the years, as he became what the world knew as "Beethoven," the importance of his legitimacy was further magnified. To be stripped of his family name would have been the ultimate desolation.

Whatever its origins in pathology and despair, Beethoven's family romance is a creative fantasy, an imaginative attempt to rewrite the past, or at least to hold reality at bay, while he reaches for a more satisfactory future. Its essence is reparative, but it is inherently incapable of fulfillment, for it emerges from and magnifies a permanent psychic disequilibrium. Thus it is a voracious fantasy, hungering for new materials to absorb, to shape, to build upon. Endlessly it drives toward a fancied fulfillment, a chimerical *telos*. Its ramifications spill over from the biographical and psychological spheres into Beethoven's intellectual and creative life as well.

Beethoven was locked within an endless loop of finding and losing, of claiming and rejecting, of expectation and disenchantment. The family romance is founded upon uncertainty, doubt, incompletion: it drives to repair injustice (of birth circumstances, of being the second-born, of not being a "real" Beethoven); it seeks vengeance for real and imagined wrongs against himself and his family. The fierce energies that attached to Beethoven's private quests stood ready to be transmuted, not only into the idealizations of art and a kaleidoscopic variety of personal and aesthetic wish-fulfillments, but also into strivings for the transformation of society. They became a source of creative rebellion against every aspect of the old order, an attempt to capture the most elevated strongholds—social, ideological, and aesthetic. The family romance pursuit of an ideal ancestry, with its unrelieved pattern of hopeful encounters terminating in disappointment, somehow metamorphosed itself into a complex quarrel with artistic tradition, into a propulsive tension between conformity and originality, classicism and modernism. Beethoven was drawn toward art forms and modes of thought that aggressively disrupted established patterns, revolutionized reality, transformed consciousness.

Both the family romance and the "fever of the Revolution," as Beethoven called it, represented ruptures of social decorum, breaches of conformity.[1] Not only was the young Beethoven's social idealism—his identification with the ideals of the Enlightenment and the French Revolution—a way of sealing off the eruptive and delusional forces within him, but the delusions themselves drove him to the ideal, into a romance with the world. Beethoven's search for an ideal self fused with the search for the "good prince"—the loving brother who would legitimize his birth and fulfill his, and mankind's, aspirations for fraternity. The image of Bonaparte mobilized Beethoven's fantasies: for, in 1804, this supreme embodiment of the selfless good prince proclaimed himself emperor, thus living out the family romance, transforming the fantasy of royal birth into reality. Bonaparte, formerly Beethoven's cohort in defiance of legitimized authority, had seized authority, separated himself from the band of brothers, and substituted the anxious solitude of kingship for the comradeship of fraternity. "What would Monsieur nôtre père have said to this, if he could have been here today?" Napoleon asked his brother Joseph during the coronation ceremony at Milan. Joseph's answer is not preserved, but Beethoven—another brother—reacted with a violence whose tremors are still being felt.

Later, the fading of the Enlightenment, with its rigorous prohibitions against superstition and religion, permitted Beethoven to seek the realization of his family romance in the hermaphroditic gods of India and Egypt, in nature worship, and in the multitude of mysterious and nocturnal forms opened up by German Romanticism. The polytheistic imagination of the Romantics embodies a refusal to accept the bland certainty of a single father-deity, just as the unresolved family romance represents the unending Romantic quest of the hero for legitimacy and a final homecoming or resting place.

E VER Y homecoming presupposes a point of departure. Johann van Beethoven took charge of Beethoven from a very early age, certainly no later than five or six, when he began to train his son in music, a pedagogic exercise not free of brutal, even sadistic episodes. Whether his motive was to achieve a dominance in the family which he could not otherwise achieve as a musician and citizen of the Cologne electorate is unclear, but it is clear that, for a time, he converted Beethoven into his reluctant but thoroughly obedient disciple. Because of the absence of any sign of protest on the part of Beethoven's mother, it may seem that she acquiesced in Johann's treatment of their son; but it is also possible that Maria Magdalena van Beethoven, who is known to have found fault with her husband for his alcoholism and ineffectuality, actually encouraged Beethoven to distance himself from his father. Beethoven would inevitably face the rending question: should he, in line with his mother's criticisms of Johann, join her in repudiating his father's moral example, his alcoholism, his failure of family responsibilities, and his suppressive pedagogical methods? The price of this proposed alliance against his father was for a long time more than the boy Beethoven was willing or able to pay. Apparently he did not readily accede to the rejection of his father; in his early years, he resisted his mother's injunctions and continued to submit to Johann, perhaps receiving some obscure compensation from his father's brutal attentions.

The signs of this conflict in Beethoven's first decade are difficult to read with certainty, but they are implied in his withdrawal from friends and social life and his total immersion in music. These, coupled with his failure to advance in school, his resistance to education, and his inhibition to learn basic arithmetical skills, may signify, "I refuse to be anything other than a musician, like my father." Moreover, his submission to his father, an identification with a mediocrity whom society scorned and his own family pitied, caused Beethoven to retard his development as a composer in order that he not appear to surpass his own father. Beethoven's "Bonn moratorium"—his period of drastically lessened compositional activity between 1786 and late 1789—may represent, at least in part, his resistance to carrying out his mother's creative mission; and the ending of his period of silence may reflect his determination to become the hero she wanted him to be.

A curious dialectic is at work here: even if Beethoven could not bring himself overtly to repudiate his father, Maria Magdalena, by her criticisms of Johann, had helped to instill in her son the family romance fantasy (a partial one, to be sure, in which only his father was replaced, while she was retained), along with an exquisite sense of moral altruism, and a hunger for greatness. Beethoven's family romance is in some sense an elaboration of his mother's unfulfilled ambitions for a more suitable husband and her daydreams of heroism and romance. Maria Magdalena's imperatives to her son combined extreme aggressiveness with altruism, implying a desire to rearrange the order of things, to change history, to overthrow tradition. The revolutionary impulse in Beethoven is born out of a mother's dissatisfaction and ambition. But in refusing wholly to surrender to the seductions of the family romance, with their patricidal implications, Beethoven rebelled against the maternal injunction as well. In other words, the seeds of disobedience, even rebellion, were present in his very refusal to assume the exemplary role that was thrust upon him.

To complicate matters even further, in accepting his father's abuse, Beethoven accepted a passive role in the family, in society, and in his sexual development, a role that was later reinforced by his conformist stance as a court musician and composer during the second decade of his life. In his passivity to his father, Beethoven emulated his mother, who, despite her complaints, remained the suffering model of submission. Equally ironic is the fact that, even without an overt effort, the simple pursuit of his father's occupation soon passed into transcendence of his father's achievement. A torrent of confluent forces was set in motion which eventually caused a wholesale rejection of his father's precepts, indeed of his very fatherhood. Thus, the patricidal role was one that Beethoven could not avoid, whatever his choices and options. All roads led to the same center. All he could do was to delay somewhat the inevitable moment when he would give way to his destiny.

The death of his mother in 1787 overwhelmed Beethoven's reluctance and ignited the heroic—patricidal—flame. Now he asserted his right to be his mother's son, to be a separate individual, and to be a creative rather than an imitative musician. Family power was settled upon him; he was compelled to put his father out to pasture and to take charge of his salary. Beethoven launched his twin careers as a composer and virtuoso pianist in earnest. Compliant to his father until Maria Magdalena's death, Beethoven now fully incorporated her image into his ego and pursued her ideals as his own. But before he could take up the task she had set for him, he also had to go through the process of mourning. Inevitably, he never completed that process, for it would have signified separation from his mother. Rather, she lived on in him: Beethoven continued his dialogue with her, his never-ending conversation with the "dumb likenesses of her which my imagination fashions for me."[2] Her somber radiance guided him from within.

T HE child Beethoven had been an object of strife between his father and mother, his person the battleground of a failed marriage, his allegiance the prize of a silent struggle. Too early, he had learned to read the undercurrents of his mother's fears about unspecified dangers, the subtext of her warnings against marriage and sexuality, just as he had learned to understand his father's warnings that a son may try to surpass his father only at his peril. He groped through a dark labyrinth from which there was no exit, for each alternative route was paved with a different kind of pain. To follow his father's path was to accept condemnation to personal passivity and permanent limitation on creative achievement. To accede to his mother was not only to break with his father but also to foreclose the possibilities of a fulfilled sexual and family life. However, to refuse her bidding was to give his mother pain; and above all, perhaps, he wanted to make her happy, for she was unhappy. To grasp the dolefulness of her personality, listen to her young neighbor Cäcelia Fischer's recollection:

> Madam van Beethoven once told Cäcelia that she was once travelling from Koblenz to Bonn and met many honest people on the boat, and the talk turned to troubles and fateful occurrences. There was one respectable woman who remained silent, serious, and sad, although, as one could see, she herself was also suffering. This woman listened to all the tales of sorrow and fate and then she said, "I have had an even harder destiny, I believe that none harder can exist . . ." They all paid great heed to this woman, this woman who lamented that she sensed she could look forward only to sleeplessness, affliction, and an early death. Madam van Beethoven said that she could not forget this poor woman; she said all parents should protect their children from so painful a destiny.[3]

Incapable of external action to resolve a constellation of dilemmas, Beethoven at first turned against himself: his misanthropic disposition and his negligent, dirty appearance toward the end of the 1770s, on which his contemporaries strikingly commented, were his way of casting himself out of his own family, rejecting his mother's care, declaring himself an orphan. At the same time, he was engaged in elaborating a complicated web of birth and illegitimacy fantasies by which he "explained" to himself his parents' attitudes and his own condition. "Unsatisfied wishes are the driving power behind fantasies," observed Freud; "every separate fantasy contains the fulfilment of a wish, and improves on unsatisfactory reality."[4] Childhood trauma gives rise to magical denial, to grandiose compensatory and explanatory fantasies.

Central to these fantasies is Beethoven's identification with his brother Ludwig Maria. Beethoven's birth-year delusion—his repeated rejection of the plain fact that he was the Ludwig van Beethoven who was baptized on 17 December 1770—was the plainest confirmation of his deeply rooted family romance; and this delusion, which provides his fantasy with its remarkable individual configuration, was itself founded upon a confusion of identity between Beethoven and the dead Ludwig Maria. In the crucial document that makes this confusion manifest, Beethoven insists: "But one thing must be borne in mind, namely, that there was a brother *born before me*, who was also named Ludwig with the addition Maria, but who died. To fix my age beyond doubt, this brother must first be found."[5] On the back of an authentic copy of his certificate, Beethoven notes: "The baptismal certificate seems to be incorrect, since there was a Ludwig born before me."[6] In wrongly asserting that his own birth certificate belonged to Ludwig Maria, Beethoven was yielding up his own identity. He no longer had either a baptismal certificate or a birth date, both of these being the property of another. At the very least this displacement disclosed his inner certainty that a substitution had taken place, which left him bereft of the basic external insignia of selfhood. Moreover, the possibility of establishing his own ancestry and identity somehow hinged on locating Ludwig Maria; perhaps that is why Beethoven remarks to Wegeler, "this brother must first be found." This is not a mere slip but an expression of his inner conviction that Ludwig Maria, though somehow present, remained to be discovered. Beethoven was unaware that Ludwig Maria's hiding-place was closer to home than he could have imagined.

Beethoven's baptismal certificate belonged, he thought, not to himself but to the first-born, to whom everything is granted—mother, father, power, knowledge of origins, access to the central mysteries—to whom belong the symbols of legitimacy—Beethoven's own name and proof of birth. Ludwig Maria van Beethoven seemed to have taken possession of the objects of Beethoven's desire, preempting his very identity. Evidently there were powerful compensations for these displacements, for Ludwig Maria had usurped the birth documents and set up house within his younger brother's inner self only with Beethoven's own connivance. Beethoven's survival as an individual apparently had come to hinge upon an accommodation with his powerful predecessor.

No one can detail the process by which Ludwig Maria began his posthumous life. The naming of a child after a deceased infant potentially creates an uncanny bond between them, a bond even more powerful in Beethoven's case because the name of the deceased infant combined not only the given names of the paternal grandparents (Ludwig and Maria) but also those of the paternal grandfather and the mother (Ludwig and Maria Magdalena). How or when Beethoven learned of Ludwig Maria's existence is not known, but if one reads from results to causes (impermissible as that may be), Beethoven's entanglement with Ludwig Maria presumably was somehow derived from his comprehension of his parents' attitudes, perhaps of his mother's repeated lamentations about her life's "chain of sorrows," which may have included—even centered—on a perpetual mourning over a lost infant.[7] To Beethoven, this may have signified that he was an inadequate replacement for a brother with whom his mother had forged a special bond, that he found himself on the outside of a mother-child circle apparently impenetrable to him.

BEETHOVEN is not the only creative artist whose life and work is colored—even invaded—by the "presence" of a departed brother, though particular configurations of his fantasy appear to be unique. Many artists have borne the names of deceased brothers. Sometimes the reverberations of this circumstance are silent, as with van Gogh; sometimes they merely serve to confuse biographers, who learn to their surprise that they have been celebrating the birthday of the wrong Francesco Guardi. Sometimes, however, the consciousness of an uncanny tie is quite on the surface: "My brother and I resembled each other like two drops of water, but we had different reflections," wrote Dalí.[8] And in his pseudonymous autobiography, Henry James, Sr., opaquely observed that the year of his birth "is not a fact embraced in my own knowledge."[9] The desire to repair a brother's death, or to take his place, is found in other lives. Faulkner pretended to be his wounded hero-brother "Jack," even walking with a limp and falsely claiming to have been shot down in World War I action; he thereby offered himself as his brother's surrogate to his troubled parents.[10] Poe and his brother William mirrored each other in a curious exchange of identities, William apparently publishing certain of Poe's poems under his own name, and Poe embellishing his autobiography with the exotic travels and experiences of his brother.[11] The afterlife of Blake's brother Robert, an artist who died at nineteen in 1787, is recorded in a letter: "Thirteen years ago I lost a brother & with his spirit I converse daily & hourly in the Spirit and See him in my remembrance in the regions of my imagination. I hear his advice & even now write from his Dictate."[12] On another occasion, Robert stood before his brother "in one of his visionary imaginations" and imparted to Blake the secret methods of illuminated printing.[13]

BEETHOVEN'S birth-year delusion and family romance suggest that he believed the facts of his ancestry had been concealed and he was an illegitimate outcast in his own family. He was cast adrift: nothing is what it appears to be; everything is flux, constantly metamorphosing; I am not I; my parents are not my parents; apparently all identity is mistaken identity. Defiance and rejection—the refusal to deny rumors of his royal lineage—were ineffectual methods to compensate for this disturbance in identity. A more effective method was to hold fast to his tenuous family ties by allying himself with— even "becoming"—Ludwig Maria, who was, without any doubt, a Beethoven. Ludwig Maria was taken in as Beethoven's protector, his good brother, his "twin," from whom he received reassurance, consolation, and inseparable companionship. Arlow observed that the "bond of complete understanding which is missing with the parent unites the twins in the wish fantasy."[14] To provide "an escape from loneliness and solitude" and a compensation for oedipal disillusionment, argued Burlingham, twinning fantasies enable the child to create an imaginary constant companion with whom he shares everything, a twin who is endowed with "all the qualities and talents that he . . . desires for himself."[15]

This was a peculiar kind of symbiosis: Beethoven feeds upon a dead infant (though one who remained somehow his elder), gains power from a helpless child who had predeceased him. But the dead and departed are still with us, as precipitates within our egos, as identifications that we cannot or will not abandon. In melancholia and the formation of the self, Freud noted, "an object which was lost has been set up again inside the ego."[16] You are what you eat: we defend against feelings of persecution and melancholia by absorbing into ourselves ambivalently regarded or hostile objects. Thus, Beethoven invites Ludwig Maria into his ego so that he can keep him under surveillance. Fenichel analyzed this double aspect of introjection: "The introjection, then, is not only an attempt to undo the loss of an object. Simultaneously it is an attempt to achieve the *unio mystica* with an omnipotent external person, to become the lost person's 'companion,' that is, food comrade, through becoming his substance and making him become one's own substance. Ambivalence, however, gives this introjection a hostile significance. The wish to force the object to give his consent to the union ends in the attainment of punishment for the violence of this wish."[17]

Beethoven's "mystic union" with Ludwig Maria was a creative fantasy; it constantly changed its shape, appearing in a multiplicity of forms which were limited only by the reaches of its author's imagination. I paraphrase the inner monologues which may have accompanied this chaotic cluster of fantasies:

• "If I were their real son, they would not treat me as they do." From some such grievance came the family romance, with its passionate reaction to a perceived vital affront. The beloved, confident child knows who his parents are. For Beethoven, the ultimate threat of extinction was to be expelled from his family by one or the other parent. His family romance was a pre-emption of that feared action, as well as a denial of its very possibility, for thereby he renounced his membership in the threatening family.

• "I am not strong enough to carry out my mother's wishes." Thus in his fantasy Beethoven constructs a heroic self who can accomplish her mission. This self is modeled on the image of the firstborn, who died in April 1769 but was reborn several years later to commence his posthumous life. Beethoven has given Maria Magdalena two sons instead of one to carry out her mission. He has not only repaired the loss of Ludwig Maria but also, through identification, fused his personality with that lost child.

• "If I were my brother, they would love me as they love him." In this version Ludwig Maria emerged as Beethoven's creative companion and ideal self, his defense against an intolerable reality.

• "I am not helpless, bleeding, destroyed. On the contrary, I am bigger and better than anyone else."[18] The circle of helplessness and invulnerability is forged here. "I too am a king!" cried Beethoven in his last years, when a trivial rebuff from the Prussian court (the seat of his rumored father) reminded him of archaic disappointments.

Maria Magdalena's mourning elicited in Beethoven a permanent and powerful desire to make her whole, and this could be done only by bringing her lost child back to life. From this need flowed Beethoven's drive to resurrect the dead brother and to assume his identity, a substitution leading to a complex of rescue fantasies as well as to the impostorship of the nobility pretense. His hero and rescue fantasies are often fantasies of restoring the lost brother to their mother, the accomplishment of which is attended by feelings of triumph and elation:

> The brother seeks his brother
> And if he can, he'll gladly help him. (*Fidelio*, 1814)

Beethoven charged his friend Wegeler: "Search out Ludwig Maria and the present Ludwig who came after him."[19] This private preoccupation was sublimated into Beethoven's altruistic quest, his apotheosis of brotherhood which was fed by, but went far beyond, the commonplaces of revolutionary and post-Enlightenment ideology.

Brother rescue, however, is also rescue *from* the parents. Perhaps Beethoven felt that his parents—or one of them—were responsible for Ludwig Maria's death, that they let him die, that, at a minimum, the omnipotent parents could have prevented his death. In that case, the fusion with his brother appears as an altruistic alliance with a victim—the mythic abandoned foundling—who is both himself and other. Incessantly, repeatedly, Beethoven arrives to thwart filicide.

• "If I were dead, they would mourn for me as they do for Ludwig Maria." In order to find the departed brother, one must journey into death and bring him upward from the depths. The heroic mission itself is perceived as self-consuming, even suicidal (a Hamlet journey). A mother's mandate to fulfillment and greatness is perceived, like all heroic missions, as an impossible burden, even as an urge to self-destruction, particularly here, for Maria Magdalena has placed her child in critical opposition to his own father. From this arise not only Beethoven's impulse toward suicide but also, perhaps, his extraordinary receptivity to the death-and-resurrection dialectic which becomes a central component of his art.

Constantly changing his form, the internalized Ludwig Maria is not only Beethoven's fantasy twin but also his "double" and his "imaginary companion." As his double, he is simultaneously Beethoven's benevolent ego ideal and his hostile rival, both a mirrored self and a competitor for a limited fund of love and power. Beethoven repeatedly tries to externalize or even to expel or destroy him, so as to provide a lightning rod for his own fancied transgressions.[20] Similarly, the imaginary companion fantasy serves to turn a rival into a partner, as security against ego destruction.[21] The imaginary companion has many faces: he may be scapegoat, playmate, protector, mother substitute. Ludwig Maria was Beethoven's "anti-matter self," as Myers expressed it, the "oedipal brother who would be acceptable to both parents."[22] All of these apparitions—imaginary companions, fantasy twins, doubles—are part of a continuum of incorporative fantasies wherein the ego is occupied—in an unstable mixture of acquiescence and resistance—by an alien introject or ego ideal. As Arlow observed, "The existence of another individual who is a reflection of the self brings the experience of twinship in line with the psychology of the double, of the mirror image and of the shadow."[23] Because their existence is predicated upon uncertainty, all of these forms and faces are in constant flux, and the boundaries between them are drawn and erased almost at will. But they all arise from an attempt to repair a disturbance of identity by multiplication—by mirroring, twinning, shadowing, doubling. Whether as twin, double, or creative companion, Ludwig Maria becomes Remus to Beethoven's Romulus, doubling his strength. This stratum reaches the common denominator of the fantasies of introjection and of the family romance. In all of them there is a doubling: of the self in introjection, of the parents in the family romance. In the family romance, the individual retains both sets of parents, the real and the ideal; he has doubled his ancestry. In the process he has perhaps been split into two separate individuals as well, thereby forcing himself to maintain a delicate balance on those borderlines where fantasy may slip, first into delusion, and thence into pathology.

IN trying to navigate those slippery borderlines, Beethoven more than once fashioned biographical reality out of fantastic or delusory materials. Uncertain of his identity, he became an impostor who, instead of wearing the mask of an omnipotent stranger, assumed his own name, which is to say, assumed the identity of the brother who owned the baptismal certificate that bore Beethoven's name.[24] He wants to be a Beethoven but fears (believes) that he is not; to become Beethoven, he must therefore usurp the characteristics and name of a true Beethoven. The impostor's "sense of helplessness or incompleteness" is offset by a seizure of identity or, more accurately in this instance, a sharing of identity.[25] Impostorship is central to Beethoven's nobility pretense, his quarter-century dissimulation that he possessed an aristocratic pedigree. Through that deception he claimed to "prove" in reality what he inwardly "knew" or desired—that he was not of mean birth. Through it he fulfilled the family romance fantasy of elevated ancestry. Through it he seized the superior power of nobility, the attributes of aristocracy, the lineaments of kingship. And in some obscure way, Beethoven could take Ludwig Maria's place—or rise to his level of supremacy—through the nobility pretense, just as he had compounded their identities by means of the birth-year delusion.

Similarly, Beethoven's appropriation of his nephew was an attempt to act out the family romance by raising a Beethoven child to the level of nobility. But the pathological guardianship struggle touched on every point in the galaxy of Beethoven's fantasies. In one stroke he had taken control of the Beethoven family, for Karl was the family's only child, the embodiment of its potentiality for biological continuation. Simultaneously Beethoven was contending with Ludwig Maria, whom he had objectified as Karl, trying to neutralize his power. In Beethoven's delusion, he perhaps viewed Karl as an amalgam of the two Ludwigs. He had somehow given birth to, "fathered," his elder brother: "I am now the real physical father of my deceased brother's child," whom he could now treat as he himself wanted to be treated by his own parents.[26] He identified himself with Karl, loving him for his "illegitimacy" (Karl was conceived out of wedlock) and his partially orphaned status (Beethoven repeatedly calls Karl "a poor orphan"), for these remind him of his own condition.[27] Moreover, Beethoven's delusion that he was the "real physical father" of his nephew is an inversion of his earlier fantasy that his own father was not Beethoven's "real physical father." His unconscious now insists that a false father (himself) is a true father, thereby repairing by identification his repudiation of Johann van Beethoven (thereby also reiterating and proving the family romance subtext that all fathers are false fathers). The real Karl falls in the interstices of these multiple delusions. Beethoven is entangled in the web of his ancestry fantasies.

In an attempt to make himself whole, Beethoven had long before set up Ludwig Maria within his ego, and his "possession" of this treasured family object had magnified his own strength, permitting him to withstand some of the shocks of adversity. But in the course of time, particularly after the shattering of his brittle facade of invulnerability by a concatenation of biographical and creative events between 1812 to 1815, he experienced a multiple failure of his defenses. And inasmuch as Beethoven's middle-period styles had reached a point of depletion at a moment when the nature of their replacement was still obscure, there was a failure of sublimation as well, an inability to nullify anxiety by symbolic reparation and preservation.[28] With the creative failure, Ludwig Maria came to menace his younger brother from within. The "benign circle," to use Klein's term, of reparation by identification was broken; "the objects which were to be restored change again into persecutors, and . . . the ego has to resort again and again to obsessional and manic defences."[29] Because the equilibrium by which Ludwig Maria was maintained within Beethoven's ego had been disrupted, he now had to be reconstituted in the real world, both as creative twin and as fraternal persecutor. Beethoven's nephew, aged nine years old, had the misfortune to be available for this purpose in the wake of his father's death.

With the cunning of the helpless, however, Karl undermined Beethoven's enveloping thrust by means of a variety of strategies, appeasing the aggressor even as he tenaciously refused to give up his mother and the memory of his father. Karl's struggle to be free of his impostor father and to reunite with his real family endangered Beethoven's ego, for it threatened his power to contain Ludwig Maria. Beethoven's deep irrationality had a rational basis—to preserve the intactness of his self from the imagined hostility of the occupying introject. He had to keep Ludwig Maria under control at all costs, and he had to keep him alive as well, for his existence was deeply entwined with Beethoven's very self. They had entered into an interior version of a primitive union—a blood brotherhood—whereby two individuals, "being destined to live or to perform some dangerous act together" in Crawley's words, undergo a "mutual inoculation," thereby taking a part of the other into his own body.[30] An identity of interests is thereby secured, with each holding the other hostage against the possibility of treachery.

In the end, the twice-born Ludwig Maria had to die. But he did not die alone. Beethoven had carried the image of a dead brother within him and had thereby rescued him from the embrace of death. From the start, Ludwig Maria's image had been tinged with death, carrying a resonance of the grave, a hint of a state beyond life. Thus, occasions when Ludwig Maria's presence threatened to rise into Beethoven's consciousness were often accompanied by thoughts of death or of suicide. Or rather, issues bearing on mortality often brought in their train a suggestion of Ludwig Maria's unconscious presence. Such cases include the mysterious omission of a brother's name in the suicidal Heiligenstadt Testament; the postscript of the Testament's farewell to life, "Thus I take leave of Thee," which no longer addresses two living brothers but is addressed to only one unnamed person, who may be Ludwig Maria or may be the fused, condensed image of the fraternal principle; Beethoven's curious inscription on a sketch of the Adagio of his String Quartet, op. 59, no. 1, "A Weeping Willow or Acacia Tree on the Grave of My Brother"; and the words "On the death of the dead Beethoven," which the composer penned a fortnight after the attempted suicide of his nephew. Ludwig Maria was dead, or about to die—the play was ended—for when Beethoven lost Karl, the two Ludwigs surrendered their hold upon each other. Their blood brotherhood had been canceled. Beethoven bid farewell to his imaginary companion, who during his posthumous life had helped to alleviate Beethoven's sufferings, to fulfill his familial longings, and to keep alive the creative flame.

We devise odd strategies to frustrate death. Doubling is one such strategy, the fashioning of a second self-representation—"an insurance against destruction," as Freud put it—who will be offered up as a sacrificial scapegoat.[31] The difficulty is that the sacrifice of an imaginary twin may also be a suicide. That is why, in tales of the double, the hero rids himself of his uncanny mirror-image and only succeeds thereby in killing himself.

But the references to Ludwig Maria are saturated with generative as well as death imagery. Beethoven had rescued his brother from a region in which birth and death are fused. The willow and acacia grow from the soil of his brother's grave. And Beethoven's primal dream is of generation and birth: "I dreamed last night that your parents were begetting you for this world . . . I congratulate you on your existence."[32] The fraternal introject had always been the open channel to Beethoven's mother, for Beethoven's internal resurrection of Ludwig Maria had been, in part, his way of consoling Maria Magdalena for her lost infant.

Beethoven's creativity was a family affair, in which more than one Beethoven participated—a Flemish kapellmeister, his alcoholic wife, their mediocre son, his somber wife, and her children, alive and dead. Maria Magdalena's mourning elicited in Beethoven the permanent desire to make her whole by bringing her lost child back to life, even at the cost of sacrificing his own identity. Dying, too, is a family affair. Freud concluded that the necessity of death can be accepted only if it is cloaked in the imagery of birth and love, if death is seen as reunion, homecoming, fulfillment of desire.[33] Beethoven had not really expelled Ludwig Maria; he had let him go, as he let

Karl go, with resignation and understanding. He had released his nephew from his dubious role as a surrogate for a lost brother and was now free to unite with that brother, dying together, joining him and his parents in forming, at last, the benign circle which no longer admits pain.

6

On Beethoven's Deafness

DURING his childhood, Beethoven often wrapped himself in a cloak of silence as a shield against both the vicissitudes of external reality and the traumatic events within his family constellation. The reports of contemporaries who knew him toward the end of his first decade repeatedly describe his withdrawal into a world of fantasy, his penchant for isolation, his monosyllabic replies to adult questioners, his happiness at being left alone by his parents, his "deafness" when a young neighbor tried to disturb his daydreams.[1] Silence and solitude had great utility to this lonely young genius, permitting a condition of "wakeful dreaming" within a noiseless protective world woven of his own rich fantasies (or filled with music of his own creation). In Abraham's formulation, the individual "withdraws into the depth of the night in order to know nothing of the external world, that is, in order to be alone with himself and his phantasies."[2] This region of "magical-hallucinatory omnipotence" served another purpose as well: to isolate Beethoven from the reach of external commands and injunctions as well as from fearful sounds overheard or imagined.[3] For the auditory sphere is "the nucleus of the super-ego," according to Isakower, a zone of conscience accessible to the verbal prohibitions and imperatives of parental and social authority.[4] In Knapp's words, the auditory mechanism "keeps us oriented in the world of conduct."[5]

This aspect of the function of hearing was long ago perceived by Protestant theologians: they avowed that the benevolent God dwells within the heart, whereas the God of wrath enters through the "open," "receptive" sense of hearing. Luther, who (like Beethoven) suffered from a tormenting buzzing in the ears, observed: "In the Church of God nothing is demanded but hearing." Perhaps this is why Ludwig Feuerbach called the ear "the organ of terror" and asserted that "if man had only eyes, hands, and the senses of taste and of smell, he would have no religion, for all these senses are organs of critique and scepticism."[6]

There is some evidence that sound, especially loud sounds capable of transformation into tactile sensations, produced anxieties in Beethoven. During the French bombardment of Vienna in 1809, he "spent the greater part of the time in a cellar in the house of his brother Caspar, where he covered his head with pillows so as not to hear the cannons."[7] It might seem that Beethoven was here merely protecting his sensitive organs of hearing from the cannons' roar; however, long before the first signs of his deafness appeared—toward the close of his third decade—Beethoven had abandoned playing the organ because, as he told the organist Freudenberg, "my nerves could not stand the power of the gigantic instrument."[8] This might imply that Beethoven feared what Niederland called "auditory extinction."[9] Loud noises may mobilize memories of fearful sounds stemming from an early stage in the individual's development "when noise was something material, perhaps of an acutely threatening or . . . engulfing or devouring corporeal nature."[10]

Clinical research has demonstrated the close association between fear of noise and the memory of being maltreated and beaten in childhood. In general, Niederland noted, many traumatic events "are accompanied by frightening and often extremely intense noises such as screaming, moaning, shouting for help, etc. This acoustic aspect of the traumatic event . . . may . . . play a much larger role than the sight of an object of anxiety."[11] The linguistic connections between sound and beating appear in such metaphorical expressions as "beat," "strike," "blow," "bang," and "hit." In light of contemporary reports that Beethoven was repeatedly beaten by his father and probably also by his teacher at the Bonn grade school, Johann Krengel, who habitually used "harsh corporal punishment" to correct "the smallest transgression,"[12] it may well be that certain forms of auditory stimulation were perceived by Beethoven as threatening, reviving painful memories and reawakening the dread of physical maltreatment. As Kohut and Levarie observed, the exposure to severe auditory stimuli "must create an early, close (or 'symbolic') association between sound and the threatening external world, as opposed to quiet and security. Hence, in the regressive psychological states . . . in which hypersensitivity to noise is revived, the danger reacted to is, on the deepest level, the greatest and earliest of all: the danger of total psychobiological destruction."[13]

Medical studies of tinnitus have shown that patients like Beethoven who suffer from annoying buzzing and humming sounds in their ears perceive the auditory intrusions as persecutory. This may partially explain Beethoven's choice of metaphors for his deafness: "I should be happy, one of the happiest of mortals, if that *fiend* had not settled in my ears," and again, "My bad hearing *haunted me everywhere like a ghost,* and I fled from mankind."[14]

Several routes are open to one seeking to master the anxieties generated by fearful sounds: withdrawal into physical seclusion, selective hearing or the refusal to listen, retreat into daydreaming, replacement of chaotic and disturbing sounds by meaningful and pleasurable auditory experience, and deafness. There is copious evidence that Beethoven utilized the first four of these avenues. As for the last avenue, Beethoven's deafness, whether or not it was "willed" or generated through some obscure psychosomatic mechanism,[15] served to protect his creativity from the assaults and seductions of the external world and from the memories of a submissive past at a moment when he was about to embark upon what he termed his "new path," a path that would lead him to transform the parameters and procedures of the Viennese Classic tradition and to establish new boundaries and norms for the future development of music.

Soon after he learned in 1801 that his infirmity was incurable, he told his brothers and several of his intimate friends that he wished his encroaching deafness to be kept secret. However, this "great secret," as he called it, may have been not his deafness but his acquiescence in the necessity of deafness as a condition of his creativity, that is, of his competition with God and with the omnipotent parents of archaic memory.[16] Weber described the "notion that certain kinds of suffering and abnormal states provoked through chastisements are avenues to the attainment of superhuman, i.e., magical power."[17] Beethoven's deafness may have been such a form of magical asceticism, a rite of passage, a prelude to an ecstatic and "holy" state from which emerged the masterpieces of his maturity.

II

THROUGH a process of psychological displacement, the ear may be invested with the characteristics of other bodily organs, in a fluid and perplexing interchange. Knapp observed the phallic attributes of the ear, not only as a protruding organ but also, in its active function, "as a probe, a weapon, or a sensitive antenna, with which we extend the boundaries of the visible world and grasp important data for the formation of ego and superego."[18] The sharply protuberant ears of Bacchus and Lucifer are the most obvious confirmations of this metaphor in the mythological consciousness. This equation was not far from Beethoven's consciousness as well. Advising his intimate friend Karl Amenda of the onset of his hearing difficulties, he wrote: "Know that my most vital part, my hearing, has greatly deteriorated."[19]

Thus, even without the explicitness of a van Gogh's self-mutilation, deafness tends to be perceived as a form of castration, displaced upward and inward. But the matter does not end here: the mythological consciousness also includes the Madonna's impregnation through the ear and, through that same channel, the curious birth of Gargantua and the poisoning of Hamlet's father. In a sense, deafness stands for all the regions of the interior: the soundless world of dream and the unconscious, the cavities of the body, and the places of burial and of birth. Beethoven's music came to maturity within a silent space carved out of his own body, perpetually secluded, and in permanent symbiosis with a nourishing female principle. An inner darkness that has the double significance of birth and death also supplied the ground for a creativity which partook of opposed generative forces. By means of his exile from the auditory world, Beethoven's creativity was able to compete, not only with God and the father, but with the teeming mother as well.[20]

Beethoven's musical powers were scarcely impaired by his deafness. Perhaps that is why he even appeared for a time to acquiesce in it, as a condition favorable to his creativity, by way of its elimination of all outlets competitive to composition, such as continued public performance as a keyboard virtuoso.[21] But these compensations could not diminish the affliction of Beethoven's deafness. He perceived his deafness as a wounding, a punishment, and a retaliation ("that *fiend* [which] settled in my ears"). And perhaps because of its implication of feminization, he viewed it as a shameful malformation. "I must live as an outcast," he observes in the Heiligenstadt Testament. "If I appear in company I am seized by a burning anxiety, and I fear being exposed to the danger that my condition might be noticed."[22] To Amenda, he complains: "I am cut off from everything that is dear and precious to me."[23] In his copy of Sturm's *Reflections on the Works of God in Nature* he makes special note of a passage dealing with physical deformity and its transcendence: "How unjustly do those act, who . . . despise, or treat with asperity, those of their fellow-creatures who have bodily defects . . . The perfections of the soul alone give man true merit, and render him worthy of admiration . . . Have we not seen persons, who were neither distinguished by birth nor fortune, render the most important services both to church and state? Often crippled or deformed persons have shown more magnanimity of soul, than those who were favoured with the most beautiful and majestic form."[24]

Beethoven's innermost responses to his deafness cannot be easily known or summarized. But it is fairly certain that at first he reacted to the onset and progress of his hearing loss by a narcissistic distancing; indeed, deafness was Beethoven's main rationale for his withdrawal from society, from sexual relationships, and from the prospect of founding a family of his own. Ferenczi once described this kind of "narcissistic regression" as stemming from "an injury to a part of the body especially powerfully charged with libido, with which the ego as a whole easily identifies itself."[25]

However, as Beethoven's hearing worsened and total deafness came into prospect, the narcissistic defenses increasingly proved insufficient to contain the anxieties and the accompanying feelings of persecution and impotence induced by his condition. He needed to return to the world, to find human contact, somehow to compensate for the auditory void. He fully recognized his need, lamenting to his brother Nikolaus Johann: "With my poor hearing I surely need to have someone always at hand. And whom am I to trust?"[26] Similarly, he addresses himself in his Tagebuch in 1817: "To live alone is like poison for you in your deaf condition."[27] Perhaps this desire to be "in" and "of" the world is precisely what encouraged Beethoven into sexual activity with prostitutes beginning around 1810, expressing the need physically to "reach out," to touch, to communicate with other human beings.[28] Music had always served this compensating function for Beethoven, but with the passage of years he required something more than the symbolic sharing of experience with others. Somehow, sexual communication demonstrated Beethoven's wholeness, repaired his physical defect, by permitting him to explore in reality the geography of the feminine.

Beethoven's proposal of marriage to Therese Malfatti in 1810, his profound love beginning in 1810 or 1811 for the woman he called his Immortal Beloved, his "seizure" of his nephew after 1815, and his lengthy entanglement with that boy's mother—all these testify to the intensification of his drive to establish passionate and concrete human relationships at a time when deafness was closing him off from the world. True, his Tagebuch begins with the outcry: "For you there is no longer any happiness except within yourself, in your art," and in that same diary Beethoven exhorts himself: "Live only in your art . . . the *only existence* for you."[29] But the painful prospect of an existence locked within the spheres of the aesthetic and the imaginative was never wholly accepted by Beethoven, who continued to reach out, striving to take up residence beyond as well as within the secluded circumference of his own creativity.

BIOGRAPHY AND CREATIVITY

7

Thoughts on Biography

Few would altogether deny the presence of a "personal" factor in creativity. But many minimize its importance or assert that it cannot be adequately measured. And certainly no discussion of the biographical dimension of art can proceed without acknowledging both its limitations as an explanatory factor and its difficulties of application as a critical principle. To begin on the most basic level: every work of art is only partially an individual creation. The composer cannot invent the scale or the poet the alphabet. The creative act unites extremes of subjectivity and collective experience; even the most inimitable of psychic materials—dreams and fantasies— belong to a common stock; art is never "freely" created but issues from a multiplicity of antecedent events which are quite independent of the artist's personality—including the prior history of art, the level of development of its languages and forms, and the needs or demands of its patrons or audiences.

Among the many who have stressed this point in various contexts, T. S. Eliot observed: "We shall often find that not only the best, but the most individual parts of [a poet's] work may be those in which the dead poets, his ancestors, assert their immortality most vigorously."[1] Or in the words of an African aphorism, reported by Ernst Bloch: "If this story is worthless, then it belongs to the man who tells it; if it is worth anything, then it belongs to us all."[2]

We cannot deduce the particular work of art from the universals which surround and penetrate it. Dewey recognized that, despite the fact that the material in art "came from the public world and so has qualities in common with the material of other experiences, while the product awakens in other persons new perceptions of the meaning of the common world," the artwork itself, because it has "passed through the alembic of personal experience," has "no precedents in existence or in universal being."[3] Just as every superior artist creates values that transcend the limitations of his own personality, and just as he is an agent for the transmission of a common heritage which presents itself to him as a "given," so is it equally certain that his works bear the unique impress of his personality. They can belong to no other historical individual. Even prior to Romanticism's urgent call for "originality" (which in turn generates its own uniformity), even in works created in those eras in which Aristotelian, theological, or Enlightenment ideologies encouraged the production of works in imitation of ideal models, the singularity of every creative artist's work is apparent not only to the trained observer but even to many observers of relatively slight sophistication.

Sainte-Beuve long ago specified the still uncharted region of relative freedom within which this singularity arises: "After making every allowance for general or particular elements and for circumstances, there still remains room and space enough round men of talent for freedom of movement and change of place. Besides, however circumscribed the line round each, every man of talent and genius . . . possesses a secret, which is his alone, for producing marvels in that space, and for bringing wonders to light."[4] We sense that the artist's personality is reflected in his work—that his "individual style" reflects not only his technical preoccupations and his assimilation of available styles but also his psychological attitudes, conscious choices, and unconscious mental processes. However, the tracing of biographical or psychological experiences within a given artwork presents many difficulties. The idiosyncratic experiences may be so deeply embedded in the work, or so disguised, that they cannot be retrieved, except, perhaps, through the psychoanalysis of the living artist. Furthermore, since all psychological processes are fusions of contradictory drives, a given stimulus may produce a diversity of symptoms or responses. Often a work of art reflects its author's personality only as a negative image, in the same way that a visionary work may be an inverted reflection of its epoch. Art embodies wishes and striving as well as actual events and experiences; one usually cannot distinguish between the real and the imagined, between direct representation and sublimated transformation.

Thus one cannot formulate any theory which justifies the reading of the life from the work. Moreover, in a work of many dimensions the artist symbolically enacts roles which are at once within and beyond his immediate experience; the multiple characters of the novelist and the imaginative range of a symphonist's ideas do not necessarily, or merely, result from the splitting of the artist's ego into "many component egos," as Freud suggested.[5] "In the creative process," argued Slochower, "the artist at once draws on his immediate and personal experience even as he transcends it. In short, the artist moves on a thin borderline of delicate imbalances."[6]

The difficulties are not minimized when an artist claims a specific subjective intention and significance for his work. Goethe, who once asserted that his works were but "fragments of a great confession," is a classic case, and even Beethoven during his last years, when he came under the influence of Romanticism, wrote about the "innate summons to reveal myself to the world through my works," a conception at odds with his ingrained Enlightenment attitudes.[7] Mahler, too, firmly believed in the autobiographical substratum of his work. "My whole life is contained in my two symphonies," he wrote in 1893. "In them I have set down my experiences and suffering . . . To anyone who knows how to listen, my whole life will become clear."[8] More recently, Berg scholars discovered that he understood the *Lyric Suite* to be a literal description of his beloved's domestic life—a meaning that no reasonable listener could possibly have suspected. The more primitive examples of the "intentional fallacy" (more accurately termed "autobiographical reductionism") apparently have their source in the feelings of awe and grandiosity that an artist's own creativity arouses in himself, feelings which, in the Romantic and post-Romantic period in particular, lead to an overvaluation of the personal factor in the creative equation.

The psychoanalyst K. R. Eissler pointed out that, even apart from the tendency of artists either to overestimate or to underestimate their achievements, it is impossible to tell whether an artist's conscious statement about his art also represents his unconscious intention. And, like many others, Eissler emphasized that in any case the meanings of a completed work of art are in constant flux: "A work of art, once created, is a structure that has become entirely separated from its creator, that has started to live its own life. Its value is now utterly independent of its originator's intentions."[9]

In the face of such difficulties, can we continue to pursue the naive belief of Shakespeare's first biographer, Nicholas Rowe, that "The knowledge of an Author may sometimes conduce to the better understanding his Book"? [10] If so, we must be able to show that there is indeed a network of correlations between biography and art, and that these correlations are significant in the origination of art as well as in its appreciation. But in order to do so, we must acknowledge several further difficulties: first, that the definition of a "biographical event" is by no means a self-evident one; second, that many different kinds of biographical events have a bearing upon artistic creation.

I shall not dwell upon the problems of definition except to note that it is only in theory that one can isolate biographical events from the profusion of active forces which are at play in artistic creativity. For if "biography" is "the life-course of an individual," then the "events" that constitute biography embrace a vast spectrum, extending from the biological and ancestral inheritance, proceeding through the various layers of personality structure as determined by the totality of external phenomena impinging upon the individual, together with the sum of his physical actions and mental processes, and merging ultimately into the nexus of relationships that bind him to society both retrospectively and prospectively. A biographer's task is to maintain a constant awareness of "background" and "foreground." He must resist two temptations: to dissolve his subject into his sources, and to isolate him from his context and treat his life as a self-contained universe. The creative significance of an artist can best be revealed by his juxtaposition against tradition—the extent to which tradition is available to him, shapes him, is disrupted by him, and ultimately is reconstituted in the light of his contribution. For biography exists in the tensional interplay between the individual and the diverse global "backgrounds" against which his experiences must be projected in order for them to have any significance beyond the merely solipsistic.

BIOGRAPHICAL "causation" of art takes place on many simultaneous levels. These are simultaneous only in the sense that the human psyche is historical, retaining the impress of archaic patterns of behavior while constantly being reconstituted through its assimilation of present experience and its anticipation of future events. The biographer may seek to gain access to different levels of this genetic network through a variety of strategies and at any of the levels of motivation. For example, he may begin with more "distant" events and attempt to trace their putative reverberations in long-term patterns of creativity and, eventually, in finished works of art. Or he may begin with what appear to be biographical precipitates in a given work and seek their analogues in experiences of the author. A particularly tempting approach is to construct a dynamic model of the artist's personality out of the interplay between known biographical data and the psychological materials embodied in his works.

Still another possible strategy involves analysis of a certain type of mundane and often readily verifiable biographical datum—the catalytic event which gives rise to the conscious decision to make a work of art. That is, the biographer-critic may begin with the seemingly simple, external factor closest in time to the creative act. I will pursue the implications of this approach for a moment, not because I advocate it as a methodology but because it may help to demonstrate the intricate interweaving of biography with other determinants of creativity.

In Beethoven's case, virtually every one of his compositions may be traced to such a simple proximate cause. Usually this is a patron's commission, a performance opportunity, a publication offer, or (particularly after the patterns of his patronage changed after 1814) the anticipation or ready availability of one or a combination of these. By way of rapid example, and in view of the fact that we do not know all of the details, the piano sonatas through "Les Adieux," op. 81a, and at least the first four piano concertos were written for performance by Beethoven on various occasions; the first two versions of *Fidelio* sprang from a commission from the Theater-an-der-Wien, and the third version from anticipation of the 1814 revival at the Kärntnertortheater; the incidental music to Goethe's *Egmont* was suggested by the directors of the Hoftheater; the first six symphonies were written with specific concert opportunities in mind; Beethoven needed the Cello Sonatas, op. 5, for performance at the court of Friedrich Wilhelm II; and publishers desired, if they did not actively solicit, the early sets of variations in order to satisfy a ready market in sheet music.

Less frequently the proximate cause may be "celebratory" in nature: a love offering ("An die Hoffnung," op. 32; "An die Geliebte," WoO 140; perhaps opus 98); a token of friendship or esteem ("Hochzeitslied," WoO 105); or an affirmation of belief, whether ideological ("Der freie Mann," WoO 117; the "Friedelberg Songs," WoO 121-122) or religious ("Gellert Lieder," op. 48; "Opferlied," op. 121b). Sometimes the commodity and celebratory character of a work cannot be readily differentiated, as in works composed in honor of a patron (*Missa solemnis*, op. 123; "Lobkowitz Cantata," WoO 106). In any event, the precipitating factor is almost always the emergence of a concrete opportunity; and since there are many such opportunities that Beethoven rejects, an opportunity, if it is to become a catalyst, must mesh with his desires, leading to a conscious decision. An "offer" emerges from the welter of social relations and presents itself as a single biographical opportunity. Beethoven confronts the opportunity, weighs the possibilities, and exercises what is apparently a "free" choice.

The "occasion" provides Beethoven with both opportunity and limitations, for the work must to some degree be suited to the occasion; it must be composed for a specified combination of instruments or for an available ensemble, and it must accommodate to the tastes of the patron, whether that be an individual, an audience, or a publisher seeking to satisfy an intended market. The imaginative and problem-solving aspects of Beethoven's creativity now function within these limitations, which have been set up by this "simplest" biographical event. This is not to say that the imaginative process begins only when an external opportunity is at hand. An extended gestation often attends Beethoven's most important innovations; the general "idea" of a composition or the specific notion of a technical innovation may well long precede the occasion for its realization.

Thus the proximate cause of each of Beethoven's compositions immediately engages underlying and neighboring generative universes. The surface event usually arises from a sociological dimension, from the conditions of patronage and the opportunities for social communication. A social "offer" and private "acceptance" set Beethoven's productivity in motion and shape its general direction within the framework of evolving contemporary musical styles and the complex of ideological and emotional attitudes of certain audiences at a given moment in Austrian history.

We have quickly reached a crossroads in the network of intersecting and interacting genetic forces. The biographer whose main interest is in the historical determination of ideology may at this point choose to explore Beethoven's place in the cultural milieu, his connection to trends in the history of European (more specifically, German and Austrian) thought. The music historian will almost automatically be drawn into such issues as Beethoven's relation to his predecessors and contemporaries, his musical innovations, his location in the evolution from Classicism to Romanticism, and his influence upon later composers. The biographer who hopes to give a more comprehensive portrait of the composer will combine these lines of investigation, aware that in attempting so much, he risks the superficiality of eclecticism.

Each of these (in any event overlapping) levels of investigation appear to lead away from the specific issues of biography. Actually, however, an enriched study of either the ideological or the musical genesis of a composition involves the constant referral of data to the composer's biography. The ideological issues cannot be solved without knowledge of Beethoven's ideas; that is, we cannot begin to deal with the "intentional fallacy" so long as we remain ignorant of the composer's intention. And to know Beethoven's thought, it is necessary to study his letters, conversation books, and other private documents and to evaluate the extent of their congruence with the apparent ideological stances of his music. Beethoven's tangled attitudes toward his patrons must be acknowledged before the critic can begin to answer the question of how closely his works conform to their requirements. These are specifically biographical issues which cannot be inferred from the work of art.

Nor can musical issues be adequately confronted in the absence of biographical data. To take only one example, the scholar who wants to understand Beethoven's special synthesis of musical sources has to answer such (random) questions as: What music did he have access to in Bonn and Vienna? What did his various teachers offer to teach him? How did he regard his contemporaries? Were his attitudes toward French music in part derivatives of his attitudes toward French historical developments? Did his religious renewal in later years motivate his exploration of various traditions of ecclesiastical and religious music? And did his Enlightenment faith or readings in Romanticism influence his choice or treatment of texts? At nearly every juncture the biographical and musical issues supplement and reinforce one another.

The more adventurous biographer will wish to continue the "descent" through interrelated generative levels of experience. Depending upon the biographer's own ideological or psychological predispositions, he may attempt to uncover the archetypal which lies behind the iconological, the economic issues which underlie the ideological standpoints, or the infantile and unconscious roots of his subject's adult behavior. (And he will find that the search for ultimate origins is both futile and obsessional: futile because we cannot uncover first causes without finding that further causes—natural, biological, cosmic—lie beyond them; and obsessional because the quest for knowledge rises under the sway of our most powerful compulsions, which can never be fully satisfied.) Of these three regions—mythic, economic, psychological—the last is a directly biographical category, but the first two are also inextricably involved with issues of individual being and praxis. For the archetypal embodies those relatively universal mythic symbols wrought by mankind in its search for orientation, while the economic consists of material interactions between man and nature, of individuals in association acting upon the external world.

In short, the "biographical" element cannot be disengaged from the network of art's origins without undermining the entire structure or at least leading to an impoverishment of meaning. The strictly "biographical" is inseparable from all other modes of experience that contribute to art's formation because art is a form of human activity and not the operation of any abstract principle, either spiritual or material. Thus the simplest biographical fact—the commission, opportunity, or psychic "event" which brings about the compositional decision—meshes with underlying universes of experience. And such a biographical fact—apparently so superficial, belonging solely to the surface of the creative process—properly explored, permits entrance to the multidimensionality of art's causal nexus.

Ehrenzweig described the unity of the internal and external in creativity: "The exploration of the medium and the exploration of his own self . . . becomes one and the same process; the outside and the inside merge in unity. The artist himself does not know of this. His passionate interest in the outside world, in the functional properties of the material in which he works, makes him forget that he is also at grips with himself."[11] Ehrenzweig called this "the artist's self-deception, the externality illusion of art, which turns the artist's attention from his inner to the outer world." The phrasing is seductive but misleading. Beethoven's ongoing receptivity to a broad range of Enlightenment and early Romantic ideas reflects his emotional attitudes and his conflict-ridden psychological makeup; but the ideas also have an independent value. Similarly, although art may be a cloak for or an externalization of private fantasies, it does not thereby surrender its autonomy. Though a capacity for creative form-building may rise as a counterphobic or defense mechanism, the forms themselves do not thereby lose either their plasticity or their permanence. Though an altruistic cultural model may serve as an idealization to mask a personal woundedness, its ethical values are not thereby diminished. Beethoven's tragic family circumstances reverberated throughout his life; they were a source of a psychological disequilibrium that motored his creative quest, incessantly causing him symbolically to reenact archaic catastrophes, driving him to embody these—and to transcend them—in musical structures. But music is not reducible to its origins: the revelation of sources, even those at a core level, does not annihilate the surface. As a symbolic structure, art points within and beyond itself; surface and core are fused in unity.

In the last analysis, the pursuit of a significant "personal" element which can be distilled from the work of art may itself be a chimerical one. What can most readily be isolated are the inarticulate, often unconsciously produced style elements that constitute an artist's "fingerprints," those idiosyncrasies of style that Morelli used as the foundation for his theories of art-historical attribution. The musical equivalents of these are certain repeated musical patterns and word-music associations such as an older generation of musicologists were delighted to find in Bach, Beethoven, and other masters. (As Shakespeareans can testify, the study of recurrent imagery and associated image-clusters generates its own equivocal meanings, even where the subjective source is unmistakable.) But it would be ironic indeed if biographers, with their implicit and explicit claims for the significant explanatory worth of biographical research, were to settle for so small a dividend.

Perhaps the miscalculation here is that biographers often seek concrete associations between biography and art, whereas it may be sufficient only to understand the *necessity* of the tie, to set the life alongside the work and thus to throw the outlines of the interchange into relief—especially the broad patterns of creativity, the relationships between psychological crisis and style evolution, and the biographical conditions conducive or inimical to productivity. It is an unexpected bonus to trace an image to its specific life-source. But art's sources are as fugitive as art itself; they cannot be blueprinted, fixed, or dominated. "Art, when it is persecuted, finds asylum everywhere," Beethoven wrote. "Why, Daedalus when confined to the labyrinth invented the wings which lifted him *upwards* and out into the air."[12]

Artistic productivity exemplifies in superlative form the distinctively human quality of the labor process in Marx's sense, its creative-teleological aspect. "At the end of every labor process," wrote Marx, "we get a result that already existed in the imagination of a laborer at its commencement."[13] Or in Lukács's reformulation: "A design conceived in thought reaches material reality by adding to it something qualitatively and radically new."[14] In a fragmented labor process and alienating social environment, art is, of course, the exemplar of such imaginative effort, and its very existence constantly reaffirms the possibilities of human self-realization and social transcendence. Wartofsky described, in Feuerbachian terms, some of the implications of this process for our attitudes toward the artist: "The artist thus becomes a model of the potentialities of human nature, of human creativity, in which the appreciator realizes his own species-capacity for creation, not necessarily in himself, but in another."[15] We recognize in the creative act the breakthrough of repressed human powers. We sense, even if we cannot demonstrate to the skeptic, that the transcendent note, the anticipatory flash of insight, the symbolization of the new, in short, the element of the productive imagination is largely rooted in the personality and experience of the artist.

But creativity is a threatening subject. Through it man not only competes with the divine and the ancestral (which are sufficiently fraught with danger) but also throws tradition itself into question. Creativity disturbs the world's peace by its insistence that we have both the opportunity and the responsibility to change the world—at least to alter our way of perceiving it. Creativity disrupts the existing order: it speaks of rotten states to contented citizens; it is hopeful and despairing, accepting and rejecting; it is filled with expectation but always suffused with the inevitability of tragedy. Moreover, the artist is himself a dangerous child. Permitted access to taboo realms— incest, parricide, revolution, the varieties of Utopia—he delineates the ways in which we may, by his example, participate in the forbidden. Little wonder that he arouses extremes of ambivalent feeling—

hostility and adoration, rage and awe, hate and love. Little wonder that those critics who speak for their own timidities, as well as for fearful social orders, have undertaken to neutralize him and his work by every conceivable strategy.

I TURN, briefly, to a final issue—whether any aesthetic or critical significance can be ascribed to biographical knowledge. In a widely-read text, Wellek and Warren asserted flatly: "No biographical evidence can change or influence critical evaluation."[16] Such antibiographical positions remain commonplace, not only among the successors to the New Critics but also among the purveyors of alternative genetic theories. I think, for example, of psychoanalysts who, following Freud's lead, are eager to lay down their arms in the presence of the creative process, and of those analytical critics who approach the work of art as does the lepidopterist his still-fluttering specimen or the anatomist his cadaver.

But in order to maintain the hypothesis—one which, although easily stated, cannot be empirically validated—the critic must be prepared totally to insulate evaluation from perception, an improbable task. For there is no such thing as an unconditioned apprehension of an artwork. Its effect is inseparable from the aura through which we perceive it, an aura, compounded of our accumulated experience, projecting some aspect of the work's meaning and shaping our receptivity even before a single note has been sounded. We hear every musical composition as a member of its genre, as one segment of the œuvre of its composer, as a product of its historical period, as symbolic action whose meanings are filtered through the judgment of prior generations—and as an emanation of the (presumed) personality of its composer. We approach every work of art with a more or less extensive set of preliminary assumptions (perhaps only vaguely formulated), and our critical evaluation of the work is conditioned by those assumptions.

We listen to Beethoven's *Eroica* Symphony differently than to his other symphonies because of its extramusical associations—its title, its subtitle, its funeral march, and its quotation from *The Creatures of Prometheus.* Beethoven has attempted to shape our responses, to direct them along avenues selected by himself. We listen to it differently, *nolens volens*, because of Ries's story about the rending of the inscription to Bonaparte. Now we will hear it differently because of what we have learned about Beethoven's intended journey to Paris as the proximate cause of the symphony and of its original dedication, and about Beethoven's intention to use the piece as his musical passport to France. Listening to the *Eroica*, can we expel from our consciousness our knowledge of Beethoven's hero and rescue fantasies, his suicidal thoughts, his family romance, and his nobility pretense?

It is doubtless true that we need have no knowledge whatever of a composer's biography, or knowledge of any other motivating factor of any kind, to appreciate the artwork on some fundamental level. Beautiful forms, sensuous materials, and the psychological universals embedded in art's subject matter are sufficient to achieve a certain kind of unmediated response in the untutored individual, assuming his existence *in abstracto*. But such responses do not exemplify a higher form of appreciation. Because his aesthetic sensibility is insufficiently formed, the "innocent" will respond "naturally" to melodramatic or highly sensuous works but not to exquisite or formally demanding works. And he will respond, for example, quite as intensely to Seneca's *Oedipus* as to Sophocles', to Beethoven's *Wellington's Victory* as to his Fifth Symphony. Such responses are often to elemental feelings: to variations upon family-romance myths, to simple oedipal conflicts writ large, or to works which arouse extremes of feeling—whether of altruism or of sexuality— via manipulative ruses rather than aesthetic processes.

If it were merely the untutored response to art which is diminished by knowledge, there would be little reason to mourn the loss of such innocence. But there are highly sophisticated critics who deny the value of biographical and psychological exegeses. Some object to such studies because they prefer to stress other, nonbiographical kinds of genetic factors—religious or archetypal, intellectual or cultural, economic or historical. Such critics minimize the role of the individual in his own creativity; that is, they have in common the notion—which may take platonic, Romantic, theological, or utilitarian forms—that the artist is a more or less passive medium through whom speaks some incarnation of an ideal—variously the deity, the collective, the race, the myth, the unconscious, or the social class. Still others maintain that the significant determinants of art are the artist's conscious responses to the traditions, inherited materials, and technical demands of the medium, and that it is to these areas that study should be directed. And there are those who believe in the absolute autonomy and inviolability of art, passionately advocating a pure, unconditioned aesthetic response to the work of art. In a review of a recent musical biography, Siegmund Levarie writes:

> In relation to the essence of a work of art, historic as well as psychological data are irrelevant . . . Composition, like all true artistic creation, is a spiritual process; and physiological or psychological research will never touch the essence of it any more than that of life itself. My knowledge of Beethoven, such as it is, derives from my having heard and studied his scores. To the spiritual power represented by them, external and internal biographic data remain tangential and secondary. In no case do they explain the spirit that carries and gives life to a work of art. The *creator spiritus* defies analysis.[17]

This attitude, familiar enough in the New Criticism and among the so-called "neo-Aristotelian" critics at the University of Chicago several decades ago, belongs to a long and significant tradition, one that Abrams analyzed as deriving from the "heterocosmic" view of poetry, which takes its point of departure from the analogy of artistic to divine creation. Some of the earlier proponents of the "divine analogy" actually magnified the biographical factor in creativity, holding that the artwork is a disguised self-revelation. But a variant tradition—extending from Sidney to Lessing, Bradley, and the New Criticism—emphasized the metaphor of the artwork as a self-contained universe of discourse. It is, in Abrams's words, "a second creation, and therefore not a replica nor even a reasonable facsimile of this world, but its own world, *sui generis*, subject only to its own laws, whose existence . . . is an end in itself."[18] It follows that we neither need nor wish to know anything about the work's sources, external or internal. As Abrams observed, "the appropriate attitude to Divinity, of course, is one of adoration."[19]

"The *creator spiritus* defies analysis." Adoration, yes; but perhaps fear as well. The Protestant will have no book other than Scripture lest he learn that which is forbidden. The uncovering of origins can be bewildering and fearful, whether of the libidinal sources of sublime masterworks, the economic motivations of abstract thought, the evolutionary lineage of mankind, or even the ancestry of an individual. The heterocosmic view aims to decontaminate art of its "lower" sources, to segregate sexuality from spirit, pathology from the intact ego. It sunders art from the body, from the social nexus, and from the mythic context. Art achieves a virgin birth. Life is thrown overboard.

One somehow shares the sense of loss. All of us have shuddered at the clumsiness of genetic analyses not of our own devising; all of us resist the reduction of art to its origins, the denial of its specificity, its transformation into a handmaiden of other disciplines. But the alternative, as Praz pointed out, is to regard the work as an *individuum ineffabile*, self-enclosed and perfect, leaving the critic frozen in "a mystical, admiring silence."[20]

To retrace our steps once more: it is clear that knowledge of a creative artist's biography is not a necessary condition for the enjoyment or understanding of his works. The absence of an adequate biographical record of Shakespeare's life is often adduced to demonstrate this. But is it not the case that we now comprehend Shakespeare's poems and plays as, in part, the very emanation of a personality whose biographical record is defective, and that our perception of the works is therefore actually shaped, perhaps even heightened, by our awareness of their author's biographical ambiguity? Do we not somehow fill in the outlines of his identity with projections of our own making?

> Lovers and madmen have such seething brains,
> Such shaping fantasies, that apprehend
> More than cool reason ever comprehends . . .
> And as imagination bodies forth
> The form of things unknown, the poet's pen
> Turns them to shapes and gives to airy nothing
> A local habitation and a name.

I do not offer to justify such ectoplasmic projections; I merely suggest that they exist as fantasies whether or not any biographer has objectified them. If this is true, then the biographer's task appears to be not only to establish a documentary record but constantly to clear away the accumulated fantasies and romances which have filled the void created by ignorance. In any event, and in summary, to the extent that biographical data exist, they—like knowledge of history, of culture, of the anatomy of forms—alter the state of awareness within which we perceive art. And this in turn cannot fail—regardless of our will—to affect aesthetic and critical judgment, if these terms are to mean something other than the merely analytical or taxonomic.

Of course there is something to be said for withholding from an uneasy mankind knowledge both of its origins and of the possibility of transcendence. "For in much wisdom is much grief," said the Preacher, "and he that increaseth knowledge increaseth sorrow" (Eccl. 1 : 18). But knowledge increases whether we will it or not. We had better come to terms with its consequences and try to put them to good use.

8

The Creative Periods
of Beethoven

CONFRONTED with the immense range of formal and expressive problems in Beethoven's works and with those qualitative changes in his style which are turning points in the history of music itself, his early appreciators must have experienced a great sense of relief when, only ten years after his death, an apparently valid periodization hypothesis was proposed within which his works might be classified. This was the theory of the three stages or periods, which, remarkably, was suggested as early as 1818 by an anonymous writer and worked out in rudimentary fashion a few months after Beethoven's death by his hasty first biographer, but which was significantly formulated only in 1837 by Fétis in his *Biographie universelle des musiciens*.[1]

The "three stages," analogous to biographical childhood, manhood, and old age, were a commonplace of European thought by the 1830s—in Hugo's *Preface to Cromwell*, the positivism of Comte, and the dialectical trinity of German classical philosophy. Anticipated by Forkel, evolutionist music-historians almost universally insisted upon a three-part division of their subject.[2] Fétis, working from incomplete listings of Beethoven's works and partially unaware of the actual chronology of composition, divided Beethoven's music into three "classes of production," the first extending from opus 1 to the *Waldstein* Sonata, op. 53; the second from the *Eroica* Symphony and the Sonata, op. 54, to the Seventh Symphony, op. 92; and the third period from the Eighth Symphony, op. 93, to opus 137.

In 1840, Schindler organized his biography of Beethoven into three periods, namely 1770 to 1800, 1800 to October 1813, and November 1813 until Beethoven's death.[3] Schindler's division, like that of Fétis, was based on style periods rather than biographical considerations.

The pivotal works inaugurating the second and third periods respectively were given as *Christ on the Mount of Olives,* op. 85 (which Schindler erroneously believed to have been composed in 1800), and *Wellington's Victory.*[4]

In 1843, C. T. Seiffert divided the sonatas and symphonies into three groups.[5] In 1850, Paul Scudo disposed of the seeming incomprehensibility of late Beethoven by proposing that the three styles corresponded to youth, maturity, and decadence.[6] And in 1853, Czerny offered an intriguing subdivision of the late works according to the progressive stages in the evolution of Beethoven's deafness.[7] The three-stage hypothesis was so firmly entrenched by 1852 that in that year it found its way into Brendel's *Geschichte der Musik in Italien, Deutschland und Frankreich.*[8] In that same year Wilhelm von Lenz's *Beethoven et ses trois styles* appeared, a work which is often credited with the discovery of the three styles, although Lenz specifically granted priority to Fétis and to one Count Mikhail Yurevich Vielgorsky.[9]

Here, and in his later *Beethoven: Eine Kunst-Studie* (Kassel & Hamburg, 1855–1860), Lenz divided the periods into, first, opus 1 to opus 20 plus the First and Second Symphonies; second, opus 21 to opus 100; and third, opus 100 to opus 137, with significant exceptions. Lenz's originality, as Newman noted, was that he attempted "to find out the causes for the changes from one style to another, and did not accept the divisions as watertight; he pointed out instances of reaching out in an early work to a later style, and of reversions in later works to an earlier style."[10] Lenz's opponent, Alexandre Oulibicheff, continued this line of exploration in his *Beethoven: ses critiques et ses glossateurs,* perceptively stressing the distance that separated the last quartets from earlier third-period works (even suggesting that the quartets by themselves might constitute the third style), pointing out difficulties of dating the close of the second style, and calling attention to the apparent disparity between biographical milestones and the boundaries of the style periods.[11]

The three-style classification, or variants thereof, has since been accepted to a remarkable degree.[12] Virtually all those who have contributed to the special literature on the quartets, sonatas, and symphonies have dealt with these genres in terms of the traditional three groupings, into which the works seem to separate themselves with what Kerman called "ominous ease."[13] However, scholars disagree as to which works properly belong within each style period.

And many of the more profound commentators on Beethoven's music have not specifically taken up the three-style periodization, or have regarded it as simple and restrictive. "The traditional division of his music into three periods is not untenable," noted Rosen, "but it can be as misleading as it is useful . . . It is a fiction for the purposes of analysis, a convenience for understanding, and not a biographical reality."[14]

Franz Liszt was perhaps the earliest to object to the three-style classification as a diversion from more serious issues. Liszt suggested that Beethoven's music might more fruitfully be divided into two categories mirroring the dialectic between "freedom and necessity." In the first category, he wrote, "conventional and traditional forms contain and govern the master's thought," whereas in the second, "the thought stretches, breaks, recreates and fashions forms and style."[15]

For many years, the theory failed to evolve significantly and, despite its apparently wide acceptance, was actually falling into disuse. However, in recent decades increased attention to Beethoven's pre-Vienna music and new datings of some of his later works aroused new interest in the subject. In 1963 William S. Newman suggested a new division of Beethoven's works into five periods: A "student" period, 1782–1794; "virtuoso" period, 1795–1800; *Appassionata* period, 1801–1808; "invasion" period, 1809–1814; and "sublimation" period, 1815–1826.[16] In particular, Newman's suggestion that the Bonn works constitute a separate—fourth—creative period found a hospitable reception. Fétis, Schindler, and Lenz all began their chronology with the Trios, op. 1, of 1794, not taking into serious account the earlier works. Most later researchers merely added the Bonn compositions to the first period—seen as the "student" or, as d'Indy would have it, the "imitative" period—thereby minimizing the advance in formal mastery evidenced by the Viennese works of the 1790s. But Nohl and Thayer treated the Bonn years as a separate biographical entity; and Wyzewa, Bekker, Prod'homme, and Riemann dealt with the Bonn piano compositions as a distinct class.[17] Beethoven himself was unwilling to grant his first opus number to any of the pre-Vienna works.

It is time to discard Nottebohm's conclusion that Haydn's instruction of Beethoven was defective.[18] A Haydn was not needed to point out parallel fifths in Beethoven's exercises. To study with Haydn was to learn not merely textbook rules of counterpoint and part writing but also the whole range of Viennese high-Classic musical ideas and techniques. Beethoven's successful mastery of these styles and forms—of sonata form and the sonata cycle—sharply separates the early Vienna works from the Bonn compositions.

Other subdivisions of the traditional three periods may also be necessary. We will want to study what Beethoven termed his "new path" and to determine whether it differs from the "heroic" or *Appassionata* manner. Newman is right to call attention to the stylistic issues raised by Beethoven's works of 1809–1814. There are powerful intimations of late Beethoven in the Violin Sonata, op. 96, the Sonata, op. 90, and the String Quartets, op. 74 and op. 95, but it is questionable whether these are hallmarks of a distinct style. Equally problematic is whether such patriotic potboilers as *Der glorreiche Augenblick, Germania,* and *Wellington's Victory* can be considered as legitimately falling within the boundaries of any of Beethoven's authentic style periods.

Implicit in reopening the question of chronology is a call for a clearer delineation of the musical elements that make up Beethoven's stylistic manner at each stage of its evolution. No period, no matter how restrictively defined, is wholly given over to a single manner; rather, conflicting and simultaneous styles are in a dynamic process of evolution. In each period, moreover, there are strong stylistic contrasts between works according to the genres that are used. There is often a disproportion between intent and realization, with musical ideas arising at very early stages, prior to the possibility of their formal solution. As Blom noted, "Form and subject matter do not always progress simultaneously in Beethoven's music."[19] Thus, for example, the germ of the heroic manner is already present in the *Joseph* Cantata of 1790 and perhaps even in the choice of a pathetic funeral march by Dressler as a subject for variation in Beethoven's first published composition, but it was more than a decade before Beethoven was competent (or daring) enough fully to explore the implications of these ideas.

Other examples of these anticipatory elements in Beethoven include the Bonn origins and intricate evolution over four decades of the finale of the Ninth Symphony; the Bonn origins of the program of the *Pastoral* Symphony; and the reverberations of the 1790 Cantatas not only in the *Eroica* but also in *Coriolan, Fidelio,* the *Pastoral* Symphony, *Egmont,* and the Ninth Symphony. Frimmel called attention to Beethoven's appropriation of a motif composed by Sacchini in the mid-1780s as the main theme of the Allegro con brio of the Sonata, op. 111.[20] Beethoven's late-period interest in Bach may also constitute an at least partial return to Bonn, for Neefe described him in 1783 as playing "chiefly The Well-Tempered Clavier of Sebastian Bach." Perhaps, with Ernest Newman, we can presuppose the germinal existence at an early stage of musical impulses which underlie all Beethoven's styles. A convergence of biographical, historical, and musical catalysts was necessary to develop their latent potentialities and to master the structural problems adequate to express these ideas.[21]

THE division of Beethoven's works into style periods is not an end in itself. Rather, classification is worthwhile only if it assists in the exploration of the dynamics and genesis of Beethoven's creative process, if it throws light on the potential connections between the style periods and genetic factors such as Beethoven's biographical circumstances, modes of patronage, musical influences, ideological outlook, and the historical background.

The modes of Beethoven's patronage divide into four fairly distinct stages which closely mirror the broad contours of the traditional style periods. Throughout the Bonn years and until the spring of 1794 in Vienna, Beethoven was in exclusive service in the traditional sense for the feudal electorate of Cologne. From 1794 to around 1800 he found patronage among the most enlightened segments of the Viennese nobility, inaugurating the transition to "freelance" semifeudal composer and virtuoso. In the third stage, dating roughly from 1800 to 1815, he achieved an unusual degree of independence from aristocratic patronage, paradoxically brought about mainly by way of two generous annuities granted him, first by Prince Karl Lichnowsky in 1800 and then, in 1809, by a princely consortium on behalf of Viennese culture. This independence was furthered by income from Beethoven's first major contacts with continental publishers and from his first public concerts for his own benefit. Finally, after 1814, Beethoven was almost wholly liberated from personal patronage as such. Emergent hedonistic trends in Viennese society and the turn toward new, less rigorous musical styles; the accelerated attrition of Beethoven's former patrons through death, emigration, and personal estrangement; the liberal terms of the princes's annuity, which made no specific demands on

Beethoven's productivity—these freed Beethoven from the necessity of composing to order, for specific occasions, or standardized tastes. He was enabled, therefore, to confront musical and aesthetic issues of the highest order, largely unaffected by economic and patronage factors. The transition "from artisan to artist," as Hess put it, had been completed.[22]

Several scholars—among them, Schmitz, Bekker, and Leichtentritt—have called attention to evident parallels between the evolving forms and styles of Beethoven's music and the historical background against which they were created. In one such model, Beethoven's predominant Bonn styles might plausibly correspond to the untroubled aestheticism of the enlightened Cologne electorate, ruptured momentarily by French revolutionary currents, which left their impress on the *Joseph* Cantata. The Napoleonic Wars in the course of time gave rise to the national, public, declamatory style of the *Eroica* period—a period of national defense against repeated onslaught and invasion. The final defeat of French forces contributed directly to the Congress of Vienna works, including the revision of *Fidelio*. And the post-Congress climate—with its heightened censorship and repression—accompanied a turn to more subjective modes of expression.

Scholars have long delighted in tracing parallels between the Beethoven style periods and the successive influences he underwent. Thus, they have uncovered influences of Neefe, C. P. E. Bach, Mozart, and Haydn in the Bonn works, and the influences of the Mannheim School, Haydn, Mozart, Clementi, and Dussek in the early Vienna works. The middle period is bound up with the accelerated entrance of elements of French revolutionary music into the high-Classic Viennese style. Finally, the renewed contrapuntal studies, the sudden interest in the ecclesiastical modes, the return to Bach, and the discovery of Handel all played an important role, however sublimated, in the late Beethoven synthesis. And it can reasonably be argued that the four major stages of Beethoven's career reveal a progression from Classic, to high-Classic, to late-Classic, and finally to Romantic styles and forms.

Although it is useful to maintain a healthy skepticism about our ability to establish causal relationships between Beethoven's life and his works, tracing the biographical and psychological sources of his long-term patterns of creativity may hold some promise. Obviously there can be no certainty in such matters, but many of us are responsive to the suggestion that the onset of the *Eroica* period is somehow connected with the revelations of the Heiligenstadt Testament; and we sense it is not fortuitous that the late style emerged more or less concurrently with the long emotional crisis whose boundaries are marked by the Immortal Beloved affair of 1812 and the conclusion of the struggle for guardianship of Beethoven's nephew in 1820. "My heart is contracted and the lights of my imagination are extinguished. I am in need of a crisis," Schiller once wrote. "Nature brings about a destruction in order to bring forth anew."[23] With Beethoven, the completion of each new musical problematic, that is, of each style period, is somehow connected to a shift in his psychic equilibrium, simultaneously engaging both the past and the future. Archaic materials re-emerge at every such critical point in his biography, with attendant malaise and anxiety resulting from a deepening access to repressed memories and feelings. But Beethoven emerges from each crisis having momentarily mastered both his anxieties and his new structural and expressive issues.

T HE interaction between crisis and creativity has implications for a revision of Beethoven's style periods. In this model, I suggest that Beethoven's works may be divided into four major periods of high productivity: the Bonn period, 1790–1792; the Haydn years, 1794–c. 1799; the middle period, 1803–1812; and the last period, 1820–1826. These periods are inaugurated by "transitional periods," when the prevailing style either reaches its outer limits of development or undergoes a process of disintegration or exhaustion, while a new style, which will predominate in the succeeding period, may begin to emerge. Most often, the transition period shows a pattern of diminished or blocked productivity. The transitional periods tend to coincide with the critical junctures of Beethoven's psychological development, whereas the full flowering of the new style tends to take place during periods of relative tranquillity in Beethoven's life.

The Bonn crisis includes all those tragic events that Schiedermair grouped under the heading "the family catastrophe," including the death of Beethoven's mother and sister in 1787, the decline of his father into a state of hopeless alcoholism, and Beethoven's assumption of a heavy burden of responsibility.[24] The crisis also includes the failure of Beethoven's 1787 trip to Vienna and his return to Bonn to resume the duties of a simple court musician. Beethoven probably abandoned his career as a composer between 1786 and late 1789.[25] His resumption of composition is perhaps signaled by his 1789 petition to the elector to dispense with the services of court tenor Johann van Beethoven and to pay his salary over to himself. Following this audacious petition, which signaled Beethoven's assumption of the breadwinner's role in the family, Beethoven resumed composition at a high level of productivity, which lasted from early 1790 until his departure for Vienna.

Beethoven perhaps underwent another crisis during 1793—a year in which, as Unger observed, not a single work of importance was created.[26] My guess is that the move to Vienna, the death of Beethoven's father, and his deep ambivalence toward Haydn brought about a diminution in productivity reminiscent of the post-1785 years. In this year he deceived Haydn by palming off Bonn compositions as newly written works, borrowed money from him on false pretenses, and engaged Schenk to do his counterpoint homework without his teacher's knowledge (certainly without his consent). The transition to the second period thus may be dated from late 1792 to early 1794, and the consolidation of Beethoven's new style properly begins with the Trios, op. 1, largely the product of 1794 and early 1795. These years are marked by apparent biographical contentment—by great outward accomplishment, public appreciation, and financial reward.

The features of the next crisis are recorded in the Heiligenstadt Testament of October 1802, with its thoughts of suicide and death, its revelation of the first, greatly exaggerated signs and progress of his deafness, and his consequent withdrawal from society. This period also includes the ill-fated flirtation with Giulietta Guicciardi and the departure of Beethoven's closest friend, Karl Amenda, from Vienna. In these transition years, which begin in approximately 1799 and end in late 1802, fall those works that mark Beethoven's greatest mastery of the high-Classic styles and media, and the clearest signs that he was in transition toward a wholly new line of development. As Thayer wrote, it was beginning in about 1800 that Beethoven "asserted his claims to a position with Mozart and the still living and productive Haydn," and from 1800, the year of his first public concert for his own benefit, can be dated Beethoven's major conflicts with Haydn, his attempts to break away from his influence in order to assert his own individuality.[27] Unlike the earlier and later crises, there was no interruption of productivity during this transition; rather, there was a remarkable acceleration in Beethoven's stylistic evolution, in which the new and the superseded styles thoroughly intermingled.

The consolidation of the middle period, with its "heroic" manner, took place during a decade of relative peace in Beethoven's life—a period rich in friendship, achievement, recognition, and the beginnings of international fame. True, signs of stress appear, particularly in relation to conflicts concerning women and his inability to carry through his marriage project.

The crisis that brought the heroic period to a close and laid the groundwork for the last style is the most complex of all. It has its origin in the aftermath of the Immortal Beloved affair, which was brought to an unsuccessful conclusion in the summer of 1812. Having completed the Eighth Symphony in October and the Sonata for Violin and Piano, op. 96 (a work which contains strong anticipations of the last period) in December, Beethoven lapsed into silence. His creativity had come to a full stop. His sense of impotence and of the failure of his manhood rise to the surface in the Tagebuch: "You must not be a human being," he wrote, "not for yourself but only for others." He went to Linz and violently interfered in his brother's love life. Evidence of mental confusion and emotional stress appears in his letters. Beethoven's Tagebuch of this period contains several references to suicide, and it is possible that Beethoven actually attempted suicide during 1812 or 1813.[28] His feelings of impotence and despair had brought him to, or even beyond, the edge of emotional breakdown. In the summer of 1813, he fell into a state of helplessness and personal disorder which reduced his musical productivity to nil.

The transition to the last style took place over an extended period of time. Beethoven's productivity was restored in late 1813 and through 1814 in connection with the Congress of Vienna: rather than moving forward to the late style, he regressed to a pastiche of the heroic style in occasional works for the assembled monarchs. The year 1814, however, does contain the revision of *Fidelio* as well as the significant transitional Sonata, op. 90. From 1815 through 1819 Beethoven's crisis was at its most intense, in connection with the final stages of his deafness, the death of his brother Caspar Carl, and particularly his irrational battle with his sister-in-law over the guardianship of her son. During these years, Beethoven slowly gropes his way, one painful masterpiece at a time, into the world of the last period. The consolidation of the late style at a high level of productivity took place only after the guardianship struggle had at last been concluded, early in 1820. The long crisis came to an end, unleashing Beethoven's creativity and bringing the last style to full fruition in the completion of the Sonatas, opp. 109–111, the *Missa solemnis*, the Diabelli Variations, the Ninth Symphony, and the late quartets.

KERMAN has advanced an alternative periodization scheme, consisting of four style periods each of which is further divided into two subperiods. The Bonn subperiods cover the years 1782–1785 and 1790–1791; those of early Vienna include the years 1793–1799 and 1800–1802; the middle period covers 1803–1812, with a subdivision at 1809; and the late period is subdivided into 1813–1818 and 1820–1826.[29] Worked out with great subtlety, Kerman's is a valuable framework for an overview of Beethoven's music. Moreover, the notions of purely stylistic "subperiods" and critical "transition periods" are not mutually exclusive. As Kerman subsequently noted, "Isn't the fact really that subperiods work best for Bonn and 1803–1809, while transition periods work best for early Vienna and especially for 1813–1819."[30] In a sense, all of Beethoven's work is transitional, in process, constantly pressing toward new metamorphoses. And his oeuvre is a single oeuvre, which we segment out of a penchant for classification, a need to clarify—and at our peril.

9

Beethoven's Creative Process:
A Two-Part Invention

As is to be expected, a great deal more is known about Beethoven's working procedures than about his creative process. His sketches and autographs chart, in immense detail, the extended and often tortuous path by which his musical ideas were formulated, along with their subsequent elaboration and development. What they cannot possibly hint at, of course, are the mental states that preceded and accompanied the compositional act. In particular, the sketches and autographs are mute on a crucial issue: whether they document the path by which the work is "created" or by which it is "discovered." Perhaps it is not altogether fair to pose the question in this way, for artistic activity doubtless involves both creation and restoration: the finished work of art is surely something different from the image it had presented to its creator at the initial moment of inspiration. In *A Defence of Poetry* Shelley took a pessimistic view of the matter: "The mind in creation is as a fading coal . . . When composition begins, inspiration is already on the decline, and the most glorious poetry that has ever been communicated to the world is probably a feeble shadow of the original conceptions of the poet."[1] Earlier, in a letter to Goethe of 27 March 1801, Schiller had recognized the same difficulty: "In experience the poet likewise begins only with the unconscious, indeed he may count himself lucky if, through the clearest consciousness of his procedures, he gets so far as to rediscover undimmed the totality of his first dark idea in the complete work."[2] Unlike Shelley, however, Schiller did not exclude the possibility that the finished work might be an improvement upon the idea of which it is in some way an imitation, for it has, in the process of composition, shed much of its purely personal character and become a social possession.

In the few documented instances where Beethoven rather obliquely referred to these issues, it seems probable that he felt his labors to represent stages in the rediscovery of an idea or image that had preceded any serious technical preoccupation with its realization. At least that is what may be implied by his reported comment to Neate, "I have always a picture in my mind, when I am composing, and work up to it," and by his remark to Treitschke, "For my custom when I am composing even instrumental music is always to keep the whole in view," and by his report to A. M. Schlesinger in 1821, "I merely jot down certain ideas as I used to do, and when I have completed the whole thing in my head everything is written down, but only once."[3] To be sure, these remarks may be interpreted in other ways. In regard to several of these quotations, Tyson suggested that when Beethoven attempted to describe his working methods, he may have had "a tendency to glide over the 'private' labours in the sketchbooks and to focus on the perfecting of the autographs."[4]

Unfortunately, the only detailed description of Beethoven's creative process by any of his contemporaries can no longer be relied upon. It was supplied by the Darmstadt kapellmeister, Louis Schlösser (1800–1886), who in the early 1820s studied in Vienna and, between March and May 1823, briefly made Beethoven's acquaintance. Beethoven took a liking to the young man and met him on several occasions in Vienna and Baden. Upon Schlösser's departure for Paris Beethoven gave him an introductory letter to Cherubini and entered in his farewell album a copy of a canon on Goethe's "Edel sei der Mensch," WoO 185. Schlösser's "Recollections of Ludwig van Beethoven" were first published in December 1880; five years later, in 1885, a considerably reworded and somewhat abridged version of the same material was published as "Personal Recollections of Beethoven," and this version has made its way into the major biographical source books of the Beethoven literature.[5] Both essays contain a statement that Schlösser claimed to have taken down verbatim from Beethoven:

> I carry my thoughts about with me for a long time, sometimes a very long time, before I set them down. At the same time my memory is so faithful to me that I am sure not to forget a theme which I have once conceived, even after years have passed. I make many changes, reject and reattempt until I am satisfied. Then the working-out in breadth, length, height and depth begins in my head, and since I am conscious of what I

want, the basic idea never leaves me. It rises, grows upward, and I hear and see the picture as a whole take shape and stand forth before me in my mind as though cast in a single piece, so that all that is left is the work of writing it down. This goes quickly, according as I have the time; for sometimes I have several compositions in labor at once, though I am sure never to confuse one with the other. You will ask me whence I take my ideas? That I cannot say with any degree of certainty: they come to me uninvited, directly or indirectly. I could almost grasp them in my hands, out in Nature's open, in the woods, during my promenades, in the silence of the night, at the earliest dawn. They are roused by moods which in the poet's case are transmuted into words, and in mine into tones, that sound, roar and storm until at last they take shape for me as notes.[6]

With characteristic caution, Thayer warned against accepting Schlösser's claim to have taken down Beethoven's words "verbatim," but he believed that the "sense" of the passage is right, however much one must allow for memory slips or the intrusion of an old man's imagination.[7] Thayer's successors did not heed his warning. The passage has been cited approvingly in many of the leading biographical and critical studies of Beethoven, including those of Riezler, who avowed that it "touched the deepest secret of [Beethoven's] creative work," and Ernest Newman, who believed that it proved "the Sketch Books represent not the first but a relatively advanced stage in the making of the music."[8]

The authenticity of the passage has not heretofore been questioned, perhaps because it contains several details that are consistent with reliable information on Beethoven's working methods. It is known that he often worked on compositions over a span of years, that he extensively revised his themes (not in his head, to be sure, but on paper), that he was often occupied with several compositions at a time, and that he was wont to sketch and even to compose in the open air. These "characteristic traits" of Beethoven were well known to the readers of Wegeler and Ries, Seyfried, Schindler, Breuning, Nohl, Nottebohm, and Thayer, whose writings had long been published when Schlösser took pen in hand toward the end of his life. But if, as I suspect, Schlösser relied on these publications for many of the persuasive details of his "Erinnerungen," it was to another famous document that he turned as prototype for his lofty and Romantic description of Beethoven's creativity. It, too, was represented to be a literal account of a great composer's creativity. It, too, is an invention, and has long been known to be one.

> Concerning my way of composing, and what method I follow in writing works of some extent: I can really say no more on this subject than the following; for I myself know no more about it, and cannot account for it. When I am, as it were, completely myself, entirely alone, and of good cheer—say, travelling in a carriage, or walking after a good meal, or during the night when I cannot sleep; it is on such occasions that my ideas flow best and most abundantly. *Whence* and *how* they come, I know not; nor can I force them. Those ideas that please me I retain in memory, and am accustomed, as I have been told, to hum them to myself.
>
> All this fires my soul, and provided I am not disturbed, my subject enlarges itself, and I expand it ever wider and ever clearer; and the whole, though it be long, stands almost complete and finished in my head, so that I can survey it in my mind, like a fine picture or a comely form at a glance . . . All this inventing, this producing, takes place in a pleasing lively dream . . .
>
> When I proceed to write down my ideas, I take out of the bag of my memory, if I may use that phrase, what has previously been collected into it in the way I have mentioned. For this reason the committing to paper is done quickly enough, for everything is, as I said before, already finished; and it rarely differs on paper from what it was in my imagination. At this occupation, I can therefore suffer myself to be disturbed; for whatever may be going on around me, I write, and even talk, but only of fowls and geese, or of Gretel or Bärbel, or some such matters.[9]

The passage was first published as part of "A Letter by Mozart to the Baron von . . ." in the Leipzig *Allgemeine musikalische Zeitung* for 23 August 1815, with a brief introduction and fifteen annotations by the editor, Johann Friedrich Rochlitz (1769–1842), who assured his readers that so "noteworthy and instructive" a document must be published "with diplomatic exactitude."[10] It rapidly became the best known of all Mozart letters. Each time it was reprinted, translated, and retranslated during the following decades, assurances were given as to its authenticity.[11] The editor of the first Viennese reprint, in the *Allgemeine Wiener Theaterzeitung* of 16 November

1824, was pleased "to vouch for the genuineness of the original letter," and Edward Holmes, who reprinted the letter in his 1845 *Life of Mozart* from the translation in the *Harmonicon,* claimed that "the original letter is in the possession of Mr. [Ignaz] Moscheles," a claim later denied by Moscheles.[12] Although Otto Jahn called its authenticity into question in 1858, many decades would pass before the letter was excluded from serious Mozart literature.[13] In the meantime it made its way into writings on philosophy, psychology, and aesthetics, where it is still often cited as an example of unconscious artistic creation. For William James it demonstrated that "great thinkers have vast premonitory glimpses of schemes of relation between terms, which hardly even as verbal images enter the mind, so rapid is the whole process."[14]

The letter survived for so long because, despite clear indications that it was spurious—the glaring factual errors, the use of Saxon rather than Austrian dialect expressions, the absence of an autograph—Jahn had been loath to forsake it entirely, as were Nohl, Schenker, and even, it seems, the most recent editors of Mozart's collected letters.[15] Jahn concluded that the letter as presently known "cannot be by Mozart," but he added, with excessive caution: "I do not assume that the whole letter is forged; probably at its basis was a Mozart letter which was reworked."[16]

Otto Erich Deutsch betrayed more than a tinge of grudging admiration when he noted that what Rochlitz wrote about Mozart's manner of composition "does him much credit."[17] And well it might, for Rochlitz was ideally qualified for his task. He had allegedly met Mozart in Leipzig in the spring of 1789 and written an extensive series of "Verbürgte Anekdoten" (Authentic anecdotes) about him for the first volumes of the *Allgemeine musikalische Zeitung,* of which he was editor-in-chief until 1818 and coeditor until 1835.[18] Moreover, he combined a talent as novelist and short-story writer (his works include, it must be said, several volumes of fairy tales) with a serious knowledge of philosophy and aesthetics. A Kantian in earlier years, he published two monographs on aesthetics in the late 1790s, and in 1815, simultaneous with his composition of the "Mozart" letter, he renewed his interest in the subject when he prepared a four-part anthology of quotations from contemporary and Classical philosophers on creativity and music.[19]

Rochlitz's description of Mozart's creative process struck so responsive a chord because it echoed one of the central notions of Romantic aesthetics, namely, that the artist creates his masterworks almost as a silkworm produces silk—automatically, intuitively, and without conscious effort. Of course, the philosophers understood that inspiration must be leavened by judgment and reason—that, as Novalis put it, creation involves a "double activity of creating and comprehending, united in one moment; a mutual perfecting of image and concept."[20] But the readers and followers of Novalis, Schelling, the Schlegels, and Goethe were little interested in the dialectics of the matter; they were enraptured by the image of the spontaneous artist in a state of innocence, entering into communion with a divine principle and transmuting his experience into perfect designs and rapturous sounds.

In his autobiography (1814), Goethe marveled at the process by which he had created *Werther:* "I had written this little work without previous deliberation: it was like an act of sleepwalking [*einem Nachtwandler ähnlich*]; and on revising it, I was myself struck with the connected form which it presented.[21] Here, Schiller's notion of unconscious creation and Schelling's Neo-Platonic idea of visionary intuition had found a striking and popular formulation. Soon Schubert's fecundity and genius were explained in terms that closely parallel Goethe's remark; Vogl wrote to Stadler: "I learnt from Schubert that there are two kinds of composition, one which, as in Schubert's case, comes into existence during a state of clairvoyance or somnambulism, without any conscious action on the part of the composer, but inevitably, by act of providence and inspiration."[22]

ROCHLITZ appropriated several of the details for his "Mozart" letter from F. X. Niemetschek's life of Mozart, published at Prague in 1798: "Mozart . . . could see the completed work clearly and vividly when it came to him . . . We rarely find anything corrected or altered in his concerto scores. This does not mean that he just wrote down anything that came into his head. In his mind the work was already complete before he sat down at his desk . . . That is why he found the writing itself so easy. While at work on it he would often joke and chatter."[23] Niemetschek's dramatic eyewitness report about Mozart's postmidnight composition of the Overture to *Don Giovanni* "within a few hours" was often cited by the composer's Romantic admirers. "But do you not believe," asked Hoffmann's Kreisler, "that this overture of overtures . . . was just as complete as the whole work, even before the master set about writing it down?"[24]

Outside the Mozart literature, the possible sources for Rochlitz's formulations are numerous. Wackenroder described Raphael's creativity as taking place "in a pleasant dream."[25] Friedrich Schlegel wrote that at the conclusion of a poem "the whole must stand clearly like a picture in one perception before the listener's or reader's eyes."[26] Ultimately such conceptions go back to the Classical writers, who debated the ways in which the imagination could contain "notiones anticipatae" which simultaneously precede experience and improve upon the deficiencies of nature. In his *Metaphysics*, Aristotle stated that "the form of a work of art is present in the soul of the artist long before being translated into matter."[27] The issue was taken up, refined, and reformulated by Cicero, Seneca, and Plotinus, and later in the Middle Ages it was transformed into the theological question: Does God have ideas or antecedent images of created things?[28]

Clearly, then, the forged letter to the elusive "Baron von . . ." is based on a long-standing trope about Creation and creativity. Perhaps that is why it is so remarkably similar to Porphyry's description of his master's working habits: "Plotinus . . . worked out his train of thought from beginning to end in his own mind, and then, when he wrote it down, since he had set it all in order in his mind, he wrote as continuously as if he was copying from a book. Even if he was talking to someone, engaged in continuous conversation, he kept to his train of thought. He could take his necessary part in the conversation to the full and at the same time keep his mind fixed without a break on what he was considering."[29]

Whatever the specific point of departure of Rochlitz's invention, his portrayal of Mozart creating in a dreamlike and effortless manner appealed strongly to nineteenth-century Romanticism. Apparently, Schlösser could not resist it when he set about composing his "Reminiscences of Beethoven." He rewrote Rochlitz's paragraph extensively, carefully avoiding direct plagiarism. He also thoroughly rearranged the order of the materials and, for the sake of verisimilitude, added several details. A comparison of the two passages demonstrates how he revised his imaginative predecessor's fable:

ROCHLITZ'S "MOZART"	SCHLÖSSER'S "BEETHOVEN"
Concerning my way of composing . . . I can really say . . . no	You will ask me whence I take my ideas? That I cannot say

more about it, and cannot account for it. When I am, as it were, completely myself, entirely alone, and of good cheer—say traveling in a carriage, or walking after a good meal, or during the night when I cannot sleep; it is on such occasions that my ideas flow best and most abundantly. *Whence* and *how* they come, I know not; nor can I force them.

with any degree of certainty: they come to me uninvited, directly or indirectly. I could almost grasp them in my hands, out in Nature's open, in the woods, during my promenades, in the silence of the night, at the earliest dawn.

The committing to paper is done quickly enough, for everything is . . . already finished.

All that is left is the work of writing it down. That goes quickly, according as I have the time . . .

My subject enlarges itself, and I expand it ever wider and ever clearer; and the whole, though it be long, stands almost complete and finished in my head, so that I can survey it in my mind like a fine picture or a comely form at a glance.

Then the working-out in breadth, length, height and depth begins in my head . . . It rises, grows upward, and I hear and see the picture as a whole take shape and stand forth before me in my mind as though cast in a single piece.[30]

On closer examination, Schlösser's Beethoven reminiscences turn out to be a patchwork stitched together from the published standard literature. No personal knowledge was needed to testify to Beethoven's reverence for his grandfather, his disdain for Italian opera, his admiration for Homer and Goethe, his habit of scribbling columns of figures on his window shutters, his ownership of a Broadwood piano, his difficulties in finding a good libretto, and his plan to compose Grillparzer's *Melusine*. Nor was Schlösser a close reader of his sources. For example, in 1823 he clearly observed on Beethoven's piano "the de luxe edition of Handel's works" which Stumpff would not ship from England until late 1826, and he heard Beethoven complain about reductions in his annuity payment years after his legal battles to restore its full value had been won. It is doubtful that Schlösser's memory was sufficiently accurate to recall, after sixty years, that Beethoven was dressed one day in a "blue frock coat with yellow buttons, impeccable white knee-breeches, a vest to match, and a new beaver hat." But Schlösser, having virtually identical published descriptions of Beethoven's clothing readily at hand, had no need to strain either his memory or his imagination.[31] One would like to believe that Schlösser met "his faithful friend" Schubert at the revival of *Fidelio* on 4 November 1822 and that they saw there Beethoven, Schindler, and Stephan von Breuning; but Schlösser is the only witness to this event, which is difficult to reconcile with Breuning's known estrangement from Beethoven at the time. Probably this anecdote should be rejected, just as Schubertians have long rejected Schlösser's fabricated reminiscences of that composer, published in 1883.[32] The residue of possibly authentic material in Schlösser is little enough; it is to be used, if at all, with extreme caution.

Evaluation of Rochlitz's extensive writings on Mozart and his famous letter to Leipzig concerning Beethoven is far more important. A keen observer and brilliant journalist, Rochlitz wrote fascinating descriptions of both composers, filled with apparently authentic details. In pursuance of his plan to write Mozart's biography, he obtained rich materials, including many letters, from Mozart's wife and sister and had opportunities to interview many of the composer's contemporaries and fellow musicians. Rochlitz is a source of many important stories: about the commissioning and composition of the Requiem and *Die Zauberflöte*; about Mozart's pinched finances and excessive, almost profligate generosity; and about his eccentricity and abstracted manner in later years, bordering, it is implied, on something close to mental breakdown.

Unfortunately, however, with Rochlitz one cannot always tell what is true and what is invented. He described a visit by Mozart to C. P. E. Bach in Hamburg in 1789; but Mozart never visited Hamburg, and Bach had died in the previous year. Rochlitz certainly made up the story that Mozart refused an offer to serve Friedrich Wilhelm II as kapellmeister out of loyalty to Emperor Joseph II. And Jahn discovered among Rochlitz's effects a manuscript containing a detailed account—but wholly invented as to "time, place, persons and events"—of the circumstances of Mozart's courtship and marriage, which Rochlitz claimed to have written down from Mozart's own narrative of the events to him.[33]

There is an extensive pattern of fabrication in Rochlitz's contributions to the Mozart literature that would lead a prudent observer to reject the whole. Nevertheless, many of his characterizations and reports remain inextricably woven into the fabric of Mozart biography.

Even Jahn, despite his dismay at finding that Rochlitz was contributing to the formation of an "unhistorical fantasy portrait" of Mozart, did not refrain from utilizing and accepting a good deal of his testimony. And it must surely give pause to the skeptic that crucial passages from Rochlitz's writings on Mozart, including his moving portrait of the composer's burning creativity and disturbed mental state in the months preceding his death, are reproduced in Nissen's biography of Mozart, issued under the supervision and apparently bearing the approval of Constanze Mozart.[34]

To evaluate Rochlitz's account of his three alleged meetings with Beethoven in 1822, it is necessary to take into consideration the fact that the relationship between the two men was scarcely free of complications. Rochlitz early entertained the hope that Beethoven would set one of his poems or librettos to music. In Beethoven's only letter to him, dated 4 January 1804, the composer seems not displeased to have an opportunity to reject a libretto by the editor of a journal, the *Allgemeine musikalische Zeitung*, whose reviews of his early works had rankled: "I could feel a little angry with you for having so many false reports about me inserted, but no—I realize that you are doing this purely out of ignorance of the conditions prevailing in this city."[35] In a letter to Breitkopf & Härtel of 9 October 1811 Beethoven ridicules Rochlitz for his criticism of a chorus in *Christus am Oelberge*: "Well, you may go on reviewing as long as you like; and I wish you much enjoyment. Even if the composer feels something like a gnat biting him, well the pain is soon gone."[36]

Beethoven's irritation over negative notices in the *Allgemeine musikalische Zeitung* never entirely passed, despite the many favorable reviews of his music published there over the years. As late as 24 August 1825, in a letter to Karl Holz, he refers to Rochlitz as "Mephistopheles" whom "Beelzebub, chief of the devils, will shortly seize . . . by the ears" (a conversation-book entry of that year shows that Rochlitz was more than once called "Mephistopheles" in Beethoven's circle).[37] Busy with the *Missa solemnis*, the Ninth Symphony, plans for the Sonatas, op. 110 and op. 111, and the Diabelli Variations, the composer surely was not pleased to read in an 1821 issue of the journal: "Beethoven occupies himself, as father Haydn once did, in the arranging of Scottish songs; for larger undertakings he seems to be completely written out."[38]

Rochlitz should not have been surprised if Beethoven failed to regard his arrival in Vienna in late May 1822 as an occasion for jubilation. Indeed, Rochlitz admitted that he approached the composer with great trepidation, through an unnamed intermediary, and that their first meeting was a fiasco, for Beethoven spoke not a word and was unable to hear anything that Rochlitz said. Subsequently, according to Rochlitz, Schubert took him to Beethoven's favorite tavern, where Beethoven allegedly spoke to him at great length about a variety of subjects, from the dearth of Viennese performances of his music to his literary tastes and future plans. Rochlitz described yet a third meeting, at Baden, which sealed their friendship. His account of these meetings is contained in a letter of 9 July 1822 from Baden, curiously addressed "to my home" and apparently written to his wife but containing several passages directed to G. C. Härtel, who died in 1827, prior to the letter's first publication.[39] No autograph of the letter has ever been produced.

Rochlitz's letter contains more than a few inconsistencies and errors. In it Beethoven is heard to complain of the Viennese neglect of his symphonies and *Fidelio* at a time when they were frequently performed; he appears to have forgotten that the violinist Schuppanzigh had been absent from Vienna for some years; and he tells Rochlitz that he wrote his *Egmont* music (1809–1810) following his meeting with Goethe in 1812. Thayer attributed such errors to Rochlitz's "propensity for embroidery and invention,"[40] and it is difficult to deny his strong inclination to fabulation, but they can be explained even more plausibly by the hypothesis that Rochlitz's second and third meetings never took place, or even that he never met Beethoven at all.

Certainly there is no documentary verification of any meeting between them. Rochlitz claimed that he was commissioned to transmit Breitkopf & Härtel's offer that Beethoven should compose incidental music for Goethe's *Faust,* but there is no hint of such a commission in the publisher's archives. Indeed, at the very time of Rochlitz's visit to Vienna, Härtel asked Georg August Griesinger to approach Beethoven about a renewal of his association with the Leipzig publisher: "Mr. Härtel has written to me from Leipzig [to ask] whether you could not find and set to music an opera book worthy of your art before you hang up your harp for good."[41] In late July Beethoven wrote to his brother about Breitkopf & Härtel's approach through Griesinger but made no mention of a similar, almost simultaneous offer through Rochlitz. In this letter, too, Beethoven first mentioned his plan to go to Baden in late summer, yet Rochlitz's July meeting was placed in Baden, at a time when Beethoven was spending his holiday elsewhere—in Döbling. Possibly Rochlitz chose Baden as the locale for his last encounter with Beethoven because J. R. Schultz in "A Day with Beethoven," published in 1824, described it as the village where Beethoven "usually resides during the summer months." [42] In fact, comparison of Rochlitz's letter with Schultz's report reveals a surprising number of other details in common, including a walk in the Helenenthal, high praise for Handel and Mozart, unrestrained discourse on politics, a favorable opinion of the British, and remarks about friendship with Goethe. [43]

Rochlitz retained his old desire to have Beethoven set one of his poems. On 10 September 1822, he wrote to Tobias Haslinger from Leipzig asking the young publisher to suggest that Beethoven should set Rochlitz's "Der erste Ton." He expressed his disappointment at Beethoven's refusal in another letter to Haslinger, of 28 December 1822. [44] In view of his claim of friendly relations with Beethoven in the summer of 1822, it is difficult to account for this approach through an intermediary and for the absence of any correspondence between him and Beethoven.

Even more difficult to reconcile with Rochlitz's description of his meetings with Beethoven and their discussion of Goethe and *Faust* is a lengthy letter to Goethe, dated 18 September 1822, which Rochlitz wrote shortly after his return to Leipzig. [45] Although the letter is almost wholly given over to Rochlitz's impressions of his Viennese visit, there is in it no mention of Beethoven or of Härtel's *Faust* commission. Another letter from Rochlitz, written to Friedrich Kind from Leipzig on 21 August 1822, contains a detailed description of musical events in Vienna during Rochlitz's sojourn, but again there is no reference to any meetings with Beethoven. [46] These letters appear to be clear evidence that Rochlitz's reminiscences of Beethoven are a tribute, not to the historian's craft, but to the art of the storyteller.

Perhaps it was only to be expected that one source would "confirm" Rochlitz's meetings with Beethoven. Anton Schindler wrote: "Friedrich Rochlitz saw Beethoven three times in the summer of 1822. I was present at two of these meetings." [47] Here Schindler, who became Beethoven's amanuensis only in late 1822 or early 1823, was attempting in his usual manner to "document" his asserted earlier contact with Beethoven. Unfortunately for Schindler, he assumed that Rochlitz was a reliable observer. Thus, following Rochlitz, he erroneously placed Beethoven (and himself) in Baden in June and July 1822, where—he claimed—he had the unique opportunity to observe Beethoven as he put the "finishing touches" to the *Missa solemnis*.[48]

To return to our point of departure: it was not to be expected that Beethoven would leave a verbal or prose key to the mysteries of his creative process. Indeed, on more than one occasion he seemed to express the feeling that his creativity was not wholly accessible to conscious understanding, let alone to verbal description. To Wegeler in November 1801 he wrote: "Every day brings me nearer to the goal which I feel but cannot describe."[49] Formulating the same idea somewhat differently in a letter to Wilhelm Gerhard of July 1817, he took note of the different realms of experience inhabited by poet and musician. He observed: "My sphere extends further into other regions and our empire cannot be so easily reached."[50] The investigation of that empire will have to rest on firmer evidence than Schlösser's variation on a theme by Rochlitz.

10

Beethoven and His Nephew: A Reappraisal

IMMEDIATELY following the death of Caspar Carl van Beethoven on 15 November 1815, Ludwig van Beethoven, in direct contravention of his brother's express wish, moved to assume the sole guardianship of his nephew, Karl, to the exclusion of the boy's mother. Naturally Johanna van Beethoven resisted Beethoven's claim, but his substantial influence in aristocratic and judicial circles ultimately prevailed, so that he was permitted to supervise his nephew's upbringing and education until the summer of 1826, when the long cycle of violence reached its crest, freeing Karl from his uncle's domination and leaving Beethoven with a crushing realization of failure, curiously leavened by a sense of great relief.

That there was a pathological and irrational component in Beethoven's love for his nephew and in his exaggerated charges against Johanna has long been recognized. True, certain biographers sought to minimize, explain away, or even justify Beethoven's behavior by heaping blame upon his sister-in-law, his brothers, and his nephew, and by purveying Beethoven's own view that he was merely a good uncle who strove to rescue an ungrateful child from an unfit mother. ("I have fought a battle for the purpose of wresting a poor, unhappy child from the clutches of his unworthy mother, and I have won the day—Te Deum laudamus.")[1] However, even the most apologetic of the early biographers had mixed feelings on the subject. Schindler, for example, though he concluded that Beethoven "was led to adopt this course by the most cogent reasons," admitted that Beethoven "may have been over-severe towards the mother";[2] and he furnished the interesting information that Beethoven's "reputation as a woman-hater grew, another effect of the same lawsuit, in which large numbers of the female general public had been vocal in their sympathy with the sister-in-law."[3] Nohl characterized Beethoven's affection for Karl as "a passion which tormented the boy to death,"[4] and incidentally confirmed that "during the later law proceedings, [Johanna] had the 'sympathy of the public' entirely on her side."[5] Thayer, whatever his view of Johanna's character and Beethoven's motivations may have been, disapproved of Beethoven's exclusion of the widow from the guardianship: "a child of that age needs a woman's care and tenderness."[6] In summary, he wrote: "Very questionable . . . if not utterly unpardonable, were the measures which Beethoven took to separate the boy from his mother in spite of the dying wishes of the father."[7]

With the publication in 1907–1911 of most of the essential documents in the final volumes of Thayer-Riemann and in the editions of Beethoven's letters by Kalischer-Frimmel, Prelinger, and Kastner, few could fail to sympathize with the plight of a mother from whom her son was torn by her eccentric and famous brother-in-law, with young Karl's efforts to achieve a reunion with his mother through flight or surreptitious visits, and with Johanna's valiant efforts to see her child at the Giannatasio Institute by disguising herself as a chimney sweep or to receive news of her boy by secret arrangement with Beethoven's own servants. Nor did the serious post-Thayer biographers overlook the negative implications. Ernest Newman characterized Beethoven's actions as "an obsession bordering on the insane" and dwelt on the matter at some length.[8] Bekker, though believing the boy unworthy of Beethoven's affection and the mother "frivolous and deceitful," called Beethoven "passionate, ruthless and determined . . . in attempting to separate mother and son," and he commented that, with age, "Beethoven showed signs of a deliberate, calculating, and cold egoism."[9] In a similar vein Sullivan described Beethoven's "idolatrous love for his nephew" as "blind, irrational, pitiful."[10] Riezler noted temperately that Beethoven was unsuited to bring up a child and that "in the end he failed, for he succeeded neither in permanently alienating his nephew from his mother, nor in instilling into him any idea of his own conception of life."[11] Rolland decried "the long, ugly and cruel judicial combat" in which Beethoven's humanity was diminished. He described Beethoven as "without consideration, without pity."[12]

Clearly, then, the main biographers did not approve of Beethoven's actions on either pragmatic or ethical grounds, nor was the eccentricity of his behavior lost upon them.[13] However, it was only with the publication in 1954 of Richard and Editha Sterba's *Beethoven and His Nephew: A Psychoanalytic Study of Their Relationship* that an attempt was made to explain the psychological genesis and the psychical consequences of this critical series of events and relationships in Beethoven's life.[14] To summarize the Sterbas' conclusions: the basic conflict in Beethoven's character arose from "the polarity between the male and female principle, which he vainly sought to reconcile in his behavior" (p. 305). This polarity was partially manifested in unconscious homosexual tendencies which had earlier found their outlet in his devotion to his brother Caspar Carl, whom he tried to control in the manner of a jealous and overprotective mother (pp. 21, 28, 32). With the death of Caspar Carl, Beethoven grasped the opportunity of appropriating his child "as a suitable substitute . . . as an object of maternal love" (p. 52). In order to accomplish this, it became necessary to supplant the boy's real mother, whom Beethoven persecuted as a rival and as the embodiment of feminine evil. He was therefore acting out a rescue fantasy, attempting to save a "close male relative . . . from woman's fatal claws" (p. 52); in the process his apparently innate aggressive and sadistic tendencies overwhelmed his ego, causing a "regression in his erotic development" (p. 208), disturbing his psychic equilibrium, "to such a degree that composition became almost impossible" (p. 117) for several years, and, ultimately, following Karl's suicide attempt, leading to his death (pp. 281, 294–295).

Whether one agreed with this psychological reconstruction or not, it would no longer be easy to hold the positions that the Sterbas had undermined, or merely to characterize Beethoven's actions without explaining them. As Forbes pointed out, the book arose in response to a need for a serious "re-examination of this phase in Beethoven's life."[15] To deplore his behavior while praising his motives, as Krehbiel had done, would no longer suffice.[16] To be sure, such eminent Beethoven scholars as Ludwig Misch, Willy Hess, and Paul Nettl rejected the book's thesis entirely, but they did so without attempting to formulate alternative explanations of the more arcane aspects of the guardianship battle.[17] An astute critic in the *Music Review*, although he felt that there was nothing in the book "that we all did not know" from the earlier literature, nevertheless found the book "gripping and disturbing" and was forced to retreat into undocumented references to "the very real case against Frau Beethoven," as though the missing evidence of her maternal unfitness would dispose of the matter.[18]

Other commentators were wholly enthusiastic. MacArdle called the Sterbas' thesis "potentially the most important contribution to our understanding of Beethoven that has appeared in the past forty years."[19] Mosco Carner maintained that it moved "into the sharpest possible focus the startling and, hitherto, mysterious discrepancies between the exalted ethos of [Beethoven's] greatest creative achievements and the crass defects of his private personality."[20] Cooper accepted significant elements of the Sterbas' interpretation, although he believed they had "greatly exaggerated and unnaturally isolated" the homosexual component in Beethoven's character.[21]

In the psychoanalytic literature, the book was received with praise tempered by the caution with which psychoanalysts habitually view pathographies of great men that operate "beyond the bounds of the basic rule," that is, the rigorous analysis of transference supported by the cooperation of the subject. Several specialists in applied psychoanalysis were more critical. Although Kohut considered the book an "outstanding contribution" to psychoanalytic biography,[22] he objected to the Sterbas "becoming Beethoven's accusers" and to their uneven crediting of sources: "The work of those biographers of Beethoven whose idealization contrasts most unfavorably with the authors' realistic outlook is presented at length in the text; Ernest Newman's outspoken objections to the hero worship of the biographers are, however, relegated to the appended notes."[23] Eissler criticized the Sterbas' failure to explore the probability that Beethoven's apparent irrationality might be "connected with, or perhaps is a prerequisite, or even a manifestation of the creative process."[24] He stressed the "infinite" love for the nephew expressed by Beethoven, "which despite all temporary tragedies resulted in the education of an able citizen."[25] Above all, he objected to the application of ordinary psychological parameters to the analysis of genius: "What appeared as dissociality, rudeness, brutality, in Beethoven's everyday life was the cornerstone of his creativity. A mastered emotion would never have led to those musical compositions which we admire."[26]

Eissler here touched on a basic flaw in *Beethoven and His Nephew*, perhaps *the* basic flaw in terms of an understanding of the psychology of genius, although Kohut's allusions to the Sterbas' hostile and biased attitude toward Beethoven are, I believe, equally significant.

But there is a great deal in the book which quite rightly impressed its original reviewers and which is of lasting value. Central to its importance is an excellent chronological narrative of the guardianship struggle, a thorough treatment of Beethoven's relationship to his brother Caspar Carl, and a detailed presentation of the main data concerning Beethoven and his nephew during the 1820s. The materials necessary for an understanding of these subjects were drawn together from Thayer, the letters, the published conversation books, and the reminiscences of contemporaries.[27] A sketch of Beethoven's biography prior to 1815 and a separate study of his conflicts with women are less successful; the latter, though it claims to exhaust "the biographical material which demonstrably refers to an erotic relationship with a woman" (p. 107), fails to mention Magdalena Willmann, Josephine Deym, Bettina Brentano, or any of the "crushes" of the Bonn period. The well-known references in the conversation books of later years to Countess Guicciardi, Therese Malfatti, Frau Peters, Frau Janitschek, and others are also omitted, which may explain the Sterbas' erroneous claim that in his final decade "we find no further signs in him of any erotic interest in a woman" (p. 111). Nevertheless, the Sterbas' perception of a defensive pattern in Beethoven's relationships with women—alternating between desire and aversion, and invariably terminating "in a withdrawal to a womanless solitude" (p. 101)—is convincing and has influenced, as Kerman pointed out, "most recent biographers in their treatment of this matter."[28]

The book also contains other interesting interpretations of the biographical data. Considerable light is cast upon Beethoven's relations with his brothers, which alternated between melodramatic quarrels and effusive familial affection. The full range of Beethoven's emotional responses to his nephew is shown, and the Sterbas observe that Beethoven's conscious love for him "was so ambivalent that the slightest occasion undermined its positive elements" (p. 207). The book contains a thorough description of Beethoven's possessive jealousy of Karl in 1824–1826 and of Karl's suicide attempt (pp. 232–234, 282). Beethoven's extreme fear of poverty, his "traits of petty economy, of exaggerated interest in figures and sums of money" (p. 120), are thrown into high relief. Nanette Streicher's importance as Beethoven's "motherly protectress and counsellor" (p. 112) is underscored, so that she emerges as a key figure in these critical years.[29] The Sterbas' defense of Johanna, though tending to transform her into a one-dimensional "good mother," is a valuable corrective to the misstatements about her in the literature.[30]

Furthermore, the Sterbas were the first to call attention to the subtle signs of Beethoven's ambivalence toward his mother. His difficulties with women are linked to "disillusionments in the first exemplary love-object" (p. 100). His identification with his mother is demonstrated by his fear of tuberculosis, the disease of which she had died (pp. 77–78, 183), as well as by his almost literal repetition of her cheerless attitudes toward marriage (p. 81). The authors theorize that it was the invalidism of Princess Lichnowsky and Countess Erdödy (they might have added, of Josephine Deym and Antonie Brentano) which "made it easier for him to re-experience his own mother in them" (pp. 107–108). As for the negative side of Beethoven's attitude to his mother, this is deduced from his expressions of hostility to Johanna, which the Sterbas believe to be a derivative of "his earliest relationship to his own mother," with Johanna representing a "substitute-figure for his own mother" (pp. 183–184). "Ludwig's attitude and conduct towards women, not least his bitter hatred of Johanna, show that his love of his mother . . . had a large admixture of hostility and negativism. The cause of this negative element remains obscure" (p. 81). Although this may be overstated and omits the father complex which lies, as Max Graf pointed out,[31] on the surface of Beethoven's biography, the Sterbas are to be credited for opening so suggestive a line of inquiry, one which illuminates a number of problems concerning Beethoven's attitudes toward women, especially the apparent tendencies toward misogyny of his last years.

For the specialist, then, there is much that is of interest in *Beethoven and His Nephew*. The problem arises when we approach the book not for its individual insights and interpretations but for its synoptic picture of Beethoven's personality. Here grave reservations must be entered, for the Sterbas fail conspicuously to present a balanced picture. On the most superficial level, this results from their failure to place Beethoven's relationship with his nephew in the full context of his later life. In their concentration upon one important series of biographical events they omit or minimize virtually all of the other major events of Beethoven's life between 1815 and his death: the composition, rehearsals, and performances of the *Missa solemnis*, the late sonatas and quartets, the Ninth Symphony; his pride at the receipt of honors and diplomas, including his election to the Swedish Academy; projected journeys; negotiations with publishers; and plans for a collected edition of his works. During these years, we know of Beethoven's meetings with Rossini, Moscheles, Liszt, Weber; the conversations with Czerny, Grillparzer, Kanne, and a host of others. As Arnold Schmitz wrote, "The conversation books of this period are rich in conversations about theology, pedagogy, philosophy, politics," and other subjects.[32] These are the years of a turn to the ecclesiastical modes, of the rediscovery of the polyphonic masters and a new appreciation of Handel and Bach. They are also the years during which Beethoven invented and consolidated one of the major stylistic advances in the history of music. In the Sterbas' presentation all of these manifestations of a secure and intact ego are dissolved. Beethoven's musical, social, political, and intellectual interests disappear, together with the numerous manifestations of his wit, tenderness, and warmth.

Nor have the Sterbas fairly represented Beethoven's relationships with his friends and contemporaries. It is surely a measure of Beethoven's character that those who knew him during this difficult period withheld neither their love nor their sympathy from him. Grillparzer, who was no sentimentalist, told of "the sad condition of the master during the latter years of his life, which prevented him from always distinguishing clearly between what had actually happened, and what had been merely imagined,"[33] but this recognition did not dim his compassion: "and yet," he wrote, "for all his odd ways, which . . . often bordered on being offensive, there was something so inexpressibly touching and noble in him that one could not but esteem him and feel drawn to him."[34] And Beethoven was loved not only by the somewhat sycophantic members of the conversation-book circle but by his brother Nikolaus Johann, sister-in-law Therese— the Sterbas feel "a certain astonishment" (p. 213) at a manifestation of her warmth for him—numerous visitors, fellow-musicians, patrons, and friends. Fanny Giannatasio never revealed her "secret love" but movingly recorded it in her diary.[35] Antonie Brentano wrote in 1819 of Beethoven's "soft heart, his glowing soul," adding that "he is natural, simple, and wise, with pure intentions."[36] He was cherished and humored by his close friends as a "wayward child," and his childlike qualities aroused loving, motherly feelings in Nanette Streicher.[37] That he could not be the sole object of his nephew's love is comprehensible to us, as it was not to Beethoven. At the Blöchlinger Institute, Beethoven was once overheard shouting at his nephew: "I am known all over Europe; don't you dare disgrace my name."[38] The pathos of the incident wars with its tragic overtones. Nevertheless, Karl, along with feelings of a negative kind, showed deep affection for his uncle on more than one occasion. And despite extreme provocation, it is nowhere recorded that Johanna van Beethoven ever spoke ill of her brother-in-law.

THAT Beethoven was a man of high eccentricity was not unknown to his contemporaries. The early biographical literature is filled with examples of his sudden rages, uncontrolled emotional states, suicidal tendencies, melancholic disposition, and frequent feelings of persecution.[39] Many of his contemporaries drew attention to the disorder of his surroundings, his constant changes of lodgings, his reclusiveness, and his occasional turn to physical violence toward friends, relatives, pupils, and servants. The belief that Beethoven was something more than eccentric gained wide currency during his first decades in Vienna, as may be gathered from references in the Fischhof Manuscript and from comments by William Gardiner, Magdalena Willmann, Max Ring, Ludwig Spohr, and J. F. Reichardt.[40] Dr. Aloys Weissenbach, a leading surgeon from Salzburg who met Beethoven during the Congress of Vienna, wrote of "the decay of his nervous system" in clinical terms: "His nervous system is irritable in the highest degree and even unhealthy. How it has often pained me to observe that in this organism the harmony of the mind was so easily put out of tune."[41]

It was, however, following the appropriation of his nephew that the reports of Beethoven's supposed insanity became common currency in Vienna. To be sure, Dr. Karl von Bursy, who visited Beethoven in 1816, made careful inquiry and found "no grounds for the assertion that he is sometimes insane."[42] But Bursy was surprised by Beethoven's garrulousness, his readiness to pour out his inner feelings to a stranger, and described this as "exactly the *signum diagnosticum* of hypochondria."[43] Later in that year Charlotte Brunsvik wrote in some dismay: "I learned yesterday that Beethoven is going crazy."[44] Zelter wrote to Goethe on 29 July 1819: "It is said that he is intolerably *maussade*. Some say he is a lunatic."[45] Grillparzer told Thayer that Beethoven was "half crazy."[46] A Viennese lady who met Beethoven during the 1820s told Felix Weingartner that many then viewed the composer as "crazy" or "foolish."[47] Beethoven's manner and appearance during later years did nothing to slow the spread of this belief. The story of his arrest in 1821 or 1822 by the Wiener Neustadt police, on the grounds that he had been peering into windows and looked like a tramp, surely was widely circulated.[48] On the street, his broad gestures, loud voice, and ringing laugh caused passersby to take him, according to Marie von Breuning, "for a madman."[49] Violent scenes with street urchins added fuel to the fire.[50]

And Beethoven was well aware of his reputation. He warned Dr. W. C. Müller in 1820 "not to be misled by the Viennese, who regard me as crazy," and added: "If a sincere, independent opinion escapes me, as it often does, they think me mad."[51] Schindler, though he claimed that Beethoven "took no notice" when he was assigned "a place, sometimes in one mad-house, sometimes in another,"[52] nevertheless reported Beethoven's concern over "the apprehension of his friends touching his mental condition."[53] In private correspondence, however, Beethoven did not hesitate to confess his own feeling that the stresses of the guardianship struggle had caused him to cross the boundaries of normality. In 1816, he wrote to the Archduke Rudolph: "Notwithstanding my healthy appearance, I have all this time been really ill and suffering from a nervous breakdown."[54] On 18 June 1818 he addressed Nanette Streicher: "Everything is in confusion. *Still it won't be necessary to take me to the madhouse.*"[55] Shortly thereafter, he wrote to her again: "May God grant that I shall be able again to dedicate myself entirely to my art. Formerly I used to be able to make all my other circumstances subservient to my art. I admit, however, that by so doing I became a bit crazy."[56] And on New Year's Day, 1819, he wrote to Rudolph that "a terrible event took place a short time ago in my family circumstances, and for a time I was absolutely driven out of my mind."[57]

The description of Beethoven in his last period as "a sublime madman" became a commonplace of conservative French music criticism after 1840, in writings of Paul Scudo, Henri-Louis Blanchard, and Édouard Garnier.[58] But with the publication in 1864 of Cesare Lombroso's sensational psychiatric study of genius and insanity, the assertion that Beethoven was insane passed from the Beethoven literature into the public domain, to be reinforced by Tolstoy's diatribe against the "abnormality" of late Beethoven and by Lange-Eichbaum's similar characterization of the composer as pathological.[59] Frimmel devoted several pages of his *Beethoven-Handbuch* to the subjects of Beethoven's alleged insanity and eccentricity.[60] And in 1927, Ernest Newman, whose voice was an influential one, wrote flatly that Beethoven's "conduct in the affair of his nephew is hardly consistent at all points with normal sanity."[61] The argument of the Sterbas (who make no reference to any of the foregoing data) is therefore in a long tradition which does not lack documentation or proponents. It is not a matter of dispute that Beethoven's life exhibited pathological tendencies. These are evident not only in the post-1815 period but in several other definite episodes of psychological and functional breakdown, including the period leading to the Heiligenstadt Testament of 1802 and the year 1813, following the Immortal Beloved crisis, when his creativity came to a full stop for a time and he was reduced to an abject, helpless state.[62]

Although the mechanisms of the matter are far from clear, research into the creative process has repeatedly demonstrated the close connection between apparent psychopathology and the highest creativity. Psychoanalysts variously view art as defense against instinctual danger, sublimation of inner conflict, symbolic transcendence, or reparation of loss. And they recognize that all of these factors may be simultaneously operative in the psychology of genius, for, as with all important issues, any absolutist explanation is bound to fall short. The foremost psychoanalytic student of the subject, K. R. Eissler, believes that "one of the prerequisites for the creation of great art is a tendency—even a strong tendency—towards psychosis . . . which is mastered or diverted by (automorphic) counter-mechanisms that transform this tendency towards psychosis into the molding of an artistic product. Or, in other words, we may say that if the genius were prevented by external forces from creating art he would become psychotic." It is "a grave error," however, to equate "psychopathic personality and genius," for in the former "life destructiveness prevails," whereas in the latter "we encounter the sublimest examples of constructiveness."[63] Kris similarly insisted that psychosis and creativity, though connected, are to be sharply differentiated: "Inspiration—. . . in which the ego controls the primary process and puts it into its service—need be contrasted with the opposite, the psychotic condition, in which the ego is overwhelmed by the primary process."[64] Glover put this view most trenchantly: "Whatever its original unconscious aim, the work of art represents a *forward* urge of the libido seeking to maintain its hold on the world of objects. Its instinctual compromises are not the result of a pathological breakdown of the repression system." We should therefore suspend judgment on the "correlation of psycho-pathological manifestations with the attributes of genius."[65] Further, as Eissler noted: "It is only during the fiery storm of a profound regression, in the course of which the personality undergoes both dissolution of structure and reorganization, that the genius becomes capable of wresting himself from the traditional pattern that he has been forced to integrate through the identifications necessitated and enforced by the oedipal constellation."[66] These comments may provide a clue to the tremendous surges in Beethoven's creativity which followed the crises of the Bonn "family catastrophe," Heiligenstadt, and the guardianship struggle—and which played some role in initiating the profound style changes of "late Bonn" (the Cantata on the Death of Emperor Joseph), the "heroic period," and the "last style."

The issue raised by the Sterbas is of a different order. Rather than seeking to establish the dynamic linkage between Beethoven's psychic structure and his creativity, they interpret his manifestations of irrationality and psychopathology after 1815 as "a psychological deterioration" such that "one can almost speak of a breakdown of the ethical structure of his personality" (pp. 209, 211). This characterization tends to create a disjunction between Beethoven's personality and the masterworks of his final period. The Sterbas, aware of this difficulty, insist that "there must be unity between man and work" (p. 305), but are content to resolve the antinomy by referring to the ego's capability for autonomous activity (Hartmann's "conflict-free sphere") in which sublimation can bring about a symbolic solution to an otherwise irreconcilable psychological conflict (pp. 307–308). While this interpretation is hypothetically possible, it is difficult to accept that Beethoven's late works could have been composed by a cruel and unethical human being.[67]

It seems to me that the facts of the guardianship struggle do not compel so painful a conclusion. Moreover, a close look at the Sterbas' characterization of Beethoven shows it to be so fundamentally flawed that it cannot serve as a reliable basis for interpretation. In a chapter entitled "Rebel and Tyrant," Beethoven is pictured as an anarchistic despot, whose "rebellion exhibits an unmistakable element of sadism" (p. 91). In a repeated phrase, the epitome of their characterization, they present Beethoven as a "Führer-personality":

> It is to the rebel's titanic resistance to all political and civil order, his disregard of all social norms and customs, and the fearlessness and lack of hesitation with which he sets himself

against authorities and obligations, that we must ascribe a great part of the fascination which Beethoven's personality exercised and still exercises upon many people.

Personalities like Baron von Zmeskall-Domanowecz and Prince Karl Lichnowsky were practically his slaves. Upon such natures he had the sinister effect which a certain type of Führer-personality produces . . . Toward themselves . . . they require absolute submission, and they obtain it because such submission appeases the unconscious feelings of guilt which accompany rebellion against legal or conventional authority in the average person (pp. 91–92).

This is followed by assertions that "there is no doubt that his circle feared him" (p. 92), by references to "his sinister influence over so many small personalities" (p. 93), and by a claim that "terror of him simply forced his intimates to agree with him. He tolerated no contradiction, and no admonition to reason" (p. 94). We are told that he was consumed by unmitigated "blind hatred" of his sister-in-law (p. 145), that he was imbued with a "baleful drive to destroy" (p. 276), that his nephew was subject to "the whole gruesome power" (p. 244) of his personality. This power extended beyond Beethoven's lifetime and has continued to exert its force: "Even Freud . . . could not escape the influence of Beethoven," whom Freud placed "on a plane with the powerful Führer-personality of Moses, with whom Beethoven has in common, among other things, lack of self-control, violence of wrath, rebellion against civil authority, and the inexorable insistence that others submit to him" (p. 95).

In the Epilogue to their study the Sterbas claim that they attempted "as far as possible, to avoid evaluations" (p. 303), such neutrality being, of course, a fundamental tenet of psychoanalytic method. They have, rather, chosen to pass judgment on Beethoven in highly charged terminology filled with the sense of moral outrage that Beethoven's actions and alleged personality traits arouse in them. The imputation of a sadistic component (pp. 91, 232, 269) to Beethoven's character is grievous, since the prime characteristic of sadistic aims "is a specific kind of pleasure; pleasure not at the discharge of aggression and at destruction only, but . . . at the infliction of pain, at the suffering or humiliation of others."[68] *Beethoven and His Nephew* is not an objective and sympathetic exploration of the psychological drives and conflicts of a great creative figure, but a tendentious attempt to shatter his (supposedly) hallowed and idealized image.

The Sterbas, who had begun with an "ideal image of Beethoven" (p. 11), found that previous biographers had clothed him "in a halo of glory" (p. 12). They determined to pierce the veil of hero worship. In fact, however, their portrait of Beethoven is the dialectical underside of the heroizing approach which they abjure: the description of him as a titanic and sinister rebel—a Lucifer or Moses figure—is manifestly a reversal and continuation of the mythologizing attitude. Essentially, it is a modern version of Richard Wagner's wish-fulfilling transformation of Beethoven into a Wagnerian hero: "The world was obliged to accept him as he was. He acted like a despot toward his aristocratic benefactors, and nothing was to be had from him, save what, and when, he pleased."[69] This finds its echo in the Sterbas' claim that Beethoven revolted against "every sort of authority" (p. 83); that he "openly expressed his opposition to all authority and to the governmental and social hierarchy" because "he was embittered by the higher position which his aristocratic friends held in the order of society . . . It is hardly credible how badly he treated his highly placed friends and patrons" (p. 86).

But this is a much oversimplified picture, which cannot account for the young Beethoven who proudly wore the gala uniform of the Bonn court, who wrote the Cantatas on the Death of the Emperor Joseph II and on the Elevation of the Emperor Leopold II, and who gratuitously identified himself in his correspondence as a servant of the elector of Cologne. It does not convey the Beethoven who dedicated the Septet to the Empress Maria Theresa and closed his public concert of 5 April 1803 with a set of variations on "Gott erhalte Franz den Kaiser [God preserve Emperor Franz]." The Sterbas' Beethoven could never have composed the Congress of Vienna works or dedicated the Ninth Symphony to Friedrich Wilhelm III or dubbed himself the minstrel Blondel to Archduke Rudolph's Richard Coeur-de-Lion.[70] Like many human beings, Beethoven was highly ambivalent toward authority and authority figures. The biographies record many intemperate outbursts by Beethoven against the Viennese, the imperial court, and his patrons. In general, however, Beethoven's personality embodied a clear tension between obedience and rebellion. Both elements coexisted within him in an unstable balance: seldom was an eruption of rage not followed by penitence and remorse.

A single example suffices to indicate the Sterbas' misreading of the evidence on this point. They write that his close association with the Archduke Rudolph, who was his pupil for about two decades, was "an intolerable constraint" and that he "rebelled against it almost as if it were a monstrous injustice" (p. 90). They further assert that he could not complete the *Missa solemnis* because "the fact that the Mass was dedicated to [Rudolph] called up all the inward resistance which was so characteristic of the great rebel" (p. 210). Rudolph, however, received more dedications from Beethoven than any other person, and in the very years during which the *Missa solemnis* was being composed (1819–1823) Beethoven dedicated several other major works to him, the Sonatas, op. 106 ("Hammerklavier") and op. 111, as well as a canon, "Alles Gute, alles Schöne," as an affectionate New Year's greeting on 1 January 1820. That the "delay" in completing this unprecedented and complexly structured composition could be attributed to alleged resistance to dedicating the Mass to Rudolph is an indication of the caution with which we must read the Sterbas' judgments of Beethoven's character.

The Sterbas give as examples of the "sinister effect" of Beethoven's "Führer personality" his relations with Zmeskall and Karl Lichnowsky. They were "practically his slaves," from whom he required "absolute submission." This, too, is wide of the mark. Lichnowsky was Beethoven's leading patron for more than a dozen years after his arrival in Vienna. He took the young virtuoso and composer into his home, treated him as a son, subsidized the publication of his opus 1, conferred a handsome annuity upon him, gave him expensive presents, introduced his works to the advanced segments of the nobility through performances in his home, and arranged for and accompanied him on a tour of foreign cities. As a generous but stern father-surrogate, Lichnowsky gained Beethoven's deepest affection and gratitude. But he was never submissive to Beethoven, let alone his "slave." If anything, he and his wife controlled and guided Beethoven to such a great extent up to the first revision of *Leonore/Fidelio* in late 1805 that Beethoven found it necessary to loosen the bond in order to avoid being totally engulfed. Lichnowsky interfered in Beethoven's love affair with Josephine Deym in 1805. The break came when Beethoven refused Lichnowsky's demand that he perform for a group of French officers at his Silesian country estate in 1806. Beethoven "grew angry and refused to do what he denounced as menial labour"; he immediately left Lichnowsky's estate, returned to Vienna, and dashed the bust of his patron to the floor.[71] His submission to Lichnowsky's will thereupon came to an end, although their relationship was later resumed and continued until Lichnowsky's death in 1813. In a word, the Sterbas have misrepresented the nature of the relationship.

As for Zmeskall, his friendship with Beethoven endured without interruption on a level of absolute equality from about 1793 until the composer's death. When Beethoven dedicated his F-minor Quartet, op. 95, to Zmeskall in 1816, he sent a warm letter: "Well, dear Z, you are now receiving my friendly dedication. I want it to be a precious memento of our friendship which has persisted here for so long; and I should like you to treat it as a proof of my esteem and not to regard it as the end of what is now a long drawn out thread (for you are one of the earliest friends I made in Vienna)."[72] Beethoven often asked Zmeskall for small favors, and Zmeskall apparently was a source of free quills from the Hungarian Chancellery for many years. Their fascinating and many-sided relationship shows no trace of the "sinister effect" that Beethoven supposedly exerted upon this beloved friend.

CENTRAL to the Sterbas' portrait of Beethoven as a sadistic and authoritarian personality is their inflexible description of his relationship to Johanna van Beethoven. They are somewhat at a loss to explain Beethoven's occasionally benevolent actions toward his sister-in-law, his passionate expressions of remorse and guilt, and his later efforts at atonement. They surmise that certain indications of mildness stemmed from his having "found a better object for his misogyny in Therese" (p. 230), his other sister-in-law, who "had drawn all his hatred of women upon herself" (p. 243). They assert that "it was [Johanna's] money which made him feel more kindly toward her" (p. 128). Such explanations do not get us very far, having only the virtue of consistency with the authors' monolithic view of Beethoven's character.

An alternative reading of Beethoven's relationship to Johanna has to take account of his profound underlying ambivalence toward her—a volatile mixture of fear and desire, aversion and guilt, hatred and love. Beethoven's entanglement with Johanna van Beethoven was not merely an incidental byproduct of his single-minded drive to fashion himself as the father of a Beethoven child. The entanglement with his sister-in-law was itself a primary object, a distorted expression of Beethoven's unresolved attitudes toward mothers and wives, and even a delusory way of fulfilling his thwarted longings to participate in family life. For by his seizure of Karl and his involvement with Johanna, Beethoven unwittingly created a "fantasy family," one that was held together by conflict for four or five years until it dissolved in exhaustion. Far from evidencing the unalloyed hatred—"blind," "burning," "bitter," "passionately hostile," "relentless"—of which the Sterbas wrote, the data leads into a tangled web of conflicting feelings, whose unraveling may permit a fuller and more generous understanding of Beethoven's actions during the guardianship struggle.[73]

THE IMMORTAL
BELOVED

11

Recherche de
Josephine Deym

THE identity of the woman Beethoven called "my immortal beloved" in his letter of 6–7 July 1812, but whose name he incon-
veniently neglected to provide, continues to attract interest. Antonie
Brentano, née von Birkenstock (1780–1869), was the likely recipient
of the letter, which was written from Teplitz, a Bohemian spa, to a
woman with whom he was intimately associated in Vienna and who
was then vacationing in neighboring Karlsbad, having arrived there
by way of Prague, where a meeting with Beethoven apparently took
place. Frau Brentano meets all of the conditions of chronology, prox-
imity, and topography required to identify the addressee of the letter, and inasmuch as no data speaking against her candidacy has
emerged since her name was put forward in 1972, the case in her
favor has advanced from plausibility to near certainty.[1] Nevertheless, there are those who continue to be committed to the candidacy
of Countess Josephine Deym-Stackelberg, née Brunsvik, with whom
Beethoven had been in love for several years beginning in 1804. It is
therefore worthwhile to take stock of the arguments for her as Beethoven's Immortal Beloved.[2]

Countess Deym's supporters, though they have scrutinized police
records, resort guest-registers, and contemporary newspaper listings
of prominent travelers, as well as the voluminous Brunsvik family
papers, have been unable to provide a single item of direct evidence
that she and Beethoven sustained any kind of relationship—personal, epistolary, or through intermediaries—after 1808 at the latest;
that she and Beethoven had any contact during the period of the Immortal Beloved letter; or that she was in Prague, Karlsbad, or elsewhere in the Bohemian spas during the first part of July 1812—all

these, of course, being essential to the identification of the woman to whom Beethoven addressed his letter.

One must bear in mind that, in the Hapsburg realms at that time, traveling almost inevitably left traces: passports were required for crossing borders; police registration was compulsory for persons arriving at the Teplitz and Karlsbad spas; newspapers reported the comings and goings of notable—especially aristocratic—visitors. Any travels between Vienna, Prague, and the Bohemian resorts by the prominent Countess Deym would very likely have been noted somewhere in contemporary letters, accounts, or diaries, especially those of the Brunsvik family itself. Consider the rich documentation of Antonie Brentano's movements between Vienna and Bohemia— and how those movements precisely intertwined and intersected with Beethoven's own—at that time. Consider, moreover, the materials documenting Josephine Deym-Stackelberg's family vacation a year earlier. On 10 August 1811 the arrival of "Countess Stackelberg, en route to Karlsbad" was announced in the *Prager Oberpostamts-Zeitung*; two days later her arrival at Karlsbad with one of her daughters was recorded on the compulsory registration list under her husband's name, with her husband's arrival announced for later; on 18 August her husband's arrival in Prague was published; on 24 August his name appeared on the Karlsbad registration lists; and finally, on 29 August he was recorded as traveling through Prague to Vienna.[3] Furthermore, Therese Brunsvik's contemporary letters and diaries independently confirm that her sister and her sister's daughter Victoria indeed went to Karlsbad in 1811 to take the cure and later were joined there by Baron von Stackelberg.[4]

By contrast, the arguments by her advocates concerning the "possibility" that Countess Deym was in Bohemia in early July 1812, where she could meet or plan to meet Beethoven, are necessarily attempts to prove a hypothesis by the assertion that no evidence exists to the contrary.[5] The very paucity of information about her whereabouts for several weeks in late June and early July 1812 becomes the mainstay of a series of pyramiding speculations. Responding to Kaznelson's melodramatic question, "Where was Josephine?" her proponents feel free to place her at any location suggested by their fancy. It is postulated that she, separated now from Baron von Stackelberg, had traveled incognito to Prague, where she could have stayed with her first husband's sister; in Prague, she engaged in a tryst with Beethoven and promised to meet him in Karlsbad, but she subsequently changed her mind and returned to Vienna. As a recent account has it: "One unplanned night of fulfillment and ecstasy. It must have been in Prague . . . Josephine, estranged for a month from her second husband, Baron von Stackelberg, after a disastrous two-year marriage and relieved of care of her children for a time by her sister Therese, was very likely staying in Prague with Victoria Golz, her first husband's sister and her own best friend."[6]

There are no facts in this scenario. Another approach, abjuring a total embrace of the fictional, takes the very unavailability of hard evidence as a spur to further pursuit: "The slightest piece of paper that would constitute proof that Josephine was in Prague on 2–3 July, or in Karlsbad around 7 July, would better serve our case. As long as that proof has not been supplied we believe that the inquiry must continue."[7] The certainty of success is assured by a circularity of method. "Inasmuch as the letter of 6–7 July could only have been written to Josephine," observed Tellenbach, "she must have been in Bohemia in the summer of 1812."[8]

However, unacknowledged by Countess Deym's advocates, substantial evidence does exist concerning Countess Deym's whereabouts and activities during the summer of 1812. On 14 June 1812, her husband wrote to his mother in Talinn, Estonia: "Your kind letter has made both of us indescribably happy . . . This summer we have undertaken to travel to Reval [Talinn], but I can't permanently return to my homeland for several more years, because I am involved in business here and have taken on responsibilities which I am, in honor, bound to fulfill . . . Little Theophile can already walk very well, and is even beginning to talk; all of her teeth have come in painlessly and until now, thank God, she hasn't been sick. My wife and . . . the children send a thousand greetings and we often speak about our joy at the prospect of seeing you this summer in Reval."[9] This letter is the first of three documents establishing that the Stackelbergs were living together as a family in Vienna during the period surrounding the Immortal Beloved letter. It describes their plans for a summer vacation in Estonia and dissolves all speculations about a planned journey by the Stackelbergs to the Bohemian spas. Although it touches on one of the main points of conflict between the couple, Stackelberg's desire to return to Estonia, it also suggests that the problems leading to the couple's eventual separation in 1813 had scarcely reached a critical point in mid-June 1812.

The second document is Franz Brunsvik's letter of 25 July 1812 to his sister, "Madame la Baronne de Sta[c]kelberg, née Comtesse Brunsvik a Vienne": "I received your letter in which the receipt of the first bond is confirmed; I hope that you have meanwhile also received the second one. I haven't heard a syllable from Stak[elberg]; hasn't he yet presented the letter? What good is it, that the money is already located in Russia, if we don't get it . . .?"[10] Franz goes on to describe plans for a commercial shipment of wine and advises that, if he does not "receive instructions to the contrary within a week," he will make the shipment. Goldschmidt, without real conviction, tries to leave open the possibility that this letter never reached Countess Deym; but Franz's references to an ongoing correspondence with the Stackelbergs about financial issues requiring immediate attention make it obvious that the couple was in Vienna—and Franz knew them to be there—during most, if not all, of July.[11]

The third document is a letter from a certain Hager to Josephine Deym, dated 13 August, confirming a social visit to the Countess and her husband: "Madame! Since Count Traun arrived last night, Madame la Comtesse, we must pay our calls today at 11 o'clock before dinner, and also hope to find Monsieur de Stackelberg there."[12]

Thus, there is every reason to agree with Brandenburg that the prospects for the candidacy of Josephine Deym as the Immortal Beloved have not improved: "On the contrary, it has become rather probable that Josephine was to be found in Vienna during the time in question at the beginning of July 1812 and not in Prague and in the north-Bohemian spas at that time."[13] The supposed separation of the Stackelbergs prior to the spring of 1813 is a fiction. And Stackelberg's proven presence in Vienna also indicates that the lurid speculation that Beethoven fathered Minona von Stackelberg, Josephine's last child, born on 9 April 1813, should at last be laid to rest.[14]

OTHER circumstances speak against Countess Deym's candidacy. Even before her first marriage, Beethoven made two joint dedications of minor works to her and her sister when they were his young students, but no separate dedications to her either then or thereafter; there are no presentation copies to her of his autographs or publications, either with or without a dedicatory message, no gifts to her or her children, no exchange of portraits, and not even an expression of condolence to any member of her family upon her premature death in 1821. In mid-1812, the two youngest of her six children were barely out of infancy, having been born in November 1810 and October 1811 respectively. Her deeply troubled marriage did not altogether disintegrate until April 1813, when the homesick and debt-ridden Stackelberg left her to "begin a new life" in the "service of the Lord."[15]

Furthermore, the initials of Countess Deym's name and the dates of her association with Beethoven do not conform with several other clues to the identity of the Immortal Beloved provided by the composer's diary, letters, and spoken remarks. Clearly, she could not have been either the "A" or the "T" of several cryptic entries in Beethoven's Tagebuch which may refer to the letter's recipient. The Tagebuch's "T"'s are therefore interpreted by Countess Deym's supporters as references to Therese Brunsvik, the alleged intermediary for suspected meetings between Beethoven and her sister. And her advocates read the "A" of Beethoven's diary entry in a variety of ways favorable to her. "This initial, which the copyist hesitated to read as an 'A' could in reality have been a 'J' (Josephine), 'P' (Pepi), 'B' (Brunsvik), 'D' (Deym), 'S' (Stackelberg) or even the beginning of a pet-name," wrote Kaznelson; and in Goldschmidt's opinion: "If the letter is not an 'A' it can only be an incorrectly read 'J,' as letters in Beethoven's hand from the Leonore years confirm 24 times."[16]

This strategy is now outmoded, because the recent publication of the only copy of the Tagebuch made from the original—copied by Anton Gräffer shortly after Beethoven's death—shows an unmistakable "A."[17] But Tellenbach, not quite grasping that Fischhof's manuscript of Beethoven's Tagebuch is directly copied from Gräffer's and has no separate authority, wrote: "The recently rediscovered Anton Gräffer copy has an 'A.' But Fischhof's 'A' is not certain. The hypothesis that Beethoven's original contained 'J' is possible after all, considering all the known relationships."[18]

More centrally, inasmuch as Beethoven had known Countess Deym since the late 1790s, she could not have been the beloved woman of whom he spoke in 1816, whose acquaintance he said he had made "five years ago" and whom he still loved "as on the first day."[19] The "five years" reference appears definitely to exclude Countess Deym from being the Immortal Beloved, and this difficulty has of course not been overlooked by her proponents. To keep her candidacy alive, they now must either claim Beethoven's remark to be apocryphal or propose that there was a "second beloved" to complement the Countess; this is a bitter irony for those who wish to regard her as Beethoven's "only beloved" (*einzige Geliebte*), as he had referred to her in earlier years.[20] Combining the "five years" reference with the Tagebuch's "with 'A' everything goes to ruin," several Deym advocates have recently proposed Amalie Sebald—who clearly could not have been the Immortal Beloved—as the second beloved, thus displacing Rahel Levin from the role in which Kaznelson cast her.[21] The improbability that Beethoven conducted two simultaneous love affairs in 1812 is glossed over. Why Beethoven, in 1816, should have recalled so feelingly a love affair with a "second beloved" rather than with the Immortal Beloved is not clarified.

Beethoven's association with Therese Brunsvik and Franz Brunsvik continued into the second decade of the century, but research has failed to disclose a single unambiguous item of evidence directly linking Beethoven to their sibling Josephine Deym after 1807 or 1808, let alone demonstrating an intimate connection with her. Goldschmidt's discovery of Therese Brunsvik's remark, in an undated letter of 1814 or later, "with Beth: it is nothing to do" later turned out to have nothing to do with Beethoven but with another person altogether.[22] Similarly, there is no reason to accept Tellenbach's identification of Beethoven as the addressee of a letter sketched in Josephine Deym's diary on 8 April of an unspecified year, for the letter contains nothing that might connect it to the composer.[23] In summary, the material evidence for Josephine Deym as Beethoven's Immortal Beloved does not exist, and the circumstantial evidence speaking against her is considerable.[24]

Even the authentic correspondence of 1804–1807 between Beethoven and Countess Deym does not show a grand passion on her part during the years of their closest association. Indeed, the correspondence suggests a friendship which, on her side, cooled inversely as Beethoven became more amorous. With the arrival of serious suitors for her hand, this friendship ultimately became an impediment to her romantic and matrimonial plans—an impediment that she removed by refusing to see him. The relevant passages from Beethoven's side of the correspondence are painful:

> I called on you *twice*—but I was not so fortunate—as to see you—That hurt me deeply—and I assumed that your *feelings* had *perhaps* undergone some change . . . I could almost deliver this letter myself—if I did not suspect—that I might for the third time fail to see you. (20 September 1807)

How sorry I am not to be able to see you—But it is better for your peace of mind and mine not to see you—You have not offended me. (Autumn 1807)

Since I must almost fear that you no longer *allow yourself to be found* by me—and since I do not care to put up with the rebuffs of your servant any longer—well, then, I cannot come to you any more . . . Is it really *a fact*—that you do not want to see me any more—if so—do be *frank*. (Autumn 1807)

I thank you for wishing still to appear as if I were not altogether banished from your memory . . . You want me to tell you how I am. A more difficult question could not be put to me—and I prefer to leave it unanswered, rather than—to answer it *too truthfully*. (Autumn 1807)[25]

With these words, Beethoven's correspondence with the reluctant Countess came to a conclusion in late 1807 or perhaps sometime in 1808. There simply is no reason to believe that she later changed her mind about him, or even that he wanted to renew the friendship. In fact, Beethoven usually did not continue to associate with the women who had rejected him. Magdalena Willmann, Giulietta Guicciardi, and Therese Malfatti are examples of women who, after being loved or courted by Beethoven and failing to respond to his attentions, essentially disappeared from his life. Beethoven, unlike Josephine Deym's advocates, learned to take no for an answer.

Thus, although Therese Brunsvik, upon first reading the Immortal Beloved letter after its publication by Schindler in 1840, asserted that the letter "must be to Josephine, whom he loved passionately," she made no mention of a reciprocal passion on her sister's part.[26] And inasmuch as Countess Therese accepted Schindler's false assertion that the letter was dated 1803, her comments clearly refer to an earlier period, around the time of her first husband's death in 1804, rather than to 1812. Confirming this fact is her diary entry of 4 February 1846: "Why didn't my sister J take [Beethoven] as her husband *when she was the widow Deym?*" "Together," she later mused of Beethoven and her sister, "both of them might have been happy," adding, parenthetically, a faltering "Perhaps."[27]

"He lacked a woman," Therese Brunsvik continued accurately, if bluntly, "that is certain, just because he did not know how to act."[28] Beethoven did not treat Josephine well, even during the time of their close friendship. His unconcealed suspicions caused her abundant anguish. "How could you wound me?" she wrote, "Your heart does not protest, when you accuse me of certain things"; "You treat me quite wrongly"; "Often you do not know what you are doing—how deeply I feel"; "I cannot express how deeply wounding it is to be equated with low creatures."[29] On a more superficial level, Beethoven neglected her when it suited him: "Surely no proof is necessary—of how gladly I would have gone to you today—but—only an overwhelming amount of work has prevented me."[30] And the adored Countess Deym may not have managed to see only the humorous side of Beethoven's habit of taking back his love offerings to her:

> I am sending you herewith for the present six bottles of eau de cologne which belong to me—You can return them to me when you have received yours . . . (Spring 1805)
>
> Here are *your—your*—Andante—and the sonata . . . (Spring 1805)
>
> Please send me the Andante and the two songs—I promise you that you will have all three compositions back the day after tomorrow.—I would not take the last two from you, were it not really a fact that I must send some songs to the *widowed Empress of Russia* . . . (Spring 1805)
>
> Now *I need the sonata in A as well* . . . (1805)
>
> Please send me back the book in which I enclosed my lines to you—I was asked for it today. (Autumn 1807)[31]

IN closing, a curious issue: Countess Deym's advocates read fanciful allusions to their heroine into a vast number of Beethoven's compositions—as though music were a composer's private cipher rather than an aesthetic structure. They seek—and invariably find— "secret" dedications to Josephine Deym of numerous Beethoven works over the last quarter-century of his life, and everywhere they discover encrypted references to her in the music itself. Thus, the Massins—who began this trend—attributed "silent" dedications not only of "An die Hoffnung" (first version) and the *Andante favori*, both of which Beethoven loaned to Countess Deym, but also of *Leonore/Fidelio*, the Fantasia, op. 77, and the Sonatas, op. 54, 57, 78, 96, and 109. The Bagatelles, op. 126, are seen as Beethoven's "Tombeau de Josephine," after which his piano "remained forever mute."[32] Goldschmidt accepted many of these suggestions, added numerous others, and concluded that the C-minor Sonata, op. 111, is not only Beethoven's "farewell to the piano sonata" but also a "re-

a. *Sonata, op. 111, Movt. I, mm. 117–119.* b. *Andante in F major, WoO 57, mm. 1–3.*

quiem for Josephine." Goldschmidt offered an irresistible solution to his own riddle of why Beethoven would have wanted to dedicate to Antonie Brentano a requiem for Countess Deym: "The transcendence of this discrepancy is only possible at a plane upon which the images of both women flow together into one."[33] He also discovered long-concealed textual references to Josephine throughout the late sonatas, as well as in earlier works (figs. a, b).[34]

Tellenbach's list of works "dedicated" to or inspired by Josephine also includes such works as the Cello Sonata, op. 69, the String Quartet, op. 95 ("the year 1810 stood under the impact of Josephine's second marriage ceremony"), the Eighth Symphony (themes in the Allegretto scherzando and finale show "a certain affinity" with melodies from Countess Deym's native Hungary), the Ninth Symphony, the last sonatas, and the *Missa solemnis,* which "came into being against the background of his relationship to Josephine, her sufferings and death."[35] By elaborating the assumption that all music is concealed autobiography, Josephine Deym advocacy comes close to the most extreme speculations on the identity of the "onlie begetter" of Shakespeare's sonnets; and those who resort to deciphering secret codes and hidden texts in Beethoven's instrumental music bid fair to become the new Baconians and Oxfordians. The pursuit of Josephine Deym threatens to convert the works of Beethoven into a new "great cryptogram," whose mysteries may be plumbed only by the initiate.

12

Antonie Brentano and
Beethoven

JOHANN Melchior Edler von Birkenstock (1738–1809) was the father of Antonie Brentano.[1] He was born in Heiligenstadt, Austria. After completing his studies at the universities of Erfurt and Göttingen, he entered the diplomatic corps, serving in various cities, including Paris, where he was attached to the imperial embassy in 1767. He was a protégé of both Prince von Kaunitz and the Empress Maria Theresa, and subsequently he became the devoted court secretary of Emperor Joseph II, whom he accompanied to Frankfurt in 1780, on the occasion of the emperor's coronation. Ultimately, as director of the ministry of education, he was permanently stationed in Vienna. His strong identification with Josephinian reforms and ideals may have led to his partial retirement from court service upon the inauguration of Emperor Franz in 1794; he was permanently retired in 1803. An art collector of world rank, he held numerous master drawings and paintings, among them important works by Dürer, Holbein, Van Dyck, Cranach, Rogier van der Weyden, Rembrandt, and Raphael. The atmosphere of the Birkenstock mansion at 98 Erdbeergasse in the Landstrasse was evoked by Bettina Brentano in a letter to Goethe: "Here I live in the house of the deceased Birkenstock, surrounded by two thousand copperplate engravings, as many hand-drawings, as many hundred antique urns and Etruscan lamps, marble vases, antique fragments of hands and feet, paintings, Chinese garments, coins, geological collections, sea insects, telescopes and countless maps, plans of ancient buried empires and cities, skilfully carved walking-sticks, precious documents, and finally, the sword of the Emperor Carolus."[2]

Birkenstock also wrote several books in Latin, one of which was later rendered into German; his last book was posthumously published by his daughter in 1813. He was a well-dressed, grave-looking man with prominent features, who walked with a measured, stately gait.[3] In later years his daughter advised two prospective visitors: "Pay attention solely to him, not to his surroundings, because he knows nothing of modern elegance and is solely preoccupied with antiquities. You will enjoy his company. He knows an immense amount and can be very charming."[4]

Birkenstock married Carolina Josefa von Hay (1755 or 1756–1788) on 1 March 1778. They had two children: Hugo Konrad Gottfried, born 15 December 1778, and Johanna Antonie Josefa, born 28 May 1780. Carolina von Birkenstock died in May 1788 during an influenza epidemic. In an undated diary entry, the young Antonie Brentano summarized the key events of her life, all of which, she thought, were somehow bound up with the number "8": "My father was born in 1738; in 1778 he got married; in 1780 I was born; on 28 May 1788 my mother died and I came to the Cloister."[5] Her loneliness at the Ursuline Cloister in Pressburg, where she boarded for seven years, and her deep attachment to her father during these trying years are recorded in her prayer-book entries as well as in her letters from the cloister: "Farewell, dear, dear, dearest Papa, please write to me soon. It is my happiness and my consolation."[6] Her father, in turn, wrote his daughter loving verses, assuring her of his devotion: "Come, come to your father's arms, after so long a parting, sweet child!"[7]

Antonie Brentano returned to Vienna in 1795 and lived at home during the next three years, assisting her father and taking an active interest in his pursuits. An undated diary entry of around 1798 expresses both her deep contentment and her resistance to any change in her condition: "Remain in your homeland. Remain even in your hometown. If possible, remain in your father's house. Blessed is the house where the industriousness and the virtues of the parents never depart. Who lives by the good name of the father is like a new fruit of the same tree. Happy is the daughter who does not live far from her mother, who in the evening can secretly return to her, to the old hearth in which the flame burns as if it had never been extinguished."[8] However, her father had other plans for her. When she was not yet eighteen, four suitors for her hand came forward. She apparently was in love with one of them but did not reveal this to her father, who shortly thereafter arranged her marriage to Franz Brentano, a sympathetic and wealthy Frankfurt merchant fifteen years her senior. Brentano's wealth may have been a factor in the selection of a nonaristocratic merchant as Antonie's husband, for contemporaries commented on Birkenstock's parsimonious tendencies.

Franz Brentano (1765–1844) was the second of six children of Peter Anton Brentano (1735–1797) and his first wife, Paula Maria (1746–1770). At an early age he entered his father's mercantile business in Frankfurt-am-Main as a salesman, and in 1792 he established a division of the firm specializing in the sale of spices and dyes and the fulfillment of drafts and commissions. Upon his father's death in 1797, Franz Brentano merged the family businesses and, together with his half-brother Georg, ran a prosperous banking, import, and trading firm until its dissolution on 31 December 1840. Twelve children survived from his father's three marriages, and as the eldest son, Franz became their guardian, a position that he fulfilled with his characteristic sober responsibility. Several of the children, including Bettina Brentano (1785–1859) and Clemens Brentano (1778–1842), were to figure significantly in the history of German Romanticism; another child, Kunigunde ("Gunda," 1780–1863), married Karl von Savigny (1779–1861), the celebrated historian of jurisprudence; and Bettina, who enchanted Goethe for a time, later married the author Achim von Arnim (1781–1831). Franz was universally respected and beloved by friends and family alike. Bettina called him "my dearest brother," and Clemens wrote of him in 1804, "I even owe to him the feeling—of having a father—which, without him, would have remained unknown to me."[9]

It was not until just before his father's death that Franz Brentano began seriously to entertain the prospect of marriage. Toward the end of 1796 he visited Vienna, where he made the acquaintance of Antonie von Birkenstock. In the following summer his sister Sophia and his stepmother Friederike Brentano, née von Rottenhoff, went to Vienna expressly to appraise Antonie's suitability to be Franz's bride. Her suitability established, they faced a more difficult task: to persuade the seventeen-year-old Antonie to accept him. The protracted negotiations with Herr von Birkenstock are documented in more than twenty letters written by Franz between the summer of 1797 and the spring of 1798. The letters show Brentano fearful about the long delay in reaching agreement with Birkenstock, who postponed his final decision because of the French occupation of the Rhineland and the uncertainties created by the war. From the beginning he had said that he would not send his daughter into a war zone. However, Franz suspected that there were other motives, such as questions about the family fortunes, as he wrote on 16 December 1797 to Friederike von Rottenhoff, or even the possibility that Antonie was in love with another, as he suggested on 4 October 1797. "I open the mail with a beating heart and if there is no letter fear enters my soul and I feel depressed," he wrote to Frau von Rottenhoff on 11 March 1798. "I cannot suppress the fear that once you and Sophie are no longer there he might come to my Toni with other ideas and make her unhappy." [10]

A NTONIE Brentano's recollections of her early life, marriage, and first years in Frankfurt-am-Main were related by her to the Frankfurt artist Karl Theodor Reiffenstein (1820–1893) during two interviews, on 4 May 1865 and 25 January 1866. [11] "One day," she recalled, "I was told that I was engaged to Brentano." "I didn't know other than that my father would do what was right for his daughter's future well-being," she said, "but to this day I still don't know how I bore everything that I had to go through, and I would not have been able to bear it had I not been so young and inexperienced." They were married on 23 July 1798 at St. Stephen's Cathedral and immediately left for Frankfurt. She related that she knew "from rather certain sources" that her "true love" remained standing behind a church pillar at St. Stephen's, weeping "bitter tears" at their separation. And she remembered that Franz "was still so alien to her that it was only after months that she grew accustomed to the Thou (*Du*) with him."

Young Antonie, as the wife of the eldest brother, was placed in full charge of the large Brentano house in the Grosse Sandgasse in Frankfurt. "I went up the stairs into my new home with a fearfully beating heart and fearful feelings. Everything was absolutely strange to me." Franz's eldest sister Pauline, who had headed the household until then, turned the account books and the keys over to Franz's young wife. It was a great burden, involving not only the heavy and unaccustomed household duties but also the task of keeping the Brentano "geniuses" under control. She wept "endless hot tears" in solitude: "I did not want to let my husband know how hard it was for me, because he was always so loving and friendly toward me." She recalled the birth, in 1799, of her first child, Mathilde: "I forgot all my pain, and I was delighted with my new happiness." But Mathilde died suddenly early in 1800, throwing Antonie into despair.

Apart from her periodic visits to Vienna, vacations at fashionable resorts, and summers at the Brentano family residence, "Winkel," on the Rhine, Antonie Brentano remained in Frankfurt until the autumn of 1809. By 1806 she had given birth to four more children, all of whom survived infancy.[12] Because of her rare beauty and strength of personality, she soon became a force within the Brentano family, strongly affecting Clemens, Christian, Sophia, Kunigunde, Bettina, and the others and arousing strong feelings, both loving and hostile, often within the same individual. Antonie's role as head of the household and substitute mother inevitably engendered mixed feelings toward her by the Brentano siblings. Bettina resisted her authority; Gunda, who married Savigny in 1804, for a time may have regarded her as a rival for his affections; Clemens incorporated her into his 1801 novel, *Godwi*, as a "slender, gentle, pale beauty" and entered into a tender correspondence with her between 1800 and c.1804.[13] He wrote about her to his sister Gunda in mid-January 1803: "Just this minute I received one of the most beautiful letters which I have ever been sent in my life; and you may tell Toni that it is hers, that I sincerely thank her and will soon answer her, and that I love her very much."[14] However, only a few weeks later he wrote to Savigny, in an access of rage: "I could strangle these vermin. Toni is a scoundrel and Gundel a carrion."[15] And in 1805 he wrote to his wife, Sophie Mereau, that "Toni's character is ever more developing into that of a cold and slanderous wife."[16]

Of course, such rapid and extreme reversals of attitude may tell us more about Clemens Brentano than about his sister-in-law. But her temperament was scarcely more placid than his own. Moreover, from the first she felt that the Brentano family's consideration for her was solely because she was Franz's wife: "Everybody hugged the returning brother—who was venerated by everyone—in joyful commotion, and I stood there alone, abandoned in the midst of the room and was regarded with curiosity." A letter to Sophia Brentano of 8 September 1799 is tinged with bitterness: "Tell everybody around you 'all the best from Franz's wife.' Only under this heading might they accept my greetings and friendship."[17] She was painfully aware of negative perceptions of her character. "My coldness is only an appearance, dear Savigny," she wrote in a letter of 1803. "This coldness has developed through the circumstances in which I found myself in the first years of my marriage, when I was seen as an exotic plant."[18]

From the first days in Frankfurt, the signs of an eventual crisis were present in her letters. "We have to move heaven, hell, and the sun, otherwise we cannot enjoy life," she wrote to Sophia in 1799.[19] And in a letter to Gunda of 3 September 1803 she expressed her inability to conform to traditional feminine stereotypes—"God grant that I will find joy in housewifely everyday life"—but recognized the dangers of "wanting to live as one would love to live," of departing "from the beaten track."[20] Naturally, however much she was wont to complain about the monotony of her existence, moments of happiness and fulfillment contended with days of melancholy and even despair.[21] She pursued self-education: already fluent in several languages, she studied English and Italian, read the Classics as well as the German and English Romantics, received some vocal training, and was a fairly accomplished amateur pianist and guitarist.

She managed to present a controlled exterior to visitors during the early years. A touring Englishman described her in 1801 simply as "Madame Brentano, a beautiful Viennese," who graciously took time from her family obligations to initiate him into German poetry.[22] Achim von Arnim was able to write in 1805 that "Toni Brentano is, as always, the well-bred hostess."[23] However, as early as 1802 Clemens Brentano commented that "Toni is like a glass of water which has been left standing for a long while."[24] And Bettina expressed concern in a letter of June 1807 to Savigny, which gives the impression that Antonie was going through a period of withdrawal and depersonalization: "Toni is in a bizarre correspondence with me; she has rouged and painted herself like a stage set, as though impersonating a haughty ruin overlooking the Rhine toward which a variety of romantic scenes advance while she remains wholly sunk in loneliness and abstraction."[25]

Frau Brentano's malaise soon manifested itself in physical symptoms. In 1806 she wrote to Clemens: "I have a lot of headaches, and my damned irritability doesn't leave me."[26] An undated letter to Savigny refers to a nervous condition that prevents her from traveling.[27] In mid-1808 she wrote to the Savignys: "the pains in my chest increased to such a degree that it almost cut my breath off. No position in bed was tolerable, until this terrible seizure dissolves in compulsive crying." Ominously, she continued, "A deathly silence

(*Todesstille*) reigns within my soul."[28] Two days later Bettina wrote to Arnim that "Toni is sickly and desolate, without any female society whatsoever; this will perhaps keep me here for a long time."[29]

Antonie Brentano's unhappiness centered on her inability to accept the separation from her native city. Her longing for an altered condition and especially for a return to Vienna tempered even her expressions of delight in her growing children. "These dear and lively children mean everything to me," she wrote to her father, "and my striving to have them develop good qualities is the highest tendency of my life. From the piano I go with them to see that marvelous Madonna with the wondrous child and a feeling of bliss drives out another feeling in my heart. I often think, then, if only my good father would enter, that would be an excess of bliss, but I would bear it so gladly."[30] She told Reiffenstein, "Through all these ceaseless difficulties, the expectation of my trips to Vienna, where I went regularly every two years, sustained me . . . this was the ray of hope in a difficult life . . . because when I look back upon all that has passed it is incomprehensible to me that I was able to withstand so many difficulties."

Closely related to her yearning for Vienna was a revulsion against Frankfurt. One gains the impression that her only moments of happiness in Germany came when she was on holiday or visiting the family country estate, "Winkel," far removed from the Brentano house on the Sandgasse. A letter from Frankfurt to her son's tutor, Joseph Merkel, in late 1808 conveys her mixed feelings about the two residences: "Here one is pressed constantly, without enjoyment. There is enjoyment without stress. There is sunshine; here we follow the will o' the wisp. There truth; here deception. There frugality with little; here debauchery. There present; here past. There rest; here unrest."[31] Drawing back from the implications of this contrast, she concluded: "But these are not my words, because there means separation for me from the best of all men, and here is beautiful reunion." Nevertheless, in another letter to Merkel, she summed up the heartsickness that Frankfurt engendered in her. "The shadows of the Sandgasse," she wrote, "are the gloomy backdrop to the painting of my life."[32]

IN June 1809 Antonie learned that her father was dying. She wrote to Merkel: "When the leaves fall in the autumn, I will no longer have a father, and before he goes to his eternal rest he shall rest in my arms and I near to his heart."[33] Antonie Brentano and her children arrived in Vienna in early autumn 1809 and took up residence in the Birkenstock house. Her husband followed shortly thereafter and established a branch office of his firm in Vienna, leaving the Frankfurt home office in the care of Georg Brentano. In Vienna she cared for her father until his death on 30 October, and thereafter she dedicated herself for several years to the settling of his estate, particularly the disposition of his vast and valuable art collection. In her devotion to the arts, Antonie Brentano showed herself to be not only an authentic Romantic of her generation but her father's daughter as well. Her homesickness for Vienna, which is so evident in her memoirs and letters from Frankfurt, is also a homesickness for her father, toward whom she maintained an attitude of total deference—identifying with his intellectual enthusiasms, arranging for publication of his posthumous book, even acquiescing, as revealed by a letter of 1807 to Savigny, in his repudiation and disinheritance of her beloved older brother Hugo:

> As a girl I gave him every penny I saved, and as a woman I did it a little more cautiously . . . I wanted to counteract my father's frugality . . . Hugo is sinking deeper every day. He has indulged in the most abominable vices and, through drinking and debauchery, has acquired the most abominable illness to the disdain of everyone . . . He turns up everywhere to oppose his father and to ask for pity, to beg for pity. We don't want him to remain in military service, but what else is left for him: the terrible retrospect of the bygone years of his life, the complete desecration of everything good in him? What prospect for the future? I know well his hypocritical manner. He is good with words and he has never looked anyone in the eye, which is a proof of his heavy conscience . . . If you, dear Savigny, could know how many thoughts and memories fill my heart when I hear the name of Hugo, and how unbearably heavy are the clouds of sorrow, you would have to weep with a sister who sees a marvelously gifted brother so completely debased.[34]

However, it would not be surprising if, beneath Antonie Brentano's seemingly automatic obedience to her father, including his choice of husband, lay deep resentments which could surface only after his death. These may have been mobilized by the auction and sale, which Antonie Brentano personally supervised, of Birken-stock's collection, a sale that was her rationale for delaying the fam-ily's return to Frankfurt for three full years. Clemens Brentano was distressed by the sale. "I am moved to tears," he wrote on 10 January 1811, and he accused her of "nullifying her father's entire life and work."[35] However, she would not be dissuaded, offering a fully rea-sonable explanation: "Father collected for a whole long lifetime and often bought worthless rubbish. The forty-room house is crammed full and I cannot leave everything and live in Frankfurt or take the risk of transporting more than I have room for there. I have the guid-ance of true friends of art to help me separate the wheat from the chaff, and to keep the most beautiful part for my life."[36] The disposal of the collection was the means by which Antonie finally separated herself from her father and completed the process of mourning. Her identification of the collection with mortality itself is described in her letter to Clemens on the eve of the first auction, in February 1812: "And so, the dear possession scatters; everything dissolves, we pass on and the stream of time engulfs the traces."[37]

Frau Brentano's inner conflicts generated a flight into illness. She told the biographer Otto Jahn that, following her father's death, she was "frequently ill for weeks at a time."[38] "My health is completely shattered," she wrote to Merkel on 5 June 1811," and that prevents me from having a pleasant life, and makes me acquainted with mor-tality."[39] By her illness, however, she succeeded in prolonging her residence in Vienna where, all things considered, she was able to find a happiness not available in Frankfurt: "I am kept in my home town by sweet necessity longer than in the home town of my chil-dren, and I enjoy the real contentment and well-being which are cre-ated through circumstances free of compulsion."[40]

In light of the foregoing, it is surely not fortuitous that the letter to the Immortal Beloved was written only a few weeks after the final auction of the Birkenstock collection. At this juncture, Antonie Brentano faced the imminent prospect of returning to Frankfurt, of being compelled to leave her childhood home and all that it repre-sented to her. It is my assumption that she fled to Beethoven seek-ing salvation from that prospect—to one who represented for her a higher order of existence, who embodied in his music the spiritual essence of her native city. At the same time, she may belatedly have been asserting her right to choose her own beloved.

BEETHOVEN had become acquainted with the Brentano-Birkenstock family in May 1810 in connection with Bettina Brentano's visit to Vienna, and he soon became a frequent visitor and close friend of the family. Schindler mistakenly asserted that Beethoven became acquainted with Antonie and her father "when he first arrived in Vienna in 1792."[41] Seeking to verify Schindler's assertion, Thayer made inquiry of the Brentano family through the United States consul in Frankfurt, W. P. Webster, who responded on 18 October 1872: "I understand that Hofrath Birkenstock was a friend of Beethoven's; that Beethoven was very often in the Birkenstock house; and that the acquaintanceship of the daughter with him began prior to her marriage with Herr Brentano."[42] This compounding of Schindler's error turned out to be based on Webster's misreading of a detailed summary supplied by an unidentified Brentano family member, which correctly stated the year in which Beethoven's association with the Brentano family actually began:

> The friendly relations of Beethoven with the Brentano family of Frankfurt/Main, with respect to Frau Antonie Brentano *née* Birkenstock . . . and her husband, Herrn Franz Brentano, merchant, then magistrate and Senator of the free city of Frankfurt . . . had their origin in the friendly intercourse between Beethoven and Frau Brentano's father, Imperial Councillor Johann Melchior von Birkenstock . . . which had existed since the time when Frau Brentano with her three oldest children visited Vienna in 1809, because her father, Councillor von Birkenstock, had been in seriously bad health for some time. This friendly association was maintained after the death of von Birkenstock on 30 October 1809 in Vienna and during the three-year residence in Vienna of the Brentano family. Beethoven came often to the Birkenstock—later the Brentano—house, attended the quartet performances which were given there by the most distinguished of Vienna's musicians, and he himself often delighted his friends with his masterful playing. The Brentano children sometimes brought fruit and flowers to him at his lodgings; in return, he gave them bonbons and always showed them the greatest friendliness.[43]

Although the Brentano report improbably stated that Beethoven first met Birkenstock on his deathbed, it clearly placed Antonie Brentano's meeting with Beethoven in the period after her arrival in Vienna. Further, no references appear in either Beethoven's letters or the reminiscences of his contemporaries to connect him with any of the Brentanos or Birkenstocks prior to 1810. Birkenstock was not among the 123 illustrious subscribers to the Trios, op. 1, in 1795.[44] Beethoven was not in attendance at the wedding of Franz and Antonie, nor is his name mentioned among those who gave presents to the bridal pair.[45]

Antonie Brentano herself was interviewed by two eminent music biographers. Jahn, who interviewed her toward the end of her life, implied that she came to know Beethoven only after her father's death. And to Ludwig Nohl she "categorically asserted" that she had met Beethoven for the first time in 1810, when she and Bettina together sought out Beethoven at his lodgings at the Pasqualati house.[46] Bettina, who enchanted Beethoven, left Vienna within a few weeks, but the friendship between Beethoven and the Brentano family was firmly established. As Jahn wrote:

> A tender friendship bound him . . . to Frau Antonie Brentano . . . This young woman, who did not feel at home in Frankfurt, made Herr Brentano move to Vienna, where she spent several years in the Birkenstock house, which Bettina so beautifully described. Beethoven, as a friend, frequented this house, where there was much music-making, and his "little friend," for whom, in 1812, he wrote the little Trio in one movement [WoO 39] "to encourage her in playing the piano" [*zu ihrer Aufmunterung im Klavierspielen*, as the dedication reads], was Antonie's daughter, Maximiliane (later, Frau von Blittersdorf), to whom he dedicated the Sonata in E major [op. 109] ten years later. After Birkenstock's death (1809), he also sought to act as a practical friend, trying to negotiate the purchase by the Archduke Rudolph of a part of the Birkenstock estate.[47]

The first reference to Beethoven in Antonie Brentano's correspondence, as well as the first indication of her profound feeling for him, appears in her letter of 26 January 1811 to Clemens Brentano, who had sent her a cantata text which he wanted set to music. She wrote: "I have read your cantata and was moved by it, and therefore I feel as if it were dedicated to me. If I have to give it to the one for whom you have destined it, it would have to be printed, or at least the dedication would have to be from your hand . . . I will place the original in the holy hands of Beethoven, whom I venerate deeply. He walks godlike among the mortals, his lofty attitude set against the mundane world, and his sick digestion aggravates him only momentarily, because the Muse embraces him and presses him to her warm heart."[48] At what point this worship was transformed into love is not yet known. The romance was apparently well under way by December 1811, when Beethoven composed the first version of "An die Geliebte" (To the beloved), WoO 140, the manuscript of which he soon presented to Antonie. The score is dated in Beethoven's own hand. In light of its date and content, the song was certainly written for the Immortal Beloved. In the upper right-hand corner of the first page of the autograph are the words, in Antonie Brentano's hand: "Requested by me from the author on 2 March 1812."[49] Beethoven presented to Frau Brentano several other compositions with dedicatory messages in late 1811.

Toward the end of her life Antonie Brentano recalled that only one person had been able to console her during her most desolate moments in Vienna. She told Jahn that during her long periods of illness, she withdrew from company and remained "in her room, unfit to see anybody." There was one exception. Beethoven used to come in regularly, "seat himself in her antechamber without any further ado and improvise; when he had 'said everything and given solace' to the suffering one in his own language, he would depart as he had come, without taking notice of anybody else."[50]

The letter to the Immortal Beloved may now be read as a document addressed to a real person rather than to a mysterious unknown. The overt ethical implications of Beethoven's renunciation become apparent. His love for Antonie is in conflict not only with his deeply rooted inability to marry but also with the prospect of the betrayal of a friend. Beethoven had warmed himself at the family hearth of the Brentanos, partaking vicariously of their family life. He loved them both, and he could not separate them. At the critical moment of the letter's composition, his anguish is apparent. And his answer is clear: he will continue to love both of them, as a single and inseparable unit.

The precise date of the Brentanos' departure from Vienna is not yet fixed, but it was probably in November 1812. On 6 October Franz wrote to Clemens from Vienna about their imminent return to Frankfurt: "Toni as well as I are still ailing very much . . . For quite a time I have not been well. I cannot stand this climate, but I hope to regain my health on the Rhine . . . If it had not been for my impending journey, which depends on Toni's recovery, I would have invited you to come here to stay with us. But I have a strong impulse to go home, and my errant, unquiet life has lasted much too long."[51] Beethoven may have prolonged his stay with his brother in Linz until their departure was assured. Despite occasional revivals of his desire to see his birthplace on the Rhine, he never made the journey that might have reunited him with the Brentanos, nor, as far as I can determine, did Antonie Brentano ever again visit the city of her birth.

WHEN the Brentanos left Vienna in late 1812, there was no rupture in their relationship with Beethoven. On the contrary, for a decade thereafter they remained among his most loyal and dedicated supporters. Frau Brentano's love for Beethoven was sublimated into an attitude of devotion and utter fidelity. There is much evidence of this. An entry in Beethoven's Tagebuch for 1814 reads: "I owe F. A. B. [Franz & Antonie Brentano] 2300 florins."[52] This sum probably includes one of the loans that she told Nohl was given to Beethoven "when she learned of his condition through her doctor."[53] Similarly, Beethoven wrote Frau Brentano in early November 1815 a request that she aid his brother Caspar Carl in "disposing of" (surely a hint that she purchase) a pipe bowl at an exorbitant price.[54] It is safe to assume that the Brentanos' loans were converted into outright gifts; Beethoven made no attempt to repay them, despite the good state to which his finances reverted during the Congress of Vienna.

Far from complaining, Franz and Antonie were eager to assist Beethoven in every way. Believing that he was still in difficult straits, they later sent him an unsolicited check, which he felt rather guilty about accepting.[55] On 22 February 1819 Antonie wrote a letter to her spiritual mentor, Bishop Johann Michael Sailer, requesting that he accept Beethoven's nephew Karl at his school in Landshut. (No response from Sailer survives.) The letter shows her to be deeply—almost fiercely—committed to Beethoven's viewpoint in the contest between him and his sister-in-law concerning the guardianship of her son:

> I am chosen as a mediator to ask you for a favor, even for a good work (it deals with doing good works, even with saving someone), so I do not hesitate, with all the confidence that you have inspired in me, to ask you for your counsel and action.

I must say this about my glorious, beloved home town: Vienna, though full of great advantages, nevertheless has, especially today, the great disadvantage of making it virtually impossible to educate a normal child properly, because of the great economic instability and the resulting bad consequences for morality among all classes. It is almost impossible to educate a child who has been born under an unlucky star, whose salvation can be achieved only by the act of removal. An only son, eleven to twelve years old, fiery, the child of poor parents, whose father is dead, and whose mother has openly been declared a thief and a morally debased creature, full of intrigues, living in the most straitened circumstances. The courts annulled her rights as a mother and this boy, who has been described to me as talented, showing great promise, with great facility at learning, as well as with an indescribable thoughtlessness, has been put under the care of his uncle (the father's brother), following his father's death, which occurred three years ago. This great, excellent person, whose name I enclose herewith, who is greater as a human being than as an artist, has made it the greatest concern of his life to provide the best possible conditions, but with his soft heart, his glowing soul, his faulty hearing, with his deeply fulfilling profession as an artist, and considering the very limited means which are at the disposal of educators there, and the isolation of the boy in his uncle's house, and the inadequacy of public institutions of learning, and the incessantly active, dangerous intrigues of the mother, so far not even a tolerable patchwork has resulted. And he wants to send this talented but frivolous boy to a Catholic university, one not too costly where, along with the invisible guardian angel he will have a visible one who will lovingly attend to his sustenance and salvation; Heaven inspired him to think of Landshut, and he has learned through one of my relatives that I am in the happy position of knowing you personally, you whom he has venerated for so long, and he urgently desired that I make you aware of these facts and ask if the boy's salvation can be achieved there, and if he, who is now in his third school can learn drawing and French when he continues his studies, and how high the costs are for boarding such a student.

As you well know how everybody feels, dear Sailer, so you likewise know what you must reply to a person who, like this

B[eethoven], asks you with warm will and hearty confidence. He is natural, simple and wise, with pure intentions, and the best and surest way of approaching him is to write to him as he deserves, as if you knew him for a long time, as the singer of pious songs. The fastest way is to send a letter directly to him. He is expecting it, because I have indicated to him that from you one can predict the loving deed.[56]

In the same year the Brentanos commissioned the fashionable portrait painter Joseph Stieler—who a decade earlier had painted portraits of each of them as well as of their daughter Ludovica—to execute an oil portrait of their beloved friend. After four sittings over a period of two months, the oil portrait was completed in April 1820. Although Stieler assured Beethoven that it would be sent to the Brentanos immediately following a planned exhibition, whether they ever received it is not known, for its early provenance is obscure.[57] If the Brentanos did receive the portrait, as is likely in view of their having commissioned it, they evidently gave it up at an early date. However, Antonie Brentano retained an ivory miniature copy painted especially for her by Stieler.[58]

Unfortunately, in 1820 Franz agreed to act as Beethoven's agent in negotiations with the Bonn publisher Simrock regarding publication of the *Missa solemnis*. Franz was thus placed in the position of trying faithfully to carry out a sale on Beethoven's behalf which the composer did not honor, for despite Simrock's good faith, the Mass was not delivered to him. This failure resulted in a loss of 900 florins to the Brentano firm, which had advanced this sum to Beethoven out of Simrock's escrow payment. In a letter of January 1823 Beethoven expressed the hope that he would "not put the generosity of my exceptional friends, the B[rentanos], too severely to the test."[59] Indeed, his letter to Brentano of 10 March 1823 refers to a repayment of 300 florins—that is, one-third of the advance on the Mass.[60] But Beethoven's good intentions were not fully translated into the funds that would have healed the breach. The burden of Beethoven's actions went far beyond the limits of Franz Brentano's practical outlook (in *Godwi*, Clemens Brentano dubbed Franz *der Deutliche*, "the blunt one"). The correspondence and all further contact between Beethoven and the Brentanos appears to have ended with, or shortly after, Beethoven's letter of 2 August 1823, which coolly evaded the question of repayment while audaciously requesting that Brentano continue to serve as his unpaid agent and freight forwarder.[61]

Beethoven, though he evidently did not attempt to resume the correspondence, had not forgotten his debt. On 1 August 1824 he wrote concerning his will to his attorney, Johann Baptist Bach, instructing him, in the event of his death, to remit "the first 600 florins" from the sale to Schotts' Sons of the *Missa solemnis* "to two of the most noble persons who, when I was nearly destitute, lovingly assisted me with this sum, lending it to me without interest."[62] This sum—which together with the previously paid 300 florins would have discharged the debt on the Mass—was never paid. Franz (the Rhenish bourgeois patrician) and Antonie (the devoted and beloved noblewoman) had for Beethoven somehow become transformed into nourishing surrogate parents, from whom everything was expected but to whom too little was given in return.

Yet Beethoven did attempt to repay them for their devotion—in his manner. He sent Antonie Brentano his portrait on 6 February 1816, with the inscription: "Most respectfully to Frau von Brentano, née Birkenstock, from her admiring friend, Beethoven." He forwarded to the Brentanos copies of a number of his works. On 6 December 1821 he dedicated to their daughter, Maximiliane, the Piano Sonata, op. 109, accompanied by a beautiful dedicatory letter in which he recalled the good times he had shared with the Brentanos at the Birkenstock house:

> Well, this is not one of those dedications which are used and abused by thousands of people—It is the spirit which unites the noble and finer people of this earth and which *time* can *never* destroy. It is this spirit which now speaks to you and which calls you to mind and makes me see you still as a child, and likewise your beloved parents, your most excellent and gifted mother, your father imbued with so many truly good and noble qualities and ever mindful of the welfare of his children. So at this very moment I am in the Landstrasse—and I see you all before me . . . The memory of a noble family can never fade in my heart. May you sometimes think of me with a feeling of kindness.[63]

He intended also to dedicate to Antonie Brentano two other sonatas, op. 110 and op. 111, but a mixup caused op. 110 to appear in Paris without any dedication, and external pressures caused op. 111 to be dedicated to the Archduke Rudolph.[64] Beethoven therefore intended to dedicate all three of his final piano sonatas to Antonie Brentano and her daughter. The London edition of op. 111 was actually published on 25 April 1823 with a dedication to Frau Brentano.[65]

Beethoven may have had some reluctance formally—and publicly—to dedicate one of his works to Antonie Brentano. True, he dedicated two compositions, the Sonata, op. 109, and the Trio in B flat, WoO 39, to her daughter, who was the only friend's child to be honored in this way by Beethoven. He composed the love song "An die Geliebte" for her in 1811, and he probably also wrote his song cycle *An die ferne Geliebte* (To the distant beloved), op. 98, for her in 1816. Furthermore, presentation copies of several of his works bear dedicatory messages to her. Two of these are publications of October 1811, which may therefore be viewed in relation to the events of the following summer: the *Drei Gesänge*, op. 83 ("to my excellent friend, Toni Brentano, née Edle von Birkenstock, from the author") and the piano transcription of *Christus am Oelberge*, op. 85 ("to my revered friend, Toni von Brentano, née Edle von Birkenstock, from the author"). Finally, the lied "So oder so," WoO 148, published in early 1817, bore the inscription, "For my esteemed friend, Antonie Brentano, from the author."[66]

These, however, were not dedications. The first and only full dedication to Antonie Brentano was in June 1823: "Thirty-Three Variations on a Waltz [by Diabelli] for Pianoforte, respectfully dedicated to Frau Antonia von Brentano, née Edle von Birkenstock, and composed by Ludwig van Beethoven, op. 120." Frau Brentano had at last received a dedication—and of one of Beethoven's greatest works. That he was not wholly unambivalent concerning even this dedication is shown by the fact that in March 1823 he briefly considered dedicating the variations to Franz rather than to Antonie.[67]

There is no record of Antonie Brentano's reaction to this dedication. Her conversations with Reiffenstein are silent on Beethoven. Not a single one of the letters she wrote to Beethoven has survived. Nor have a large proportion of his numerous letters to both Antonie and Franz—such as the nine letters mentioned in his Tagebuch for 1817—survived.[68] Each of the four surviving letters to Antonie are, as MacArdle observed, "in fact as much to her husband as to herself."[69] But this is not very surprising, for Beethoven loved Franz more deeply than was ever understood by any of the participants in this drama of love and abnegation. He made this feeling sufficiently explicit in one of his final letters to Franz, dated 10 March 1823: "My most ardent wish is to be able to show you how much I honor and love you,"[70] and he expressed it most movingly in his letter of 15 February 1817:

> Some time ago I sent you several musical works in order to recall myself to your friendly remembrance. All the members of the Brentano family have ever been dear to me; and you especially, my esteemed friend, I shall always remember with sincere regard. I myself would like you to believe that frequently I have prayed to Heaven for long preservation of your life so that for many years you may be usefully active for your family as its esteemed head . . .
>
> I very greatly miss your company and that of your wife and your dear children. For where can I find anything like it here in our Vienna? Hence I hardly go to see anyone, for I have never been able to get on with people unless there is some exchange of ideas—Well, all my very best wishes. I hope that all possible good and beautiful things may come to you during your lifetime to crown your merits. May you now and then call me to mind; and may you not think me unworthy of your remembrance—

At the foot of the page Beethoven added as an afterthought: "All my best greetings to my beloved friend Toni and to your dear children."[71]

ANTONIE Brentano gave birth on 8 March 1813 to her sixth and last child, Karl Josef. I think it is prudent to regard the Immortal Beloved letter as having been written without knowledge of Antonie Brentano's pregnancy. In the event, the subsequent awareness of her pregnancy sealed all the issues. She and Beethoven now could pledge their eternal love and devotion without suffering the consequences that an actual marital rupture would bring upon a Catholic mother of four young children and a composer married to his art. She now *must* return to Frankfurt to bear her child; he may now retire with honor from a challenge to which he was not equal, retaining in his possession the extraordinary letter that is the irrefutable proof of his capacity for love.

Antonie Brentano, too, had been engaged in a great Romantic charade, a pretense that her grand passion for a supreme artist, for the composer who "walks godlike among the mortals," would lead her to an heroic overthrow of convention. It seems clear that, like Bettina Brentano (who in 1810, while engaged to Arnim, permitted Goethe to stroke her breasts),[72] Caroline Schelling, Dorothea Schlegel, Caroline Günderode, and Rahel Levin, Antonie wanted to serve as a muse to genius, to replace propriety with passion, and above all to achieve a perfectly harmonious union. Although she was at the center of a celebrated Romantic family, she was scarcely a liberated Romantic heroine. If anything, she was more constrained by convention than her models. When the critical moment arrived, neither she nor Beethoven was capable of taking a drastic step. Oddly enough, however, by a circuitous route thickly paved with discretion and resignation, they ultimately arrived at an ideal Romantic love, an infinite yearning for an eternally postponed union, each moment of which was its own fulfillment. Doubtless they remained eternally grateful to each other for permitting themselves to transcend the commonplace gratifications of desire in favor of this extraordinary renunciation.

I have been able to find only one reference to Beethoven in Antonie Brentano's late correspondence. Writing from her favorite spa, Schlangenbad, in August 1854, she described the various recreational activities there: "fireworks, balloons, improvisations, Beethoven's music has been announced." To which she adds, rather opaquely: "Poor Schlangenbad, what will become of you. Don't lose your innocence."[73] We do not, however, require a superfluity of references to Beethoven in order to document her feelings for him. As Sophia Brentano once wrote to Clemens Brentano: "The heart may speak very intensely to someone, even if the tongue and the quill are silent."[74] Or as Antonie Brentano herself suggested in an undated diary entry: "There exists between people a spiritual and emotional community which need not be prepared. They understand each other in an instant. Their lives contained related points of contact even before they knew each other. People and events evoke in them the same thoughts. Reflections about themselves have brought them to similar convictions and conclusions which do not have to be verbalized. Ordinary people do not enter into such relationships, even if one strives to bring them in. They do not grasp these elective affinities."[75]

The documents do partially record, however, the reverberations of Beethoven's death upon Antonie Brentano. A Viennese friend, Moritz Trenck von Tonder, who knew of her closeness to the composer, wrote to her within forty-eight hours of Beethoven's death and again on 7 April and 10 May 1827, giving her full details of the event and enclosing newspaper clippings, the text of Grillparzer's funeral oration and other materials. In his letter of 28 March 1827 he wrote:

> I hesitate to bring you sorrow through the sad news concerning our friend Beethoven, and I did not write partly because I did not want to make you sad and also because I hoped that providence and the human art of the physicians might have restored the health of our hero. But the book of Fate ruled differently. Ludwig van Beethoven entered the land of peace on the 26th of March in the evening between 5 and 6 o'clock. The weather itself was dreadful: at the time of his death there was a terrible thunderstorm, with lightning and thunder and a heavy snowfall, almost as if the elements were rebelling against the death of this great mind. The sufferings of Beethoven in the course of his last year were really more than terrible, and made his death desirable. I saw him often, but his shattered appearance—a consequence of his pain—his complete deafness, always made me sad. Now he rests in God. He is at peace and all those who saw him during the last period of his life and loved him were relieved to see him freed from the torture of such an existence . . . Tomorrow we will bury him, as you can see from the attached announcement. His obituary from the Wiener Zeitung is also enclosed . . .
>
> I will keep you informed as I learn more details with regard to B. because I know what great interest you, honored lady, take in his Fate.[76]

Tonder's final letter to Frau Brentano stressed Beethoven's sufferings and eccentricities during his last years: "His irregular life-style contributed to his Fate, but he refused all advice. I myself talked to him—and urgently—about a year ago and warned him, but with his stubborness it was no use. He could have lived on his income but he neglected everything and was betrayed and robbed by his servants. His own nephew (his heir) cost him dearly and caused him grief, on top of his deafness; and his misanthropical nature, which often made him seem rougher than he was on the inside, made him an orphan, so to speak, during the last span of his life."[77]

Frau Brentano avidly followed the obituary and celebratory notices in the European press, making extracts from these in her own hand and adding her own marginal comments.[78] Beethoven's death impelled her to begin noting down the names of her friends who had died. By the end of her long life, in 1869, the yellowed sheets of paper were filled with names, each followed by the date of death. The first entry reads: "Beethoven, 26 March 1827."[79]

A NEW chapter in Antonie Brentano's life opened after her return to Frankfurt in late 1812. As she told Reiffenstein, her husband's brothers and sisters had moved out of the family house, and this brought her "quieter times." In 1816 her husband was elected a senator of Frankfurt. The Brentano town house and country estate, "Winkel," became gathering places for numerous friends and famous contemporaries. Goethe, who first met Antonie at Karlsbad in early July 1812, visited the Brentanos and spent a memorable week at Winkel between 1 and 8 September 1814.[80] In 1820 the family moved into a new mansion, 22 Neue Mainzerstrasse, built for them in neo-Renaissance style by the outstanding Romantic architect Karl Friedrich Schinkel. Continuing her father's tradition, Antonie Brentano's home became famous for its "art evenings," at which connoisseurs and collectors would gather to examine and admire her collection. Goethe reminded her of her blessings: "If ever you feel restless in your lovely family circle, you have only to stand in front of your Van Dyck and there, surpassing all earthly and celestial pictures, including the most famous of all hares, be absolutely restored."[81] She presided over balls, festivities, theatrical productions, and other cultural events at the Brentano residences. She became "the most esteemed lady in Frankfurt, simultaneously honored for her refinement as for her moral worth and genuine piety."[82] Both Goethe and Bishop Sailer dedicated editions of their collected writings to her. She was co-founder of a society for the support of needy and unemployed women. Her later public life was devoted to philanthropy, the furtherance of the arts, and the Catholic Church. She was noted for her generous financial grants and her support of missionary and social organizations. In Frankfurt she was called "the mother of the poor."[83]

Antonie's devotion to good works and to the Cross sustained her during fresh sorrows which far surpassed any that she had yet undergone. At an early age her youngest child, Karl Josef, was stricken with partial paralysis of the legs. More seriously, in his fourth year

he showed signs of severe mental retardation, coupled with epilep-
tiform seizures and violent behavior, requiring that he be constantly
watched and restrained. During the last fifteen years of his life (he
died in 1850) he was perpetually under the care of three attendants.
His mother took him from one doctor to another in a vain search for
a cure. "I am begging for help," she wrote to Savigny on 25 October
1820, "I call for help to God and to people, and the sympathetic
friend will understand my urgency and will not deny me what is in
his power."[84] And again, on 10 April 1821 she wrote to Savigny:
"Oh, when one has to drink such a bitter cup of sorrow daily, hourly,
how can there remain a last bit of joy and strength."[85]

Frau Brentano traveled to Paris with her son. Bettina Brentano
wrote to her husband in October 1821 that Gall "gives great hopes
for a cure for her child, and that is why Toni still remains in Paris."[86]
But the efforts were unsuccessful. As Karl's room was directly above
his mother's, his fits and paroxysms caused her unceasing anguish
and sleeplessness. The sole means by which she could temporarily
tame his behavior was through a repetition of Beethoven's treatment
of her depression in Vienna: she would play the piano for her son,
and "the playing soothed the sufferer so that he would lean his head
upon her shoulder"; but this would last for only the briefest time,
after which "he would spring up and rave so wildly that she herself
was forced to flee."[87]

In the 1820s her first-born son, Georg, also began to show pathological tendencies. Earlier, Franz had described the boy, perhaps
understating the matter, as "a little difficult to handle."[88] Later,
Georg had become a foolhardy horseman, with tendencies toward
violence. Now he began to play the classic profligate, much like Antonie's brother Hugo. Bettina reported that he was "plagued with
shameful sicknesses" and that he wasted 80,000 florins in one year
alone, thereby "almost bringing his father to the grave." He would
mock Franz publicly, "pulling his nose, screaming through the whole
town like a lunatic."[89]

Antonie found comfort and expiation in the church. Bettina, com-
menting on the effects of Karl's illness upon his mother, wrote to
Arnim on 20 March 1822: "Tonie, through this child, has changed
from a scheming, mocking woman into an angel of sorrow."[90] From
this comment it is clear that Antonie's relationship with the Brentanos had not become free of conflict. She and Clemens had been
temporarily reconciled when he dedicated *Die Grundungs Prag* to

his "beloved sister-in-law Antonie Brentano" in 1815. But following his emergence from a six-year residence in a monastery and his conversion to a fanatic piety, Clemens raged against her: "He told Franz things concerning Toni for which Franz was entitled to throw him out of the house," Bettina informed her husband on 31 August 1824.[91] And on 19 October Arnim was witness to a similar scene; he wrote to Bettina that Clemens "says the harshest things about Toni based on mere conjecture, and without forbearance."[92]

Antonie Brentano had the full measure of tragedy that comes to one who outlives not only her husband but all except one of her children as well. "How I have suffered, wept, bemoaned in this past fateful year," she wrote to Christian Brentano in 1845; "I can still see the hand of the Father who has glorified good Franz before the increasing insanity of the times . . . Here, incredible stupidity has reached its peak: persecution and viciousness of all types exists; but all the more we can save ourselves by returning to the womb of the mother, sinking our Catholic heart in the unending fund of blessings of the true salvation."[93] "The old trunks are broken," she wrote to Gunda Savigny in 1852, "and the young branches are helpless without love, shrouded in sadness."[94] However, her losses were counterbalanced by her faith, her family, and her many warm friendships and associations. She viewed love as a healing and restorative power. Years before, she had written to her father's friend, Johann Isaak von Gerning, that the consecration of art is beautiful, "but more beautiful is the art of love, having been taught by nature," and "the most beautiful is the mutual interchange of happiness between two people."[95] Her oft-repeated motto was "Alte Liebe rostet nicht [Old love does not wither]," and she wrote to Savigny that "the most beautiful thing is to become gray in love and fidelity."[96]

She remained, according to all reports, the unwavering center of the Brentano family until the end.[97] She mediated family quarrels and guided its affairs. Many of her eleven grandchildren and thirteen great-grandchildren would gather in reunion each Sunday at her house until she suffered an incapacitating stroke in late 1868. "They are all about me. They knock at the door and at my heart," she wrote to Savigny around 1860.[98] Occasionally her matriarchal role seemed futile: "I, a poor old woman, gave audiences like a king, although just as with real kings, nothing came of it, and it is very tiring and without comfort."[99] Her contemporaries wrote of "Frau Schöff [Mrs. Magistrate]" in glowing and superlative terms. Her late correspondence reveals a woman of deep moral convictions and religious faith, leavened by a sharp wit and strong human concerns.

Ludwig Grimm described Antonie Brentano in his memoirs quite simply: "She had the bearing of a Queen."[100] A younger contemporary, although looking back upon the days of "Old Frankfurt," still recalled her as a child of Vienna:

> But she was not only a child of Vienna: she was not the waxen, soft, sentimental, funny, sad, today elated, tomorrow deathly sad Viennese nature-child . . . All hearts in the cold financial aristocracy of Frankfurt were conquered by [her]. Thus, she soon became mistress and queen over the very large family in the house of Brentano. But beyond this she soon was also the center of spiritual life of the old federal city of Frankfurt, owing to her irresistible graciousness and her intellect.
>
> I still see her before me, as she sat on her corner sofa, facing the Gallus Gate, absolutely erect, without leaning back . . . next to her home-grown rubber tree, behind which her Weber birds, black and yellow (good Austrian!) made a frightful noise.[101]

Antonie Brentano died on 12 May 1869 at the age of eighty-eight.

SOME VARIETIES
OF UTOPIA

13

Beethoven's
Magazin der Kunst

I N 1800, Franz Anton Hoffmeister (1754–1812), the prolific Austrian composer who headed the long-established Viennese music publishing concern which bore his name, moved to Leipzig, leaving his wife and an administrator in charge of the firm.[1] In Leipzig he joined forces with the organist Ambrosius Kühnel in a new publishing venture and almost immediately entered into negotiations with Beethoven for publication of his latest compositions. In Vienna, Hoffmeister had been fortunate enough to publish first editions of the very popular *Sonate pathétique*, op. 13, and the Six Variations for Piano on Süssmayr's *Tändeln und Scherzen*, WoO 76. Now he gained rights to such accessible works as the First Symphony, op. 21, the Second Piano Concerto, op. 19, the Sonata in B flat, op. 22, the overture to *Die Geschöpfe des Prometheus*, op. 43, and the immensely successful Septet, op. 20.[2] None of the seven surviving letters from Beethoven to Hoffmeister predates Hoffmeister's departure from Vienna; nor are there any reminiscences or anecdotes describing an earlier association between them. However, it is clear from the extremely friendly tenor of Beethoven's letters, which were written between December 1800 and September 1803, that the two men had already become well acquainted, albeit not sufficiently intimate to use the "*Du*" form. Beethoven even addresses his fellow composer repeatedly as "my beloved and worthy brother and friend."[3] Furthermore, their relationship was such that Beethoven felt free to express nonconformist social and political views to Hoffmeister, an evident sign of ideological sympathy between them.

For example, it was Hoffmeister to whom Beethoven in 1802 wrote a letter turning aside a proposed commission of a program sonata in praise of the French Revolution's ideals or leaders. "Has the devil got hold of you," he demurred, "that you suggest that I should compose such a sonata?"[4] He explained his refusal in terms of his belief that the "time of the revolutionary fever" had already passed, as evidenced by Bonaparte's negotiations for a reconciliation with the Vatican. The same letter contains the politically dangerous comment, "There are rascals in the Imperial City as there are at the Imperial Court." Again, in his final letter to Hoffmeister, Beethoven sardonically complains about the court and the improbability of his ever obtaining an appointment there: "Heaven help us! What appointment at the Imperial Court could be given to such a *parvum talentum com ego?*"[5] These passages are all the more unusual in that Beethoven rarely risked political comments in his letters during his first Vienna decade: indeed, these are the first such references to be found subsequent to the letter of 2 August 1794 to Nikolaus Simrock in Bonn, in which Beethoven disdainfully predicts that a Viennese is unlikely to revolt so long as he can get his "brown beer and little sausages."[6]

In the absence of Hoffmeister's side of the correspondence, it is impossible to tell precisely what views were shared by the two composers, although it is clear that both men had once succumbed to the "revolutionary fever" and that neither had much use for Hapsburg rule. Perhaps they were also united by a common inclination to Freemasonry, which could not be openly avowed, because in contemporary Austria Freemasonry and Illuminism were readily equated with Jacobinism by the police and by those who contributed to the pages of such counterrevolutionary journals as the *Wiener Zeitschrift* and *Eudæmonia.*[7] Hoffmeister, a good friend of Mozart, who was a noted Mason, wrote a number of Masonic songs, and his first business partner, the bookseller Rudolf Gräffer, was a Freemason.[8] Reasonably enough, Specht took the "Dear Brother" references in Beethoven's letters to Hoffmeister as frankly Masonic.[9] Despite the numerous signs of Beethoven's sympathy with Masonic ideals and rituals, it is doubtful that he himself ever belonged to a Masonic lodge. However, the Lesegesellschaft, with which he was closely associated in his late teens, was manifestly a haven for the proscribed organizations of Illuminati and Freemasons. This linkage was not unusual. As Brunschwig noted, "Almost from the start, the lodges associated themselves with the reading clubs," forming cultural associations which served as "nurseries of the *Aufklärung.*"[10]

Our subject is a particularly striking passage in Beethoven's second letter to Hoffmeister, written in mid-January 1801, in which Beethoven offered the publisher his First Symphony, Septet, Second Piano Concerto, and B-flat Sonata, op. 22, for a total fee of 70 ducats. Partly by way of apology for being forced into the unwelcome role of negotiating financial terms with a fellow artist, Beethoven added: "Well, that tiresome business has now been settled. I call it so because I wish things were different in the world. There just ought to be in the world a *storehouse of art* (*ein Magazin der Kunst*) to which the artist would only bring his artworks in order to take what he needed; as it is one must be half businessman, and how can one be reconciled to that!"[11] It has scarcely escaped notice that Beethoven's suggestion, though limited by him to works of art rather than goods in general, resembles the socialist ideal which Louis Blanc described in his epigram, "*la distribution des travaux selon les facultés, et la répartition des fruits selon les besoins,*" and which Marx later condensed into "from each according to his ability, to each according to his needs."[12] But Beethoven's visionary recommendation also has possible sources in the writings of the forerunners of modern socialism and, more particularly, in eighteenth-century French utopian thought.[13]

First, we ought to rule out the possibility that the phrase "*Magazin der Kunst*" refers to a publishing establishment. There were several publishers, such as the Musikalisches Magazin auf der Höhe in Brunswick, who used the term *Magazin* to designate their firms, but from the phrasing and context of Beethoven's letter it is clear that he is not merely expressing his desire for a more equitable publishing arrangement. Similarly, there is no reason to connect his phrase with the Magazin de musique à l'usage des fêtes de la Révolution, a cooperative publishing house formed in 1793 by fifty-one composers of the Revolution, with substantial underwriting from the French treasury, primarily to issue their large-scale ceremonial works, in which commercial publishers had until then been wholly uninterested.[14] Beethoven's suggestion is far more radical: he is proposing as a universal principle the exchange of the products of creative labor for livelihoods guaranteed by society as a whole.

THE ideal of a social system founded upon the community of goods and the equitable satisfaction of needs has ancient roots: according to Plutarch, Lycurgus founded such a commonwealth in Sparta, one that Plato hoped to revive in his Republic and which bears a marked resemblance to the lost Golden Age mourned in the writings of Seneca and the Church Fathers. An extensive literature is devoted to the description and advocacy of such societies, whether historic, mythic, or prospective. However, it appears to have been Sir Thomas More who, in 1516, first described the simple distributive system of an imaginary commonwealth in phrases that resemble Beethoven's:

> Every city is divided into four equal parts or quarters. In the midst of every quarter there is a market place of all manner of things. Thither the works of every family be brought into certain houses. And every kind of thing is laid up several in barns or storehouses. From hence the father of every family, or every householder fetcheth whatsoever he and his wife have need of, and carrieth it away with him without money, without exchange, without gage, pawn, or pledge.[15]

A strikingly similar form of distribution is pictured in a work that originated outside of the utopian tradition but which had some effect upon its seventeenth- and eighteenth-century development: Garcilaso de la Vega's *Royal Commentaries of the Incas and General History of Peru*, part one of which was published at Lisbon in 1609:

> Throughout the whole kingdom there were three sorts of storehouses to hold the harvest and tribute. Every village, whether large or small, had two storehouses: one was used to hold the supplies kept for the use of the people in lean years, and the other was used for the crops of the Sun and of the Inca . . . The supplies that were not consumed in warfare or by the court were kept in the three kinds of storehouses . . . and distributed in years of want among the people, whose well-being was the first care of the Incas.[16]

Several new French editions of More's *Utopia* appeared in the early eighteenth century;[17] a French translation of Garcilaso's history was published in Amsterdam in 1737.[18] It is highly probable that these writings influenced the book which, I believe, is the main source of contemporary formulations of Beethoven's utopian idea: the *Code de la nature* (Paris, 1755), written by the Abbé Morelly (1715?–1755?), a little-known French essayist and *philosophe*.[19] In part four of the *Code de la nature*, Morelly set down the laws upon

which his ideal society was to be founded. The third of these "fundamental and sacred laws" reads: "For his part every Citizen will
contribute to the public weal in accordance with his strength, his
talents, and his age; these will determine his obligations, in conformity with the Distributive Laws."[20] In turn, article six of the "distributive and economic laws" regulates the distribution of durable
"products of Nature and Art": "Now, all these durable products will
be collected in public storehouses [*magazins publics*] for distribution, some daily or at stated times to all Citizens, for the ordinary
needs of life and for carrying on their various occupations; others
will be supplied to people who make use of them."[21]

Because the *Code de la nature* was published unsigned and because Morelly's life was extremely obscure, the work had a curious
publishing history—a history that actually magnified its impact
upon French intellectuals and radicals during the succeeding decades. In 1757 the influential *France Littéraire* mistakenly attributed the *Code* to Diderot, an attribution which led to its inclusion
in two pirated editions of Diderot's works: *Œuvres philosophiques
de M. D**** (Amsterdam, 1772) and *Collection complète des œuvres
philosophiques, littéraires et dramatiques de M. Diderot* (London,
1773).[22] The misattribution was widely accepted, partly because of
Diderot's failure to disclaim authorship and the absence of any claim
for Morelly—of whom no proven trace exists after 1755.

Whether or not under the direct influence of Morelly-Diderot,
shortly thereafter the French social critic and moralist Gabriel Bon-
not de Mably (1709–1785) included a suggestion similar to Morelly's in his *De la Législation, ou Principes des lois* (Amsterdam,
1776). Elaborating his vision of a republic in which private property
did not exist, he wrote: "I see public storehouses everywhere which
contain the wealth of the republic; and the magistrates, who are
really the fathers of the country, have scarcely any other function
than to maintain morality and to distribute the necessaries of life to
each family."[23]

The forecasts of Morelly and Mably, including their blueprints of
social distribution, were taken up by several leading ideologists during the French Revolution. In a letter of November 1793, Jacques
Grenus of Mont Blanc described a system of commonly owned property: "It will be necessary to set up national storehouses to receive
the surplus of foods and manufactures, to be subsequently distrib-
uted in equal shares. We thus arrive at the threshold of a system of

common ownership, where everyone brings the product of his efforts into the common pool to be apportioned among everyone."[24] However, these protocommunist ideas achieved their most dramatic impetus from the speeches and writings of the French revolutionist François Noël (Gracchus) Babeuf (1760–1797) and his followers. In mid-1795 Babeuf turned his attention to issues of economic production and social distribution of goods. He worked out his solutions to these issues along Morellyan lines in a letter of 28 July 1795 to Charles Germain, in which he envisaged a time when "all those engaged in production and manufacture will work for the common storehouse" and each citizen will receive his share of society's collective product.[25] Babeuf first publicly elaborated this doctrine in his *Manifeste des plébéiens*, published in November 1795 in his revolutionary journal, the *Tribun du Peuple*. There he addressed the strategies necessary to prevent any individual from acquiring more than his "fair share of the fruits of toil and the gifts of nature": "The only way to do this is to organize a communal regime which will suppress private property, set each man to work at the skill or job he knows; to require him to deposit the fruits [of his labor] in kind at the common storehouse, and establish a simple administration of distribution, an administration of needs, which, keeping a record of all individuals and all things, will distribute these with the most scrupulous equality."[26]

The advocacy and organization of armed insurrection against the Directory by the Conspiration pour l'Égalité, headed by Babeuf, led to the mass arrest of the Babouvists in 1796 and to their trial, commencing 20 February 1797, before a specially constituted High Court of the Vendôme at the Palais de Justice. Babeuf and his co-conspirators were found guilty on 24 May 1797, and he was executed three days later.

Denied the right of counsel, Babeuf had conducted his own defense, the culmination of which was a three-day address in which he sought to justify the conspiracy by appealing to the interests of the nation as a whole and by placing his revolutionary ideas in the tradition of French social thought, exemplified by Rousseau, Mably, and Diderot, to whom he attributed Morelly's *Code de la nature*. Quoting at length from his own *Manifeste des plébéiens*, including the passage quoted, he insisted that his ideas are "mere pallid paraphrases of our three great philosophers and lawmakers."[27] Babeuf ascribed to Mably not only the passage "I see public storehouses everywhere" but also another description of the good society, writing that it "will be composed of all in complete equality—all rich, all poor, all free, all brothers. The first law will be a ban on private property. We will deposit the fruits of our toil in the public storehouses. This will be the wealth of the state and the property of all. Every year the heads of families will elect stewards whose task will be the distribution of goods to each in accordance with his needs."[28]

Although there are doubtless other references to communal storehouses in the literature of the French Revolution, in contemporary accounts of Babeuf's trial, and in commentaries on the writings of Mably and Morelly-Diderot, these are the main precursors of the phrase in Beethoven's letter to Hoffmeister. Which of them, if any, were known to Beethoven, we cannot tell. Morelly's *Code de la nature* went through a minimum of five editions, including those where it was identified as a work of Diderot. Mably's *De la Législation* had at least three separate editions and was also included in its author's collected works, of which at least five editions (with further reprints) appeared between 1789 and 1798.[29] A German translation, *Ueber die Gesetzgebung, oder über die Grundsätze der Gesetze*, was published in 1779 at Nuremberg. More's *Utopia* was translated into German at least three times in the eighteenth century (1704, 1730, and 1753). The full extent of the dissemination of Babouvist ideas is not yet known. Of the passages quoted, only the one in his *Manifeste des plébéiens* was printed contemporaneously, but Babeuf's activities and writings were widely reported in the press and closely followed by many European intellectuals and radicals.[30] For example, in northern Germany, the journal *Frankreich*, edited by the composer-writer Johann Friedrich Reichardt, published two virulent articles describing Babeuf's ideas as outlined in the *Tribun du Peuple* and detailing his conspiracy against the Directory.[31] Not to be outdone, the Hamburg journal *Minerva*, edited by the liberal Johann Wilhelm von Archenholz, ran almost a dozen separate articles on Babeuf's life, trial, and martyrdom in its issues between May 1796 and July 1797.[32] These included substantial extracts from his writings, such as the "Doctrine of Babeuf"—printed under the heading "Doctrine of the Terrorist Babeuf"—and his moving, stoical farewell letter to his wife.

Like many natives of the Rhine region, Beethoven was fairly fluent in the French language, as well as receptive to ideological currents from the West. The ideas of "Diderot" and Mably would have been readily available to him during his later years at Bonn through the mediation of the politically advanced circle with which he was then associated at the Lesegesellschaft, the university, the Zehrgarten, and even the electoral orchestra. There is insufficient information about his early Vienna years to permit informed speculation; virtually nothing is known about what he read during the first Vienna decade, apart from the texts which he set—or intended to set—to music, a few later retrospective references, and a handful of books in his estate. Writings that questioned the legitimacy of private property would have made their way past the very effective Viennese censorship only with great difficulty, but that censorship was scarcely thorough enough wholly to cut off the flow of proscribed printed material—let alone of ideas transmitted verbally by the numerous visitors from Paris and the Rhineland.[33]

BEETHOVEN was deeply preoccupied with the modes of musical patronage, seeking a financially secure post or, even better, a guaranteed income to make him independent. He had very early come to feel a sense of responsibility for what he liked to call his "divine art" and this, rather than any simple desire for wealth, is what compelled him to learn the fairly complex maneuvers necessary for a "free" composer trying to make a living at the beginning of the modern age.[34] "I have to live entirely on the products of my mind," he accurately observed toward the close of his career, and he was proud that he managed to do so.[35] Although he lived quite well, he never became wealthy; nor did he ever seek wealth as an end in itself.[36] As he wrote to the publisher Heinrich Albert Probst in 1824, "I really must thank Heaven which so blesses me in my works that, though admittedly I am not rich, I have yet been enabled by means of my compositions to *live for my art*."[37]

Beethoven's economic concerns are prominent in his correspondence throughout his life, but especially in the years prior to 1809, the year in which several members of the high nobility committed themselves to pay him a substantial lifetime annuity. It is easy to imagine that such concerns were the subject of much discussion between him and his fellow artists; hence it is not unlikely that the Morellyan-Babouvian suggestion of such a guarantee by the state as an alternative to traditional, aristocratic patronage became a lively topic of speculation among his contemporaries, especially those who had once felt the pull of French revolutionary ideas, even those who were repeatedly disenchanted by the Terror, by Thermidorian reaction, and by Bonapartist military export of "freedom" to France's recalcitrant neighbors.

There seems little reason to doubt that the *Magazin der Kunst* conception belongs to, and probably also derives from, the utopian tradition of Morelly, Mably, and Babeuf and that Beethoven, at least momentarily, was fascinated by its implications as a panacea for his economic and creative needs. But it does not follow that Beethoven accepted the central economic and social doctrines of this tradition, such as the abolition of private property (or at least, the concentration of property in the hands of the state) or the formation of an austere welfare state along neo-Spartan lines. There is no reason to believe that Beethoven ever favored the kind of eminently static and coercive social order which Lycurgus founded and Morelly advocated. Like most readers of Plutarch, Beethoven admired the Spartans for their dedication to the common weal. "These Lacedæmonians died ready to risk death or life for honor," he approvingly noted in his diary.[38] But his admiration for Lycurgus and his utopian descendants surely stopped far short of endorsing a hierarchically enforced egalitarianism, let alone the sexual practices and family structure characteristically associated with such societies. What would Beethoven have made of Morelly's insistence upon compulsory marriage at the age of consent?

In the closing decade of the eighteenth century, the Hapsburg persecution of dissenters as well as the repressive censorship encouraged many Viennese radicals to cultivate discretion and even conformism. Discretion is the clear imperative in Beethoven's letter to Simrock of 2 August 1794, which advised of the arrests of "various *important* people" and warned: "You dare not raise your voice here or the police will take you into custody."[39] And a concession to conformism is at least implied in Beethoven's setting of two nationalist texts by Friedelberg in 1796–1797 (WoO 121–122). For him, as for so many young idealists of the time, the rebellious impulse was deflected from politics into art, which served as a vital focus during a time of shifting ideologies, uncertain loyalties, and relentless persecution. Beethoven apparently spent these years in single-minded development of his artistic capabilities, seeking to transform music in ways no less revolutionary, and perhaps more permanent, than those by which political radicals had been able to transform society.

Nevertheless, whatever the vicissitudes of his political outlook during these years, Beethoven surely continued to hope for something more than a revolution in aesthetic sensibility. At any rate, it is certain that he entered the nineteenth century with a heightened distrust of the Hapsburg order and dissatisfaction with its forms of musical patronage, a malaise that he did not conceal from his friends. This discontent was climaxed by Beethoven's dedication, in 1801, of his Piano Sonata, op. 28, to Joseph von Sonnenfels, who was a forthright opponent of excessive police powers, and by his intended dedication of the Third Symphony to Napoleon Bonaparte, along with his never-fulfilled plan to pursue his career in Paris (the earliest oblique reference to this move may indeed be in Beethoven's first letter to Hoffmeister, dated 15 December 1800, in which he underscores that he is witholding some of his better works from publication "*until I myself undertake a journey*").[40]

That Beethoven's radicalism was not anchored in any specific, transitory political program may have been his strength, for, in retrospect, there were valid counterbalancing reasons not to regret, as Hegel, Heine, and Marx did, that Germany's revolution, in contrast to France's, was confined to the regions of the imagination.[41] Beethoven's attraction to France and to Bonaparte, however ambivalent and contradictory, suggests that the young composer, too, yearned for activity in the historical arena: it was only in his mature years that he came to rejoice that his proper realm was the "empire of the mind" or, as he put it on another occasion, that his "kingdom" was "in the air."[42] There may have been more than a tinge of defensiveness in his rejection of the "revolutionary" sonata suggested by Hoffmeister, and more than a hint of guilt feelings behind his claim to his old Masonic friend, Franz Wegeler, that he still hoped someday to practice his art "solely for the benefit of the poor."[43]

"I wish things were different in the world," Beethoven wrote to Hoffmeister. His manifest wish was that the *Magazin der Kunst* might exist for all artists, not merely for a lone refugee from Bonn of Flemish ancestry. In the letter to Hoffmeister he envisaged a system under which artists might achieve freedom from the fettering imperatives of the marketplace. Elsewhere, in an inchoate and emotion-laden draft statement for a proposed complete edition of his works, he expressed his determination "to show that the *human brain* cannot be sold either like coffee beans or like any form of cheese." He continued: "The human brain in itself is not a saleable commodity"—a maxim which, had it been known in Beethoven's own time, might have been inscribed as an epigraph of nineteenth-century Romanticism.[44]

Underlying Beethoven's resistance to the treatment of artists as mere purveyors of salable merchandise, as well as his concern for the sanctity of the artist as a creative individual, is his adherence to the ideas of freedom and fraternity. His devotion to every manifestation of freedom—political, artistic, religious, and intellectual—was unwavering throughout his life, from his Bonn setting of *Wer ist ein freier Mann*, WoO 117, to his inscription of Schiller's words, "To love liberty above all else," in the album of a friend shortly after his arrival in Vienna, to his magisterial statement to Archduke Rudolph in 1819: "*Freedom, progress*, these are the main objectives in art as in the whole of our great creation."[45] Beethoven did not come by chance to the prisoners' choruses of *Fidelio* or to Egmont's climactic monologue and its instrumental apotheosis. Similarly, the resonances of the idea of brotherhood are richly documented in Beethoven's work—from his *Joseph* Cantata to the setting of "An die Freude" in the Ninth Symphony—and in his life as well, where the emotions generated by fraternal feelings enriched his relationships, though they more than once overwhelmed his better judgment.

Liberty and fraternity—but not equality. It is on the issue of equality that Beethoven parts company with the slogans of the French Revolution and the eighteenth-century utopian *philosophes*. He regarded servants as "inferior" persons and even as "beastly rabble."[46] He counseled himself that he should never "*outwardly* show people the contempt they deserve."[47] He regarded the ordinary "burgher" as unworthy for him to associate with, preferring the company and status of "higher men."[48] In the very letter to Hoffmeister containing the utopian phrase he contrasts "genuine and true artists" with "mere tradesmen" (whom he elsewhere sometimes derogates by their racial or national origins) to the detriment of the latter. He engaged in a nobility pretense for a quarter-century in Vienna. Beethoven's egalitarianism did not extend very far beyond his "brothers in Apollo," his dearest friends, or those few nobles whom he considered worthy of their estate. Having spent his life in the development and defense of his creative gifts, he could not acknowledge anything less than the equality of excellence, which he usually defined in terms of an aristocratic ideal.

Perhaps Beethoven could have accepted in principle Rousseau's distinction between those "natural inequalities" deriving from "age, health, bodily strength, and the qualities of the mind or the soul" and the "political inequality" which derives from the institutions of private property and civil society.[49] However, it is nowhere recorded that he in fact adopted as his own creed such distinctions, let alone accepted the virtually unmediated egalitarianism and monastic leveling of More, Morelly, or Babeuf. At a time when Babeuf was formulating the central slogans of his doctrine around the issue of equality—"Nature has given to each individual an equal right to the enjoyment of all its goods . . . The purpose of society is to defend this equality . . . The goal of the French Revolution is to destroy inequality and to reestablish the general welfare"—Beethoven was writing to his friend Zmeskall: "*Power* is the moral principle of those who excel others, and it is also mine."[50] One can only imagine Beethoven's dismay—and disdain—at the Babouvist slogan, formulated by Silvain Maréchal in the *Manifeste des égaux* (1796) and endorsed—albeit uncomfortably—by Babeuf in the *Défense*: "If necessary, let all the arts perish, as long as we have true equality!"[51]

B Y now the reader will have sensed that this essay will close without having successfully disentangled the ideological from the personal motivations underlying Beethoven's *Magazin der Kunst*, let alone having demonstrated that either of these is more decisive than the other in giving rise to his idea. This may not really be surprising, for Beethoven's actions often display a perplexing blend of altruism and self-interest. However, these twin levels of motivation are perhaps reconciled by the fact that Beethoven's deepest self-interest was, after all, to create the conditions under which he could most profoundly and effectively fulfill his altruistic impulses—in his music.

14

Beethoven and Schiller

FRIEDRICH Schiller's "An die Freude" was written in 1785 and published in February of the following year in the second volume of his magazine, *Thalia*. Written during the decade that saw the culmination in German-speaking lands of the Enlightenment ideal of a benevolent social order devoted to spiritual freedom and secular reform, it achieved instantaneous popularity through its quasi-religious evocation of a condition in which all conflicts were dissolved in brotherhood, love, and reconciliation. Schiller was then an adherent of *Glückseligkeitsphilosophie* (philosophy of happiness), a doctrine derived from Locke, Shaftesbury, and other philosophers of the English Enlightenment, which saw joy and love as the motive forces and goal of creation, overseen by a loving father who seeks to bring his creatures to perfection and enjoins them to promote the welfare of their fellow man. The ode's appeal to young idealists was reinforced by its similarity in tone and outlook to poems that were then current in the lodges of German Freemasons, a similarity not altogether accidental, for Schiller was then living in Dresden within a circle of Freemasons that included his closest friend, the jurist and amateur composer Christian Gottfried Körner.[1]

Körner almost immediately wrote what appears to have been the first musical setting of the "Ode to Joy."[2] The poem rapidly became a popular subject for German composers: more than forty settings are known, mostly for solo voice and piano, but also including several for mixed choir, mixed choir with soloists, and male chorus.[3] More than a few of these were written in the late 1780s and early 1790s, so it was not an occasion for surprise when in January 1793 Schiller's disciple and friend, Bartholomäus Ludwig Fischenich, wrote to Schiller's wife from Bonn with the news that yet another composer was contemplating a setting: "I am enclosing with this a setting of the 'Feuerfarbe' on which I would like to have your opinion. It is by a young man of this place whose musical talents are universally praised and whom the Elector has sent to Haydn in Vienna. He proposes also to compose Schiller's 'Freude,' and indeed strophe by strophe. I expect something perfect, for as far as I know him he is wholly devoted to the great and the sublime."[4] The details of Beethoven's friendship with Fischenich are not fully known, but they both frequented the Josephinian reading society (the Lesegesellschaft) and the widow Koch's literary tavern (the Zehrgarten), and they probably were associated at the university as well.[5] Although Fischenich was only two years older than Beethoven, the young professor of philosophy and jurisprudence apparently regarded Beethoven as his protégé and attempted to impart to the young composer his own passion for Schiller's works and ideas.

There is no reason to believe that Beethoven's attraction to Schiller— or his devotion to "the great and the sublime"—began only in late 1792, when he told Fischenich of his resolve. Schiller's first dramas, *The Robbers* and *Fiesco*, were presented at Bonn as early as the season of 1782–1783 by the Grossmann and Helmuth theater company, a troupe that is closely intertwined with Beethoven's early life.[6] Its director was a frequent visitor, with his wife, at the Beethoven lodgings, and its music director, Christian Gottlob Neefe, was Beethoven's teacher. Schiller's early works were widely circulated in Bonn, and his first applications of Kantian ideas to aesthetic and literary subjects contributed to the Kant fever that swept German intellectual life during the period. So great was Schiller's popularity that, upon Beethoven's departure for Vienna in 1792, no fewer than three of his friends chose passages from *Don Carlos* (1786) for their entries in his farewell album (Stammbuch).[7] That Beethoven shared this enthusiasm for Schiller's exuberant blend of Sturm und Drang sentiment and enlightened aestheticism is evident from his own inscription of quotations from *Don Carlos* in the autograph albums of friends during his early Vienna years. For example, on 22 May 1793, he wrote in one such album: "I am not wicked—Hot blood is my fault—my crime is that I am young. I am not wicked, truly not wicked. Even though wildly surging emotions may betray my heart, yet my heart is good" (act 2, sc. 2).[8] And to his dearest friend, Lorenz von Breuning, he wrote on 1 October 1797:

> Truth exists for the wise,
> Beauty for a feeling heart.
> They belong to each other.   (Act 4, sc. 21)[9]

There was no personal contact between Beethoven and Schiller, nor is there any mention of Beethoven in Schiller's writings.[10] In addition to Fischenich, however, Schiller and Beethoven had another close mutual friend, the Viennese piano manufacturer and musician Johann Andreas Streicher, who was one of Beethoven's unwavering friends for three decades, beginning in the mid-1790s. He and Schiller had studied together at the military academy in Stuttgart during the early 1780s, and in 1782 Streicher assisted Schiller in deserting from his regiment and accompanied him to Mannheim, where he provided him with sorely needed funds to maintain himself. They separated permanently in 1785, vowing, according to Streicher's memoirs of the relationship, "not to write to each other till Streicher was a kapellmeister and Schiller a minister of state."[11]

O N E of the Schiller entries in Beethoven's Bonn farewell album might have been inscribed as an epigraph on the Ninth Symphony:

> Tell him, in manhood, he must still revere
> The dreams of early youth, nor ope the heart
> Of Heaven's all-tender flower to canker-worms
> Of boasted reason,—nor be led astray
> When, by the wisdom of the dust, he hears
> Enthusiasm, heavenly-born, blasphemed.
>
> (*Don Carlos*, act 4, sc. 21)

Ultimately, Beethoven indeed proved that he had not forgotten "the dreams of early youth." But evidently he could not pursue such dreams until he had first achieved maturity and until the past had been—or seemed to be—irrevocably lost. The reaffirmation of early enthusiasms could perhaps occur only after those enthusiasms had been tempered by experience, by doubt, and even by disillusionment. Thus it was necessary for Beethoven's "Ode to Joy" project to undergo a long process of germination. But as in the similar case of *Faust,* which Goethe claimed to have carried with him for more than half a century, completion of Beethoven's "Ode to Joy" was not simply the long-postponed maturation of an early idea. Rather, it was at the same time a qualitatively new idea, one that could not have been brought to fruition at an earlier time.

So it would have been altogether appropriate for the "Ode to Joy" to be set aside. Surprisingly, however, Beethoven probably did set the poem to music during his early Vienna years: a sketchbook of 1798–1799 contains music for one line of the poem ("Muss ein lieber Vater wohnen"), and in 1803 Ferdinand Ries wrote to Nikolaus Simrock in Bonn, offering for publication Beethoven's "Ode to Joy" as one of eight lieder which had been composed within the preceding "four years."[12] If the song was indeed composed, it has disappeared without a trace. Although Beethoven may have withdrawn this song as musically unworthy, political factors may also have been at play in the failure to publish it. Schiller's works were banned for fifteen years by the Habsburg censors, beginning in 1793, when *The Robbers* was declared "immoral" and "dangerous." Beethoven had written to Simrock in 1794: "You dare not raise your voice here or the police will take you into custody."[13] For some years he apparently exercised caution in the expression of his antifeudal, rebellious attitudes, and perhaps he moderated his enthusiasm for Schiller in deference to Emperor Franz's imperial censor, if not his police. Schiller's early radicalism, too, had long been tempered by discretion and by a more stoical view of historical events. He had repudiated the consequences of the French Revolution, found safe havens (first at Jena and then at Weimar), and had both sought and obtained the insignia of princely approval, including in 1802 a patent of nobility. Thomas Mann observed with a mixture of curiosity and regret that Schiller "always transposed his enthusiasm for liberty and liberation to other nations: to the Netherlands in *Don Carlos,* to France in *The Maid of Orleans,* to Switzerland in *William Tell.*"[14]

But neither Schiller's nor Beethoven's art was seriously affected by such matters as political timidity. Although Schiller had long since abandoned the fervent tone of his early rebellious dramas, he remained true to his antityrannical sentiments and to his recurrent themes of fraternity and national liberation. During these very years,

1803 and 1804, Beethoven not only contemplated dedicating his Third Symphony to France's first consul but apparently seriously considered taking up residence in the capital of revolutionary France. And despite the censorship, in 1805 the closing quatrains of Sonnleithner's text to *Fidelio* contain a slightly modified couplet from the second verse of Schiller's "Ode":

Wer ein holdes Weib errungen
Mische seinen [stimm in unsern] Jubel ein.

It was for aesthetic rather than political reasons that Schiller seems to have lost his passion for the "Ode to Joy" during his later years. In September 1800, he sent Körner a new edition of his poems, advising him that he would "look in vain for several of them."[15] Körner, who often acted as Schiller's literary and political conscience, wrote reproachfully on 10 September: "Many will not forgive you for having excluded the 'Artists' and the 'Ode to Joy.'"[16] Schiller responded: "I regard the 'Ode to Joy' . . . as decidedly faulty; and although it has a certain quantity of fiery enthusiasm to back it, it is nevertheless a bad poem, and denotes a degree of cultivation which I must leave far behind me if I am to produce anything at all decent; but as it is written against the bad taste of the age, it has acquired a certain degree of popularity." He concluded, wistfully, but firmly: "Your admiration of this poem may be attributed to the time at which it was written; but that is its only merit, and that only *for us*, and not for the world, or the art of poetry."[17] Despite his seeming firmness, Schiller not long thereafter once again took up the "Ode to Joy." In 1803, two years before his death, he published a revised version of the poem. This revised version is what provides the basis for Beethoven's eventual setting of the ode in the Ninth Symphony.

Apart from the ode, Beethoven set only a few texts by Schiller: a single verse of a ballade, "Das Mädchen aus der Fremde," in 1810; a twelve-bar setting of "Song of the Monks" (WoO 104) from *William Tell* in 1817; and two canons on the closing lines of *The Maid of Orleans*, one written in 1813 (WoO 163) and the other in 1815 (WoO 166). Beethoven told Czerny: "Schiller's poems are very difficult to set to music. The composer must be able to lift himself far above *the poet;* who can do that in the case of Schiller? In this respect Goethe is much easier."[18] Nevertheless, when in 1809 Beethoven was offered a choice of composing incidental music to either *William Tell* or *Egmont*, he chose *Tell*, but he was assigned the Goethe play by theater director Joseph von Hartl. At this time the censorship of Schiller virtually came to an end in Vienna, and his dramas soon dominated the programs at the Theater-an-der-Wien. Perhaps this is one reason why Beethoven wrote to Breitkopf and Härtel in August 1809 for editions of Goethe's and Schiller's complete works: "These two poets are my favorites, as are also Ossian and Homer."[19] Beethoven did not receive the editions from his Leipzig publishers; they rather advised him of the cost, overlooking his broad hint that he hoped to receive them gratis. He did acquire a volume published in 1810 that included *The Maid of Orleans* and *William Tell*.[20] And in a letter to Bettina Brentano of early 1811, he sought to impress that literary lady with several allusions to Schiller. Referring to the frustration of his marriage plans, he sighed "'Pity my fate,' I cry with Johanna."[21] And when he was questioned about the sketchbook that he invariably carried on his walks, Beethoven was wont to paraphrase Schiller's Joan: "Without my banner I dare not go."[22]

In 1812, the "Ode to Joy" project was momentarily rekindled. Beethoven interrupted the sketching of his Seventh and Eighth Symphonies to jot down some ideas on "Freude schöner Götterfunken," intended either for a D-minor symphony or a choral overture. In 1814–1815, this thematic material was utilized in the *Namensfeier* Overture, op. 115.

During the last fifteen years of Beethoven's life, passages from or allusions to Schiller's works appear frequently in his correspondence, his conversation books, and his Tagebuch. These show that Beethoven was quite familiar with Schiller's poetry, with at least some of his essays, and with such plays as *The Maid of Orleans, William Tell, Maria Stuart, Fiesco*, and *The Bride of Messina*. Three Schiller quotations appear in Beethoven's Tagebuch in 1817.[23] The first of these is the transcription of the "Song of the Monks" from *William Tell*—in anticipation of the setting for three male voices in memory of Beethoven's friend, the violinist Wenzel Krumpholz. Also from *William Tell* is the phrase, "He who would reap tears should sow love," an apparent reference to Beethoven's relationship with his nephew, Karl. And perhaps as an expression of his remorse over separating Karl from his mother, Beethoven noted these rather pre-Freudian lines from the close of *The Bride of Messina*:

This one thing I feel and clearly perceive:
Life is not the sovereign good,
But the greatest evil is guilt.

Schiller's essay "The Mission of Moses" also was known to Beethoven, for he copied from it three Egyptian ritual inscriptions, which he kept under glass on his desk until the end of his life.[24]

Those who knew Beethoven in his later years indicated that Schiller remained one of Beethoven's favorite German writers. Franz Grillparzer reported that Beethoven "held Schiller in very high regard," and Karl Holz recalled that Beethoven "had underlined everything in Schiller's poems that constituted his [own] confession of faith."[25] Aloys Weissenbach and Johann R. Schultz related that Beethoven habitually equated Schiller and Goethe, as was conventional at the time, but several members of Beethoven's conversation book circle—a group not often given to disagreements with Beethoven—expressed their own preference for Schiller. "Goethe is more of an egoist," wrote Karl Bernard; Holz declared that Schiller is "more exalted" in his attitude toward humanity.[26] And Schiller was the special passion of Beethoven's nephew. Karl memorized many of his poems and declaimed them at school; he preferred Schiller, not only to Goethe but to Shakespeare as well. Beethoven would not go quite that far, and one of their conversations closed with Karl grudgingly acknowledging Shakespeare's preeminence: "That is generally said, but Schiller is much dearer to me."[27]

As early as May 1820, Beethoven determined to buy an edition of Schiller's works for Karl.[28] The boy repeatedly brought up the subject, chiding his uncle on the condition of his library, and on several occasions Schindler was reminded to pursue the matter with the booksellers. But Schindler, who despised Karl, was in no hurry to bear him gifts. Not until the appearance in 1824 of the Grätz pocket edition of Schiller's *Werke* by the Viennese publisher Jacob Mayer did the works of Schiller in twenty-one volumes, plus three brochures of engravings, find their way into Beethoven's library.[29]

Whether the striking convergence between Schiller's and Beethoven's ideas is a matter of affinity or of direct influence remains an open question. Naturally they shared a common intellectual heritage, one that included worship of classicism and the ancients, adherence to German varieties of Enlightenment philosophy (especially Kantian conceptions of morality, religion, and art), and rejection of tyranny and arbitrary rule in favor of government by an idealized aristocratic elite.[30] Neither man was a democrat. Goethe said of Schiller that he was "far more of an aristocrat than he himself."[31] Schiller's phrase "The majority is nonsense" finds its echo in Beethoven's "They say *vox populi, vox dei*. I never believed it."[32] Both men placed their faith in princely saviors to rectify injustice and to cleanse society of irrational tyranny. Schiller's Karl Moor decried "this weak, effeminate age" and called for a sword that he might "strike this generation of vipers to the quick."[33] Similarly, Beethoven raged, "Our epoch requires powerful minds to scourge these frivolous, contemptible, miserable wretches of humanity," adding—for he was really a gentle soul—"repulsive as it is to my feelings to cause pain to any man."[34] Both men insisted that excellence and genius could not be measured by ordinary standards of morality. Beethoven once declaimed: "*Power* is the moral principle of those who excel others, and it is also mine."[35] And Schiller, in the Preface to *The Robbers*, insisted: "An exuberance of strength which bursts through all the barriers of law, must of necessity conflict with the rules of social life."[36] The simultaneous acceptance and defiance of necessity is a striking characteristic of these men. Schiller's thought, "Happy is he who learns to bear what he cannot change!" has its parallel in Beethoven's "Plutarch has shown me the path of resignation," as well as in his Tagebuch notation from the *Iliad*: "Fate gave man the courage to endure."[37] Despite such sentiments, neither man consistently advocated the acceptance of suffering. Beethoven's affirmation of free will, "I will seize Fate by the throat; it shall certainly not bend and crush me completely," has its close equivalent in Schiller's "Let evil destiny show its face: our safety is not in blindness, but in facing our dangers."[38] It is also echoed in Schiller's "On the Pathetic," in which he claimed: "The first law of the tragic art was to represent suffering nature. The second law is to represent the resistance of morality to suffering."[39]

There is a deep kinship between Beethoven's touching Tagebuch entry, "All evil is mysterious . . . when viewed alone; it is all the more ordinary the more one talks about it with others; it is easier to endure because that which we fear becomes totally known; it seems as if one has overcome some great evil," and Schiller's aesthetic universalization of this thought: "Man rises above any natural terror as soon as he knows how to mold it, and transform it into an object of his art."[40] And although Beethoven left no formal expression of his religious theory, the many passages that he extracted from a wide range of religious texts show that he fully agreed with Schiller, who wrote: "Religion itself, the idea of a Divine Power, lies under the veil of all religions; and it must be permitted to the poet to represent it in the form which appears the most appropriate to his subject."[41]

Schiller may have influenced Beethoven's decision to close the Ninth Symphony with a choral movement. In 1818, Beethoven planned what he called a "symphony in the ancient modes" which would utilize two innovations. It would unite pagan and Christian style elements—"Greek myth" and "Cantique Ecclesiastique"—and it would use a chorus.[42] Both of these innovations were possibly inspired by a reading of the central ideas of the preface to Schiller's *Bride of Messina*. That preface, entitled "The Use of the Chorus in Tragedy," urges that the tragic poet reinstate the chorus of the Attic tragedians as a means of penetrating "to the most simple, original, and genuine motives of action." The chorus, explained Schiller, "appeals to the sense with an imposing grandeur. It forsakes the contracted sphere of incidents to dilate itself over the past and future, over distant times and nations, and general humanity, to deduce the grand results of life, and pronounce the lessons of wisdom." Although Schiller made reference here to a dramatic rather than a musical chorus, the musical implications of this theory are readily apparent. Schiller noted that the chorus infuses a "bold lyrical freedom" into tragedy and that it achieves its effect "in conjunction with the whole sensible influence of melody and rhythm, in tones and movements." As for the fusion of Greek mythology and Christianity, Schiller observed: "I have blended together the Christian religion and the Pagan mythology, and introduced recollections of Mohammedan superstition."

Beethoven never composed his "Adagio Cantique," as he called it in 1818, but the notion of using a chorus to climax a symphony was not forgotten. Furthermore, the fusion of pagan and Christian religious motifs in the text is central to the "Ode to Joy" and gives it much of its emotional power. And although Beethoven's Ninth is not his "symphony in the ancient modes," the "Seid umschlungen Millionen" passage of its finale is firmly rooted in the ecclesiastical modes.

This connection is highly speculative, for there is no direct evidence that Beethoven read the introduction to *The Bride of Messina*, although his Tagebuch for 1817 shows that he knew the play, which was customarily printed with the introduction. There is also no evidence that Beethoven actually read or was influenced by Schiller's major aesthetic writings, such as *Letters on the Aesthetic Education of Man*, in which Schiller elaborated on his theories of art's humanizing function and of the "play impulse," or "Concerning Naive and Sentimental Poetry," which set forth clearly for the first time the distinction between Classic and Romantic art.[43]

But if Beethoven was not directly influenced by Schiller's visionary writings on art and politics, certain of his compositions can in a sense be regarded as musical embodiments of Schiller's aesthetic utopianism. Schiller, in his desire to heal what he described as the "wounds" that civilization had dealt to an innocent humanity, in his quest for a social condition that would restore man's harmony with nature and permit the unfettered development of human creativity, proposed that art's function was to hold out the "effigy of [the] ideal" as a goal toward which mankind could strive.[44] He proposed that the idyllic vision of such a future condition was modeled upon memories of a lost paradise: "All nations that have a history have a paradise, an age of innocence, a golden age. Nay, more than this, every man has his paradise, his golden age, which he remembers with more or less enthusiasm, according as he is more or less poetical."[45] However, Schiller insisted that the artist's responsibility was not to advocate a contemplative return to Arcadia but to portray a future Elysium, a condition of harmony and joy that would transcend both the idealizations of memory and the malaise of an alienated present: "A state such as this is not merely met with before the dawn of civilization; it is also the state to which civilization aspires . . . The idea of a similar state, and the belief of the possible reality of this state is the only thing that can reconcile man with all the evils to which he is exposed in the path of civilization." It is therefore "of infinite importance for the man engaged in the path of civilization to see confirmed in a sensuous manner the belief that this idea can be accomplished in the world of sense, that this state of innocence can be realized in it."[46]

This yearning for a paradisiacal condition was not without its biographical sources, experiences that predisposed both Schiller and Beethoven to their passionate desire for brotherhood and reconciliation, to their shared dream of a world of innocent joy. Beethoven's life and his art can be envisaged as a search for Elysium, for "one day of

pure joy" as he phrased it in the Heiligenstadt Testament, for fraternal and familial harmony, as well as for a just and enlightened social
order. With the "Ode to Joy" of the Ninth Symphony, that search
found its symbolic fulfillment, though not its conclusion. And it was
both fitting and inevitable that Beethoven turned to Schiller for assistance in mapping the geography of Elysium.[47]

15

The Quest for Faith

LITTLE is known about the nature or extent of Beethoven's religious beliefs during his Bonn years. He was born and baptized into a Catholic family, but apart from neighbors' conventional references to his mother's piety there are no reports that his parents were practicing Catholics, let alone that they instilled any of their sons with religious feeling. The grade school—the Tirocinium—which Beethoven attended for several years (and where he learned so little) was a Catholic institution, and in later years he approvingly told the Giannatasio del Rio family that he had been brought up "with proverbs" by a Jesuit teacher.[1] Before he was ten years old Beethoven frequented a number of the local churches: he had organ lessons and training in church ritual from Friar Willibald Koch of the Franciscan monastery and from Zenser, organist of the Münsterkirche. His venerable teacher, Gilles van den Eeden, is said to have sent the boy to play organ at High Mass, and a certain Pater Hanzmann arranged for him to play organ at six o'clock morning Mass at the cloister of the Minorites. Although these events primarily reflected Beethoven's endeavor to broaden his musical education, their religious implications cannot be wholly overlooked.

Beethoven composed no religious music at Bonn. Appropriately enough, his only Bonn music to a religious text was a harmonization of the *Lamentations of Jeremiah,* written as a practical joke intended to prevent the singer from locating the final cadence.[2] However, a hint of the young composer's desire to believe in God appears in the text of one of his very first lieder, "An einen Säugling," WoO 108, composed when he was twelve years old: "You still don't know whose child you are . . . There is some occult giver who cares for all of us . . . After the years have gone by, if I am pious and a believer,

216

even He will be revealed." Whether this is a quest for God or for a father is less than clear; nor will it ever be clarified, for to Beethoven, who spent much of his life seeking a noble and worthy replacement for the mediocre and alcoholic tenor who had begotten him, the notions of deity and fatherhood were inextricably intertwined.

Beethoven came to manhood during the enlightened decade of Emperor Joseph II, and for him and many of his compatriots religion occupied a position subordinate to Enlightenment, especially Kantian, conceptions of morality. The electorate of Cologne was itself a Catholic principality; most of the elector's subjects were Catholic, and the external forms of the religion were observed there. But what Schiedermair called "enlightened electoral Catholicism" was really a compromise ideology that permitted a relatively peaceful coexistence between the church and a rationalism that was unsympathetic to religious dogma, though it did not exclude religious faith.[3] Although many of the leading intellectuals and artists of Bonn—with whom Beethoven associated at the Lesegesellschaft, the university, and the Zehrgarten—were anticlerical Freemasons and Illuminists, they were by no means atheists. As with most adherents of the German *Aufklärung*, they did not seek to *Écrasez l'infâme* in the manner of the followers of Voltaire and the Encyclopedists; rather, they proclaimed moral consciousness as the standard of conduct, rejecting the primacy of dogmatic, biblical, and hierarchical authority in favor of a universal, humanistic religion. The Kantians among them believed that, although man, possessing free will, required neither the idea of God nor any incentive other than law to comprehend his duty, this very freedom served to confirm his subjective belief in the existence of God. Beethoven's principal teacher, Christian Gottlob Neefe, was a Protestant believer despite his Masonic and Illuminist propensities. Even the revolutionary Eulogius Schneider preached in December 1789 against the divinity of Christ, not as a disbeliever but, like Lessing, as a proponent of Jesus the sublime teacher of mankind.[4]

Beethoven was not the only composer to be affected by the antidogmatic temper of the Josephinian decade. Between 1782 and 1790 neither Mozart nor Haydn received commissions for church music; it was not until after the death of Joseph II in 1790 that Mozart wrote his *Ave verum* and his Requiem, and not until 1796 that Haydn returned to church music with his first mass in fourteen years, expressing regret that he had theretofore spent so much time in the composition of sonatas and symphonies. Unlike Haydn, Beethoven wrote no religious music during his first decade in Vienna. Nor is there any hint in his correspondence or in the reminiscences of his contemporaries before the turn of the century that he held religious beliefs. Reportedly Haydn, in a fit of pique, once called him an atheist, and although this may merely express Haydn's resentment at his pupil's unwillingness to acknowledge a musical rather than a heavenly deity, it may also reflect the prevailing view of Beethoven's religiosity.[5] And there is more than a hint of contempt for Roman Catholicism in one of Beethoven's letters of this period. Writing to Hoffmeister on 8 April 1802, Beethoven imperiously rejected a proposal that he write a sonata celebrating the French Revolution (or Bonaparte: the reference is not altogether clear): "Now that Bonaparte has concluded his Concordat with the Pope—to write a sonata of that kind?—If it were even a Missa pro Sancta Maria a tre voci or a Vesper or something of that kind—In that case I would instantly take up my paint-brush—and with fat pound notes dash off a Credo in unum. But, good Heavens, such a sonata—in these newly developing Christian times—Ho ho—there you must leave me out."[6]

However, at this very time, with the onset of serious signs of his deafness, appear the first intimations that, in Cooper's words, "the natural springs of religious feeling in him were unspoiled."[7] At first Beethoven lashed out in anger: "I have often cursed my Creator"; "I have cursed Him for exposing His creatures to the slightest hazard, so that the most beautiful blossom is thereby often crushed and destroyed."[8] He also reaffirmed his adherence to the Stoicism of the Romans: "*Plutarch* has shown me the *path of resignation.*"[9] But in the Heiligenstadt Testament he appealed directly to a personal and protective deity: "Almighty God, you look down into my innermost soul, you see into my heart and you know that it is filled with love for humanity and a desire to do good."[10] It was during these critical years that Beethoven composed *Christus am Oelberge*, op. 85, which seems to embody his identification with a suffering savior.[11] At this time he also wrote the Gellert Songs, op. 48 (composed in 1801 or early 1802), which were settings of religious poems, including a prayer, a celebration of the works of God in nature, a psalm, and a plea for forgiveness:

> Against Thee only, against Thee have I sinned, and often done
> evil in Thy sight.

Thou seest the guilt which proclaims the curse upon me.
See also, O God, my wretchedness.

Composed in 1803 is another lied, "Der Wachtelschlag," WoO 129, containing pastoral invocations to fear, love, thank, and trust in the Lord. Of course, it is dangerous to try to connect a composer's beliefs, religious or otherwise, with the texts that he happens to set to music.[12] In the present instance, however, there may be some justification for suspending skepticism, for these works were not commissioned, so far as is known, but, like most of Beethoven's lieder, were freely chosen because of his affinity for their texts.

The deep personal, musical, and ideological crisis that Beethoven underwent during these years seems to have momentarily brought his religious feelings to the surface. But with the subsidence of the crisis and the consolidation of his stylistic "new path," the external manifestations of his religious impulse waned once again. In any event, religious music disappeared from Beethoven's workshop for half a decade, despite the popularity of *Christus am Oelberge,* which clearly called for, but never received, a sequel. Beethoven remained deeply involved in "Enlightened" projects on secular themes—the *Eroica* Symphony, *Fidelio,* and *Egmont*—and his search for faith remained centered on the standard Enlightenment precepts of humanity, universal brotherhood, progress, morality, and reason. However, the rending in 1804 of the Bonaparte inscription of the *Eroica* Symphony signaled that Beethoven had begun to question the infallibility of enlightened leaders and was beginning to search elsewhere for an immutable anchor for his beliefs.

There seems little doubt that Beethoven's worship of nature had deeply religious overtones. This worship went far beyond the conventional pastoral and arcadian evocations characteristic of the followers of Rousseau and Schiller to border upon religious fervor: "Every tree in the countryside said to me: 'Holy! Holy!' In the forest, enchantment! Who can express it all?"[13] Even more explicit is the passage on a leaf of sketches: "Almighty in the forest! I am happy, blissful in the forest: every tree speaks through you, O God! What splendor! In such a woodland scene, on the heights there is calm, calm in which to serve Him."[14] Viewed in this context, the *Pastoral* Symphony (1807–1808), with its closing song of thanks to a benevolent deity, may be counted among those works that give expression to Beethoven's religious feelings.

Around 1808 and 1809, Beethoven showed renewed interest in

church music. He began to consider an oratorio on a religious subject, *Die Höllenfahrt des Erlösers*, and he asked Breitkopf & Härtel to send him Mozart's Requiem and Haydn's masses.[15] His only religious work of these years, however, was the commissioned Mass in C, op. 86, a work that he termed "especially close to my heart" but which initially met with a negative reception and was published only after much persuasion and a reduction in his fee. In a letter to Breitkopf & Härtel, Beethoven referred to the "utterly frigid attitude of our age to works of this kind," and this may well have been one factor in his avoidance of religious music for another decade.[16]

Beethoven's deep attachment to Christian Sturm's *Reflections on the Works of God in Nature* may have represented his attempt to strike a compromise between nature worship, enlightened ideas, and Christianity. He probably knew this book from his Bonn days, perhaps through Neefe, but the heavily marked and annotated copy that has survived dates from an edition of 1811.[17] Sturm's *Reflections* is a voluminous series of miniature essays on the wonders, great and small, of natural law and universal phenomena. These marvels are ascribed to the actions of God, to whom the author composes devout hymns of praise and of thanksgiving. Sturm, whose avowed purpose was the reconciliation of science and religion, was a staunch friend of the Enlightenment, of which he asked only that it make room for his God: "You know how much I honor the religion of Reason, but that cannot be at the cost or to the diminution of the religion of Christ, which . . . must be taught and praised."[18] Sturm took from the eighteenth-century philosophers the view of God as a purposeful and divine watchmaker delicately adjusting the mechanisms of nature and supervising the movements of the heavenly spheres. Beethoven was evidently much taken by Sturm's view of God as the supreme engineer of natural phenomena, by his conception of nature as "a school for the heart," and by his proposition of direct and unmediated contact between man and God which required no intervention of church or priest.

For Beethoven had little use for organized religion. Apart, perhaps, from his feebly accepting the last rites upon the urging of friends and family and from his having once taken his nephew to confession in order to avoid charges of negligence as Karl's guardian, he was never a formal observer of any religion, let alone a churchgoer. He was completely lacking in piety toward the icons and assumptions of Christianity and even displayed, on at least one occasion, a brash irreverence for the divinity of Christ.[19] There is more than one sign that he regarded hierarchical religion and churchmen with disdain. Meeting the Catholic composer Abbé Stadler once at Steiner's music shop, he knelt before him and jestingly asked his blessing. The abbé exaggeratedly mumbled a prayer and said, "If it does no good, 'twill do no harm." Beethoven thereupon "kissed his hand amid the laughter of the bystanders."[20] One can also hear the scoffing raillery of the freethinker in Beethoven's Canon, WoO 178, for the good abbé: "Signor Abate! I'm ailing. Holy Father, hasten to give me thy benediction. Unless you hasten, go to the devil!" And there was surely more mockery than naiveté in Beethoven's reported recommendations to Catholic priests that they read Sturm's *Reflections*—the sermons of a Lutheran minister—from their pulpits.[21]

THE long crisis that inaugurated Beethoven's late style, though it coincided with the fading of the Age of Reason and accompanied the undermining of Beethoven's own rationality during the battle over the guardianship of his nephew, did not lead him to reject Enlightened ideals as such. He never consciously gave way to the blandishments of mysticism. He abjured the intrusion of the miraculous and supernatural into art and literature because, he wrote, "it has a soporific effect on feeling and reason."[22] In his Tagebuch of 1812–1818, which includes his intimate communion with a variety of deities, he wrote: "One should not seek refuge in melancholy against the loss of riches, nor in friendlessness against the loss of friends, nor in abstention from procreation against the death of children, but in Reason against everything."[23]

Beethoven continued to exalt "Sovereign Reason" as that which counteracted the weaknesses of the flesh and tendencies toward moral error.[24] When Moscheles wrote under the last bars of his piano arrangement of *Fidelio*, "Finished with God's help," Beethoven scathingly added, "O man, help thyself!"[25] However, the Enlightenment's optimistic commonplaces were now insufficient to one who had glimpsed both the irrational and the divine within himself, who had witnessed the terrors of invasion, war, social disruption, and Metternichean repression. Beethoven was no longer wholly satisfied with the reasonable platitudes of the Enlightenment, nor was he alone in his search for a spiritual touchstone in an age of inquietude. The Romantic poets and the idealist philosophers alike were then involved in an exploration of the collective beliefs of the past; they sought meaning in medieval communality, in the *Volksgeist*, in the idea of nationhood. As Heine observed, the Romantics "wished to restore the Catholicism of the Middle Ages, for they felt that in this Catholicism there still survived many sacred recollections of their first ancestors, many splendid memorials of their earliest national life."[26] Schleiermacher's and Schelling's pantheism, Hegel's phenomenology of the phases of the human spirit, Fichte's nationalist evocation of a transcendent utopian future, and Novalis's glorification of the miraculous and the irrational—all may be seen as efforts to discover new patterns of belief to replace outworn, defeated, and fragmenting ideologies. Catholicism itself once again became a living force among the educated—especially among the Romantics—who were attracted, not primarily by its theology, but by its serene world-view and its deep sense of human fellowship.

During the period following the close of the Napoleonic Wars a religious revival swept through Vienna. An order of latter-day Redemptorists (called Liguorians) was founded in 1816 by Clemens Maria Hofbauer, who preached a consoling personal religion with mystical overtones and who successfully played upon the yearnings for salvation among those—especially the poor, the lesser nobility, and the intellectuals—who felt excluded from or unsympathetic to the official imperial version of Josephinian Catholicism. Hofbauer's leading disciple was the dramatist Zacharias Werner, a former Freemason, whose emotionally overheated sermons attracted large audiences for several years. Beethoven merrily told his young friend and publisher Tobias Haslinger to "go every Sunday to Pater Werner, who will show you the little book by which you may go to heaven in a jiffy," but unlike such Romantic writers as Collin, the Schlegels, and Clemens Brentano, he was repelled by the revivalist and mystical character of this movement, if the negative comments by members of Beethoven's conversation-book circle are evidence of his views as well.[27] However, he was apparently more tolerant of, and perhaps leaned toward, the teachings of Bishop Johann Michael Sailer, who was a leading representative of a form of Catholic Fideism of the day and who headed a school at Landshut in Bavaria to which Beethoven hoped to send his nephew. Sailer, an "adversary of literal orthodoxy, partisan of a religion of sentiment, who put the Christian in direct contact with the revealed verities of God," admired Sturm's works and preached a religion of the heart that bears a strong resemblance to spiritual trends in Protestantism.[28] Although there is no evidence, apart from Beethoven's ownership of several of Sailer's books, that the composer was an adherent of his or of any other theological tendency or school, Beethoven may well have been drawn to the ecumenical and sentimental Catholicism of his friend Antonie Brentano's spiritual guide.

It was during this critical period that Beethoven freely gave expression to his yearnings for solace and to his feelings of dependency upon a supernatural being; and he now began a complex, apparently random search for religious meaning in Eastern and Egyptian ritual, Classical mythology, and Christian theology. Some of the outlines of this inner journey can be traced in his correspondence, his Tagebuch, and his choice of texts.

The opening recitative of his second setting of "An die Hoffnung," op. 94 (1815), contains the tremulous question: "Is there a God? May he some day grant the promise of our tearful longings? May he, this enigmatic being, reveal himself on some judgment day? Man must hope! He may not question!" But such doubts are not present in the Tagebuch where he wrote: "All things flowed clear and pure out of God. If afterwards I became darkened through passion for evil, I returned, after manifold repentance and purification, to the elevated and pure source, to the Godhead—and to your art."[29] And again: "God, God, my refuge, my rock, O my all, you see my innermost heart . . . O hear, ever ineffable one, hear me, your unhappy, most unhappy of all mortals."[30]

In another Tagebuch entry Beethoven expressed the hope of finding tranquillity and fulfillment in composing for "a small chapel" where he would dedicate his works to "the glory of the Almighty, the eternal."[31] Elsewhere he is concerned to define his conception of God, perhaps seeking to find a rational explanation for his faith: "God is immaterial and that is why he surpasses every conception; as he is invisible, he cannot have a form. But from what we perceive of his works we can deduce that he is eternal, almighty, all-knowing, and all-present."[32] Appropriately, the Tagebuch closes, in late 1818, with these words, copied from Sturm: "Therefore, calmly will I submit myself to all inconstancy and will place all my confidence in your eternal goodness, O God! My soul shall rejoice in Thee, immutable Being. Be my rock, my light, forever my trust!"[33]

Beethoven's religious beliefs were scarcely limited to Christian forms, however. A Tagebuch notation of 1816 shows that the Classic-

Stoic conception of fate retained its hold upon him: "Show your power, Fate! We are not masters of ourselves. What has been decided must be, then so be it!"[34] Here Beethoven has relegated the god of wrath to Greek mythology, perhaps so that he may unambivalently look upon other deities as untainted gods of love and mercy. Always, Beethoven's desire to find a mode of accommodation to society warred with his equally strong rebellious tendencies. He sought the approval of the great and the powerful while—often simultaneously—lashing out against authority and its representatives. Perhaps this internal warfare found its theological analogy in a splitting of Beethoven's personal pantheon into sharply differentiated images of loving benevolence and relentless persecution.

Beethoven's religious search now began to extend to the more exotic religions as well. Like many of his contemporaries—virtually all of the Romantic poets and philosophers among them—he became for a time receptive to Indian philosophy, especially to its poetic evocations of an immaterial and omniscient God. He copied into the Tagebuch a translation of Sir William Jones's Vedantic "Hymn to Narayena":

> Spirit of Spirits, who through ev'ry part
> Of space expanded and of endless time,
> Beyond the stretch of lab'ring thought sublime,
> Badst uproar into beauteous order start,
> Before Heaven was, Thou art:
> Ere spheres beneath us roll'd or spheres above,
> Ere earth in firmamental ether hung,
> Thou sat'st alone; till, through thy mystick Love,
> Things unexisting to existence sprung,
> And grateful descant sung.[35]

The suppression of libidinal interest in reality, which is one of the central tenets of Indian thought, had special appeal to Beethoven. "Blessed is he who has suppressed all passions," he wrote in the Tagebuch.[36] Another entry refers to the extended, enforced silence of Brahman novitiates.[37] He was perhaps attracted to the Eastern religions because of their teaching of the need for systematic withdrawal of all attachment to the outer world as a precondition of wisdom and achievement. For it was especially in Beethoven's last decade that a sacrificial element, a notion of attainment through suffering, manifested itself. He wrote in June 1819 to Archduke

Rudolph: "There is hardly any good thing which can be achieved—without a sacrifice; and it is precisely the nobler and better man who seems to be destined for this more than other human beings no doubt in order that his virtue may be put to the test."[38] Even more expressively, in May 1816 he wrote to Marie Erdödy: "Man cannot avoid suffering; and in this respect his strength must stand the test, that is to say, he must endure without complaining and feel his worthlessness and then again achieve his perfection, that perfection which the Almighty will then bestow upon him."[39] On a personal level, Beethoven regarded the guardianship of his nephew as a divinely ordained mission, a burden that he was compelled to assume in accordance with some unspecified moral or religious imperative.

The East had no monopoly upon either asceticism or sacrifice. Beethoven wrote in his Tagebuch: "Endurance—Resignation—Resignation. Thus we may yet prevail over the most extreme misery."[40] Actually, Catholicism itself had developed the idea of sacrifice and abstinence to a fine art. As Feuerbach wrote: "God has sacrificed himself for man; therefore man must sacrifice himself to God . . . Hence the high significance attached to the denial of sexual love."[41] Beethoven's Tagebuch contains references to his vain struggle to remain chaste—a chastity that was both his expression of obedience to the moral law and, he firmly believed, a necessary precondition of his creativity.

From the East, Beethoven turned to ancient Egypt. Preserved under glass on his work table were his copies of two inscriptions from monuments to Egyptian mother goddesses, along with a third inscription from a later, patriarchal stage of Egyptian civilization:

> I am that which is.

> I am everything that is, that was, that will be. No mortal man has lifted my veil.

> He is of himself alone, and it is to this aloneness that all things owe their being.[42]

We cannot tell what attracted Beethoven to these passages. The Sterbas claimed that they expressed Beethoven's "grandiose narcissism." The juxtaposition of matriarchal and patriarchal views of the generative process may have constituted part of their appeal.[43] However, the religious import of these phrases is scarcely less fundamental. The reiterated "I am" originated in Egyptian and Babylonian ritual and later appeared in the Hebrew God's injunction to Moses: "I am that I am" (*Exod.* 3:13–14), which Cassirer described as the final form through which language elevates the deity to the realm of the absolute, "to a state that cannot be expressed through any analogy with things or names of things."[44] In these inscriptions and in his citations from Indian philosophy, Beethoven simultaneously encompasses conceptions of a timeless, immutable deity and of a protean deity whose nature is in a process of emergence—that which is, was, and shall be.[45] He was able to reach out toward the horizon of possibility as well as backward to a petrified and changeless conception of a perfected God, to unite the God of origins with the Messianic concern for what Isaiah called "the things that are not yet done" (*Isa.* 46:9–10). This spiritual cleavage perhaps mirrors the unceasing interplay in Beethoven (and in his art) between tradition and modernism, between his restless dissatisfaction with the present order of things and his reverence for the cultural and historical heritage. Just as Beethoven in his art is never content with any single manifestation of perfection, his striving for faith perpetually presses onward to embrace and to unify new territories of spiritual perception, and his faith is always leavened by a skepticism that made his an unending spiritual journey which could find provisional way stations but no final resting place.

DESPITE the private and unique shape of Beethoven's quest for belief, his religiosity belongs firmly in the mainstream of Enlightenment thought, which had sought to free religion from the sway of metaphysical thinking and the appeal to dogma, opening the way to a conception of the manifold nature of divinity and, with Hegel, to the transformation of divinity into a transcendent idea. In his rejection of the authority of Bible and church Beethoven shows his independence of all schools of Catholic and Reformation thought, which are postulated on dogma as the core of theology. In this and in his receptivity to a variety of religious views and experiences Beethoven is representative of advanced Enlightenment tendencies, for as Cassirer noted, the Enlightenment "emphatically proclaims the identity of religion amid all its different rites and despite all controversies regarding ideas and opinions."[46] Beethoven's acceptance of pagan and Eastern religion parallels the efforts of Leibniz, Montesquieu, Voltaire, and Herder to expand the concept of divinity to include the totality of its manifestations, each of which is accorded independent value. These efforts culminated in the mythological and philosophical writings of the early German Romantics, especially those who viewed themselves as inheritors of the rationalist traditions of the departed century. Like them, Beethoven sought to remove the veils that differentiate diverse forms of belief and to locate a substratum where they are fundamentally united—in a humanistic conception of an omniscient, omnipotent, ubiquitous, and benevolent father-God whose teachings are in conformity with the demands of morality and of reason. His personal journey recapitulates, and preserves, the collective strivings of the Age of Reason at the moment of its supersession.

As Beethoven's search proceeds, he does not abandon his older beliefs—in reason, in nature, in the divinity of mankind. He adopts as his own outlook young Kant's reconciliation of the existence of God with natural law: "When in the state of the world order and beauty shine forth, there is a God . . . Since this order has been able to flow from universal laws of Nature, the whole of Nature is inevitably an effect of the highest wisdom."[47] Beethoven wrote to Archduke Rudolph: "God . . . sees into my innermost heart and knows that as a man I perform most conscientiously and on all occasions the duties which humanity, God and Nature enjoin upon me."[48] "Humanity, God, and Nature"—here is Beethoven's spiritual trinity, which remains as the foundation of an ever-ascending superstructure of faith and of expectation.

Beethoven's circumnavigation of the world's religious systems is perhaps symbolically summarized in the dream that he related in a letter of 1821 to Haslinger: "Yesterday, as I found myself in the carriage on the way to Vienna, I was overcome by sleep . . . While thus slumbering, I dreamed that I was taking a very long journey, as far even as Syria, as far even as India, back again, as far even as Arabia; finally I came, indeed, to Jerusalem."[49] There would be a certain symmetry here if Beethoven's dream foreshadowed his literal return to the religion in which he had been baptized. However, Beethoven's reconciliation with Catholicism in his last years was at best partial and ambivalent.

THE liberation of the religious impulse during these years of crisis seems to have brought Beethoven to attempt the composition of his sole masterpiece in a religious musical form, the *Missa solemnis,* op. 123. This was not his only sacred project of these years. One or more additional masses, a Requiem, an oratorio, and several smaller works were planned as well, though none was actually composed. His last lieder, especially his "Abendlied unterm gestirnten Himmel," WoO 150, of 1820, are saturated with religious imagery and senti-ment. In 1818 he sketched in words the idea for a grandiose sym-phony which would combine Greek and Christian ecclesiastical elements, perhaps in an attempt at a musical union of diverse faiths paralleling that which he was seeking to form for himself. This was to be his "Adagio Cantique": "Pious song in a symphony in the ancient modes—Lord God we praise Thee—alleluia—either alone or as in-troduction to a fugue . . . In the text of the Adagio Greek myth, *Can-tique Ecclesiastique*—in the Allegro, feast of Bacchus."[50]

This idea found its fulfillment in the Ninth Symphony, which was conceived almost simultaneously with the *Missa solemnis.* To-gether they exemplify Beethoven's desire to hold both religious and secular-humanist ideas in one hand, so it is not surprising that the anachronistic Enlightenment model of "An die Freude" is penetrated by religious motifs, and the archaic liturgical model of the mass by secular elements. "Socrates and Jesus have been my models," he wrote in a conversation book in 1820, indicative of the evenhanded-ness with which he drew upon exemplary models from Christian and Classic sources.[51] In the end Beethoven drew no distinction be-tween the city of man and the City of God.

There was in Beethoven a deep yearning for immortality, but he was too much a child of the Enlightenment fully to yield to the com-forting promises of religion.[52] Thus, Beethoven was compelled to re-main content with the more modest consolations that flowed from religious belief—the solitary moment of happiness, the "one day of pure joy," the temporary easing of pain, the conditional assuagement of life's inevitable tragedies. A prayerful strain shows itself—in his diary entries, in his Gellert Songs, in his lieder of hope, sacrifice, and longing, and in the "plea for inner and outer peace" of the *Missa so-lemnis.* "An die Freude" is itself a prayer—that "All men become brothers" and be reconciled with the "dear father" who dwells be-yond the starry vault.

On occasion, Beethoven's prayers were answered, calling forth his heartfelt expression of thanks. On the sketches of the last move-ment of the *Pastoral* Symphony he wrote: "Oh Lord, we thank thee," and following his recovery from a near-fatal illness in the spring of 1825, he wrote in a conversation book: "Hymn of Thanksgiving to God of an Invalid on his Convalescence," words that in slightly altered form are now found on the Molto Adagio of the String Quartet in A minor, op. 132.[53] Gradually, with the passage of time, Beethoven had become strong enough to set aside the armor of heroic self-sufficiency which had to some degree impoverished his middle years. He found a new ability to call for help, to pray, to give thanks, to reveal weakness, and even provisionally to accept his dependence upon an immaterial and unknowable deity.

THE TAGEBUCH

16

Beethoven's Tagebuch

DURING the years 1812–1818 Beethoven kept a kind of diary, the Tagebuch, in which he made occasional entries. Although unsystematic and sometimes obscure, these entries illuminate many aspects of his life, personality, and creativity. Indeed, the Tagebuch is an unparalleled source of information on Beethoven's life during the personal and stylistic crisis that extended from the composition of the Seventh and Eighth symphonies in 1812 to the completion of the Hammerklavier Sonata in 1818, the years spanning the transition between his middle and late styles. No comparable document survives from any other period of Beethoven's life. The notebook that he kept between the end of 1792 and the beginning of 1794 is a log rather than a diary and, despite several entries of a subjective character, is primarily useful as a record of events and expenses.[1] From time to time, even during the years of the Tagebuch's composition, Beethoven made diarylike, prose entries on his sketches and autographs and, more rarely, on individual leaves of paper.[2] Subsequently such entries appeared occasionally in the conversation books. In later years, too, he recorded items pertaining to household affairs and finances on calendars.[3] But there is no sign that Beethoven kept a diary on any other occasion, and in view of his propensity for saving personal documents, it is doubtful that he did.

A personal crisis probably provided not only the background but the motive for beginning the Tagebuch. Of course, Beethoven was scarcely a stranger to crisis. But throughout his earlier life it was characteristic of him that he could confide the details of his inner struggles to intimate friends: to such men as Franz Wegeler, Karl Amenda, Stephan von Breuning, and Ignaz von Gleichenstein, and to such women as Helene von Breuning, Christiane von Lichnowsky,

Josephine Deym, Marie Erdödy, and Antonie Brentano. A man who could write to a beloved friend, "As soon as we are together again with no one to disturb us, you shall hear all about my real sorrows and the struggle within myself between life and death," surely had little need for the catharsis provided by a diary.[4] For such confessional diaries often arise in the absence of alternative outlets for the sharing of private feelings. But by the autumn of 1812, with the departure from Vienna of the Brentano family and his estrangement or withdrawal from Gleichenstein, Breuning, Erdödy, and other close friends, Beethoven found himself in a state of heightened isolation. This isolation, along with the powerful aftermath of the Immortal Beloved love affair, may have provided a stimulus for the Tagebuch, with its pathetic opening entries. Apparently the commitment of his feelings to paper helped Beethoven to secure some perspective on the critical events that had overtaken him, for he continued to make entries in the Tagebuch from time to time during the next six years, especially at moments of great inner turmoil and self-doubt.

The Tagebuch served several simultaneous functions. It was at once Beethoven's *journal intime* and his commonplace book. In the latter capacity it records events in its author's life, documents details of his productivity and musical projects, serves as a reminder of things done and to be done, and is a repository of citations and extracts from various writings, both classical and contemporary. The specialist will find unique and valuable data on a wide variety of subjects, from the cost of music paper to the date of final revision of *Fidelio*, from the minutiae of Beethoven's fees and finances to his exploration of older religious music in preparation for the *Missa solemnis*, and from descriptions of his hearing aids to specifications of the string forces for his concerts of early 1814.

But it is largely as a *journal intime* that the Tagebuch has been valued, for such a document is the quintessential record of subjective feelings. Unlike letters, the interpretation of which must take into account the recipient's personality, the relationship between writer and addressee, and the writer's personal interest, the *journal intime* is free from self-consciousness, if not always from self-deception. And unlike the consciously crafted memoir or autobiography, with its artifices and simplifications, the intimate diary contains raw responses to immediate experience, registering in this instance its author's uninhibited reactions to intensifying deafness, to the termination of his marriage project, to his brother Caspar Carl's death, and to his assumption of the guardianship of his nephew, Karl. On a less fateful plane it also records his frustrations over the trivialities of his financial and household affairs, his illnesses and medical treatments, his dissatisfaction with his servants, and other thorny details of his everyday life.

Such documents, of course, must be used with caution and supplemented by materials on the author's personality from more "objective" sources. For, as is typical of diaries, Beethoven's Tagebuch has little to say about his moments of happiness, his periods of good health, and his sense of kinship with his community. Nor does it adequately reflect the wide variety of Beethoven's activities or the extent of his productivity during these years. Wholly omitted, too, are historical and political references. Reading it, one would scarcely imagine that it was composed during a period that embraced the closing months of the Napoleonic Wars, the Congress of Vienna, and the onset of the age of Metternich in Austrian history.

The Tagebuch is unsurpassed as a record of Beethoven's intellectual interests. It superbly documents the intermingling of Classical, Enlightenment, and Romantic threads among his literary influences. His devotion to Homer, Plutarch, Schiller, and Christian Sturm's *Betrachtungen* is known from other sources, but it is only from the Tagebuch that one learns the extent (and in some instances even the existence) of Beethoven's attraction to Indian philosophy and literature, to the poetry of Herder, the *Fiabe* of Gozzi, the dramas of Alfieri, the "fate tragedies" of Zacharias Werner and Adolf Müllner, and the cosmological speculations of the young Kant. In the Tagebuch is ample confirmation of Beethoven's famous assertion: "From my childhood I have striven to grasp the meaning of the better and wiser people of every age."[5] This is not to imply that he possessed either unusual erudition or esoteric leanings. His intellectual inclinations were firmly in the mainstream of contemporary taste, and all his enthusiasms were shared by many educated men and women of his time. Predictably, the Tagebuch includes many quotations from the ancients, and several other entries appear to be quotations but may be Beethoven's own formulations of commonplace or proverbial ideas. The presence of an extract from a given author does not necessarily imply that Beethoven regarded it as a confession of his own faith, for certain of the texts—such as those by Müllner,

Werner, Homer, Herder, and Schiller—were probably copied with a view to possible musical setting. However, Beethoven usually set only those texts that reflected his own sentiments.

The Tagebuch is equally important for its documentation of Beethoven's religious faith, which apparently was greatly reinforced during these years. It contains several direct appeals, even prayers, to a personal God and exemplifies Beethoven's undogmatic adherence to a wide variety of non-Christian religious forms. His even-handed acceptance of Christian, Eastern, and Greco-Roman religious conceptions is typical of both Romantic and Enlightenment viewpoints, which rejected the authority of the church while postulating that religious truth is independent of its formal manifestations.

Beethoven appears here to be particularly drawn to Eastern and Rosicrucian ideas of purification, asceticism, sacrifice, and the suppression of libidinal interest in the outer world. Perhaps these notions helped to enhance his ability to absorb the shocks of mortality, increasing infirmity, deafness, guilt, and disappointment. Throughout, the Tagebuch testifies to the resiliency of Beethoven's personality, for in it he not only gave vent to his feelings and set down those problems that deeply troubled him but also weighed alternatives, considered consequences, and determined upon courses of action. The Tagebuch gives evidence of Beethoven's ability to counter adversity by renewed creative activity and by devotion to a stringent, if often misguided, standard of ethical action. Indeed, creativity and morality are the underlying themes of the Tagebuch, which in some sense is Beethoven's guide to virtue and proper conduct. It serves to justify his actions to himself (or to an imaginary "better" or "future" self), to assuage his guilt, and to redeem those faults to which he so freely confesses. And virtue, in turn, is only a means to a higher purpose: the safeguarding and furtherance of Beethoven's creativity.

Beethoven's central conflict—between his longings for human contact and his devotion to art—is writ large in the Tagebuch. The opening entry laments: "for you there is no longer any happiness except within yourself, in your art" (No. 1). And as the years pass, Beethoven explicitly calls for the subordination of his personal happiness to his creative work: "Everything that is called life should be sacrificed to the sublime and be a sanctuary of art" (No. 40); "Sacrifice once and for all the trivialities of social life to your art" (No. 169). Repeatedly Beethoven exhorts himself to break his isolation; he expresses his desire to take meals with friends, to share his griefs with others, and to hold fast to the threads of social and familial kinship. But his yearnings for friendship, warmth, and love are not quite compatible with his equally strong yearnings for conflict-free surroundings in which to develop his artistic gifts: "Live only in your art . . . This is . . . the *only existence* for you" (No. 88). In the last analysis Beethoven came to believe, however ambivalently and painfully, that he must follow a sacrificial path to artistic fulfillment.

AFTER Beethoven's death the Tagebuch passed, along with those personal papers that had not been appropriated by Anton Schindler, to Stephan von Breuning, the executor of Beethoven's estate. Following Breuning's own death on 4 June 1827, it came to Jacob Hotschevar, who had previously served as Johanna van Beethoven's lawyer in the litigation over the guardianship of Beethoven's nephew and who now replaced Breuning as executor and guardian. Hotschevar left Beethoven's papers in the custody of Artaria & Co. for a brief time. Then, according to Thayer, whose authority was Karl's wife, Caroline, Hotschevar delivered them to Karl "upon the attainment of his majority," which was to occur on 4 September 1830.[6] Thayer took for granted and apparently knew as a fact that these papers included the Tagebuch. This can be assumed to have been the case inasmuch as similar documents, notably the Heiligenstadt Testament and Beethoven's 1792 souvenir album did pass to Beethoven's family around this time. But we must allow some latitude concerning the precise date and recipient, for a note on the verso of the Heiligenstadt Testament indicates that Hotschevar received it from Artaria & Co. on 21 November 1827 and transmitted it to Karl's mother rather than to Karl himself. Clearly this required Karl's approval, for he was Beethoven's sole legatee.

The original manuscript of the Tagebuch has unfortunately been lost. After Karl's death in 1858 Beethoven's papers remained for a time in his widow's possession. She appears to have been the source for Thayer's statement that "a large part of them were borrowed from her . . . and sold by the borrower for his own profit!"[7] The identity of the mysterious "borrower"—if he indeed existed—is unknown, but there is evidence that Caroline van Beethoven herself disposed of some of the documents she had inherited. The souvenir album was purchased by the Austrian National Library from Gustav

Nottebohm in early 1871.[8] Nottebohm probably was acting on Caroline van Beethoven's behalf; and it seems reasonable to assume that she sold off other Beethoven autographs—perhaps including the Tagebuch—to interested collectors, just as Karl's mother had earlier disposed of the Heiligenstadt Testament.

In any event, because the original manuscript of the Tagebuch has not been found, its translation must be based on the surviving copies. Four of these are known at present. One forms part of the Fischhof manuscript in the Deutsche Staatsbibliothek in Berlin (catalogued Mus. ms. theor. 285). A second is in the Municipal Archive at Iserlohn (papers of Ludwig Nohl) in northwest Germany. A third is in the University Library at Bonn (Sammelband Velten, catalogued as S 1665). A fourth copy, in the Deutsche Staatsbibliothek, is part of Otto Jahn's literary estate. All four contain essentially the same material, presented in the same order. There are numerous differences, however, in orthography, punctuation, paragraphing, and (occasionally) wording and content, which make it important to establish the chronology of each and their textual relationship.

A L L the copies owe their existence, directly or indirectly, to a projected but abortive "Viennese biography" of Beethoven. Writing from Vienna on 14 September 1827 to Ignaz Moscheles in London, Schindler referred to the plan: "In Prague Herr Schlosser has published a most wretched biography of Beethoven. Here, too, a subscription is circulating for another 'life,' which, I hear, will be compiled by Herr Gräffer . . . The newly appointed guardian of Beethoven's nephew has handed over Breuning's papers to Herr Gräffer."[9] This last was Anton Gräffer (1784–1852), a guitarist, essayist, and engraver, who worked for Artaria & Co. from 1815 as a clerk, auctioneer, and cataloguer. He was a specialist in Beethoven's works, having in 1827 prepared the auction catalogue of his estate and, in 1844, a catalogue of Beethoven manuscripts then in the possession of Artaria & Co. He came to know Beethoven when he compiled a *Catalogue des oeuvres de Louis van Beethoven,* which Artaria published in 1819 as a supplement to its edition of the Sonata, op. 106; a revised edition of the *Catalogue* appeared in 1828. Gräffer left valuable reminiscences of Beethoven in an unpublished autobiography (1850).[10] Karl Holz was very likely Gräffer's collaborator and even a prime mover in the projected "Viennese biography"; at all events he possessed the sole legal authority from Beethoven to write his life.

Invitations to subscribe to the biography, dated "September 1827," were circulated individually and were also published in several Viennese newspapers at the time. The announcement read in part: "With the co-operation of the guardian of Beethoven's nephew, the editors have succeeded in examining and making use of all those interesting writings of the great composer that are in his estate. Among them are a Tagebuch and a souvenir album of Beethoven's, with important chronological and other information; several documents, diplomas, manuscript letters, reviews of his most important works, etc. etc."[11] This is the first published reference to Beethoven's Tagebuch. The anonymous announcement continued optimistically: "Thus, from genuine original sources carrying the stamp of authenticity will be created the whole life history of our artistic hero."

But the biography, the publication of which had been promised for March 1828, presumably by Artaria & Co., was soon canceled for lack of an adequate response from subscribers and memoirists. With its cancellation, Gräffer was left with his copy of a Beethoven miscellany that included transcripts of letters to and from Beethoven, of Beethoven's baptismal certificate, of his annuity contract of 1809, of the Heiligenstadt Testament, and of the Tagebuch (though not, strangely enough, of the souvenir album). It also eventually included a few original documents: one autograph letter and several autograph sketches, as well as three first editions (WoO 47, WoO 63, and opus 88). Some time between 1832 and June 1835 Gräffer composed a brief history of the project and a draft biographical sketch for possible future use, woven in large part from previously published materials but also from the memoirs and documents supplied by Zmeskall, Simrock, Bertolini, Mosel, and J. B. Bach, now added to the miscellany.

Gräffer prepared an inventory of the papers and offered them for sale: "List of a remarkable collection of memoranda, etc., concerning L. van Beethoven, which may be obtained from Herr G[räffe]r in Vienna for the firm price of 50 florins C.M." Two slightly different copies of the list are in existence, one in the hand of Aloys Fuchs from Vienna and the other in the hand of Friedrich August Grasnick from Berlin, both assiduous collectors of musical autographs.[12] The surviving copies of the list were prepared in 1841 or 1842, but Fuchs, in a note appended to his copy and in a letter to Schindler of 9 September 1852, relates that the collection had been offered to him as early as 1828 or 1829. Apparently Gräffer was then unable to find a buyer, probably because the miscellany consisted almost entirely of transcripts, at a time when Beethoven autographs were in plentiful supply.

In 1842 Karl Holz, angered by the falsifications and personal attacks in Schindler's *Biographie von Ludwig van Beethoven* (1840), persuaded the Karlsruhe kappelmeister, Ferdinand Simon Gassner (1798–1851), to undertake to write Beethoven's biography. In September Gassner came to Vienna to gather documentary materials with Holz's assistance. His most important acquisition was the Gräffer miscellany, which he received from Gräffer along with the *Pastoral* Symphony Sketchbook and several other sketchleaves.[13] Simultaneously Holz gave to Gassner his own collection of Beethoven materials, and soon he formally transferred to Gassner his authorization to write Beethoven's biography.[14] Although few details are known, Holz's collection apparently included several items which had been in the fund of documents and memoirs accumulated for the "Viennese biography" and which had been withdrawn by Holz after the abandonment of the project.[15]

Perhaps in anticipation of the transfer to Gassner, Gräffer permitted Joseph Fischhof (1804–1857), a prominent Viennese pianist, music teacher, and collector, to make a copy of the entire miscellany, including the Tagebuch.[16] The date of the Fischhof copy cannot be definitely fixed. The *terminus ante quem* is September 1842, when Gassner received Gräffer's collection. A marginal reference to "Schilling Lexikon" in the Fischhof manuscript implies a *terminus post quem* of May 1835, for the first volume of Gustav Schilling's *Encyclopädie der gesammten musikalischen Wissenschaften oder Universal Lexikon der Tonkunst* (containing an entry on Beethoven) was published in that month. However, it is conceivable that Fischhof added the marginal reference only after he had copied Gräffer's miscellany; in that case a reference in the text to "Schindler in Münster" proves that the transcript could not have been made earlier than 1832, for Schindler lived in Münster between the end of December 1831 and 1 June 1835.[17]

As Viennese specialists in music manuscripts, Fischhof and Gräffer were well acquainted. Fischhof owned the catalogue of the Artaria Collection of Beethoven manuscripts which is in Gräffer's hand; indeed, at Artaria's request, he collaborated with Gräffer in its preparation.[18] There is no doubt that the Fischhof manuscript actually derives from Gräffer's miscellany (though it may contain some additional material as well), for the major portions of the manuscript correspond almost exactly to items 2–9 in Gräffer's sales list.[19] The modernization of the spelling in Fischhof's copy of the Tagebuch shows that it postdates Gräffer's copy, which retains, for example, Beethoven's habitual use of *y* instead of *i* in such words as *bei, beide,* and *sein.* That the Fischhof Tagebuch was transcribed from Gräffer's copy rather than from the original is proved by Fischhof's adherence to almost all of Gräffer's obvious misreadings of, and omissions from, Beethoven's original. Furthermore, several of Beethoven's phrases that appear in Gräffer as cancellations are lacking altogether in Fischhof. For example, in No. 37, Fischhof's copy lacks the words "in Canons," which in Gräffer's copy are crossed out with dots underneath to signify "stet." Similarly, in No. 54, the word "Akustik," which is canceled but clearly legible in Gräffer, does not appear at all in Fischhof.

In 1859 Fischhof's collection became the property of the Royal Library in Berlin; it is now in the possession of that library's successor, the Deutsche Staatsbibliothek. Both Nohl and Thayer made use of the Fischhof manuscript in their Beethoven biographies, and Nohl described it in some detail in an article of 1879.[20] Albert Leitzmann published an annotated transcription of Fischhof's copy of the Tagebuch in 1918, which has often been reprinted and extensively used.[21]

However, the first nearly complete publication of the Tagebuch was by Nohl in 1871. For it he utilized the copy made by Gräffer, which, despite his ignorance of its origin and earlier history, he recognized as a better source for his text than the version in the Fischhof manuscript. He found the Gräffer copy in the possession of Gassner's widow (Gassner had died in 1851, leaving his biography of Beethoven unwritten), whom Nohl visited in Baden-Baden on several occasions. At first he assumed that she had a copy derived from Fischhof, but on closer examination and comparison of the two documents he understood that Gassner's copy predated the transcript of the Tagebuch included in the Fischhof manuscript.[22] Accordingly, he borrowed it and used it as the basis for his annotated transcription of the bulk of the document, published in *Die Beethoven-Feier und die Kunst der Gegenwart* (Vienna, 1871), where he wrote: "It is published here . . . according to an old Viennese copy which, although it contains minor errors, represents in the main a reliable source."[23] In the final volume of *Beethoven's Leben* (1877) he specified that source: "The Tagebuch of 1812–18 is published in my book *Die Beethoven-Feier und die Kunst der Gegenwart* . . . after an old Viennese copy which came from the estate of Court Kapellmeister Gassner, and which deviates from the Berlin copy [the version in the Fischhof manuscript] in several details. Unfortunately, the publication is not free of mistakes, and where there are deviations the present final publication [the extracts in *Beethoven's Leben*] is decisive."[24]

Gassner's Beethoven materials perhaps were presented to Nohl by Frau Gassner; in any event, he never returned the Tagebuch transcript to her, and it was presumed lost until 1965 when it and other papers of Nohl's were deposited in the Iserlohn Municipal Archive. The significance of the manuscript was first understood in 1978 when Sieghard Brandenburg identified the handwriting as belonging to Anton Gräffer. Subsequently, Martin Staehelin, then director of the Beethoven Archive, graciously made it available for preparation of the present edition. The clearly traceable sequence of ownership of Gräffer's Tagebuch—from Gräffer to Gassner to Nohl to Nohl's estate—makes it certain that the manuscript now in the Iserlohn Municipal Archive is the copy that Gräffer made from Beethoven's original. The handwriting of the Iserlohn manuscript is without question that of Anton Gräffer.

The dates and derivation of the two remaining copies of the Tagebuch can easily be determined. Otto Jahn obtained a copy of it, transcribed from the Fischhof manuscript, along with other portions of the same document, for use in his projected but never written biography of Beethoven. Dated 22 September 1852, his copy bears the legend, "From Beethoven's Tagebuch, according to the copy of Prof. Fischhof," and contains on its last page a citation of material paralleling entry No. 93 derived from the *Berlin Musik-Zeitung Echo* of 4 October 1857. The fourth copy belonged to Andreas Velten, a collector of materials pertaining to Bonn history. Velten's copy was made from Jahn's. The copyist obligingly copied Jahn's date as well as the 1857 entry; on the title page he also noted that it was made from a manuscript "in the possession of Herr Joseph von Fischhof in Vienna." In 1864 Velten's collection, including his Tagebuch, was acquired by the University Library, Bonn.

Thus, a direct sequence can be established for the four extant copies of Beethoven's Tagebuch:

Beethoven's original (1812–1818; lost)
Gräffer's copy (summer 1827; Iserlohn, Municipal Archive)
Fischhof's copy (1832–1842; Berlin, Deutsche Staats-
    bibliothek)
Otto Jahn's copy (1852; Berlin, Deutsche Staatsbibliothek)
Velten's copy (1857–1864; Bonn, University Library)

In the absence of the original manuscript, the translation of the
document that appears here is based on the Gräffer copy.

A SEPARATE, consecutive number is here assigned to each paragraph of the Tagebuch. There is some possibility of error in
this procedure, for this translation follows the paragraphing of the
Gräffer manuscript, where (as is usual in German manuscripts) most
new paragraphs are not indented, so that where an entry extends to
the very end of a line, one cannot be certain whether the following
line is a new paragraph or a continuation of the same paragraph.
Such "possible" new paragraphs are printed as new paragraphs here.
Occasionally two or more separate paragraphs of closely related materials are grouped under a single number (for example, Nos. 60 and
94). In several instances, where disparate materials appear in a single
paragraph (for example, Nos. 63, 68, and 93) or where a sequence of
separate quotations from published texts is run together in one paragraph (for example, Nos. 60 and 105), further subdivisions are made,
designated by letters (a, b, c, etc.).

   The English rendering aims for the middle ground between literal-
ness and intelligibility. Orthodox punctuation is employed where it
clarifies the evident meaning of Beethoven's thought but not where it
would result in an unwarranted "interpretation" of the text. The
translation does attempt to suggest the meaning of obscure passages,
however. For in the German transcription, lacunae, incoherent sen-
tences, copying errors, and other difficulties often give rise to ambigu-
ities in meaning. In the translation, editorially supplied punctuation
is not identified. Square brackets are used for alternative readings as
well as for editorial emendations and additions. Diamond brackets
are used for some words from published texts that have been editorially restored in the Tagebuch entries. Where possible, each of
Beethoven's extracts from a published text was compared with the

edition that he is known or is likely to have used. Where a diary entry varies from a published text, the translation relies upon the published text unless the divergence has a special significance.

The process of identifying the literary extracts that Beethoven copied into his Tagebuch has been a protracted one, which is even now not at an end. Nohl identified the passages by Plutarch, Homer, Herder, Schiller, Müllner, Werner, and Sturm; Leitzmann located the sources of the passages from Kalidasa and Kant; Schubring noted the extract from the *Bhagavad-Gita;* and I identified the passages from Hesiod, Plato, Sir William Jones, Robertson, Wilkins, Kleuker, various Indian religious writings, and several proverbs, as well as specifying the actual editions that were in Beethoven's hands.

Nohl published, in *Die Beethoven-Feier und die Kunst der Gegenwart* (1871), an edition of the Tagebuch that was largely based upon the Gräffer-Gassner copy. Nohl's annotations are unreliable and fragmentary. He omitted one entry (No. 146) by accident, and twelve entries (Nos. 7e and 55–65) because he had previously published them in his *Beethovens Brevier* (Leipzig, 1870) (there, however, they were printed according to the Fischhof manuscript). Besides its incompleteness, his edition is unreliable, containing scores of significant errors—incorrect readings, word omissions, or transpositions— and hundreds of deliberate emendations in spelling and punctuation. He substituted modern spelling for the original's often archaic spelling. To complicate matters, although Nohl claimed that his edition was based solely on Gräffer-Gassner, he actually used the Fischhof copy as well. Where the texts of the two copies varied, he tacitly chose the reading that he preferred.

Although Nohl's transcription did not achieve its goal, it aimed at being a faithful rendering of the Tagebuch. As a text, it is greatly preferable to Leitzmann's, which was based primarily on the Fischhof manuscript. Leitzmann's edition is avowedly not a diplomatic transcription; but it cannot be recommended even on its own terms, for apart from its modernization of punctuation and spelling and a generous sprinkling of exclamation marks for dramatic emphasis, it lacks eight entries (Nos. 32, 33, 46, 76, 135, 146, 147, and 161), includes material drawn from non-Tagebuch sources (Leitzmann Nos. 1–6, 69, 78, and 181–184), and is untrustworthy insofar as many words have been silently changed to "clarify" obscure passages.[25]

The translation of Beethoven's Tagebuch is made from a secondary source, which contains a variety of faults. In many instances one cannot tell whether the defects are faithful transcriptions of Beethoven's own errors or whether they are to be ascribed to the copyist's inadequacies. Occasionally Gräffer struggles to find a correct reading, as in No. 60, where he renders the word *straft* as "strebt? strahlt?" Elsewhere, as in No. 106a, errors appear to result from hasty or even unthinking workmanship. Several entries are rendered opaque or even meaningless. Moreover, it is not certain that Gräffer's copy represents the complete text as Beethoven left it. Details that might have embarrassed or compromised various individuals may have been suppressed, perhaps by Hotschevar as executor of the estate.[26] Although there is no evidence of such suppression, one cannot help wondering why several pagan terms are omitted in Nos. 61, 64, and 65.

The fate of Beethoven's original Tagebuch is unknown. Based on the existence of three leaves in Beethoven's hand which duplicate material in Nos. 60 and 61/62/93, Nohl concluded that the Tagebuch had been partly or wholly dismembered and its leaves dispersed.[27] If Nohl's hypothesis were correct, however, many more leaves would probably have come to light by now. It is true that the two leaves containing excerpts from Werner's *Die Söhne des Thals*, corresponding to No. 60, were Gräffer's source and thus must have belonged to the original Tagebuch.[28] However, the leaf that combines material corresponding to Nos. 61, 62, and 93 differs significantly in content and in arrangement. The Tagebuch entries could not have been copied from it.

Thayer had the impression that the original Tagebuch was an assemblage of jottings and memoranda recorded in various calendars and notebooks.[29] The content and chronology of the entries, however, demonstrates that Gräffer's copy was made from a unified, probably bound diary rather than a miscellaneous assemblage of loose sheets. There is no reason to suppose that individual pages or entries were inserted into Beethoven's original sequence or that the sequence itself was disturbed in any way. Although establishing the precise date for every entry in the Tagebuch is not possible, the many dated or clearly datable entries make it certain that Beethoven wrote the entries chronologically and that Gräffer copied them in the order in which they appeared in the original manuscript. The approximate chronology of the entries is:

1812: Nos. 1 or 1-2
1813: Nos. 2 or 3 to 16 or 17
1814: Nos. 17 or 18 to 33-37
1815: Nos. 34-38 to 70
1816: Nos. 71-110 or 111
1817: Nos. 111 or 112-141
1818: Nos. 141-171

A Note on Money Values

1 florin (or gulden) = 60 kreuzer
1 silver florin = 2 ½ paper florins
1 gold ducat = 4 ½ silver florins = 11 ¼ paper florins
1 Reichsthaler = 1 ½ florins
1 Rheinthaler = 2 florins

Paper florins were termed "Weiner Währung" (W.W.), while silver florins were termed "Conventions Münze" (C.M.). The rates were subject to wide fluctuations and are therefore only approximate. The following abbreviations, used by Beethoven in the Tagebuch, were in common usage:

# = dukaten
f = florin
x = kreuzer

1 *1812*

Submission, deepest submission to your fate, only this can give you the sacrifices—for this matter of service. O hard struggle! Do everything that still has to be done to arrange what is necessary for the long journey. You must find everything that your most cherished wish can grant, yet you must bend it to your will. Maintain an absolutely steady attitude.

You must not be a *human being, not for yourself, but only for others:* for you there is no longer any happiness except within yourself, in your art. O God! give me strength to conquer myself, nothing at all must fetter me to life. In this manner with A everything goes to ruin.

This entry and No. 3 are usually thought to express Beethoven's reactions to the Immortal Beloved love affair of mid-1812. "A" may be the initial of the name of the addressee (Antonie Brentano?) of Beethoven's letter of 6–7 July 1812 to the "Immortal Beloved." Anderson, no. 373. Unlike the "A" at this point in the Fischhof manuscript, the "A" in Gräffer's copy cannot be taken for any other letter. The words "long journey"—if they are not a poetical reference to death—may refer to Beethoven's travels to or from the Bohemian spas in the summer of 1812, his journey to Linz in October, or his resolve to leave Vienna expressed in the Immortal Beloved letter.

2 The precise coinciding of several musical voices generally hinders the progression from one to the other.

3 *13 MAY 1813*
To forgo what could be a great deed and to stay like this. O how different from a shiftless life, which I often pictured to myself. O terrible circumstances, which do not suppress my longing for domesticity, but [prevent] its realisation. O God, God, look down upon the unhappy B., do not let it continue like this any longer.

Apparently a further reference to the termination of the Immortal Beloved affair and to the dissolution of Beethoven's long-postponed marriage plans.

4 Look through them all in the evening.

5 Learn to keep silent, O friend. Speech is like silver, but to be silent at the right moment is pure gold.

Johann Gottfried Herder, "Das Schweigen," from *Blumen aus morgenländischen Dichtern gesammlet*, which consists mainly of Herder's free renderings of didactic, aphoristic poetry from the *Būstān* and *Gulistān* by the Persian poet Sa'dī (c. 1213–1292), first published in *Zerstreute Blätter, vierte Sammlung* (Gotha, 1792), p. 11, reprinted in *Herders poetische Werke*, ed. Carl Redlich, *Sämmtliche Werke*, vol. 26/2 (Berlin, 1882), p. 374. Beethoven's canon on this text, WoO 168 no. 1, was entered in Charles Neate's souvenir album on 24 January 1816; there is also a reference to the canon in the letter to Tobias Haslinger of January 1816. See Anderson, no. 600. According to Fanny Giannatasio del Rio's reminis-

cences, Beethoven wrote a canon on the same text for her family.
See Kerst, I, 213. Six more Herder poems are copied into the Tagebuch (Nos. 6, 55–59). A large folio sheet in Beethoven's hand contains copies of five further poems from the same collection: "Die
laute Klage," "Morgengesang der Nachtigall," "Die Perle," "An-
muth des Gesanges," and "Macht des Gesanges." It was originally
in the Artaria Collection and is at present on loan from the heirs
of Stefan Zweig to London, BL, Department of Manuscripts. See
*Führer durch die Beethoven Zentenar-Austellung der Stadt Wien
1927* (Vienna, 1927), no. 529. Beethoven set "Die laute Klage" in
1814 or 1815 (WoO 135) and "Der Gesang der Nachtigall" on 3 June
(not May) 1813 (WoO 141). Eleonore von Breuning inscribed an aphorism of Herder's in Beethoven's 1792 souvenir album. Two brief
sketches for a setting of Herder's "Die Schwestern des Schicksals"
appear in the Kafka Miscellany (London, BL, Add. MS 29801), fol.
100. See also Kerst, I, 235.

6   And even if the clouds were to rain rivers of life
    Never will the willow tree bear dates.
    Don't waste time with bad people;
    Ordinary cane will never give sugar.
    Can you forge a good sword out of soft clay?
    Does the wolf's nature change when it is nursed by Man?
    Is it not one and the same ⟨rain⟩ that makes thistles and thorns
    grow here on salty ground and gives flowers to the gardens?
    So, waste not seed and precious cultivation:
    It is all one to show bad to the good and good to the bad.
        Herder, "Verschwendete Mühe," *Zerstreute Blätter*, p. 27; reprinted
        in *Sämmtliche Werke*, 26/2, 380. See commentary on No. 5.

7   a   The best way not to think of your woes is to keep busy.
    b   Mark you well, such is Man!
        Thus, when one has fallen
        Another may *weep*;
        But must not *dare to judge.*
    c   Life resembles the trembling tones
        And Man the lute:
        When it falls hard to the ground
        The true sound disappears
        And it cannot become whole again;

It can only give displeasure.
It may no longer sound together with *others;*
May it not disturb the ear's harmony
And bring discord to the pure-sounding choir.

d Dost thou ask the *cause* when
Stars rise and set?
Only *what* happens is clear
The *why* will become apparent
When the dead arise!

e *Elvira* (alone, harp in her arm, ending the music with ever quieter
and softly disappearing tones):

As the last tone dies away,
That sounds under a soft hand
From the harp's strings
Like a drop fallen
On the clear crystal pond,
The rings become steadily weaker
Until they disappear quietly
In the distance on the pond's flowery banks,
So would I, one day, like to soar on high
And fade away into the better life!—
Far from the fatherland,
In the rough cradle of storms,
Where I lie bound
By love's strong bond,
Shall, one day, the hand of fate
Carry me softly upward to my home?

(Her head bent over the harp, she rests awhile. A string breaks,
Elvira starts up in fright, the harp falls ⟨echoingly⟩ to the ground.)

　　　　—The sound, the wave,
They are surely the image of life;
But the wave, that breaks on the rock
In a fearsome surge,
Is like the wave that
Disappears on the mirror of the pond
In the white moonlight;
And the rupture of the taut strings,
As the sound softly dies away,

Is a *sound*
Which portends
The downfall of a man.

> **b-e** Extracts from *Die Schuld*—act 4, sc. 7; act 4, sc. 8; act 4, sc. 11
> (closing words of the drama); act 1, sc. 1 (opening of the drama)—a
> popular *Schicksalstragödie* (fate tragedy) by the German dramatist,
> editor, and critic Amandus Gottfried Adolf Müllner (1774–1829),
> which Beethoven considered for musical setting. *Die Schuld* was
> first produced on 27 April 1813 at Vienna's Burgtheater. Beethoven
> had access to the text before its publication in book form, *Die
> Schuld: Trauerspiel in vier Akten* (Vienna, 1816). The extracts ap-
> pear on pp. 130, 135, 146, and 11–13. In **c** lines 4–10, and **e** lines
> 25–26 ("But the wave . . ."), Beethoven's text varies significantly
> from the published text.

8 In trochaic [lines] with occasional dactyls the —∪∪ counts for no
more than —∪. They work out well in Dr Müllner's play, most of
which is in [trochaic] tetrameters. These also are well suited to musical setting.

> The reference is to Adolf Müllner's *Die Schuld*. See commentary
> on No. 7. Beethoven often marked out the meter of the texts in his
> sketches for vocal compositions. See Schmitz, *Romantisch*, pp. 76–
> 77; cf. No. 49. The text is clearly corrupt.

9 Concerning several doubts in German poetry!
The overture can be well laid out in such a way that it ends with
a *pizzicato*, which Elvira seems to sustain on the harp for a few
seconds.

> The prefatory stage directions for Müllner's *Die Schuld* specify:
> "The overture must end with a *pianissimo*, which Elvira seems to
> sustain on the harp for a few seconds." See commentary on No. 7.

10 How should Eleison be pronounced in Greek? ~~E-lei~~ E-le-ison is correct.

> This is the only sign that Beethoven contemplated a setting of the
> Mass at this time. In settings of the Kyrie, Italian composers usu-
> ally made a clear syllabic separation of the two inner vowels ("E-le-
> i-son"), whereas Germans usually treated the inner syllables as a
> dipthong (either "E-lei-son" or "E-<u>le</u>-i-son"). See Carl Maria Brand,
> *Die Messen von Joseph Haydn* (Würzburg-Aumühle, 1941), p. 7.
> In the *Missa solemnis*, Beethoven set the word as "E-lei-son."

11 Scher la a'mando la Rondinella
scherzet liebet [liebend] die Schwalbe
lieto gode la tortorella
fröhlich freut sich Turteltäubchen
io sola misera non io [?so] goder

The little swallow jokes and loves.
The little turtle-dove is merrily happy.
I alone am wretched and unhappy.
See commentary on No. 12.

12 Always translate the Italian and only if you have doubts here and there ask the Italian instructor at the University once or twice a week.
Beethoven was practicing German-Italian translation, probably German into Italian because the lines contain several rudimentary grammatical and spelling errors. The first line, for example, should be "Scherz' amando la Rondinella." However, the Italian text may have been corrupted in copying. In that case, Beethoven was translating Italian into German. The Italian instructor was Dominick Anton Filippi (1760–1817). Beethoven's library contained a packet of Italian grammars, as well as a German-Italian dictionary; the latter is now Berlin, DSB, Autograph 40,9. See also No. 120.

13 *The Sash and the Flower.*
The Steadfast Prince by Calderón.
Two dramas by Pedro Calderón de la Barca (1600–1681), *La banda y la flor* and *El principe constante,* appeared in August Wilhelm von Schlegel's translation in *Spanisches Theater: Schauspiele von Don Pedro Calderon de la Barca,* 2 vols. (Berlin, 1803, 1809; repr. Vienna, 1813; 2d ed., Leipzig, 1845), I, 155–306, II, 123–252. Several of Beethoven's contemporaries, including E. T. A. Hoffmann and Bernhard Romberg, composed operas to German translations of Calderón's plays.

14 East morning—West evening—South noon—North midnight.
In German poetic diction the parts of the day signify the four points of the compass.

15 Stock up on everything in order to control the cheating of xx. Ask x about lights; wrote to x about x.

Beethoven often thought that he was being cheated by his servants. See also Nos. 110 and 137. The missing names were probably not entered by Beethoven.

16 I have to show the English a little of what a blessing "God save the King" is. A book of music paper costs 1 florin 12 kreuzer. That one certainly writes nicer music as soon as one writes for the public is certain, even when one writes rapidly.

Beethoven composed *Wellingtons Sieg oder die Schlacht bei Vittoria,* op. 91, which includes an orchestration of "God save the King," between August and November 1813. He dedicated it to the prince regent of England. In 1803 Beethoven composed a set of variations for piano, WoO 78, on the British national anthem, and in c.1814–1815 he arranged the anthem for chorus and piano trio, WoO 157, no. 1. In 1813 he hoped to obtain an invitation to visit England. A "book" of music paper normally contained 24 *Bogen* ("sheets" or "bifolia"). See No. 157. Beethoven rapidly composed many occasional works in celebration of the Allied victories over Napoleon.

17 N. B. Always use two staves for the b—.
Show me the course where at the distant goal stands the Palm! Lend grandeur to my most exalted thoughts, add to them the truths that shall endure for ever.

The letter "b" may mean "Bassi" (cellos and double basses) or "Bläser" (wind instruments). The second sentence, in a poetic meter, is apparently a quotation (source unknown).

18 At my last concert in the Large Redoutensaal there were 18 first violins, 18 second violins, 14 violas, 12 cellos, 7 double basses, 2 double bassoons.

Beethoven gave concerts in the Large Redoutensaal on 2 January and 27 February 1814. The first concert featured *Wellingtons Sieg,* op. 91, and the Seventh Symphony, op. 92; at the second these works were repeated and the Eighth Symphony, op. 93, was added. The orchestra was greatly augmented by *dilettanti* to almost three times its normal size. For the size of contemporary orchestras, see letter to Vincenz Hauschka of 1816, Anderson, no. 716; Heinz Becker, "Orchester," *MGG,* vol. 10 (Kassel, 1962), table following col. 192; Otto Biba, "Concert Life in Beethoven's Vienna," *Beetho-*

ven, Performers, and Critics, ed. Robert Winter and Bruce Carr (Detroit, 1980), pp. 87–91. The enlarged orchestra for Beethoven's concert of 7 May 1824 consisted of 24 violins, 10 violas, and 12 cellos and double basses.

19 Shoe brushes for polishing when somebody visits.

20 For example, the diagnosis of the doctors about my life—If recovery is no longer possible, then I must use—???

To accomplish even more rapidly what was impossible earlier it is necessary to—

Consultation with x x x—

Little is known about Beethoven's serious illness early in 1814. Romain Rolland takes the suppressed words as a reference to suicide. Rolland, p. 1459. Beethoven's physicians in 1814 included Andreas Bertolini, Jakob Staudenheim, and Johann Malfatti.

21 Ask for the return of *Rosmunda* by Alfieri, Gozzi edition—Pertossi, which Therese Malfatti received from me.

Rosmunda is a tragedy in five acts by Count Vittorio Alfieri (1749–1803), Italian antityrannical dramatist. It was written in 1778–1780 and first published in *Tragedie di Vittorio Alfieri,* vol. 2 (Siena, 1783); it appeared in numerous reprints and translations. Carlo Gozzi (1722–1806) is the influential Italian dramatist and librettist. "Gozzi edition" may be *Le dieci fiabe teatrali del Conte Carlo Gozzi,* 3 vols. (Berlin, 1808). Schiller's version of Gozzi's *Turandot* was produced at the Theater-an-der-Wien in 1807. Productions of works by Gozzi were undertaken by Treitschke, Schreyvogel, Reichardt, and others in Beethoven's circle. See Hedwig Hoffmann Rusack, *Gozzi in Germany: A Survey of the Rise and Decline of the Gozzi Vogue in Germany and Austria* (New York, 1930; repr. New York, 1966), pp. 72–103. "Pertossi" is probably a misreading; it may refer to Gozzi's *I pitocchi fortunati.* Beethoven proposed marriage to Therese Malfatti (1792–1851) in 1810. He lent books to her. See his letter to her of May 1810, Anderson, no. 258. For Beethoven's study of Italian, see commentary on No. 12.

22 The opera *Fidelio* 1814, instead of March, newly written and improved by 15 May.

The final version of the opera *Fidelio* was first performed on 23

May 1814. The revision had been begun by mid-February: "My opera is also going to be staged, but I am revising it a good deal." Letter to Count Franz Brunsvik of 13 February 1814, Anderson, no. 462. The extent of the work in February is described in a letter to Georg Friedrich Treitschke of March 1814: "Before my concert [of 27 February 1814] I had just made a few sketches here and there, both in the first and in the second acts." Anderson, no. 479. See also N II, p. 296n.

23 Have the old stove cleared out of the lodgings and put in the attic.

This entry relates to Beethoven's lodgings in Baden toward late summer 1814.

24 That the affair with K is so I am prepared to swear under oath to K and B— G—.

This entry probably relates to the progress, in the summer of 1814, of Beethoven's litigation against Prince Ferdinand Kinsky's estate to restore the full value of his annuity payments. See Thayer-Deiters-Riemann, III, 440–442; Thayer-Forbes, pp. 590–591. If so, the first "K" is Kinsky and the second "K" is the curator of Kinsky's estate, Johann Kanka, who helped to negotiate a settlement agreeable to Beethoven, or Franz Anton von Kolowrat, a burgrave of Prague who, at Archduke Rudolph's urging, intervened on Beethoven's behalf. See letters to Kanka of 22 August 1814 to 24 February 1815, Anderson, nos. 486, 497, 502, 520–522, 530; letter to Archduke Rudolph of late 1814, Anderson, no. 513. "B— G—" is obscure but may refer to "Burggraf" (burgrave) Kolowrat. The matter was settled on 18 January 1815. Thayer-Deiters-Riemann, III, 489–491. For the Kinsky litigation, see V. Kratochvil, "Beethoven und Fürst Kinsky," *BJ* 1st ser., vol. 2 (1909), pp. 13–18.

25 There is much to be done on earth, do it soon!

I must not continue my present everyday life; art demands this sacrifice too. Rest and find diversion only in order to act all the more forcefully in art.

26 For Fate gave Man the courage to endure to the end.

The Iliad, book 24, line 49, *Homers Ilias*, trans. Johann Heinrich Voss (Hamburg, 1793); Beethoven cites the Vienna reprint of 1814, II, 424. The Tagebuch contains another citation from *The Iliad*

(No. 49) and three from *The Odyssey* (Nos. 74, 169, 170). There are frequent references to Homer in the conversation books and occasional references in the correspondence. Prosodic studies of hexameters from Homer appear in No. 49 and in the Scheide sketchbook of 1815–1816. SV 364; N II, p. 328. A draft canon on a text from *The Odyssey* occurs in a pocket sketchbook in the British Library. SV 189: London, BL, Egerton 2795. See Hans Boettcher, "Beethovens Homer-Studien," *Die Musik* 19 (1926–1927):478–485.

27 In October 1812 I was in Linz because of B.

An ear trumpet could be such that stars of the opening [amplify] the entrance of the sound and the sound would be transmitted around the ear and in this way could be heard towards all openings.

On 5 October 1812 Beethoven arrived in Linz, where he stayed with his brother ("B") Nikolaus Johann (1776–1848), owner of an apothecary's shop in that city. The text of the second sentence is defective. One of Beethoven's ear trumpets (now in the Beethovenhaus, Bonn) has stars near the opening. Ear trumpets were made for Beethoven by Johann Nepomuk Mälzel (1772–1838) during 1814. See letters to Nikolaus Zmeskall von Domanovecz of 11 January 1814 and to Dr. Carl of July 1814, Anderson, nos. 459, 485.

28 From today on never go into that house—without shame at craving something from such a person.

29 A good word will come true.

A German proverb. See Franz von Lipperheide, ed., *Spruchwörterbuch* (Berlin, 1907), p. 1033, col. 2.

30 Hatred recoils upon those who harbor it.

Another proverb, commonplace with "evil" for "hatred," but not located in this precise form. Beethoven once said that "he had been educated with proverbs." Ludwig Nohl, *Eine stille Liebe zu Beethoven*, 2d ed. (Leipzig, 1902), p. 63.

31 *Rule.* Don't allow copies to be made from a copied score of a work that is important to me. And they must always be on paper with 20 and 24 staves.

No time passes more quickly, rolls by faster, than when our mind is occupied or when I spend it with my Muse.

Beethoven probably means that all copies of his important works should be made from the original autograph rather than from second-generation copies. This entry may relate to the unauthorized copy of the *Fidelio* score that was sent to Mainz in the summer of 1814. See letter to Treitschke of summer 1814, Anderson, no. 488. For the number of staves in Beethoven's autographs, see Alan Tyson, "Sketches and Autographs," *The Beethoven Companion*, ed. Denis Arnold and Nigel Fortune (London, 1971), pp. 452–453; Lewis Lockwood, "The Autograph of the First Movement of Beethoven's Sonata . . . Op. 69," *The Music Forum*, vol. 2, ed. William J. Mitchell and Felix Salzer (New York and London, 1970), pp. 22–23.

32 7 pairs of boots.

33 I owe F. A. B. 2300 florins, once 1100 florins and 60 ducats.

Beethoven accepted loans from his intimate friends the merchant Franz Brentano (1765–1844) and his wife Antonie Brentano (1780–1869). He never fully repaid the loans. See Maynard Solomon, "Antonie Brentano and Beethoven," *M&L*, 58 (1977): 165–167. A letter to Antonie Brentano of c.1814 probably refers to one of the loans that is the subject of this entry. See Anderson, no. 659. Antonie Brentano told Nohl that, "when her doctor informed her of [Beethoven's] circumstances, she loaned him 300 florins C.M., equaling 200 Thalers." Nohl, III, 13; see also pp. 14, 808n5.

34 Never *outwardly* show people the contempt they deserve, because one cannot know when one may need them. The Scottish songs show how unconstrainedly the most unstructured melody can be treated by harmonic means.

Like Haydn, Pleyel, Weber, and Hummel, Beethoven prepared numerous arrangements of Scottish, Irish, and Welsh songs for the Edinburgh publisher George Thomson. See opus 108; WoO 152–157. For his work on arrangements of Scottish songs during late 1814 and early 1815, see letters to Thomson of 15 September 1814, October 1814, and 7 February 1815, Anderson, nos. 496, 503, 529; see also Kinsky-Halm, pp. 624–626, 657; Willy Hess, "Handschriftensammelbände zu Beethovens Volksliederbearbeitungen," in Dorfmüller, pp. 96, 98.

35 No copy of a score is as correct as the score the composer himself writes.
   See No. 31.

36 Every day share a meal with someone, such as musicians, where one can discuss this and that, instruments etc., violins, cellos, etc.

37 The best opening phrases in canons are built around harmonies.

   The musical notation is meaningless.

38 34 bottles from Countess Erdödy.
   After a long estrangement, Beethoven and Countess Marie Erdödy (1789–1837) were reconciled early in 1815. See letter of 29 February 1815, Anderson, no. 531. A gift of wine seems to have accompanied their reconciliation.

39 *Cortez* and *La Vestale* are performed everywhere.
   The operas *Fernand Cortez ou La conquête du Mexique* (first version 1809) and *La vestale* (1807) were composed by Gaspare Spontini (1774–1851). Frequent references to productions of these operas in Vienna, Berlin, Dresden, Breslau, and Mannheim appeared in the musical press between October 1814 and April 1815. See *AMZ* 16 (1814):706–707, 755, 788, 800–804, 866; 17 (1815):22–27, 59–60, 167, 225. One may deduce that this entry was written in late January or February 1815. Nohl entered a marginal date referring to the "grand festival production" in Vienna of 1 October 1814. See Thayer-Deiters-Riemann, III, 451. For references to performances of excerpts from the operas and to Spontini's appointment to the post of Berlin court kapellmeister, see *AMZ* 16 (1814):655; 17 (1815): 51, 191, 256, 277. Beethoven praised Spontini to Freudenberg. See Kerst, II, 114. He also regarded *La vestale* as having an exemplary libretto. See Thayer-Deiters-Riemann, IV, 465; Thayer-Forbes, p. 874.

40 Everything that is called life should be sacrificed to the sublime and be a sanctuary of art. Let me live, even if by artificial means, if only they can be found!

41 If possible, bring the ear trumpets to perfection and then travel. This you owe to yourself, to Mankind and to Him, the Almighty. Only thus can you once again develop everything that has to remain locked within you. And a small court [ein kleiner Hof]—a small chapel [Kapelle]—in it the hymn written by me, performed for the glory of the Almighty, the Eternal, the Infinite.

> Beethoven's words "ein kleiner Hof—eine kleine Kapelle" are equivocal. "Hof" could indicate a prince's residence. It was reported in 1809 that Beethoven hoped to receive an appointment as kapellmeister to Archduke Rudolph after Rudolph's enthronement as cardinal. See Johann Friedrich Reichardt, *Vertraute Briefe* (Amsterdam, 1810), II, 75–76; Thayer-Deiters-Riemann, III, 188–189. But it seems equally likely that "Hof" is to be understood as a rural dwelling or peasant hut. In this case the entry is to be viewed in connection with Nos. 66 and 86.

43 Portraits of Handel, Bach, Gluck, Mozart, and Haydn in my room. They can promote my capacity for endurance.

> J. S. Bach, Handel, Mozart, and Haydn had long formed Beethoven's musical pantheon. Although this is the earliest documentary evidence of his high regard for Gluck, there is little doubt that he had long admired him as well. See letter to Heinrich Joseph von Collin of February 1808, Anderson, no. 163; Czerny's memoranda to Otto Jahn in Kerst, I, 45, 57, 60. There is no record that Beethoven owned portraits of any composers.

44 If only one wanted to separate oneself from the past, still the past has created the present. They became terrestrial—terrible prophecies and through the poems, through their significance—rescued—

> Perhaps a reference to the myths of a polytheistic religion. The text may be defective.

45 Because you lived under a great delusion about *yourself*, I deem it necessary to take a stand on this. For it has already often happened that after you have vented your spite on me, you then tried to make it up with some friendliness. You were not absolved of your punishment; an order is appropriate for the importance in recognition of your departed spirits—and mine.

Presumably the opening of a draft letter—continued in No. 47— probably to Johanna van Beethoven, wife of Beethoven's brother Caspar Carl. See Kastner-Kapp, p. 314. "Manen" (departed spirits) is probably a misreading; possible alternatives are: "in Ansehung Ihres Mannes—und meiner [regarding your husband and me]" or "in Ansehung Ihres Namens—und meines [regarding your reputation and mine]." See MacArdle-Misch, p. 165.

46 15 bottles in the maid's room.
18 shirts.

47 You probably believe that I did not notice all this; but to disabuse you of this error I will merely mention to you that if perhaps you care to make a better impression on me this is precisely the opposite method. That is why I must again reluctantly regret that my brother has rescued you from your deserved punishment, that I alone not so your actions—

See No. 45. In 1811 Johanna van Beethoven was convicted of embezzlement and slander; she was pardoned after several days of police confinement. See Robert Franz Müller, "Aus Beethovens Verwandtenkreis," unpublished mss., Oesterreichische Nationalbibliothek.

48 Always study from half-past five until breakfast.

49 *THE ILIAD, BOOK 22, PAGE 356*

But now Fate catches me!
Let me not sink into the dust unresisting and inglorious,
But first accomplish great things, of which future generations too shall hear!

The Iliad, book 22, lines 303–305, *Homers Ilias* (Vienna, 1814), II, 357 (not p. 356). See commentary on No. 26. Beethoven entered scansion marks, evidently for a projected musical setting.

50 At the Lamb in Brühl. How nice to see the regions of my fatherland; then I must go to England and spend four weeks there.

Frimmel, *Handbuch*, I, 78, 422, suggests that this entry was written at Zum Lamm, an inn at Mödling adjoining the picturesque

Brühl region beloved by Beethoven. See also Frimmel, "Beethoven und die Mödlinger Brühl," *Beethoven-Forschung* 5 (1915):1–32; Oscar G. Sonneck, *Beethoven Letters in America* (New York, 1927), pp. 3–6; N II, p. 132. Alternatively it may express Beethoven's wish to revisit the Brühl ten miles north of Bonn ("my fatherland"), where Electors Joseph Clemens and Clemens August had built a splendid summer palace well known to Bonn's musicians. Beethoven spent the latter part of the summer of 1815 at Mödling and at nearby Baden. His desire to visit England was of long standing, possibly referred to in his 1792 souvenir album. See N I, p. 143. His first dealings with the Philharmonic Society of London, in mid-1815, raised the possibility of an early visit. Perhaps he hoped to stay in Bonn on the way to England.

51   Two divisions of my musical material: my sketchbooks [and] studies; my scores [and] fair copies.
        In 1815 Beethoven was particularly concerned about organizing his voluminous papers. See letters to Johann Baptist Rupprecht of summer 1815 and to Archduke Rudolph of 1815, Anderson, nos. 553, 592.

52   Next to the—, the Mälzel ear trumpet is the strongest. One should have different ones in the room for music, speech, and also for halls of various sizes.
        See commentary on No. 27.

53   Asked Staudenheimer what the former ear trumpet did, me concerning a good
        Jakob Staudenheim (1764–1830) was one of Beethoven's physicians from 1811 or 1812 until c.1824 and again, as consultant, in December 1826. The sentence is incomplete.

54   Consulted Chladni's *Die Akustik*—book on sound.
        Ernst Florens Friedrich Chladni (1756–1827) was an authority on acoustics and an inventor of several musical instruments. His writings include *Entdeckungen über die Theorie des Klanges* (Leipzig, 1787), *Die Akustik* (Leipzig, 1802), and *Neue Beyträge zur Akustik* (Leipzig, 1817), the last two published by Breitkopf & Härtel. An article on acoustics by Chladni appeared in the *AMZ* 17 (1815): cols. 14–15. In a letter of 10 March 1815 Beethoven asked Härtel

for Chladni's address. Anderson, no. 533. In 1819 he hoped to (and perhaps did) attend one of Chladni's lectures. Beethoven hoped to obtain advice concerning hearing aids. See Köhler-Herre-Beck, vol. 1, pp. 32, 42, 247.

55 Under the tiger's tooth I heard the sufferer pray:
"Thanks to you, sublime one, I die in pain but free of guilt."

> Herder, "Dank des Sterbenden," *Zerstreute Blätter, vierte Samm-lung*, p. 103, reprinted in *Sämmtliche Werke*, vol. 26/2, p. 404. See commentary on No. 5.

56 Do you want to taste honey without suffering bee-stings?
Do you desire the wreaths of victory without the danger of battle?
Shall the diver win the pearl from the ocean bottom if, fearing the crocodile, he tarries on the shore?
Risk everything, then! What God has granted to you, nobody can rob you of.
Indeed, he granted it to you, to you, brave man.

> Herder, "Müh' und Belohnung," *Zerstreute Blätter, vierte Samm-lung*, p. 103, reprinted in *Sämmtliche Werke*, vol. 26/2, pp. 404–405. See commentary on No. 5.

57 He who loves God does not esteem the world more highly than it deserves,
Because he knows that it does not offer a sure footing.
Cultivate learning; no path is more secure for a man
Than that which has been trodden by wiser men.
Always avoid the pain of offending a friend.
But, above all, that friend who is like no other.

> Herder, "Das Leben der Menschen," lines 21–22, 25–26, 29–30, *Zerstreute Blätter, vierte Sammlung*, pp. 98–101, reprinted in *Sämmt-liche Werke*, vol. 26/2, pp. 403–404. See commentary on No. 5.

58 "LIFE'S SOLACE"

In adversity do not despair of seeing that day
Which will bring you joy rather than sorrow and pleasure rather than grief.
How often a poisonous wind arose, but soon after
The air was filled with the loveliest of scents.
Often a black cloud menaced you and was blown away

Before the storm emptied from the dark womb.
How often smoke ascended but there was no fire!
Therefore be of good heart even when accidents befall.
Time brings miracles to light; numberless are
The graces you can hope for from the great God.
> Herder, "Trost des Lebens," *Zerstreute Blätter, vierte Sammlung,*
> p. 102, reprinted in *Sämmtliche Werke,* vol. 26/2, p. 404. See com-
> mentary on No. 5.

59 Spare even the closest friend your secrets;
How can you ask fidelity of him, when you deny it to yourself?
> Herder, "Verschwiegenheit," from *Vermischte Stucke aus ver-
> schiedenen morgenländischen Dichtern,* in *Sämmtliche Werke:
> Zur schönen Literatur und Kunst,* vol. 9, ed. Johann von Müller (Tü-
> bingen, 1807), p. 196, reprinted in *Sämmtliche Werke,* vol. 26/2,
> p. 428. See commentary on No. 5.

60

a [*Robert:*] You shall dispense not questions but deeds,
Sacrifice yourself without fame and reward!
If you wish to unveil miracles, first practice them;
Only thus can you fulfill your existence.

b In holy consciousness of duty,
He has taught me abstinence and renunciation,
And left his heaven to me!

c And if this is *really wisdom*—there still
Hovers another goal before my inner eye.
Though it be only an illusion, I believe in it, there is nothing better.
Nevertheless I do not offer it against your truth,
Against your joyless heaven.
The master, too, has sacrificed himself in vain,
But I would rather *burn* in the beautiful illusion
In order not to freeze in your truth.

d Battle for right and for the daughter of right,
Eternal freedom that is transfigured through law,
Resignation under the unbending will
Of *iron fate;* obedience and renunciation,
And unswerving fidelity until the grave! . . .
[*Molay:*] Strong Robert!

Will you practice resignation and renunciation? . . .
You are a hero—you are what is ten times more,
A real man! . . .
Only the strings of the *weakling* are torn
By the *iron finger* of Fate;
The hero bravely presents to Fate the harp
Which the Creator placed in his bosom.
It might ⟨rage through the strings⟩;
But it cannot destroy the marvelous inner accord
And the dissonances soon dissolve into pure harmony,
Because God's peace rustles through the strings.
My strong Robert!—must the strong man
Succumb or be resurrected from the dust? . . .
Is the real true man
A slave of his environment or is he free?
Does he not seize from all storms, and, what is more, from all ⟨raptures⟩
   of this life
His better self?—The world in his bosom,
It is a part of the elemental substance;
And cannot it have an effect on what often
Surges and ferments within it? *Man!* can you succumb?—
[*Robert:*] But there are moments!
[*Molay:*] Yes, they surely exist,
But, thank God! only moments, when
Man, conquered by mighty nature,
Fancies that his higher self is in the play of the waves.
At such moments the ⟨Godhead reveals
The distance between Him and us⟩;
He punishes man's sacrilegious audacity
In trying to emulate Him, and casts him into the void.
At such moments even the wise man
Sinks down into the dust—he too is the son of dust;
But he soon rises, he goes forth cleansed
Of the calamity, and through it
The holy will pronounces His omnipotence.
You too shall rise, strong Robert!
[*Robert:*] What can I do?
[*Molay:*] To be more than your fate,
To love the one who hates and to seek
The great good of self completion in creating!
You are the mirror image of the Eternal:

When men curse Him, He smiles,
And creates paradise around their huts.
Do you selfishly want to go into the desert?
[*Robert:*] Blushing, I bow before your greatness!
[*Molay:*] You should not do that! You shall surpass me . . .
Be ⟨a lord of men!
They too are lords, because they are men!⟩ . . .
Man, the individual, can often [see] more by himself
Than when he is in the company of thousands;
For the wills of men are difficult to guide,
And seldom does the superior mind triumph.

Excerpts from Zacharias Werner, *Die Söhne des Thals, I. Theil: Die Templer auf Cypern* (Berlin, 1802). **a–c** Act 4, sc. 1. **d** Act 4, sc. 2. See Werner, *Theater*, vol. 1 (Vienna, 1813), pp. 134, 136–137, 141, 153–157. The play is written in iambic pentameter. The italicized passages are not emphasized in the published text. Friedrich Ludwig Zacharias Werner (1768–1823) was a poet, Freemason, and pioneer of fate tragedy (see commentary on No. 7) who was converted to Catholicism in 1810 and became, for several years after 1814, a priest with a large Viennese following. His name appears occasionally in the conversation books. In December 1819 Karl Bernard asked Beethoven: "With regard to Werner, when are you going to set him to music?" Köhler-Herre-Beck, I, 172. Among Beethoven documents referring to Werner, see letters to Archduke Rudolph of spring 1812 and to Haslinger of 10 September 1821, Anderson, nos. 367, 1056; Frimmel, *Handbuch*, I, 197; Schmitz, *Romantisch*, pp. 31–32. The two Tagebuch pages containing these passages are still in existence. The first page, from the beginning to "or be resurrected from the dust?" is in the Wegeler Collection, Koblenz. See facsimile in Stephan Ley, ed., *Beethoven als Freund der Familie Wegeler-v. Breuning* (Bonn, 1927), p. 99. The second page, from "is the real true man" to the end, is in the Beethovenhaus, Bonn, SBH 514. Schubert's "Morgenlied," D 685, is from *Die Söhne des Thals*. A marginal note in Nohl's hand may be translated and expanded: "From Zacharias Werner's *Plays*. The *Allgemeine musikalische Zeitung* 13 (1811), cols. [241–]242, reported from Breslau that music director Gottlob-Benedikt Bierey composed a chorus and an overture to Werner's *Weihe der Kraft*. [See also the journal] *Libussa* (1847), p. 416. Caroline Pichler, *Denkwürdigkeiten aus meinem Leben*, 4 vols. in 2 (Vienna, 1844), III, 64. Julius Franz Schneller, *Ideen über Litteratur und Kunst*, ed. Ernst Münch, Hinterlassene

Werke, vol. 3 (Stuttgart and Leipzig, 1834), p. 119. *Der Sammler*, Vienna (March 1813), p. 192. [The Viennese publisher] J. B. Wallishausser published Werner's *Theater* in 5 volumes, completed by February 1814; the 1st volume is *Die Templer auf Cypern.*"

61 **a** *Free from all passion and desire, that is the Mighty One. He alone. No one is greater* than He. ⟨Brahm,⟩ His spirit, is enwrapped in Himself. He, the Mighty One, is present in every part of space. His omniscience is self-inspired and His conception ⟨comprehends⟩ every other. Of all comprehensive attributes omniscience is the greatest . . . For it there is no ⟨threefold time, no threefold⟩ type of existence . . . It is independent of everything. **b** O God . . . You are the true, eternally blessed, unchangeable light of all times and spaces. Your wisdom discovers a thousand and more than a thousand laws, and still You act ever freely and to Your honor. You existed prior to all that we revere. To You, praise and adoration! You alone are the true ⟨Bhagavan—the⟩ blessed one, the essence of all laws, the image of all wisdom of the whole present world—You sustain all things. ⟨Sun, ether, Brahma . . . ⟩

    a A commentary on the *Rig-Veda*, ch. 1, quoted by Beethoven from Johann Friedrich Kleuker, *Das brahmanische Religionssystem im Zusammenhange dargestellt* (Riga, 1797), pp. 34–35. This volume was published as a supplement to the German translation by Kleuker and Johann Georg Fick—*Abhandlungen über die Geschichte und Alterthümer, die Künste, Wissenschaften und Literatur Asiens*, 3 vols. (Riga, 1795–1797)—of Sir William Jones and others, *Dissertations and Miscellaneous Pieces Relating to the History and Antiquities, the Arts, Sciences, and Literature, of Asia*, 2 vols. (London, 1792). The passage had appeared earlier in Nathaniel Brassey Halhed, *A Code of Gentoo Laws* (London, 1776; repr. London, 1781), pp. xxxiii–xxxiv. Kleuker's translation appears to be a revision of the translation of Halhed by Rudolph E. Raspe, *Gesetzbuch der Gentoos* (Hamburg, 1778), pp. 27–28, later reprinted in Friedrich Majer, *Allgemeines mythologisches Lexicon*, vol. 1 (Weimar, 1803), p. 245. Halhed and Kleuker attribute the passage to "Visischta Mahamuni," or the Bengali equivalent "Bisesht Mahamoonee," presumably the sage and lawgiver Vasishtha. For problems relating to his identity, see F. Max Müller, ed., *The Sacred Books of the East*, vol. 14 (Oxford, 1882), pp. 11–15. The underlined words are not emphasized in the published text. **b** A hymn in praise of the attributes of the divinity, Parabrahma, recounted to Paulinus in 1779 by a Brahman, Ciangra (Ciandra?) Govinda (not further identified). Again, Beethoven's source is Kleuker, *Das brahmanische Religionssystem*, p. 37, where the passage is cited from the Latin: Paulinus a Sancto Bartholomaeo, *Systema Brahmanicum* (Rome, 1791), p. 65. Beethoven did not use the translation in Paulinus, *Darstellung der Brahmanisch-Indischen Götterlehre* (Gotha, 1797), pp. 85–86. The words in diamond brackets ("Brahm," "Bhagavan," etc.) are in Kleuker's printed text as well as in Beethoven's copy in the Royal College of Music. See commentary on No. 62. Gräffer may have omitted these words because of their non-Christian origin. The details of Beethoven's extensive interest in Eastern literature are sparsely documented. Walter Schubring, "Beethovens indische Aufzeichnungen," *Die Musikforschung* 6 (1953): 207–214, and his identically titled but somewhat different paper in Hans Otto Günther, ed., *Indien und Deutschland* (Frankfurt-am-Main, 1956), pp. 11–15, are highly inaccurate. For the literary and philosophical background, with comprehensive bibliography, see A. Leslie Willson, *A Mythical Image: the Ideal of India in German Romanticism* (Durham, N.C., 1964); see also René Gérard, *L'Orient et la pensée romantique allemande* (Paris, 1963); Raymond Schwab, *La Renaissance Orientale* (Paris, 1950), trans. as *The Oriental Renaissance* (New York, 1984).

62 Spirit of Spirits, who, through ev'ry part
   Of space expanded and of endless time,
   Beyond the stretch of lab'ring thought sublime,
   Badst uproar into beauteous order start,
   Before Heaven was, Thou art:
   Ere spheres beneath us roll'd or spheres above,
   Ere earth in firmamental ether hung,
   Thou sat'st alone; till, through thy ⟨mystick⟩ Love,
   Things unexisting to existence sprung,
   And grateful descant sung.
   What first impell'd thee to exert thy might?
   Goodness unlimited. What glorious light
   Thy pow'r directed? Wisdom without bound.
   What prov'd it first? Oh! guide my fancy right,
   Oh! raise from cumbrous ground
   My soul in rapture drown'd,

That fearless it may soar on wings of fire;
For Thou, who only know'st, Thou only canst inspire.

    The first verse of the *Veda*-like "Hymn to Narayena" by Sir William Jones (1746–1794), who wrote that the stanza pictures "the sublimest attributes of the Supreme Being." Sir William Jones and others, *The Asiatic Miscellany, Consisting of Translations, Imitations, Fugitive Pieces* (Calcutta, 1785), pp. 7–14, reprinted in Sir William Jones and others, *Dissertations and Miscellaneous Pieces Relating to the History and Antiquities, the Arts, Sciences, and Literature, of Asia* (London, 1792), II, 351–356, German translation by Johann Friedrich Kleuker in the translation of Jones and others, *Dissertations and Miscellaneous Pieces,* by Kleuker and Johann Georg Fick as *Abhandlungen über die Geschichte und Alterthümer, die Künste, Wissenschaften und Literatur Asiens,* vol. 3 (Riga, 1797), pp. 412–415. Incorrect identifications of this entry are in Thayer-Deiters-Riemann, III, 193–194; Schubring, "Beethovens indische Aufzeichnungen" pp. 212–213. Another variant copy of this and the preceding entry in Beethoven's hand is in London, Royal College of Music, 2176, facsimile in Alfred Christlieb Kalischer, ed., *The Letters of Ludwig van Beethoven,* ed. and trans. J. S. Shedlock (London, 1909), vol. 2, facing p. 124. The document first came to public notice when it was put up for auction in Leipzig on 26 October 1857. See *Berlin Musik-Zeitung Echo,* 4 October 1857, p. 311. In this copy, which covers both sides of a single leaf, the material of Nos. 61–62 is introduced without a break by No. 93b, beginning "God is immaterial," and, along with other significant textual variations, contains the additions noted in No. 61 as well as the heading "Hymn" preceding this entry. An 1819 letter to Beethoven dated "Ash Wednesday" (24 February), from the orientalist Joseph Hammer-Purgstall, refers to Beethoven's intention "to set to music an Indian chorus of religious character." See Berlin, DSB, Autograph 35,41.

63   **a** All things flowed clear and pure from God. If afterwards I become darkened through passion for evil, I returned, after manifold repentance and purification, to the elevated and pure source, to the Godhead.—And, to your art. **b** we have no private interest in the business. It is ever thus: trees are bent by the abundance of their fruit; clouds are brought low when they teem with salubrious rain; and the real benefactors of Mankind are not elated by riches. **c** When the big tear lurks beneath thy beautiful eyelashes, let thy resolution check its first efforts to disengage itself. In thy passage over this earth, where the paths are now high, now low, and the true path seldom distinguished, the traces of thy feet must needs be unequal; but *virtue* will press thee right onward.

a Appears to be Beethoven's formulation, perhaps inspired by phrases in Johann Friedrich Kleuker, *Das brahmanische Religionssystem* (Riga, 1797), pp. 35, 174ff, and/or the *Bhagavad-Gita.* b Georg Forster's translation, *Sakontala; oder, Der entscheidende Ring, ein indisches Schauspiel* (Mainz and Leipzig, 1791; repr. Vienna, 1800), act 5, p. 142, of *Sacontala: or The Fatal Ring: an Indian Drama,* trans. Sir William Jones (London, 1789; numerous reprints). Jones's work is a translation "from original Sanscrit and Pracrit" of a play by Kalidasa, the foremost Sanskrit poet and dramatist, who flourished probably in the fifth century. c *Sakontala,* act 4, p. 123. The first sentence, the words "and the true path seldom distinguished," and the closing phrase are additions to the Sanskrit original by Jones, whose translation is used here. Kalidasa's play aroused enthusiasm among Beethoven's contemporaries, including Herder, Schiller, and Goethe. Herder's "Vorrede zur Sakontala" first appeared in the second edition of Forster's translation (Frankfurt-am-Main, 1803); his letters "Ueber ein morgenländisches Drama," widely reprinted, first appeared in *Zerstreute Blätter, vierte Sammlung,* pp. 263–312, reprinted in *Sämmtliche Werke,* vol. 26/2. See commentary on No. 5. In 1820 Schubert sketched two acts of *Sakontala,* D 701.

64 a Blessed [Praised] is ⟨the man⟩, who, having subdued all his passions, performeth with his active faculties all the functions of life, unconcerned about the event. b Let the motive be in the deed, and not in the event. Be not one whose motive for action is the hope of reward. Let not thy life be spent in inaction. Depend upon application, perform thy duty, abandon all thought of the consequence, and make the event equal, whether it terminate in good or evil; for such an equality is called ⟨Yōg—⟩ attention to what is spiritual . . . Seek an asylum then in wisdom alone; for the miserable and unhappy are so on account of the event of things. Men who are endued with true wisdom are unmindful of good or evil in this world. Study then to obtain this application of thy understanding, for such application in business is a precious art.

a *Bhagavad-Gita*, ch. 3, line 7. b *Bhagavad-Gita*, ch. 2, lines 47–50, with part of line 49 omitted. This precise conflation of a and b, and the same omission, occurs in William Robertson, *An Historical Disquisition Concerning the Knowledge Which the Ancients Had of India* (Dublin, 1791), pp. 286–287. Beethoven used Georg Forster's translation, *Robertson's historische Untersuchung über die Kenntnisse der Alten von Indien* (Berlin, 1792), p. 307. Robertson cited *The Bhāgvāt-gēēta, or Dialogues of Krĕĕshna and Ārjŏŏn*, trans. Charles Wilkins (London, 1785), pp. 45, 40, used here. In 1794 Beethoven referred to Robertson's *Geschichte von Amerika* (Leipzig, 1777) in a notebook. See Dagmar Busch-Weise, "Beethovens Jugendtagebuch," p. 78.

65 Wrapt in eternal solitary shade,
Th' impenetrable gloom of light intense,
Impervious, inaccessible, immense,
Ere spirits were infus'd or forms display'd,
Brehm his own mind survey'd,
As mortal eyes (thus finite we compare
With infinite) in smoothest mirrors gaze.

Verse 2, lines 1–6, of Sir William Jones, "Hymn to Narayena," from Jones and others, *The Asiatic Miscellany*, pp. 7–14, reprinted in Jones and others, *Dissertations and Miscellaneous Pieces*, II, 351–356, trans. Kleuker in *Abhandlungen*, III, 415. See commentary on No. 62. According to Jones, the stanza "comprises the *Indian* and *Egyptian* doctrine of the Divine Essence and Archetypal *Ideas*."

66 A farm, then you escape your misery!

A contemporary, diarylike passage on a large folio sheet containing transcriptions of five poems by Herder (see commentary on No. 5) expresses similar sentiments: "If all else fails, even in winter, the country itself remains, like Baden, Lower Brühl, etc. It would be easy to rent a lodging from a peasant." The full text is in Nohl, *Brevier*, p. 104n. The original is in BL.

67 "You take the hardships as signposts in an agreeable life." Nothing is more effective to maintain the obedience of others than their belief that you are far wiser than they.—Without tears fathers cannot instill virtue in their children, or teachers the beneficial services of learning in their students; likewise the laws, by provoking tears from the citizens, cause them to strive for justice.

Evidently a quotation (source unknown). "Services" (*Dienste*) was probably "things" (*Dinge*) in the original.

68 **a** Noble and glorious deeds are performed by brave and excellent people, ignoble affairs by bad and cowardly ones. **b** For vice walks many paths full of present sinful desires and thereby induces many to follow it. But virtue leads on to a steep path and cannot attract men as easily and swiftly, especially if elsewhere there are those who call them to a sloping and pleasant road. **c** It is most troublesome to obtain anything from others if one appears to be a liar.

> **a** A quotation, of uncertain source, perhaps corresponding to Plato's *Republic*, Book I/350. See commentary on No. 87. **b** A gloss on Hesiod's "hill of virtue" passage in *Works and Days*, lines 287–292. The most famous lines in Hesiod, they are frequently cited, glossed, or imitated by the classical authors. See Heber Michel Hays, *Notes on the Works and Days of Hesiod* (Chicago, 1918), pp. 122–123. Beethoven's source is not known. **c** Possibly a quotation (source unknown). "Liar" (*Lügner*) may be a misreading, perhaps for "borrower" (*Leiher*).

69 O look down, brother, yes I have wept for you and still weep for you, O why were you not more open with me? you would still be alive and certainly would not have perished so miserably, had you earlier distanced yourself——and come wholly to me.

> Beethoven's brother Caspar Carl, born 1774, died on 15 November 1815. The missing words may refer to Caspar Carl's wife. See Sterba, p. 51.

70 About a library: large books must stand upright and in such a way that one can easily grasp them.

> See commentary on No. 51.

71 Our world history has now lasted for 5816 years.

> Presumably written in early 1816. The Freemasons habitually placed the Creation at 4000 B.C. and dated their records accordingly. Thus, this may be one of Beethoven's rare references to Freemasonry. See also No. 145.

72 He who is afflicted with a malady which he not only cannot change, but which little by little brings him closer to death and without which his life would have lasted longer, ought to consider that he could have perished even more quickly through assassination or other causes. O happy, who only for—

> Beethoven was often troubled by thoughts of his mortality. He was severely ill in the spring of 1816. On 13 May 1816 he wrote to Marie Erdödy: "For the last six weeks I have been in very poor health, so much so that frequently I have thought of my death." Anderson, no. 633.

73 Show your power, Fate! We are not masters of ourselves; what has been decided must be, and so be it!

> Possibly a quotation (source unknown).

74 CANON FROM *THE ODYSSEY*, BOOK 5

And the rosy dawn arose from the noble bed of Tithonus
> arises

And brought light to the gods and mortal men.
> brings
>
> *The Odyssey*, book 5, lines 1–2, *Homers Odüssee*, trans. Johann Heinrich Voss (Hamburg, 1781), p. 95. The words "arises" (*steigt*) and "brings" (*bringt*) were added by Beethoven with a view to changing the meter. Beethoven's marked copy of Voss's edition is Berlin, DSB, Autograph 40,3. The marked passages are given in Nohl, *Brevier*, pp. 15–31. A passage from *The Odyssey* is printed on the reverse of the title page of *Meeresstille und glückliche Fahrt*, op. 112. See Kinsky-Halm, p. 323. See also Berlin, DSB, Mus. ep. varia 6 (Grasnick 35,1); commentary on No. 26.

75 Every evening and early morning together with R [K?].

> "R" is doubtless a misreading of "K" (Karl). Beethoven was appointed guardian of his late brother's son, Karl (1806–1858), on 19 January 1816. He spent a good deal of time with Karl at the beginning of 1816. See e.g. the letter to Cajetan Giannatasio del Rio of late February 1816, Anderson, no. 614.

76 In spite of my poor n—

> The letter "n" may stand for "nephew" (*Neffe*), that is, Karl.

77 With all of your works, as now with the *cello sonata*, you will reserve the right to specify to the publisher the day of publication, without, so to speak, the publishers in London and in Germany knowing about each other. Because otherwise they pay less. It is also not necessary. You can pretend that someone else has ordered this composition from you.

The cello sonata is one of those from opus 102. Beginning as early as 1802 or 1803, Beethoven attempted to negotiate simultaneous publication of various works in different countries so that he could assure several publishers that each was obtaining first publication. See Alan Tyson, *The Authentic English Editions of Beethoven* (London, 1963), pp. 17–21. In 1815 Beethoven arranged for simultaneous publication by Steiner in Vienna and Robert Birchall in London of opus 91 (piano arrangement), opus 92 (piano arrangement), opus 96, and opus 97. The Cello Sonatas, op. 102, were published by Simrock of Bonn in March 1817. Despite Beethoven's efforts, no English publisher could be found for them.

78 Endurance. Resignation. Resignation. Thus we profit even by the deepest misery and make ourselves worthy, so that God our mistakes—

Beethoven's habitual advocacy of a stoical response to life's vicissitudes is repeatedly evidenced in the Tagebuch. See Nos. 1, 26, 43, 60, 64, 67, 73, 93a. See also his letter to Marie Erdödy of 13 May 1816, Anderson, no. 633.

79 Unfortunately, mediocre talents are condemned to imitate the faults of the great masters without appreciating their beauties: from thence comes the harm that Michelangelo does to painting, Shakespeare to drama and, in our day, Beethoven to music.

Quotation (source unknown). Beethoven's name was also linked with Michelangelo's by Johann Friedrich Reichardt, *Vertraute Briefe* (Amsterdam, 1810), I, 232; letter of 16 December 1808. His name was linked with Shakespeare's by Amadeus Wendt, E. T. A. Hoffman, and other critics.

80 Regard K as your own child, disregard all idle talk, all pettiness for the sake of this holy cause. Your present condition is hard for you, but the one above, O He is, without Him is nothing.

"K" is Karl van Beethoven. From the time that Beethoven assumed the guardianship of his nephew, he came to regard himself as Karl's father. See e.g. the letters to Marie Erdödy of 13 May 1816 and to Kanka of 6 September 1816, Anderson, nos. 633, 654; numerous letters to Karl are signed "your father."

81 In any event the sign has been accepted.
A continuation of No. 80.

82 Diabelli has the score of the three "Razumovsky" Quartets. No[s. 4
and] 5 from the score of *Prometheus* lent to Herr Gebauer [who
lives] in the Wieden.—Wine harvest and all music in the last room,
[which] opens upon a small square.

Antonio Diabelli (1781–1858) was a Viennese pianist, composer,
and music publisher. In 1816 he was an assistant at the firm of Sigmund Anton Steiner, who may have considered a reissue of the
"Razumovsky" Quartets, op. 59. Franz Xaver Gebauer (1784–1822)
was choral director at the Augustinerkirche in Vienna and a leading
member of the Gesellschaft der Musikfreunde. A partial copy of the
score of *Die Geschöpfe des Prometheus*, op. 43, survives, with corrections by Beethoven. See Kinsky-Halm, p. 102. It still lacks nos. 4
and 5, which Beethoven lent to Gebauer. Beethoven threatened
Gebauer with legal action if he failed to return the missing portions
of the score. See his letter to Gebauer of 26 July 1817, Anderson,
no. 791. The text of the closing sentence is obviously defective.

83 Decision to stay; it doesn't work out with H. It is outside the house,
but with a tutor in the house everything will be settled.

Soon after assuming the guardianship of his nephew, Beethoven
made plans to remove him from the Giannatasio Institute and educate him at home. See e.g. the letter to Marie Erdödy of 13 May
1816, Anderson, no. 633; diary of Fanny Giannatasio del Rio, entries of 4 May to 16 August 1816, Thayer-Deiters-Riemann, IV,
529–532. However, Karl remained at the Institute until 24 January
1818. "H" may be a misreading for "G" (Cajetan Giannatasio del
Rio).

84 Leave aside operas and everything else; write only in your manner.
And then a cowl to end this unhappy life.

After years of dividing his efforts between rarefied experimentation
and works of broad appeal, Beethoven was now determined to compose music without regard to popular or commercial considerations. The reference to monastic withdrawal expresses Beethoven's
ascetic impulses (see Nos. 61a, 63a, and 64a) as well as his attraction to medievalist Romanticism.

85 The song "Merkenstein" was written on 22 December 1814.

Beethoven set "Merkenstein" (text by Johann Baptist Rupprecht) for two voices and piano, op. 100, and for single voice and piano, WoO 144. Both versions were sketched in November 1814. See N II, pp. 308–309, 316. WoO 144 was completed first and published late in 1815; op. 100 was worked out in early 1815 and published in September 1816. See letter to Rupprecht of summer 1815, Anderson, no. 553.

86 For living and working, a house in the suburbs; in the country it doesn't work out with Karl.

See commentary on No. 83.

87 Just as the state must have a constitution, so must the individual have one of his own!

Apparently quoted or derived from Plato's *Republic*, in which are described five forms of government, each corresponding to "kinds of mental constitution among individuals" (Book 8/544; cf. Book 9/576). The specific edition used by Beethoven has not yet been located. There are several references to Plato in the conversation books, but the actual extent of Beethoven's knowledge of Plato is not known. "*Socrates* and *Jesus* were my models," he wrote. Köhler-Herre-Beck, I, 350. Schindler, without supporting evidence and with several erroneous details, asserted the influence of *The Republic* on Beethoven's political ideals. Schindler-MacArdle, pp. 112–113; Thayer-Deiters-Riemann, II, 65.

88 Live only in your art, for you are so limited by your senses. This is nevertheless the *only existence* for you.

89 In a thousand ways K. can be of help to you in daily life.

"K" stands for "art" (*Kunst*) or Karl.

90 Talk to Staudenheimer about B. Make haste with the trio for his Imperial Highness for 400 florins. Everything most urgent. At a pinch he will also pay an advance.—Ask Zmeskall and Czerny concerning the operation in case it is not at G's—which is nevertheless the best.—Not by [at?] P—t, better with P.—Arrange how it can best be done.

"Staudenheimer" is Jakob Staudenheim. See commentary on No.
53. The trio is the "Archduke" Trio, op. 97, which, upon its publication by Steiner in September 1816, was dedicated to Archduke
Rudolph. See letters to Steiner of 4 September 1816 and 6 September 1816, and to Archduke Rudolph of c. 12 November 1816, Anderson, nos. 651, 655, 671. Karl underwent a hernia operation on
18 September 1816. "B" may be "operation" (*Bruch*). The operation
was performed at the Giannatasio Institute ("G"). "P—t" and "P"
have not been identified. Beethoven sought advice from his friend
Nikolaus Zmeskall von Domanovecz (1759–1833) and the composer Carl Czerny (1791–1857).

91 The travel costs, all this is nothing.—Ar[tari]a can pay an advance.
Finish the sonata and the trio. Medicine at Karl's.

The journey being planned may have been related to Karl's operation. See No. 90. "Ar—a" is the music publisher Artaria & Co., of
which Domenico Artaria (1775–1842) was proprietor. The sonata
is op. 101, completed November 1816. See Kinsky-Halm, p. 279;
N II, p. 344. The trio is probably an unfinished Trio in F minor, for
piano, violin, and cello, which was being sketched at the time. See
N II, p. 345.

92 Take the pills again on Saturday or Sunday.
See also No. 130.

93 **a** The chief characteristic of a distinguished man: endurance in ad-
verse and harsh circumstances. **b** ⟨As⟩ *God is immaterial, He is
above all conception; as He is invisible, He can have no form; but
from what we behold of His works, we may conclude that He is
eternal, omnipotent, knowing all things, ⟨and⟩ present everywhere.*

a Evidently a quotation (source unknown). The thought was proverbial among the ancients. **b** The German translation of a spurious
sastra of the *Vedas* recounted to Dow by a Brahman. See Alexander
Dow, "Dissertation Concerning the Customs &c of the Hindoos,"
in *The History of Hindostan,* trans. by Dow "from the Persian
of [Muhammad Kāsim] Ferishtah" (London, 1768), I, xl. Dow's
passage, slightly altered, was reprinted in William Robertson, *An
Historical Disquisition Concerning the Knowledge Which the Ancients Had of India* (Dublin, 1791), p. 314, trans. Georg Forster as
*Robertson's historische Untersuchung über die Kenntnisse der
Alten von Indien* (Berlin, 1792), p. 337. Beethoven used Forster's

translation. The passage exists also in a copy in Beethoven's hand, where it introduces the material in Nos. 61–62. See commentary on No. 62.

94 (From Indian literature)
a There are works of architecture, the pagodas from unhewn stone mountains in India, the age of which are *estimated* at 9000 years.
b Indian scales and notes: *sa, ri, ga, ma, na, da, ni, scha.* **c** Five years of silence is required of future Brahmans in the monastery.
d For God, time absolutely does not exist.
e To someone who was offended by the idea of the lingam, the Brahman uttered, "Did not the same God who has created the eye also create the other human members?"
f There is one tribe among the Hindus that practices polyandry.

These and similar "marvels of the East" were widely reported in contemporary European writings about India. **a** The "rock-cut" and cave temples of India actually date from c. 200 B.C. to c. 900 A.D., but eighteenth-century travelers speculated that they were of much greater antiquity. **b** The Indian scale is actually *sa ri ga ma pa dha ni* (C D E F G A-sharp B). **c** "Youth destined to be Brahmans . . . are obliged also to observe the strictest silence, which continues five years." Paulinus a Sancto Bartholomaeo, *Viaggio alle Indie Orientali* (Rome, 1796), trans. William Johnston as *A Voyage to the East Indies* (London, 1800), p. 265n. See also Johann Friedrich Kleuker, *Das brahmanische Religionssystem im Zusammenhange dargestellt* (Riga, 1797), p. 212. However, the ritual austerities required of candidates for instruction in Vedanta do not include so extended a period of silence. **d** *"Time, they say, exists not at all with* God." Sir William Jones, "On the Chronology of the Hindus," *Asiatick Researches*, vol. 2 (1790), p. 115; Beethoven read the translation by J. G. C. Fick in Jones et al., *Abhandlungen über die Geschichte und Alterthümer, Künste, Wissenschaften, und Literatur Asiens*, vol. 1 (Riga, 1795), p. 355. Compare "The name time . . . does not exist in eternal substances and exists in noneternal substances." *Vaiśesika*, book 2, ch. 2, line 9, in *A Source Book in Indian Philosophy*, ed. Sarvepalli Radhakrishnan and Charles A. Moore (Princeton, 1957), p. 390. **e** The "lingam" (phallus) is a procreative symbol of the god Siva. The quotation has not been located. **f** Perhaps a reference to the "five-brother marriage" of the Pandu princes to Princess Draupadi described in the *Mahābhārata*, ch. 2, lines 12–13. Visitors to

India reported contemporary instances of polyandry. See Nathaniel Brassey Halhed, *A Code of Gentoo Laws* (London, 1776; repr. London, 1781), p. liv.

95 Hunting and agriculture make the body agile and strong.

This entry perhaps belongs with the preceding group. Indian youths are instructed "in agriculture . . . and the military arts," among other subjects. Paulinus, *Voyage to the East Indies*, p. 267 (see commentary on No. 94c for full reference).

96 Sung this way, excellent words also are expressed.

At the Nemean Games . . . the singer Pylades sang the words from the play ⟨by Timotheus⟩ entitled *The Persians:* "I give the sons of Greece the glorious jewel of freedom." And while he expressed all the nobility of these words with his excellent voice, the eyes of all listeners ⟨in the theater turned to Philopoemen and joyous applause was heard⟩.
From Plutarch.

Plutarch, *Philopoemen*, par. 11, lines 2–3, *Biographien des Plutarchs*, trans. Gottlob Benedict von Schirach, vol. 3 (Berlin and Leipzig, 1777), p. 484. The heading is by Beethoven, who abridges and partly paraphrases the passage. Beethoven ranked Plutarch with Homer, Schiller, and Goethe. See Johann Reinhold Schultz, "A Day with Beethoven," *Harmonicon* 2 (1824): 11. He frequently cited Plutarch, as in letters to Wegeler of 29 June 1801, Nanette Streicher of 1818, the publisher Bernhard Schotts Söhne of 17 December 1824, and Karl van Beethoven of shortly after 11 July 1825, and the report to the Magistrat der Stadt Wien of 1 February 1819. Anderson, nos. 51, 930, 1325, 1396, and App. C, no. 9.

97 You must have capital; in other words, acquire—

Apart from his annuity (see commentary on No. 119), Beethoven had a capital of 4000 florins C.M. (10,000 fl. W.W.), which he deposited with the publisher Steiner in July 1816 at 8 percent interest. On 13 July 1819 he used this money to purchase eight National Bank shares. See Max Reinitz, *Beethoven im Kampf mit dem Schicksal* (Vienna, 1924), p. 110; letter to Steiner of November 1816, Anderson, no. 677; Theodor von Frimmel, *Beethoven-Studien*, vol. 2 (Munich, 1906), pp. 176–177. Beethoven was much concerned about mounting expenses connected with the guardianship of his nephew. See the letter to Ferdinand Ries of 8 May 1816, Anderson, no. 632. Beethoven was slow or remiss in meeting obligations to Steiner, Giannatasio, Dr. Smetana, and others. He also sought advances from several sources. See Nos. 90–91.

98 The concert should consist of two parts, the first part a new [recent?] symphony, the second a cantata.

This perhaps has to do with the benefit concert Beethoven hoped to obtain from the Philharmonic Society of London in the 1816–1817 season. See e.g. letters to Charles Neate of 18 May 1816 and to Sir George Smart of c. 11 October 1816, Anderson, nos. 636, 664. Later in the year Beethoven wrote to Neate offering to write some new works for the Philharmonic Society—"Symphonies, an Oratorio, or Cantatas etc." Letter of 18 December 1816, Anderson, no. 683. The entry may refer, however, to a possible charity concert in Vienna that Beethoven was then considering (see No. 101), or even to the program of the forthcoming concerts of 30 and 31 March 1817 at which the Eighth Symphony and the oratorio *Christus am Oelberge* were performed. See *AMZ*, 19 (1817): 306.

99 Follow the advice of others only in the rarest cases; in a matter which has already been thought through, who knows all the present circumstances as well as oneself?!

100 These Lacedaemonians died ready to risk death or life for honor; rather, they crowned death and life with honor.

Possibly a quotation (source unknown). Lacedaemonians were the inhabitants of ancient Sparta.

101 In the event of a benefit concert for the disabled soldiers look up the *Wiener Zeitung* of 26 August 1816.

The *Wiener Zeitung*, 1816, no. 239, 26 August 1816, p. 1, reports that "two Hungarian brothers" made an anonymous gift of 4000 florins W.W. for the aid of wounded veterans and their children, which the Ministry of War gratefully accepted and brought to the attention of Emperor Franz.

102 Just as some time ago [I am] again at the piano in my own improvisations, despite my hearing [deficiency].

103 One should not seek refuge in melancholy against the loss of riches, nor in friendlessness against the loss of friends, nor in abstention from procreation against the death of children, but in Reason against everything.

Probably a quotation (source unknown).

104 With regard to T. there is nothing else but to leave it to God, never to go there where one could do wrong out of weakness; only leave this totally to Him, to Him alone, the all-knowing God!

Most Beethoven biographers link this passage and No. 107 with the emergence in 1816 of apparent references to the Immortal Beloved. See letter to Ries of 8 May 1816, Anderson, no. 632; memoirs of Fanny Giannatasio del Rio, Thayer-Deiters-Riemann, III, 564; Thayer-Forbes, p. 646. If this is accepted, "T" may be Antonie ("Toni") Brentano, as suggested in Solomon, *Beethoven*, p. 174.

105 **a** It is not the chance confluence of the ⟨Lucretian⟩ atoms that has formed the world; innate powers and laws that have their source in wisest Reason are the unchangeable basis of that order that flows from them not by chance but inevitably. **b** When in the state of the world order and beauty shine forth, there is a God. But the other is not less well founded. When this order has been able to flow from universal laws of Nature, so the whole of Nature is inevitably a result of the highest wisdom.

a Immanuel Kant, *Allgemeine Naturgeschichte und Theorie des Himmels* (Königsberg and Leipzig, 1755; repr. Zeitz, 1798), p. 108, reprinted in *Gesammelte Schriften*, ed. Königlich Preussische Akademie der Wissenschaften, vol. 1. (Berlin, 1902), p. 334. The 1798 editon was in Beethoven's library. **b** Ibid., pp. 121–122, reprinted in *Gesammelte Schriften*, I, 346. The passage is printed in bold type in the 1798 edition. For Beethoven and Kant, see Schiedermair, pp. 316–335; Köhler-Herre-Beck, I, 235, 308.

106 **a** The matter from which the inhabitants of different planets, even animals and plants, are made has to be of a much lighter and finer kind, and the elasticity of the fibers along with the advantageous design of their structure all the more perfect to the extent that they are further from the sun. **b** That the excellence of thinking creatures, the swiftness of their imaginations, their exact and vivid grasp of concepts perceived through external impressions, together with the capacity for putting them together, finally also their agility in actual practice, in short, the sum total of their perfection stands under a certain rule according to which they become ever more excellent and perfect according to the distance of their habitat from the sun. c That, on the planets from Mercury to Uranus and even beyond (provided there are other planets), the perfection of the spiritual as well as material world grows and proceeds in a graduated sequence according to the proportions of their distances ⟨from the sun⟩.

a Kant, *Allgemeine Naturgeschichte und Theorie des Himmels*, p. 133. b Ibid., pp. 133–134. c Ibid., p. 135. Reprinted in *Gesammelte Schriften*, I, 358, 359, 360. See commentary on No. 105. These passages are printed in bold type in the 1798 edition.

107 Nevertheless be as good as possible towards T; her devotion deserves never to be forgotten, although unfortunately advantageous consequences could never accrue to you.

See No. 104 and commentary.

108 Two forces, which are both equally certain, equally unitary and at the same time equally original and universal, namely the forces of attraction and repulsion.

Kant, *Allgemeine Naturgeschichte und Theorie des Himmels*, Foreword, pp. [xv–xvi], reprinted in *Gesammelte Schriften*, I, 234. See commentary on No. 105. Beethoven alters the order of the phrases and adds the word "namely."

109 Never again live alone with one servant, it is and remains hazardous; just imagine the situation where the master falls ill and the servant perhaps does so too.

Beethoven kept one servant (with whom he was very dissatisfied) from 25 April till the end of October or beginning of November 1816. He was ill and bedridden from 14 October for some weeks. See letter to Zmeskall of 3 November 1816, Anderson, no. 669. In November he engaged two new servants, one of whom was Wenzel Braun (see No. 132).

110 The shortest way to avoid the cheating is to order from a particular restaurant.

In the autumn of 1816 Beethoven several times expressed his fear that he was being cheated by his servants. See letters to Zmeskall

of 3 September and 3 November 1816, Anderson, nos. 650, 669. See
also No. 15.

111 He who will reap tears must sow love.

Friedrich Schiller, *Wilhelm Tell*, act 5, sc. 1. Beethoven cited the
passage from *Sämmtliche Werke*, vol. 6 (Vienna, 1810), p. 343. Beethoven's copy is Berlin, DSB, Autograph 40,6. Schiller was one of
Beethoven's favorite contemporary authors. There are two further
Schiller citations in the Tagebuch (Nos. 112, 118) and frequent references to him in the letters, conversation books, and reminiscences of contemporaries. Apart from "An die Freude," Beethoven
set only a few minor texts by Schiller. In 1809 he hoped to compose
incidental music to *Wilhelm Tell* but he was assigned Goethe's
Egmont instead. His library included twenty-one volumes of the
so-called "Grätzer Taschenausgabe" of Schiller's works published
in 1824.

112 THE MONKS HOSPITALLERS IN *TELL*.

They form a semicircle around the dead man and sing in a deep tone:

Death hurries on with hasty stride,
No respite Man from him may gain,
He cuts him down, when life's full tide
Is throbbing strong in every vein.
Prepared or not the call to hear,
He must before his Judge appear.

Schiller, "Gesang der Mönche," *Wilhelm Tell*, act 4, sc. 3, cited
from *Sämmtliche Werke*, VI, 330. See commentary on No. 111.
Beethoven's setting of these lines, for two tenors and bass, WoO
104, was written in the album of Franz Sales Kandler on 3 May
1817, in memory of the sudden death of the violinist Wenzel
Krumpholz (c. 1750–1817) on the previous day. Krumpholz was
one of Beethoven's earliest friends in Vienna. The translation used
here is that of Sir Theodore Martin in Schiller's *Works, Histories,
and Dramas* (London, 1846–1849), vol. 2, as quoted in *The Works
of Friedrich Schiller*, ed. Nathan Haskell Dole, 10 vols. in 5 (New
York, 1901–1902), unno. vol., p. 345.

113 I was paid in my own coin. (Pliny)

Pliny, *Epistulae*, book 3, letter 9, lines 3–4. The original reads: "Vedi
[Dedi] malum et accepi."

114 Nevertheless, what greater gift can be conferred on a man than fame and praise and eternal life? (Pliny)

> Pliny, *Epistulae*, book 3, letter 21, line 6. The original reads: "Tametsi quid homini potest dari majus quam gloria et laus et æternitas?"

115 Listen to much, but speak only a little.

> Latin proverb. See Alfred Henderson, ed., *Latin Proverbs and Quotations* (London, 1869), p. 32. The original reads: "Audi multa, loquere pauca."

116 Something must come to pass—either a journey and for this to write the necessary works or an opera. Should you still remain here during the coming summer the opera would be preferable, assuming only passable conditions. If you stay here for the summer, then you must now decide how, where?

> Beethoven had numerous opportunities to travel in 1817. Ries invited him to London, Marie Erdödy to Munich, and Karl Pachler to Graz. See letters to Ries of 9 July 1817, to Marie Erdödy of 19 June 1817, and to Pachler of September 1817, Anderson, nos. 786, 783, 823. He also considered journeys to Switzerland and Italy. See letter to Xaver Schnyder von Wartensee of 19 August 1817, Anderson, no. 803; No. 120. He consulted his attorney about the validity of his baptismal certificate in the event of his leaving Austria. See letter to Kanka of late March 1817, Anderson, no. 772. Nevertheless, he remained in Austria, spending the summer in Heiligenstadt and Nussdorf.

117 God help me, Thou seest me forsaken by all Mankind, because I do not want to commit an injustice; hear my plea to be together with my Karl, but only in the future, as there does not appear to be any possibility of that now. O harsh Fate, O cruel destiny, no, no, my miserable state will never end.

> Presumably the "injustice" is the separation of Beethoven's nephew, Karl, from his mother, Johanna van Beethoven. For Beethoven's desire to live with Karl, see commentary on No. 83.

118 This one thing I feel and clearly perceive:
Life is not the sovereign good,
But the greatest evil is guilt.

> Schiller, *Die Braut von Messina*, closing lines.

119 There is no other way to save yourself except to leave here, only through this can you again lift yourself to the heights of your art, whereas here you are submerged in vulgarity. Only a symphony— and then away, away, away. Meanwhile collect the salary, which can still be done for years.

Reference to a projected journey in 1817. Evidently Beethoven wished to escape from the strains of the guardianship of Karl. The "salary" is the lifetime annuity granted to Beethoven as of 1 March 1809 by the Archduke Rudolph and the Princes Lobkowitz and Kinsky. The annuity was liable to be canceled if Beethoven moved his domicile from Austrian territory. See Thayer-Deiters-Riemann, III, 125–126; Thayer-Forbes, p. 457.

120 Work during the summer in order to travel; only thus can you accomplish the great work for your poor nephew; later, wander through Italy, Sicily, with some artists. Make plans and be consoled for L.

Beethoven's letters of this period are silent concerning a trip to Italy. For a projected earlier visit, see letter to Breitkopf & Härtel of 19 February 1811, Anderson, no. 297. Nohl takes the "L" as a misreading of "C" (Karl).

121 In my opinion first the saltwater baths like Wiesbaden, etc.; then the sulphur baths like Aachen (warm) and [Nenndorf] (cold)—

This is another indication of Beethoven's travel plans for the summer of 1817, which were never implemented. In the ms., "Unendlich" (unending) is Gräffer's misreading of "Nenndorf," a spa in Westphalia known for its cold sulphur springs. For the medicinal and chemical properties of these spas and the temperatures of their waters, Beethoven consulted Christoph Wilhelm Hufeland, *Praktische Uebersicht der Vorzüglichsten Heilquellen Teutschlands* (Berlin, 1815), esp. pp. 173–175, 213–218, 309–314. Hufeland's book was in Beethoven's library.

122 To be in company evenings and middays is uplifting and is not tiring. Therefore lead a different life at home.

Sensual gratification without a spiritual union is and remains bestial, afterwards one has no trace of noble feeling but rather remorse.

Beethoven habitually reacted with dismay to any deviation from his high ethical standards. This entry expresses his sense of remorse concerning some unspecified sexual activity, perhaps involving the patronizing of prostitutes, as suggested in a series of letters to his friend Zmeskall which apparently contain coded references to prostitutes. See Solomon, *Beethoven*, pp. 220–221, 262–263.

123 A few days ago posted an unregistered letter, to Frankfurt. On 22 April another unregistered letter to Frankfurt. Sent by post. The same on the 26th. The same on the 29th, with a song.

Beethoven's friends in Frankfurt-am-Main were Franz and Antonie Brentano. See commentary on No. 33. None of the nine letters to them listed here and in Nos. 133, 139, and 141 has survived. The "song" was possibly the second (revised) version of "An die Geliebte," WoO 140, which was published, with "Das Geheimnis," WoO 145, by Simrock early in 1817. See Kinsky-Halm, p. 610. Another possibility is the song "So oder so," WoO 148, published 15 February 1817, of which a copy inscribed to Frau Brentano survives. Bonn, Beethovenhaus, SBH 752.

124 There must be a record in writing that I have given a deposit of 15 florins for the apartment in the Landstrasse.

In late April 1817 Beethoven took lodgings in the Landstrasse, no. 268, second floor, so as to be near the Giannatasio Institute, attended by his nephew Karl.

125 a A drop of water hollows a genuine stone.

(Really, in truth) a drop of water hollows a stone. b A thousand beautiful moments vanish when children are in wooden institutions, whereas at home with good parents they could receive the most soulful impressions that endure into the most extreme old age. a Ovid, *Epistulae ex Ponto*, book 4, letter 10, line 5, but lacking "really" (*verum*), followed by Beethoven's German translation. The original reads: "Verum gutta cavat lapidem." b Perhaps a quotation (source unknown). The entry relates to Beethoven's plan to remove his nephew from the Giannatasio Institute.

126 Tranquillity and freedom are the greatest treasures.

127 True friendship can be founded only on the connection of similar natures.

Probably a quotation (source unknown). Compare "Similarity is

the mother of friendship" (Greek proverb) and "For binding friendships, a similarity of manners is the surest tie" (Pliny). Beethoven
expressed a similar sentiment in a letter to Ries of 24 July 1804:
"The foundation of friendship demands the greatest similarity in
the souls and hearts of men." Anderson, no. 94.

128 Althaea root.

A medication: althaea officinalis is a marshmallow root used as a
demulcent or emollient to soothe irritated mucous membrane.

129 Gall observes that a cold bath is not beneficial to the growing body;
he even recommends that one should not allow young people between the ages of 14 and 21 to take cold baths, but only when the
body is fully grown.

Probably a citation (source unknown) from a publication on hy-
giene, perhaps by Hufeland (see No. 121), who was a follower of
Franz Joseph Gall (1758–1828), Austrian anatomist, author, and
founder of the immensely popular pseudoscience of phrenology.
Gall lectured in Vienna until 1802; after 1807 he made his home in
Paris. His major work is *Untersuchungen über die Anatomie des
Nervenssystems überhaupt, und des Gehirns inbesondere* (Paris
and Strasbourg, 1809). He published further volumes, and his work
appeared in numerous translations. Beethoven's concern is for his
nephew.

130 On 2 May took the powders and rubbed my chest.

Beethoven had a lingering cold from mid-October 1816 until mid-
1817. Starting 15 April, his doctor prescribed a powder to be taken
six times daily and a volatile ointment to be applied to the chest
three times daily. See letter to Marie Erdödy of 19 June 1817,
Anderson, no. 783.

131 Rent a room and take a lodging in the country.

In June Beethoven took temporary lodgings in Heiligenstadt.

132 My recently retired servant is called Wenzel Braun; he left my service on 17 May 1817.

Wenzel Braun entered Beethoven's service in late October or early
November 1816. See commentary on No. 109.

133 On 21 May to Frankfurt.

> Reference to a letter to Franz and/or Antonie Brentano. See commentary on No. 123.

134 Karl has 2 hours of Latin there every day—one hour of geography, history, natural history, religion. Karl is a totally different child when he is with you for several hours. Therefore stick to the plan to take him in with you. Your state of mind will be less uneasy, too. What absurdities there are in these things?!!

> Beethoven was deeply interested in guiding his nephew's education. This entry describes Karl's course of study at the Giannatasio Institute, where he was a boarder.

135 On 9 May 203 ducats
but 28 taken from them on 1 June
remaining: 172

> On 10 May 1817 Johanna van Beethoven paid Beethoven 2000 florins W.W. as her contribution to the cost of Karl's upbringing. See contract between Johanna van Beethoven and Beethoven of 10 May 1817, Anderson, App. C, no. 6. To this Beethoven added 200 florins W.W. See report to the Magistrat der Stadt Wien of 1 February 1819, Anderson, App. C, no. 9. The total was equivalent to approximately 203 ducats. The Giannatasio Institute's annual fee of 1100 florins W.W. was payable in quarterly installments, each equivalent to 28 ducats. See letters to Ries of 8 May 1816 and to Giannatasio of 1817, Anderson, nos. 632, 872. Beethoven often made errors in simple calculations, as here.

136 All evil is mysterious and appears greater when viewed alone; [it is] all the more ordinary, the more one talks about it with others; it is easier to endure because that which we fear becomes totally known; it seems as if one has overcome some great evil.

> Probably Beethoven's own words. Compare "Speech concerning a fatal evil is some mitigation of it" ("Est aliquid, fatale malum per verba levare"). Ovid, *Tristia*, book 5, letter 1, line 59.

137 To live alone is like poison for you in your deaf condition; you always have to be suspicious with an inferior person around you.

> Beethoven often suffered from morbid suspicions about his servants and tended to view them as "inferior" persons. For example, he wrote to Zmeskall on 23 July 1817: "it drives me to despair to

think that owing to my poor hearing I am condemned to spend the great part of my life with *this* class of people, the most infamous of all, and partly to depend upon them." See Anderson, no. 790; see also No. 15.

138 The frailties of nature are given by nature herself and sovereign Reason shall seek to guide and diminish them through her strength.
Perhaps a quotation (source unknown).

139 Wrote to Frankfurt on 6 December.
Beethoven continued to note the dates of his letters to Franz and/or Antonie Brentano. See commentary on No. 123.

140 Perhaps one would fare better with a servant and his wife.
Beethoven's conflicts with a succession of servants intensified during this period. He did not engage a servant couple.

141 Wrote to Frankfurt on 27 December. On 3 January—10 [January]—
Dates of letters to Franz and/or Antonie Brentano. See commentary on No. 123.

142 The kitchen maid receives 60 florins salary per annum and 12 kreuzer bread money daily.
The kitchen maid was either "Baberl," who left Beethoven's service on 12 January 1818, or her replacement, who arrived on the same day. See letters to Nanette Streicher of 28 December 1817 and early January 1818, Anderson, nos. 839, 885. For the cost of maintaining servants, see letters to Ries of 8 May 1816 and to Streicher of 2 October 1817 and c. 7 January 1818, Anderson, nos. 632, 824, 884.

143 I have to ask the superintendent of the Reformed [Church] about B, who had the Trio in D from me, the only important one.
Schlemmer still has a score of mine of *Christus am Oelberge.*—I have enough boards for one more window shutter. What do blankets cost?—Straw mats for the outer and inner doors.
The superintendent of the Reformed (that is, Calvinist) Church was Justus Christoph Georg Hausknecht (1792–1834). "B" is possibly J. X. Brauchle. The "Trio in D" is probably the Piano Trio, op. 70, no. 1. Wenzel Schlemmer (1760–1823) was Beethoven's most reliable copyist from as early as the late 1790s until his death. See Alan Tyson, "Notes on Five of Beethoven's Copyists," *JAMS* 23 (1970):

440–444. In preparation for his nephew's impending arrival, Beethoven purchased household items and had a carpenter in to make repairs. See commentary on No. 144; letter to Nanette Streicher of 23 January 1818, Anderson, no. 886.

144 Ask for Karl's report card from G. I have never had the last one.
Beethoven withdrew his nephew from the Giannatasio Institute on 24 January 1818 and began to educate him at home. "G" is Giannatasio.

145 Our consciousness on our planet is calculated as 5818 years.
Reference to the year 1818. See commentary on No. 71.

146 The marriage contract between my brother Caspar and his wife was concluded in 1806 on 25 May.
Other memoranda by Beethoven concerning this marriage contract are Berlin, DSB, Autograph 35,18.

147 Debts from her and my brother on the house. Grand total *16,862 florins, 20 kreuzer.*
Her son Karl is Susanna [Johanna] Beethoven's sole heir, for the two Lamatsch's notes or agreed-upon sum of 7000 florins belong, totally according to the arrangement of his grandfather, to my nephew Karl and are deposited in his mother's house—although she has the lifelong usufruct thereof.
K's mother's house was valued at about 16,400 florins, therefore one fourth for Karl. K's mother's house yields 1930 florins in rent yearly, not counting the widow's apartment and the garden [garden house?]. These last two, including the cellar, could be estimated at 600 florins yearly from the house. The mother again has the usufruct of the above 1000 [7000] florins which belong to Karl. Also half the pension.

Caspar Carl van Beethoven and his wife, Johanna, jointly owned and lived in the house in the Alservorstadt, no. 121, in Vienna. The inventory of Caspar Carl's estate valued the house at 16,400 florins W.W., subject to various debts and mortgages. See Thayer-Deiters-Riemann, III, 633, where the liabilities are greatly understated. On 2 July 1818 the house was sold for 16,000 florins W.W. to Johann Baptist Kössler and Friderike Trätte (Stadt- und Landesarchiv Vienna, real-estate register), on which no gain was realized. See also

No. 163. The "grandfather" is either Johanna's father, Anton Reiss, or grandfather, Paul Lamatsch. Beethoven's nephew, Karl, was the sole heir of Johanna's mother, Theresia Reiss (née Lamatsch), who died on 23 July 1813. See Draft of a Memorandum to the Court of Appeal, Vienna, of 18 February 1820, Anderson, App. C, no. 15; Mac-Ardle-Misch, p. 332. She bequeathed 7000 florins W.W. to Karl, payable to him upon the death of Johanna, who had the lifelong usufruct of the bequest. The 7000 florins was invested in the house, perhaps as a down payment. According to the report to the Magistrat der Stadt Wien of 1 February 1819, Karl "has 7000 gulden V.C. [i.e. W.W.] as a mortgage on his mother's house . . . and the interest on which his mother enjoys." See Anderson, App. C, no. 9; letters to Johanna van Beethoven of 29 March 1818 and to Johann Baptist Bach of 27 October 1819, Anderson, nos. 897, 979; Draft of a Memorandum to the Court of Appeal, Vienna, of 18 February 1820, Anderson, App. C, no. 15; Köhler-Herre-Beck, II, 80. Caspar Carl's will divided his property equally between Johanna and Karl, so that Karl was entitled to one-fourth of the net proceeds from the sale of the house.

148 On Wednesday 15 November 1815 my unhappy brother died. Karl van Beethoven was born on 4 September 1807.

Caspar Carl van Beethoven died on 15 November 1815 of tuberculosis. His son, Karl, was born on 4 September 1806 (not 1807).

149 Paragraph 191 of the new Civil Code.

Paragraph 191 of the *Allgemeine bürgerliche Gesetzbuch für die gesammten Deutschen Erbländer der Oesterreichischen Monarchie* (Vienna, 1814), p. 41, reads in part: "Those persons are unsuitable for guardianship . . . who are known to be guilty of a crime, or from whom a respectable upbringing of the orphan or an advantageous management of the estate cannot be expected." For Beethoven's reliance upon this clause in his attempt to exclude Johanna van Beethoven from the guardianship of her son, Karl, see letter to the Imperial and Royal Landrechte of Lower Austria of 25 September 1818, Anderson, App. C, no. 7; Draft of a Memorandum to the Court of Appeal, Vienna, of 18 February 1820, Anderson, App. C, no. 15; Köhler-Herre-Beck, I, 191. See No. 47.

150 A MAN'S MOST PRECIOUS POSSESSION
Sertorius did not mind the *appearance of dishonour that occurred, and he maintained that he would merely buy time, which is the*

most precious thing for a man who wants to accomplish important things.
> Plutarch, *Sertorius*, par. 6, line 3, *Biographien des Plutarchs*, trans. Schirach, vol. 5 (Berlin and Leipzig, 1778), p. 193. See commentary on No. 96. The heading and underlining are Beethoven's.

151 On 16 January 1818, 25 ducats at an exchange rate of 399 exchanged for 3—3 florins W.W. On the same day again 10 ducats another 10 ducats exchanged in all into this God-bestowed fund.
> Beethoven's savings were deposited in a fund with his publisher Steiner at 8 percent interest. See commentary on No. 97. According to a receipt dated 17 January 1818, he deposited 25 gold ducats with Steiner on that day. See Anderson, App. G, no. 9. The source of the money is unclear. The text is defective, making it difficult to reconcile the mathematics of the transaction.

152 How stupidity and misery remain forever paired.

153 To write a national hymn on the Leipzig October and perform this every year.
> N.B. Each nation with its own march and the *Te Deum laudamus.*
> Probably refers to the Battle of Leipzig, 16—19 October 1813, in which Napoleon's forces were decisively defeated by Austria, Prussia, and Russia. The work was never composed.

154 Such deposits, along with written acknowledgments such as Pasqualati had for [in?] his lodgings.
> Baron Johann Pasqualati (1777—1830) was a friend of Beethoven's and owner of the house in the Mölkerbastei, no. 1239, where Beethoven lived, on and off, between 1804 and 1815. He remained Beethoven's loyal friend and adviser until the composer's death. He received the dedication of the *Elegischer Gesang*, op. 118. The text is defective.

155 a Don't forget Bach's Litanies. b Frau Baumgarten of the first and second Ludwig.
> a Beethoven explored liturgical music in 1818. See No. 168. "Bach's Litanies" are C. P. E. Bach, *Zwey Litaneyen aus dem Schleswig-Holsteinischen Gesangbuch* for two choruses (Copenhagen, 1786). Beethoven had copied several passages from this work into his

Eroica sketchbook (N 1880, p. 55) and as a young man he treasured his father's copy of Bach's *Morgengesang am Schöpfungstage* (BB, SBH 745). **b** Beethoven was uncertain of the date of his birth and believed that his baptismal certificate of 17 December 1770 actually designated his older brother, Ludwig Maria (baptized 2 April 1769, died 9 April 1769). He wrote on a copy of the certificate that Wegeler had procured for him: "The baptismal certificate seems to be incorrect, since there was a Ludwig born before me. A Baumgarten was my sponsor, I believe." BB, SBH 493. And in a conversation book of 1820 he wrote: "Bongard must have been the name of my godmother, or Baumgarten." Köhler-Herre-Beck, I, 237, see also p. 225. See also the letter to Wegeler of 2 May 1810, Anderson, no. 256. Beethoven's godmother was Gertrud Baum.

156 A separate rack for Handel.
  This rack has to have a strip at each opening, which can be easily moved. Thus for larger and smaller books.

  Beethoven rated Handel among the greatest masters (see No. 43), and repeatedly referred to him as "the greatest composer who ever lived." See Thayer-Deiters-Riemann, IV, 57, 457; V, 126. In 1796, he composed Variations on a Theme from *Judas Maccabeus*, WoO 45, but Handelian influences appear particularly in such late works as the *Missa solemnis*, op. 123, the Diabelli Variations, op. 120, and the Overture, *The Consecration of the House*, op. 124. In 1818 Beethoven owned only a few volumes of Handel's works. See Thayer-Deiters-Riemann, V, 127. The word "Haendel" is written in Latin script, usually reserved for personal names; thus it cannot here signify business or legal materials, as suggested in *BS*, III, 279.

157 Music paper is bought at Stadt Nürnberg and a book costs 2 gulden. Anything from 10 to 16 staves is always the same [price].

  Theyer's Stadt Nürnberg was a Viennese retail shop in the Kärntnerstrasse, no. 961, carrying a variety of goods, including paper. For the number of staves in Beethoven's autographs, see commentary on No. 31. See also No. 16.

158 Karl's mother herself wanted to come to terms, but the basis of this was that the house would be sold, from which one could assume that all debts would be paid and, along with half of the widow's pension, along with what remained from the sale of the house, along with the joint usufruct for Karl's needs she could live not just decently but very well; but inasmuch as the house is not going to be sold! which was the main condition on which the settlement was reached, because one asserted that execution had already been levied against it, so I now have to set aside my scruples and I can indeed suppose that the widow hasn't situated herself badly, which I wish her from my heart. I have fulfilled my part, O Lord.

> This and Nos. 159–160 reveal how deeply unsettled Beethoven was about the fairness and consequences of the contract entered into between him and Johanna van Beethoven on 10 May 1817, which provided that she cede to her son, Karl, one-half of her widow's annual pension of 333 florins 20 kreuzer W.W. and the flat sum of 2000 florins W.W. See Anderson, App. C, no. 6; Thayer-Deiters-Riemann, III, 635; IV, 550. The house was Alservorstadt, no. 121, owned three-fourths by Johanna and one-fourth by Karl. See No. 147. By late March 1818 Johanna was actively attempting to sell the house, perhaps in order to pay her own and Caspar Carl's debts. See letter to Johanna van Beethoven of 29 March 1818, Anderson, no. 897; No. 163.

159 It would have been impossible without hurting the widow's feelings but it was not to be. And Thou, almighty God, seest into my heart, know that I have disregarded my own welfare for my dear Karl's sake, bless my work, bless the widow, why cannot I entirely follow my heart and henceforth—the widow—

> See commentary on No. 158.

160 God, God, my refuge, my rock, O my all, Thou seest my innermost heart and knowest how it pains me to have to make somebody suffer through my good works for my dear Karl!!! O hear, ever ineffable One, hear me, your unhappy, most unhappy of all mortals.

> This entry is a continuation of Nos. 158–159. Apparently, "my refuge, my rock" is an unconscious quotation from Gellert's "Bitten," op. 48, no. 1, which Beethoven set to music in 1801–1802. See Leitzmann, II, 373.

161 On 20 February 1818 I exchanged 12 ducats for wretched paper: 156 florins at a rate of 202, also from—

> In February 1818, Beethoven received 12 ducats from the publisher George Thomson, in payment for arrangements of three Scottish

songs. See Anderson, App. G, no. 8; MacArdle-Misch, p. 235n3. The exchange rate is incorrectly given.

162 Since 10 August Karl's mother has not seen him.

Write a—in which there is also a melodrama. To sum up, cantata with choir—spectacle so that one can show oneself in everything.

Following a quarrel between Beethoven and Johanna van Beethoven in August 1817, he and Giannatasio agreed to restrict her access to Karl at the Giannatasio Institute to two visits per year. See letter to Giannatasio of 14 August 1817, Anderson, no. 800. The planned composition was never written; it is perhaps related to the projected "Adagio Cantique" of 1818. See N II, p. 163.

163 According to the latest financial statement the widow's debts seem to amount to

> 23,100 florins
> ___925___
> 24,025 and 145 ducats,

they actually seem to have increased after my brother's death.

The "widow" is Johanna van Beethoven. The debts include those of her husband and the liabilities on her house. See Nos. 147, 158. The total exceeded by more than 8600 florins W.W. the amount realized from the sale of the house in mid-1818. The sale was apparently forced by her creditors. The income from the house did not cover the interest on the debts, assuming a rate of 8 percent. Johanna's known income thereafter consisted of one-half of her widow's pension (which she refused to draw for several years after 1818) and the interest on her son's 7000-florin inheritance. See No. 147.

164 Lamentable Fate, why can I not help you?

The reference here is apparently to Johanna van Beethoven.

165 Arrived here in Mödling on 19 May 1818. Bathed for the first time on 21 May.

Beethoven, together with Karl, a housekeeper ("Frau D"), and a kitchen maid ("Peppi"), stayed in Mödling at the Hafnerhaus in the Herrengasse. See No. 166.

166 In Mödling the new housekeeper started on 8 June 1818.

Frau D and Peppi were discharged before 8 June. The name of the new housekeeper is not known. See letter to Nanette Streicher of 18 June 1818, Anderson, no. 904.

167 Troglodytes [means] cave dwellers.

168 In order to write true church music go through all the ecclesiastical chants of the monks etc. Also look there for the stanzas in the most correct translations along with the most perfect prosody of all Christian-Catholic psalms and hymns in general.

Although the earliest surviving sketches for the *Missa solemnis* date from 1819, Beethoven apparently decided during 1818 to compose it. With the help of Friedrich August Kanne, Karl Peters, and Joseph Czerny, and with access to the libraries of the Archduke Rudolph and Prince Lobkowitz, he examined sacred music from Gregorian chant to Palestrina, Handel, and the Bachs. He also worked to improve his imperfect command of Latin prosody. See Berlin, DSB, Autograph 35,25; Thayer-Deiters-Riemann, IV, 334n1; Warren Kirkendale, "New Roads to Old Ideas in Beethoven's *Missa solemnis*," MQ 56 (1970):676–677, 699–700.

169 Sacrifice once and for all the trivialities of social life to your art, O God above all! For eternal Providence in its omniscience and wisdom directs the happiness and unhappiness of mortal men.

The second sentence is from *The Odyssey*, book 20, lines 75–76, *Homers Odüssee*, p. 387. See commentary on Nos. 74, 26.

170 To men are alloted but a few days.
Now he who is cruel in thought and deed
Everyone wishes him lifelong misfortune,
And even in death his memory is abominated.
But he who is noble in thought and deed,
His worthy fame is spread abroad by strangers
To all Mankind, and everyone blesses the righteous man.

Homer

The Odyssey, book 19, lines 328–334, *Homers Odüssee*, p. 373. See commentary on Nos. 74, 26.

171 Therefore, calmly will I submit myself to all inconstancy and will place all my trust in Thy unchangeable goodness, O God!

My soul shall rejoice in Thee, immutable Being. Be my rock, ⟨God, be⟩ my light, my trust for ever!

Christoph Christian Sturm, *Betrachtungen über die Werke Gottes im Reiche der Natur und der Vorsehung auf alle Tage des Jahres* (Reutlingen, 1811), II, 565 (closing lines and quatrain, entry for 29 December). Beethoven's marked copy of this edition is Berlin, DSB, Autograph 40,2. The marked passages are given in Nohl, *Brevier*, pp. 33–72. Sturm (1740–1786) was a Lutheran clergyman whose writings attempt to formulate a reconciliation between science, Enlightenment, and religion. Beethoven's deep attachment to Sturm is asserted by Schindler. See Schindler-MacArdle, p. 365; Schmitz, *Romantisch*, pp. 91–93.

ABBREVIATIONS
NOTES
CREDITS
INDEXES

Abbreviations

AMZ	*Allgemeine musikalische Zeitung.*
Anderson	Emily Anderson, ed., *The Letters of Beethoven*, 3 vols. (London, 1961).
BB	Beethovenhaus (Beethoven-Archiv), Bonn.
B&H	Breitkopf & Härtel.
BJ	*Beethoven-Jahrbuch*, 1st ser. (1908–1909), ed. Theodor von Frimmel; 2d ser. (1953–), vols. 1–8, ed. Paul Mies and Joseph Schmidt-Görg; vol. 9, ed. Hans Schmidt and Martin Staehelin; vol. 10, ed. Martin Staehelin.
BL	British Library, London.
BN	Bibliothèque Nationale, Paris.
Breuning	Gerhard von Breuning, *Aus dem Schwarzspanierhause* (Vienna, 1874).
BS	*Beethoven Studies*, ed. Alan Tyson, 3 vols. (New York, 1973; Oxford, 1977; Cambridge, Eng., 1982).
Conversation books	See Köhler-Herre-Beck; Schünemann.
D	Schubert's works as numbered in Otto Erich Deutsch, ed., *Franz Schubert: Thematisches Verzeichnis seiner Werke in chronologischer Folge* (Kassel, 1978).
Dorfmüller	Kurt Dorfmüller, ed., *Beiträge zur Beethoven-Bibliographie: Studien und Materialien zum Werkverzeichnis von Kinsky-Halm* (Munich, 1978).
DSB	Deutsche Staatsbibliothek, Berlin.
Fischer	Joseph Schmidt-Görg, ed., *Des Bonner Bäckermeisters Gottfried Fischer: Aufzeichnungen über Beethovens Jugend* (BB, 1971).

Freud, *Standard Edition*	*Standard Edition of the Complete Psychological Works of Sigmund Freud*, ed. James Strachey et al., 24 vols. (London, 1953–1975).
Frimmel, *Handbuch*	Theodor von Frimmel, *Beethoven-Handbuch*. 2 vols. (Leipzig, 1926).
GdMF	Gesellschaft der Musikfreunde, Vienna.
GM	Goethe Museum of the Freie Deutsche Hochstift, Frankfurt.
Hess	Willy Hess, *Verzeichnis der nicht in der Gesamtausgabe veröffentlichten Werke Ludwig van Beethovens* (Wiesbaden, 1957).
JAMS	*Journal of the American Musicological Society*.
Kalischer-Shedlock	A. C. Kalischer, ed., *The Letters of Ludwig van Beethoven*, trans. J. S. Shedlock, 2 vols. (London, 1909).
Kastner-Kapp	Emerich Kastner and Julius Kapp, ed., *Ludwig van Beethovens sämtliche Briefe*, 2d ed. (Leipzig, 1923).
Kerst	Friedrich Kerst, ed., *Die Erinnerungen an Beethoven*, 2 vols. (Stuttgart, 1913).
Kinsky-Halm	Georg Kinsky, *Das Werk Beethovens: Thematisch-bibliographisches Verzeichnis seiner sämtlichen vollendeten Kompositionen*, completed and ed. Hans Halm (Munich, 1955).
Köhler-Herre-Beck	Karl-Heinz Köhler, Grita Herre, and Dagmar Beck, ed., *Ludwig van Beethovens Konversationshefte*, vols. 1–8 (Leipzig, 1968–1983).
Leitzmann	Albert Leitzmann, ed., *Ludwig van Beethoven: Berichte der Zeitgenossen, Briefe, und persönliche Aufzeichnungen*, 2 vols. (Leipzig, 1921).
MacArdle *Abstracts*	Donald W. MacArdle, *Beethoven Abstracts* (Detroit, 1973).
MacArdle-Misch	Donald W. MacArdle and Ludwig Misch, ed. and trans., *New Beethoven Letters* (Norman, Okla., 1957).
MGG	*Die Musik in Geschichte und Gegenwart*, ed. Friedrich Blume et al., 17 vols. (Kassel, 1949–1986).
M&L	*Music & Letters*.
MQ	*The Musical Quarterly*.
MR	*The Music Review*.
N I	Gustav Nottebohm, *Beethoveniana* (Leipzig and Winterthur, 1872).

N II	Gustav Nottebohm, *Zweite Beethoveniana* (Leipzig, 1887).
N 1880	Gustav Nottebohm, *Ein Skizzenbuch von Beethoven aus dem Jahre 1803* (Leipzig, 1880).
NBJ	*Neues Beethoven-Jahrbuch,* ed. Adolf Sandberger, 10 vols. (1924–1942).
Nohl	Ludwig Nohl, *Beethovens Leben,* 3 vols. in 4 (Vienna, 1864; Leipzig, 1867, 1877).
Nohl, *Brevier*	Ludwig Nohl, ed., *Beethovens Brevier* (Leipzig, 1870).
Rolland	Romain Rolland, *Beethoven: Les grandes époques créatrices,* def. ed. (Paris, 1966).
SBH	Hans Schmidt, "Die Beethovenhandschriften des Beethovenhauses in Bonn," *BJ,* 2d ser., vol. 7 (1971).
Schiedermair	Ludwig Schiedermair, *Der junge Beethoven* (Leipzig, 1925).
Schindler-MacArdle	Anton Schindler, *Beethoven As I Knew Him,* ed. Donald W. MacArdle (London and Chapel Hill, 1966), trans. of 3d ed. (1860) of Schindler, *Biographie von Ludwig van Beethoven.*
Schindler-Moscheles	Anton Schindler, *The Life of Beethoven,* ed. Ignaz Moscheles (Boston, 1841), trans. of 1st ed. (1840) of Schindler, *Biographie von Ludwig van Beethoven.*
Schmitz, *Romantisch*	Arnold Schmitz, *Das romantische Beethovenbild* (Berlin and Bonn, 1927).
Schünemann	Georg Schünemann, ed., *Ludwig van Beethovens Konversationshefte,* 3 vols. (Berlin, 1941–1943).
Solomon, *Beethoven*	Maynard Solomon, *Beethoven* (New York, 1977).
Sonneck	O. G. Sonneck, *Beethoven: Impressions of Contemporaries* (New York, 1926).
SPK	Staatsbibliothek Preussischer Kulturbesitz, Berlin.
Sterba	Editha and Richard Sterba, *Beethoven and His Nephew* (New York, 1954).
SV	Hans Schmidt, "Verzeichnis der Skizzen Beethovens," *BJ,* 2d ser., vol. 6 (1969), pp. 7–128.
Tagebuch	Maynard Solomon, ed., "Beethoven's Tagebuch of 1812–1818," *BS,* vol. 3, and the present volume.

Thayer	Alexander Wheelock Thayer, *Ludwig van Beethovens Leben,* 3 vols. (Berlin, 1866, 1872, 1879).
Thayer-Deiters	A. W. Thayer, *Ludwig van Beethovens Leben,* vol. 1, 2d ed., ed. Hermann Deiters (Leipzig, 1901).
Thayer-Deiters-Riemann	A. W. Thayer, *Ludwig van Beethovens Leben,* ed. and enl. by Hermann Deiters and Hugo Riemann, 5 vols. (Leipzig, 1907–1917; reissued 1922–1923).
Thayer-Forbes	*Thayer's Life of Beethoven,* ed. Elliot Forbes, 2 vols. (Princeton, 1964; rev. 1967).
Thayer-Krehbiel	A. W. Thayer, *The Life of Ludwig van Beethoven,* ed. and completed by Henry E. Krehbiel, 3 vols. (New York, 1921).
Wegeler-Ries	Franz Wegeler and Ferdinand Ries, *Biographische Notizen über Ludwig van Beethoven* (Coblenz, 1838); *Nachtrag* (Supplement) by Wegeler (Coblenz, 1845).
WoO	Werk(e) ohne Opuszahl (work[s] without opus number) in the listing of Kinsky-Halm.
Zu Beethoven I	*Zu Beethoven: Aufsätze und Annotationen,* ed. Harry Goldschmidt (Berlin, 1979).
Zu Beethoven II	*Zu Beethoven: Aufsätze und Dokumente,* vol. 2, ed. Harry Goldschmidt (Berlin, 1984).

Notes

1. The Ninth Symphony: A Search for Order

1. Lewis Lockwood, personal communication.

2. Joseph Kerman, in his classic *The Beethoven Quartets* (New York, 1966), observed the parodistic relationship between the scherzo as a whole and the first movement: the symphony "points its second movement backward, as a sort of epitome to the first" (p. 320). This is not far from Tovey's classicist perspective: "After tragedy comes the satiric drama." Donald Francis Tovey, *Beethoven's Ninth Symphony* (London, 1928), p. 24. Beethoven himself may have authorized this insight in his apparent reference to the scherzo as "nur Possen [mere nonsense, a farce]." See Thayer-Deiters-Riemann, V, 29.

3. N II, 190.

4. For the currency of "the characteristic" in music of Beethoven's time, see F. E. Kirby, "Beethoven's Pastoral Symphony as a *Sinfonia Caracteristica*," *MQ* 56 (1970): 605–623; Kirby, "Beethovens Gebrauch von charakteristischen Stilen," *Bericht über den internationalen musikwissenschaftlichen Kongress Bonn 1970*, ed. Carl Dahlhaus et al. (Kassel, 1971), pp. 452–454. For a conversation between Beethoven and Karl Holz on "einen bestimmten Charakter in einer Instrumental Musik," see Köhler-Herre-Beck, VIII, 268.

5. Chrétien Urhan (1838), cited in Jacques-Gabriel Prod'homme, *Les Symphonies de Beethoven* (Paris, 1906), p. 459; Hermann Kretzschmar, *Führer durch den Konzertsaal* (Leipzig, 1887), I, 111; Sir George Grove, *Beethoven and His Nine Symphonies* (London, 1898), p. 359. In Viennese Classical sonata cycles, the trio of the minuet or scherzo is often the locus of nostalgia—whether pastoral or aristocratic, or both at once, as in Mozart's Clarinet Quintet.

6. See Rolland, pp. 918–919.

7. Wilhelm von Lenz, *Beethoven: Eine Kunst-Studie* (Hamburg, 1860), IV, 183.

8. Lockwood, personal communication.

9. See title pages of the overture *Zur Namensfeier,* op. 115, and of "Aufgabe" for Archduke Rudolph, published by Steiner and Co. in 1820; Anderson, I, 384 (no. 380, 9 August 1812, to B & H).

10. "Die letzten Symphonien Beethovens, den Geist erhabenster Heiterkeit ausatmend, stellen in seiner Vollendung dar, was Schiller als Idyll ahnte und forderte." Karl Heinrich von Stein, *Goethe und Schiller: Beiträge zur Aesthetik der deutschen Klassiker* (Leipzig, 1888?), p. 69, first published in *Monatsschrift des Allgemeinen Richard-Wagner-Vereins* 10 (May-June 1887).

11. *The Works of Friedrich Schiller: Aesthetical and Philosophical Essays,* ed. Nathan Haskell Dole (New York, 1902), II, 32.

12. *Schiller,* II, 36 (translation amended).

13. Otto Baensch, *Aufbau und Sinn des Chorfinales in Beethovens neunter Symphonie* (Berlin and Leipzig, 1930), pp. 94–95.

14. Rolland, p. 931n2; Harry Goldschmidt, *Beethoven: Werkeinführungen* (Leipzig, 1975), p. 66, see also pp. 46–48.

15. If not the underworld, at least "at world's end," for in Greek mythology Elysium is located in a distant region on the earth's surface (Homer, Hesiod). See "Elysium," *Oxford Companion to Classical Literature; Paulys Real-Encyclopädie der Classischen Altertumswissenschaft,* V, cols. 2470–2476. Baensch emphasized certain metaphoric aspects of Elysium, as "a moral state of perfect community," the (heavenly) realm of freedom, mortality, and true religion. Baensch, pp. 29, 51–52.

16. M. H. Abrams, *Natural Supernaturalism: Tradition and Revolution in Romantic Literature* (New York and London, 1971), p. 193. See also Northrop Frye, *Anatomy of Criticism: Four Essays* (Princeton, 1957), p. 161.

17. Harry Slochower, *Mythopoesis: Mythic Patterns in the Literary Classics* (Detroit, 1970), p. 23.

18. For overdetermining substructures or matrices of aesthetic form, see Susanne Langer, *Feeling and Form* (New York, 1953), pp. 240–242; John Dewey, *Art as Experience* (New York, 1934), pp. 147–150; Rudolph Arnheim, *Art and Visual Perception* (Berkeley and Los Angeles, 1969), p. 376; *The Critical Writings of Adrian Stokes,* ed. Lawrence Gowing (London, 1978), II, 160–163; III, 150–151.

19. "The symbol has no authorized interpretant. The symbol says that there is something that it could say, but this something cannot be definitely spelled out once and for all; otherwise the symbol would stop saying it." Umberto Eco, *Semiotics and the Philosophy of Language* (Bloomington, 1984), p. 161.

20. Schopenhauer, *The World as Will and Idea,* vol. 1 (Garden City, N.Y., 1961), p. 271.

21. Wagner, *Opera and Drama,* in *Prose Works,* trans. W. Ashton Ellis, vol. 2 (London, 1893), pp. 109–110.

22. Serov, "Deviataia simfoniia Bethkhovena: Eio skald i smysl," *Izbrannye stat'i,* vol. 1 (Moscow and Leningrad, 1950), pp. 429, 433. I am grateful to Richard Taruskin for the translation. Although never translated, Serov's ideas became influential through Lenz, IV, 177–178, and thence through Grove and others. See also Karl Steinfried, "Das Freudemotiv als Grundmotiv der Neunten Sinfonie . . . ," *Musik-Pädagogische Zeitschrift* (formerly *Der Klavierlehrer*) 24 (1892): 321–323; Rudolph Réti, *The Thematic Process in Music* (New York, 1951), esp. pp. 22–30; Fritz Cassirer, *Beethoven und die Gestalt* (Berlin and Leipzig, 1925), pp. 161–174.

23. See Robert Winter, "The Sketches for the 'Ode to Joy,'" in *Beethoven, Performers, and Critics,* ed. Robert Winter and Bruce Carr (Detroit, 1980), p. 180; Sieghard Brandenburg, "Die Skizzen zur Neunten Symphonie," *Zu Beethoven* II, 106–109.

24. N II, 190–191: "Auch dieses es ist zu zärtl. etwas aufgewecktes *muss man suchen"* (italics mine).

25. N II, 190–191 (italics mine).

26. Leo Treitler, "To Worship That Celestial Sound," *Journal of Musicology* 1 (1982): 165. See also Ernest Sanders, "Form and Content in the Finale of Beethoven's Ninth Symphony," *MQ* 50 (1964): 60.

27. N II, 189.

28. Heinrich Schenker, *Beethovens Neunte Sinfonie* (Vienna and Leipzig, 1912), pp. 96–97.

29. For the significance of B-flat major, see Sanders, pp. 60–69. Earlier, Vincent d'Indy stressed that the chord of B-flat is one of "the two tonal bases of the work." D'Indy, *Beethoven: A Critical Biography* (Boston, 1911), p. 114. See also Réti, *Thematic Process,* pp. 24*ff.*

30. Kerman, personal communication.

31. Solomon, *Beethoven,* pp. 309–310; Anderson, I, 73 (no. 57, 8 April 1802, to Hoffmeister).

32. *The Letters of Mozart and His Family,* ed. Emily Anderson, 2d ed. (London and New York, 1966), II, 769 (no. 426, 26 September 1781).

33. *AMZ* 12 (1810), trans. Ronald Taylor, in *The Romantic Period in Germany,* ed. S. Prawer (London, 1970), p. 287.

34. *Horn of Oberon: Jean Paul Richter's School for Aesthetics,* trans. Margaret R. Hale (Detroit, 1973), pp. 36–38, § 12: "Reflectiveness implies at every level a balance and a tension between activity and passivity, between subject and object . . . Inspiration produces only the whole; calmness produces the parts." For Hoffman's concept of "Besonnenheit," see Ronald Taylor, *Hoffmann* (New York, 1963), pp. 33–37; Hans Heinrich Eggebrecht, "Beethoven und der Begriff der Klassik," in *Beethoven-Symposion Wien*

1970: Bericht, ed. Erich Schenk (Vienna, 1971), pp. 54–56; Carl Dahlhaus, "E. T. A. Hoffmanns Beethoven-Kritik und die Aesthetik des Erhabenen," *Archiv für Musikwissenschaft* 38 (1981):79–92.

35. Anderson, I, 29 (no. 23); I, 68 (no. 54, 16 November 1801); I, 381 (no. 376, 17 July 1812, to Emilie M.).

36. Fichte, *Grundlage der gesamten Wissenschaftslehre* (1794), p. 303, cited in Oskar Walzel, *German Romanticism*, 5th ed. (New York, 1965), p. 29.

37. Nietzsche, *The Birth of Tragedy*, trans. Francis Golffing (Garden City, N.Y., 1956), p. 116.

38. A. W. Schlegel pondered this issue and concluded: "The impressions of the senses are to be hallowed, as it were, by a mysterious connexion with higher feelings; and the soul, on the other hand, embodies its forebodings or indescribable intuition of infinity, in types and symbols borrowed from the visible world." Schlegel, *Ueber dramatische Kunst und Literatur*, 2d ed. (Heidelberg, 1817), trans. by John Black and A. J. W. Morrison as *A Course of Lectures on Dramatic Art and Literature* (London, 1846), pp. 26–27.

39. Kerman considered the Adagio of the Quartet, op. 59, no. 2, as Beethoven's attempt to represent the infinite: "Timelessness for Beethoven meant motionlessness." Kerman, *Beethoven Quartets*, p. 128. Nicholas Temperley proposed that Beethoven's framing of the Seventh Symphony's Allegretto with a $\frac{6}{4}$ tonic chord is a way of "expressing in music the infinite nostalgia of the Romantics, forever unassuaged." Temperley, "Schubert and Beethoven's Eight-Six Chord," *Nineteenth-Century Music* 5 (1981):152.

40. "Mehr Ausdruck der Empfindung, als Malerey," Beethoven insisted on the title page of the *Pastoral* Symphony, even as the work itself indulged in several notorious touches of naturalistic imitation. He perhaps hoped to avoid the criticism of such imitative practices which had been heaped upon Haydn for his oratorios. See Adolf Sandberger, *Ausgewählte Aufsätze zur Musikgeschichte*, vol. 2 (Munich, 1924), pp. 211–212.

41. N II, 186; Nohl, III, 395.

42. James, preface to *Roderick Hudson*, in *The Novels and Tales of Henry James: New York Edition*, vol. 1 (New York, 1907), p. viii.

43. Georges Poulet, *The Metamorphoses of the Circle* (Baltimore, 1966), p. 309.

44. Wilhelm Heinrich Wackenroder and Ludwig Tieck, *Outpourings of an Art-Loving Friar* (1796; New York, 1975), p. 59; Ernst Cassirer, *Language and Myth* (New York, 1946), p. 48. Cassirer informs us that the Babylonian-Assyrian "myth of creation describes Chaos as the condition of the world when the heavens above were 'unnamed' and on earth no name was known for any thing" (p. 82).

45. I here follow Bakhtin's exposition of the "Romantic Grotesque,"

but without placing Beethoven's Ninth Symphony in that category. See Mikhail Bakhtin, *Rabelais and His World* (Cambridge, 1968), pp. 36–38.

46. Novalis, *Heinrich von Ofterdingen*, trans. Palmer Hilty (New York, 1964), p. 114.

47. Schlegel, *Literary Notebooks*, p. 1672, cited in Marshall Brown, *The Shape of German Romanticism* (Ithaca and London, 1979), p. 85.

48. Shelley, *A Defence of Poetry*, in *Essays and Letters by Percy Bysshe Shelley*, ed. Ernest Rhys (London, 1887), p. 12.

49. *Schubert: A Documentary Biography*, ed. Otto Erich Deutsch (London, 1946), p. 337, trans. from *Franz Schubert's Letters and Other Writings*, ed. O. E. Deutsch (London, 1928), p. 77.

50. Anderson, II, 701 (no. 805, 21 August 1817).

51. Köhler-Herre-Beck, III, 158–159.

52. "Doktor, sperrt das Tor dem Tod,/Note hilft auch aus der Not." WoO 189.

53. Anderson, III, 1141 (no. 1308, 17 September 1824).

54. In the late quartets Beethoven is preoccupied with a baroque theme type whose symbolism embraces the dualism of death and resistance to death. Erich Schenk, "Barock bei Beethoven," in *Beethoven und die Gegenwart*, ed. Arnold Schmitz (Berlin and Bonn, 1937), pp. 210–216.

55. Johann Georg Jacobi, *Winterreise* (1769).

56. Erwin Panofsky, "Et in Arcadia Ego: Poussin and the Elegiac Tradition," *Meaning in the Visual Arts* (Garden City, N.Y., 1955), p. 296.

57. N II, 190.

58. Schiller, "On the Sublime," *Schiller*, I, 131. For this atypical aspect of Schiller's aesthetics, see Leonard P. Wessell, Jr., "Schiller and German Romanticism," *Studies in Romanticism* 10 (1971): 177–198. Schiller was also perhaps the first aesthetician to describe the pathway between beauty and freedom, which he mapped in *Letters on the Aesthetical Education of Man* (1795).

59. Schiller, "The Triumph of Love."

60. "In mythical thinking there is no definite, clearly delimited moment in which life passes into death and death into life. It considers birth as a return and death as a survival." Ernst Cassirer, *The Philosophy of Symbolic Forms*, II (New Haven, 1955), 37.

61. Schiller, "Elysium."

62. Slochower, personal communication.

63. *Northrop Frye in Modern Criticism*, ed. Murray Krieger (New York and London, 1966), p. 144.

2. Beethoven's Birth Year

1. Anderson, I, 270 (no. 256).
2. Thayer-Forbes, p. 54.
3. Thayer-Krehbiel, I, 54–55. Thayer's assumptions about Johann's desire to create a *Wunderkind* along Mozartean lines are anticipated in Nohl, I, 79, 370.
4. Schiedermair, p. 132. See also Walter Riezler, *Beethoven* (London, 1938), p. 21; Willy Hess, *Beethoven* (Zürich, 1956), p. 21; Thayer-Forbes, p. 54; Joseph Schmidt-Görg, *Beethoven, die Geschichte seiner Familie* (Bonn, 1964), p. 16; cf. "Beethoven" in *MGG*, vol. 1, cols. 1513–1514.
5. Thayer-Forbes, pp. 57–58.
6. Facsimile in Pamela J. Willetts, *Beethoven and England: An Account of Sources in the British Museum* (London, 1970), plate XI. The false date "1781," penciled thereon in a hand not Beethoven's, should not be allowed to confuse the issue.
7. Kinsky, e.g., claims that the dedication shows Beethoven as "two years younger than he truly was." Kinsky-Halm, p. 493. Anderson makes the same error: "He was then 13." Anderson, III, 1410 n3. So does A. C. Kalischer in his edition of *Beethoven's Letters*, trans. J. S. Shedlock (London, 1909), I, 2. Schiedermair (pp. 130–31) makes many errors in both directions, referring to the concert of March 1778 as having been given when Beethoven was eight, to the dedication to the elector as diminishing Beethoven's age by two years, and to Neefe's biographical notice of 1783 as giving the "age of the boy as two years younger," when in fact all of these assertions are incorrect. See also *BJ*, 1st ser., vol. 2 (1909), p. 345; J.-G. Prod'homme, *La Jeunesse de Beethoven* (Paris, 1927), p. 61; Joseph Schmidt-Görg, "Stand und Aufgaben der Beethoven-Genealogie," in *Beethoven und die Gegenwart*, ed. Arnold Schmitz (Berlin, 1937), p. 306.
8. Thayer-Krehbiel, I, 55.
9. Gustav Nottebohm, *Thematisches Verzeichniss . . . von Ludwig van Beethoven*, 2d ed. (Leipzig, 1868), p. 149.
10. Ibid., p. 154. Here Nottebohm appears to have forgotten Beethoven's birth date, for he was really only nine for all but the last two weeks of 1780.
11. Thayer-Forbes, p. 66.
12. Emerich Kastner and Theodor Frimmel, *Bibliotheca Beethoveniana* (Leipzig, 1925), p. 3.
13. After Beethoven's death, Simrock contributed information concerning the composer's Bonn years for use in a proposed Viennese biography, but his statements about the dating of Beethoven's earliest compositions clearly derived from the title pages of the early publications. See Clemens Brenneis, "Das Fischhof-Manuskript in der Deutschen Staatsbibliothek," in *Zu Beethoven* II, 42.

14. Kastner-Frimmel, p. 3.

15. Thayer-Forbes, p. 82n9; Kinsky-Halm, p. 478. To compound the confusion, Schiedermair (p. 179) and Nottebohm (p. 143) mistakenly write that Beethoven's correct age at this time was fifteen.

16. Thayer-Forbes, p. 79. Thayer, seeing in this report a possible refutation of his theory about Johann's falsification of Ludwig's age, speculated that in this case "an untruth could not be risked, nor be of advantage if it had been." Thayer-Krehbiel, I, 55. Forbes, following Schiedermair, asks pointedly "whether the falsification of age could be purposely any the more risked in a dedication to the Elector." Thayer-Forbes, p. 54. The risk or embarrassment involved in discovery of such a false statement (as was the case in the Electoral Sonatas of 1783) makes it more than likely that Johann, too, believed Ludwig to have been born in 1771.

17. Köhler-Herre-Beck, VI, 321. In his diary, Karl Bursy further confuses the matter: "She first got to know Beethoven in Augsburg, where as a twelve-year-old he gave an organ concert and often improvised so magnificently on her father's instruments." Otto Clemen, "Andreas Streicher in Wien," *NBJ* 4 (1930):111.

18. Dagmar von Busch-Weise, "Beethovens Jugendtagebuch," in *Studien zur Musikwissenschaft: Beihefte der Denkmäler der Tonkunst in Österreich*, vol. 25 (Graz, Vienna, and Cologne, 1962), p. 77 (Blatt 12ᵛ); trans. by O. G. Sonneck, "Sayings of Beethoven," *MQ* 13 (1927):183, revised. This entry is often misdated, e.g. to 1797 by Sonneck, to 1796 or 1797 by Thayer, and to 1799 by Nohl, II, 464, and by Solomon, *MQ* 56 (1970):707n22. Alan Tyson called the true date to my attention.

19. Thayer-Forbes, p. 305. Anderson, III, 1352–1353, transposes the reference into the past: "At the early age of 28 I was obliged to become a philosopher, though this was not easy." Kalischer-Shedlock, I, 60, and Nohl-Lady Wallace, *Beethoven's Letters* (Boston, n.d.), I, 47, do not screen the difficulty, and both note the great discrepancy between this reference and Beethoven's real age—Kalischer-Shedlock suggesting a four-year gap and Nohl-Wallace a five-year error.

20. Anderson, I, 253 (no. 236).

21. Wegeler-Ries, p. 136.

22. Anderson, I, 270–271 (no. 256).

23. Thayer-Forbes, p. 54. The original is in BB (Sammlung H. C. Bodmer), *BJ*, 2d ser., vol. 7 (1971), p. 207 (SBH 493).

24. Ludwig Nohl, *Beethoven nach den Schilderungen seiner Zeitgenossen* (Stuttgart, 1877), p. 63; Sonneck (p. 77) mistakenly rendered "fünfunddreissig" as "fifty-three." Curiously, Bettina Brentano also remained for years under the illusion that she was younger than her actual age, believing she had been born in 1788 rather than 1785.

25. Tagebuch, No. 155.

26. Köhler-Herre-Beck, I, 237.

27. Theodor Frimmel, *Beethoven-Forschung* 1 (1911):27. Beethoven's correct age is given on a penciled note from Dr. Karl Iken, editor of the *Bremer Zeitung*, dedicating eleven pages of poetry and prose to the composer: "To Mr. Ludwig van Beethoven on his 49th birthday on 17 December 1819, from some of his admirers in Bremen." *Die Beethoven-Sammlung in der Musikabteilung der Deutschen Staatsbibliothek: Verzeichnis*, ed. Eveline Bartlitz (Berlin, 1970), p. 195 (autogr. 47,18).

28. Köhler-Herre-Beck, VI, 24, trans. from Thayer-Krehbiel, I, 53.

29. There is some difficulty with Caspar Carl's age as well. Upon his death in 1815, the *Wiener Zeitung* carried a notice: "Died on 16 November, Hr. Karl van Beethoven . . . aged 38 years" understating his age by three years. Thayer-Krehbiel, II, 321.

3. The Nobility Pretense

1. Nohl, *Brevier*, p. 18.

2. Thayer-Forbes, p. 704.

3. Thayer-Deiters-Riemann, IV, 550–554; Thayer-Forbes, pp. 708–711; Sterba, pp. 311–313.

4. Thayer-Forbes, pp. 710–711; Thayer-Deiters-Riemann, IV, 554; Sterba, p. 148.

5. Thayer-Forbes, pp. 712.

6. Schindler-MacArdle, p. 223.

7. Nohl, *Eine stille Liebe zu Beethoven*, 2d ed. (Leipzig, 1902), p. 138.

8. It is doubtful that the presumption of Beethoven's nobility dates from the Bonn years. The electoral court could have been under no such illusion: kapellmeister Beethoven conducted a wine business for many years; the van Beethovens had been shopkeepers for several generations; and Cornelius van Beethoven (the composer's uncle) was entered on the list of burghers of Bonn on 17 January 1736. Joseph Schmidt-Görg, *Beethoven: Die Geschichte seiner Familie* (Bonn, 1964), p. 210. Ironically, the Flemish van Beethovens of the thirteenth to fifteenth centuries may have been "nobles, attached as officers to one or another great lord," who were gradually impoverished by wars and ultimately "found their sustenance in the rough labor of the fields and by raising cattle." Raymond Van Aerde, *A la recherche des ascendants de Beethoven* (Antwerp, 1939), p. 10.

9. Wegeler-Ries, Supplement, p. 7.

10. Schindler-MacArdle, p. 219. A tiny manifestation of this deception lies in the substitution of the abbreviation *v* for *van* in Beethoven's correspondence. Whereas the Dutch particle might not be taken as a sure sign of nobility, the *v* was almost certain to be viewed as standing for the noble

von. Naturally, Beethoven often abbreviated his name to save time, but a tabulation reveals that his substitution of *v* for *van* was probably connected with the nobility pretense, especially during the years 1793–1799 and 1816–1819.

11. Nohl, II, 23–24.

12. Robert Bory, *Ludwig van Beethoven: His Life and Work in Pictures* (London, 1966), pp. 64–65.

13. Hanns Jäger-Sunstenau, "Beethoven-Akten im Wiener Landesarchiv," in Erich Schenk, ed., *Beethoven-Studien* (Vienna, 1970), pp. 13–14.

14. W. A. Thomas-San-Galli, *Die unsterbliche Geliebte Beethovens: Lösung eines vielumstrittenen Problems* (Halle, 1909), p. 65; Martin Cooper, *Beethoven: The Last Decade, 1817–1827* (London, 1970), p. 16.

15. Schindler-Moscheles, pp. 70–71. Schindler later modified this view somewhat: "It would be hard to say whether or not he attached any importance to the general belief that he was of noble blood . . . At any rate, it is a fact that from the time of his encounter with the civil code of Lower Austria, Vienna and its environs became too confining for our aggrieved master." Schindler-MacArdle, pp. 220–221.

16. John Russell, *A Tour in Germany and Some of the Southern Provinces of the Austrian Empire, in the Years 1820, 1821, 1822* (Boston, 1825), pp. 399–400.

17. Ilsa Barea, *Vienna* (New York, 1966), pp. 173, 84. Although Haydn never pretended nobility, he insisted that Prince Esterházy address him as "Herr von Haydn" as an expression of respect. H. C. Robbins Landon, *The Collected Correspondence and London Notebooks of Joseph Haydn* (London, 1959), p. xxiii. Weber's father added the "von" to his and his son's name. Later the young Debussy wrote his name "de Bussy" in an apparent attempt at a nobility pretense. And Bartók erroneously thought he was of the nobility.

18. See Thayer-Krehbiel, II, 377. In a conversation book entry from the spring of 1819 there is some suggestion that Beethoven might still be able to claim descent from the old nobility. See Köhler-Herre-Beck, I, 56.

19. Schindler-MacArdle, p. 223.

20. Henry Reeve, *Journal of a Residence at Vienna and Berlin in the Eventful Winter 1805–6* (London, 1877), p. 116.

21. Thayer-Deiters-Riemann, III, 518–519; IV, 554; Thayer-Forbes, pp. 624–625.

22. Thayer-Forbes, p. 254.

23. There is contradictory evidence on this point. See H. G. Schenk in Albert Goodwin, ed., *The European Nobility in the Eighteenth Century* (London, 1953), p. 109; Reeve, p. 116.

24. See Thayer-Forbes, pp. 795–796; Breuning, pp. 126–128; Köhler-Herre-Beck, IV, 265.

25. Anderson, II, 631 (no. 700).

26. Theodor Frimmel, *Beethoven-Forschung* 2 (July 1911):62–68; Frimmel, *Handbuch,* II, 341–343.

27. The letter to Baron von Türkheim, which has been variously dated 1813–1817, may be definitely dated as shortly after December 1815, for in this letter Beethoven puns on the word "Freiherr": "Remember that I too am a *Freiherr* [a "Baron" or "Freeman"] even though I may not bear the title!!!!" The certificate declaring Beethoven an "honorary Freeman" of Vienna is inscribed to "Herr Ludwig von [sic] Beethoven." Erich Kock, "Beethoven und der Adel—Beethovens Herkunft," in Kock and H. C. Fischer, ed., *Ludwig van Beethoven, eine Dokumentation* (Salzburg, 1970), p. 30.

28. Schenk, in Goodwin, p. 111.

29. W. H. Bruford, *Germany in the Eighteenth Century* (Cambridge, 1935), p. 61; Arthur Loesser, *Men, Women, and Pianos: A Social History* (New York, 1954), p. 118. Ennoblements in Prussia were so freely given "that it will be henceforward much more difficult to find a man than a nobleman in the Prussian states." Count Mirabeau, *Secret History of the Court of Berlin* (Dublin, 1789), pp. 159–160.

30. Thayer-Forbes, p. 864.

31. Wegeler-Ries, p. 109; MacArdle, marginal note in "Beethoven Abstracts" (ms. New York Public Library).

32. Schindler-MacArdle, p. 242.

33. Anderson, III, 1115 (no. 1271).

34. Thayer-Forbes, p. 926; Anderson, III, 1127–1129 (no. 1292).

35. Anderson, III, 1072–1073 (no. 1217).

36. Thayer-Forbes, p. 1021; Anderson, III, 1321–1323 (no. 1542).

37. Schindler-MacArdle, p. 241.

38. Schindler-Moscheles, p. 81. "How much truth there is in this I have no way of knowing," wrote Gerhard von Breuning (p. 114), who clearly considered the story an invention.

39. Köhler-Herre-Beck, VI, 134.

40. Köhler-Herre-Beck, VI, 135.

41. Wegeler-Ries, p. 109; Thayer-Forbes, pp. 184–185. Mozart, too, had received "100 Friedrichs d'or in a gold snuff-box" from Friedrich Wilhelm II for the Quartet in D, K. 575, during his visit of 1789. O. E. Deutsch, *Mozart: A Documentary Biography* (London, 1965), p. 346.

42. Anderson, I, 226 (no. 209), translation amended.

43. Anderson, I, 58 (no. 51).

44. Anderson, I, 97–98 (no. 82). Beethoven closed his concert of 5 April 1803 with improvisations on Haydn's "Emperor Hymn."

45. Anderson, III, 1421 (draft contract, February 1809). See also Anderson, III, 1446–1447 (draft scheme for a musical constitution, January 1809): "To share, if possible, the Imperial title in turn—with Salieri and Eybler."

46. Tagebuch, No. 41.

47. Schindler-MacArdle, p. 205.

48. Somewhat in modification of this, Beethoven's main contacts with the aristocracy were primarily with its most culturally advanced and aesthetically sensitive members. Apart from Archduke Rudolph, his access to the imperial family and to those who actually exercised political power in a direct sense was extremely limited. That he felt excluded from these circles is evidenced by his oft-expressed resentment against the highest nobility. Moreover, most of Beethoven's chief supporters among the aristocrats were non-Austrian in origin, deriving from Hungary, Bohemia, Russia, and Germany.

49. Anderson, III, 987 (no. 1121). In May 1823, there was talk of Beethoven obtaining Haydn's old position at Esterházy.

50. Thayer-Forbes, p. 841. Schindler writes that Lichnowsky tried "in vain to produce a change in Beethoven's sentiments on this point" in order "by this expedient to bring the master near to the court, and as it were to reconcile it with him." Schindler-Moscheles, p. 85. See Anderson, III, 1029, 1116 (nos. 1170, 1273).

51. Thayer-Forbes, p. 185. Nohl, II, 79, 471, however, believes that Beethoven went to Berlin in search of a position but that it was not offered him because he failed to make any particular impression.

52. Köhler-Herre-Beck, I, 252: "Abgeschlossen soll der Bürger vom höhern Menschen sein, und ich bin unter ihn gerathen." See Schindler-MacArdle, p. 221.

53. Anderson, II, 821 (no. 953).

54. In a conversation book entry of December 1819, Beethoven carefully explains the relevance of the Dutch *van* to the question of nobility: "*Van* signifies nobility and the patriciat *only* when it is placed between two proper names, e. g., Bentink van Dieperheim, Hooft van Vreeland, *etc. etc.*" Köhler-Herre-Beck, I, 165.

55. Anderson, III, 1392.

56. Anderson, III, 1049 (no. 1194). Schmitz, *Romantisch*, p. 68, asserts that Beethoven believed he belonged to a separate class of "people of rank" (*Honoratioren*) by virtue of accomplishment and character. This would be congruent with an Enlightenment view—typified by Rousseau in France and Kotzebue in Germany—that aristocracy should be elective rather than hereditary and based on merit rather than birth. See *Social Contract*, III, ch. 6; August von Kotzebue, *Vom Adel* (Leipzig, 1792), ch. 5.

57. Köhler-Herre-Beck, I, 219. Schmitz, *Romantisch*, p. 65, assumes that the "M" stands for "Magistrat," a more convincing reading than Schünemann's "common herd" (*Masse*). A letter of 27 October 1819 to Bach confirms Schmitz's reading: "Since I have raised my nephew into a higher category, neither he nor I have anything to do with the M[agistracy]. For

only innkeepers, cobblers and tailors come under that kind of guardianship." Anderson, II, 852 (no. 979).

58. The first printed report of the myth was in Alexandre Choron and François Fayolle, *Dictionnaire historique des musiciens, artistes et amateurs, morts et vivants* (Paris, 1810), I, 40: "Louis van Beethoven, said to be the natural son of Friedrich Wilhelm II, King of Prussia, was born at Bonn in 1772." This report appeared word for word in Italian translation in Giuseppe Bertini, *Dizionario, storico-critico degli scrittori di musica* (Palermo, 1814), I, 94. Brockhaus, *Konversations-Lexikon* repeated the story in its first edition of 1814 (I, 559), using Choron-Fayolle as its source but altering the royal parent to Frederick the Great. The origin of the legend is unknown. The Brockhaus *Lexikon*, which became the standard German encyclopedia, went through several more widely read editions containing the same material before it was finally dropped in the eighth edition (1833) at Schindler's request.

59. See Solomon, *Beethoven*, esp. pp. 5–6, 21–24.

60. Wegeler-Ries, p. 111.

61. Ernst Bloch, *Spuren* (Berlin, 1930), p. 47.

62. Fischer, pp. 33–34.

4. The Dreams of Beethoven

1. Sigmund Freud, "Some Additional Notes upon Dream-Interpretation as a Whole," *Standard Edition*, XIX, 128.

2. Freud, *Introductory Lectures on Psycho-Analysis, Standard Edition*, XV, 151.

3. Géza Róheim, *The Gates of the Dream* (New York, 1952), p. 428; Otto Rank, *The Trauma of Birth* (London, 1929), p. 75.

4. Wilhelm Stekel, *The Interpretation of Dreams* (New York, 1967), p. 123.

5. K. R. Eissler, *Discourse on Hamlet and "Hamlet": A Psychoanalytic Inquiry* (New York, 1971), p. 52.

6. Freud, *The Interpretation of Dreams, Standard Edition*, V, 546.

7. Paul Ricoeur, *Freud and Philosophy* (New Haven, 1970), pp. 521–522.

8. Freud, *Delusions and Dreams in Jensen's "Gradiva," Standard Edition*, IX, 91.

9. Anderson, I, 169–170 (no. 144), translation revised. The original reads:

Lieber Gleichenstein—die vorgestrige Nacht hatte ich einen Traum, worin mir vorkam, als sey's du in einem Stall, worin du von ein paar prächtigen Pferden ganz bezaubert und hingerissen warst, sodass du Alles rund um dich her vergassest.

Dein Hut-Kauf ist schlecht ausgefallen, er hat schon gestern morgen in aller Früh einen Riss gehabt, wie ich hieher bin; da er zu viel

Geld kostet, um gar so erschrecklich angeschmiert zu werden, so musst du trachten, dass sie ihn zurücknehmen und dir einen andern geben, du kannst das diesen schlechten Kaufleuten derweil ankündigen, ich schicke dir ihn wieder zurück—das ist gar zu arg—

Mir geht es heut und gestern sehr schlecht, ich habe erschreckliches Kopfweh,—der Himmel helfe mir nur hiervon—ich habe ja genug mit einem Uebel—wenn du kannst, schicke mir Baahrd Uebersetzung des Tacitus—auf ein andermal mehr, ich bin so übel, dass ich nur wenig schreiben kann—leb wohl und— denke an meinen Traum und mich—

Baaden, am 13. Juni.

> Dein treuer
> Beethoven.

Aus dem Briefe von Simrock erhellt dass wir wohl von Paris— noch eine günstige Antwort erwarten dürfen, sage meinem Bruder eine Antwort hierüber ob du's glaubst, so dass alles noch einmal geschwind abgeschrieben wird—Schick mir deine Nummer von Deinem Hause.

[On the verso] Antworte mir wegen dem Hut.

From Ludwig Nohl, ed., *Neue Briefe Beethovens* (Stuttgart, 1867), pp. 22–23.

10. Anderson, I, 219 (no. 202).

11. Anderson, I, 265 (no. 248); I, 303 (no. 291).

12. Anderson, II, 849–850 (no. 978) MacArdle-Misch, pp. 292–294. Translation combines both sources, with minor revisions. The original reads:

> . . . Steiner hat schon die Var. von I. K. H., er wird sich selbst bedanken bej ihnen, hiebej fällt mir ein, dass Kaiser Joseph unter dem Namen eines Grafen v. Falkenstein reiste, des Titels halber—Baumeister, wie ich im Diarium gesehn, hat sich in der Ewigkeit Sein Hauss gebaut—ohne den mindesten Anspruch als Empheler Zu machen, wüsste ich jemanden, der diese Stelle bei I. K. H. Zur vollkommenen Zufriedenheit bekleiden würde—ich freue mich sehr um I. K. H. morgen wieder sejn zu können, die verfloszene Nacht traümte [sic.] ich von I. K. H., dies war, obschon dabej nicht Musiciert wurde doch ein Musikal. Traum, allein, auch Wachend denk ich an I. K. H., die Mesze ist nun bald vollendet—der Himmel schicke das Füllhorn Seines Seegens tägl. und stündlich über ihr erlauchtes Haupt, ich aber bin und bleibe bis in den lezten Augenblicken meines Lebens
>
> Ihro kaisl. Hoheit Treuster
> Gehorsamster Diener
> l. v. Beethoven

Mödling am 15ten Oktob.
1819

From Theodor Frimmel, ed., *Beethoven-Forschung* 4 (February 1913): 114–115 (corrected).

13. Donald W. MacArdle, "Beethoven and the Archduke Rudolph," *BJ*, 2d ser., vol. 4 (1962), p. 41.

14. Anderson, II, 887 (no. 1016).

15. MacArdle, "Beethoven and the Archduke Rudolph," p. 55.

16. Anderson, II, 922–924 (no. 1056); Kalischer-Shedlock, II, 184–185; Thayer-Forbes, pp. 778–779. Translation combines Shedlock and Thayer, with numerous minor corrections. The original reads:

Baden am 10. Sept. 1821

Sehr Bester!

Als ich gestern auf dem Wege nach Wien mich im Wagen befand, überfiel mich der schlaf, umsomehr als ich beinahe nie (des Frühaufstehens wegen hier) recht geschlafen hatte, während ich nun schlummere, so träumte mir, ich reiste sehr weit, nicht weniger nach Siryen, nicht weniger nach Indien, wieder zurück nicht weniger nach Arabien, endlich kam ich gar nach Jerusalem, die Heilge stadt erregte den Gedanken an die Heilgen Bücher kein Wunder, wenn mir nun auch der Mann Tobias einfiel, und wie natürlich musste mir also auch unser Tobiasserl und das pertobiasser dabei in den Sinn kommen; nun fiel mir während meiner Traumreise folgender Canon ein:

Allein kaum erwachte ich, fort war der Canon, und es wollte mir nichts mehr davon ins Gedächtniss kommen, jedoch als ich mich andern Tages wieder hierher begab im selben Fuhrwerk (eines armen österreichischen Musikanten) und die gestrige Traumreise wieder jetzt wachend fortsetzte, siehe da, gemäss dem Gesetz der Ideenassociation fiel mir wieder selber Canon ein, ich hielt ihn nun wachend fest, wie einst Menelaos den Proteus, und erlaubte ihm nur noch, dass er sich in 3 Stimmen verwandeln durfte:

Lebt wohl! nächstens werde ich auch auf Steiner was einschicken, um zu zeigen, dass er kein Steinernes Herz hat. Lebt wohl sehr Bester, wir wünschen allzeit dass ihr dem Nahmen Verleger nie entsprecht und nie in Verlegenheit seid, sondern Verleger, welche nie verlegen sind, weder im Einnehmen noch ausgeben—singt alle Tage die Episteln des Heil. Paulus, geht alle Sonntage zum pater Werner, welcher euch das Büchlein anzeigt, wodurch ihr von Mund an in Himmel kommt; ihr seht meine Besorgniss für euer Seelen Heil, und ich verbleibe allzeit mit grösstem Vergnügen von Ewigkeit zu Ewigkeit

Euer treuster Schuldner
Beethoven

From Max Unger, ed., *Ludwig van Beethoven und seine Verleger* (Berlin and Vienna, 1921), pp. 65–66 (corrected).

17. Thayer-Forbes, p. 616.

18. Anderson, III, 1169 (no. 1345).

19. Anderson, III, 1304 (no. 1518), with minor corrections. The letter has no heading, but on the internal evidence—tone and phraseology, the re-

quest to pay the servant, the reference to the B-flat String Quartet—Holz is the only possible addressee. The original reads:

> Die Schwester von der Schwester kommt heute zu ihnen; sie hat mir gestern ein Zeugniss gegeben, non hai danaro, geben sie ihr also das Drangeld, zugleich sagen sie ihr, dass sie 100 fl. jährlich und wöchentlich 36 Kr. Brotgeld habe, diess alles habe ich gestern vergessen. Bringen sie doch das übrige vom Quartett mit dem B mit—ich könnte diese Nacht, da ihre Eltern sie auf die Welt beförderten, und wie viel Schweiss es sie gekostet, ein solches erstaunliches Machwerk ans Tageslicht zu bringen, ich gratulire zum Daseyn—wie? warum? usw. Die Rätsel lösen sich von selbst. Heut zu Tische sehe ich sie,
>
> > der ihrige
> > Beethoven

From A. C. Kalischer, *Beethovens sämtliche Briefe* (Berlin and Leipzig, 1908), V, 253–254.

20. Jacques-Gabriel Prod'homme, ed., *Cahiers de Conversation de Beethoven* (Paris, 1946), p. 346.

21. Anderson, III, 1243 (no. 1424, August 1825).

22. Ibid., III, 1308 (no. 1525).

23. Sandor Ferenczi, *Further Contributions to the Theory and Technique of Psycho-Analysis* (New York, 1960), p. 349.

24. Because of this, only Rudolph and Gleichenstein were recipients of Beethoven dedications, which, owing to his aristocratic identification, were rarely given to commoners, even those who were close friends. Haslinger was, however, the subject and recipient of six canons or musical jokes; Holz was immortalized by a riddle canon contained in a letter and by a musical joke inscribed in a conversation book. Beethoven addressed Gleichenstein and Haslinger in the intimate "Du" form; this form could not be utilized with Rudolph because of his status.

25. Another common element of the first three dreams is that they were written when Beethoven was absent from Vienna. Perhaps he could only permit himself to dream of the mother when he was separated from the city which was her surrogate. As we shall see later, it is of significance that the Holz dream could have been composed in Vienna.

26. Freud, *Introductory Lectures on Psycho-Analysis, Standard Edition*, XV, 157.

27. J. J. Bachofen, *Myth, Religion, and Mother Right* (Princeton, 1967), p. 36.

28. Karl Abraham, *Clinical Papers and Essays on Psychoanalysis* (New York, 1955) p. 75. That Beethoven was conscious of the phallic attributes of the horse is confirmed in the mirthful subscription of his letter to Steiner of 4 September 1816: "With all my heart I embrace the L[ieutenant] G[eneral] and wish him the penis of a stallion." Anderson, II, 594 (no. 651).

29. Ernest Jones, *On the Nightmare* (London, 1949), p. 260.

30. Jones, p. 246.

31. Thayer-Forbes, p. 727.

32. Thayer-Forbes, p. 719.

33. Thayer-Forbes, pp. 94–95, 136.

34. The work appeared under the title "Theme [*Aufgabe*] composed by Ludwig van Beethoven, varied forty times and dedicated to the author by his pupil R[udolph], A[rch] D[uke]."

35. Schindler-Moscheles, pp. 70–71.

36. Freud, *Introductory Lectures on Psycho-Analysis, Standard Edition*, XV, 161. Rank (p. 81) interprets traveling and carriages as separation from the mother.

37. This dream is saturated in religious and mythic imagery. These are not absent, however, from the 1807 and 1819 dreams. Gleichenstein's dream contains an implied reference to the stable of Christ, as well as an exhortation to Heaven. Rudolph's dream is "about" the *Missa solemnis* and arose in part from the news that "Baumeister has built for himself a home in eternity."

38. "Socrates and Jesus have been my models," wrote Beethoven in a conversation book of 1820. Köhler-Herre-Beck, I, 211. The "Holy City" (*heilige Stadt*) is ultimately the maternal womb, with its symbolic fusion of birth and death. However, Beethoven's most famous document, the suicide-haunted Testament of October 1802, was written in, and bears the name of, the Viennese suburb Heiligenstadt.

39. Rank, p. 110.

40. Anderson, I, 4 (no. 1).

41. Anderson, II, 898 (no. 1028). In this letter, Beethoven calls Simrock "My dear old Papa!"

42. Anderson, II, 918 (no. 1051).

43. Freud, *Interpretation of Dreams, Standard Edition*, IV, 245. Cf. Abraham, p. 114: "The tendency of the dream is projected into the future; the dreamer, however, forms his conception of the future in his unconscious phantasies after the pattern of his remote past," and Ferenczi, *Contributions to Psycho-Analysis* (New York, 1956), p. 90: "There lives on in all of us an undying longing for the return of the paradise of childhood; this is the 'Golden Age' that poets and Utopians project from the past into the future."

44. Jones, p. 259.

45. See also Anderson, II, 958–959, 974 (nos. 1087, 1103).

46. Beethoven copied into his Tagebuch the following passage from Hindu theology: "God is immaterial. He is above all conception; as He is invisible, He can have no form; but from what we behold of His works, we may conclude that He is eternal, omnipotent, knowing all things, and present everywhere . . . Brahm, His spirit, is enwrapped in Himself. He, the Mighty One, is present in every part of space." Tagebuch, Nos. 93, 61.

47. Abraham, p. 70.

48. Nohl, *Brevier*, p. 18

49. Anderson, II, 936–937 (no. 1068).

50. Yet since all four dreams may be interpreted as womb dreams, they may represent what Abraham (p. 73) describes as "the strange phantasy in which the son, during his life in the womb, becomes the witness of parental coitus."

51. Freud, "Fragment of an Analysis of a Case of Hysteria," *Standard Edition*, VII, 71.

52. Abraham, p. 182.

53. Leitzmann, II, 241.

54. Ludwig Nohl, *Eine stille Liebe zu Beethoven* (Leipzig, 1902), p. 215.

55. Heinz Kohut remarks of the twinning propensity of the grandiose self: "In a less archaic form of the activation of the grandiose self the narcissistically cathected object is experienced as being like the grandiose self or as being very similar to it. This variation . . . [is] the alter-ego transference or the twinship. Dreams, and especially fantasies, referring to a relationship with such an alter ego or twin (or conscious wishes for such a relationship) are frequently encountered in the analysis of narcissistic personality." Kohut, *The Analysis of the Self* (New York, 1971), p. 115.

56. Fischer, p. 61.

5. The Posthumous Life of Ludwig Maria van Beethoven

1. See Leon Wurmser, "Idealization and Aggression in Beethoven's Creativity," *American Imago* 36 (1979): 333–337.

2. Anderson, I, 3 (no. 1, 15 September 1787, to Joseph Wilhelm von Schaden).

3. Fischer, pp. 62–63.

4. Freud, "The Relation of the Poet to Day-Dreaming," *Collected Papers* (New York, 1959), IV, 176.

5. Anderson, I, 270–271 (no. 256, 2 May 1810, to Franz Gerhard Wegeler).

6. Thayer-Forbes, p. 54.

7. Fischer, pp. 61–62. Beethoven's mother had also lost another son in earliest infancy—Johann Peter Anton Leym, born 25 October 1764, in the second year of her previous marriage. Whether Beethoven ever learned about her first child, or even about her first marriage, is unknown.

8. Salvador Dalí, *The Secret Life of Salvador Dalí* (New York, 1942), p. 2.

9. Henry James, *The Literary Remains of the Late Henry James*, ed. William James (Boston, 1885), p. 141; Howard Feinstein, "The Autobiography of the Elder Henry James," *American Imago* 31 (1974): 296.

10. Joseph Blotner, *Faulkner: A Biography* (New York, 1974), I, 221–232.

11. Hervey Allen, *Israfel: The Life and Times of Edgar Allan Poe* (New York, 1926), pp. 253, 261, 262n, 274–275, 874–879. See also Allen and Thomas Ollive Mabbott, *Poe's Brother: The Poems of William Henry Leonard Poe* (New York, 1926), passim.

12. *The Poetry and Prose of William Blake*, ed. David V. Erdman (Garden City, N.Y., 1965), p. 678 (letter of 6 May 1800).

13. *Blake: Complete Writings*, ed. Geoffrey Keynes (London, 1971), p. 62.

14. Jacob Arlow, "Fantasy Systems in Twins," *Psychoanalytic Quarterly* 29 (1960): 178.

15. Dorothy Burlingham, *Twins: A Study of Three Pairs of Identical Twins* (New York, 1952), pp. 1, 4.

16. Freud, *The Ego and the Id* (New York, 1960), p. 18.

17. Otto Fenichel, *Psychoanalytic Theory of Neurosis* (New York, 1945), pp. 396–397.

18. See Annie Reich, *Psychoanalytic Contributions* (New York, 1973), pp. 294–295.

19. Anderson, I, 270 (no. 256, 2 May 1810, to Wegeler). Translation revised. The original reads: "den Ludwig Maria und den jetzigen nach ihm gekommenen Ludwig ausfindig zu machen." Kastner-Kapp, p. 167.

20. Otto Rank, *The Double: A Psychoanalytic Study* (Chapel Hill, 1971), p. 76.

21. Sheldon Bach, "Notes on Some Imaginary Companions," *Psychoanalytic Study of the Child* 26 (1972): 169. See also Otto Sperling, "An Imaginary Companion, Representing a Prestage of the Superego," *Psychoanalytic Study of the Child* 9 (1954): 252.

22. Wayne A. Myers, "Imaginary Companions . . . ," *Psychoanalytic Quarterly* 45 (1976): 505.

23. Jacob Arlow, "Fantasy Systems in Twins," *Psychoanalytic Quarterly* 29 (1960): 196–197.

24. For impostorship, see Helene Deutsch, *Neuroses and Character Types: Clinical Psychoanalytic Studies* (New York, 1965), pp. 319–338; Phyllis Greenacre, *Emotional Growth: Psychoanalytical Studies* (New York, 1971), I, 93–112; II, 553–554. See also Otto Fenichel, "The Psychology of Transvestitism," *Collected Papers*, 1st ser. (London, 1954), pp. 167–180.

25. Greenacre, I, 103. Greenacre (p. 102) observes that in the family history of impostors, the parents are often at odds, with "the mother frequently despising, reproaching, or attacking the father," thus placing the child in a position of superiority to the father and setting up "a potentially serious imbalance of the oedipal relationship."

26. Anderson, II, 597 (no. 654, 6 September 1816, to J. N. Kanka).

27. Anderson, II, 567 (no. 618, February 1816, to Archduke Rudolph).

28. See Ella Freeman Sharpe, *Collected Papers on Psycho-Analysis* (London, 1950), pp. 142–144. Sharpe (p. 144) remarks: "The artist who through sublimation maintains contact with reality does so by his libidinal and self-preservative impulses."

29. Melanie Klein, *Contributions to Psycho-Analysis, 1921–1945* (London, 1948), p. 318.

30. Ernest Crawley, *The Mystic Rose: A Study of Primitive Marriage,* 2d ed. (London, 1927), I, 285.

31. Freud, "The Uncanny," *Collected Papers,* IV, 387.

32. Anderson, III, 1304 (no. 1518).

33. Freud, "The Theme of the Three Caskets," *Collected Papers,* IV, 254.

6. On Beethoven's Deafness

1. Solomon, *Beethoven,* pp. 19–21.

2. Karl Abraham, *Selected Papers* (London, 1942), p. 203.

3. Sandor Ferenczi, *Contributions to Psycho-Analysis* (New York, 1956), p. 189.

4. Otto Isakower, "On the Exceptional Position of the Auditory Sphere," *International Journal of Psycho-Analysis* 20 (1939): 346.

5. Peter H. Knapp, "The Ear, Listening and Hearing," in *The Yearbook of Psychoanalysis,* ed. Sandor Lorand, vol. 10 (New York, 1955), p. 185.

6. Ludwig Feuerbach, *Lectures on the Essence of Religion* (New York, 1967), p. 27.

7. Wegeler-Ries, p. 121.

8. Kerst, II, 114. However, following a performance of the Mass in C, op. 86, at Prince Lichnowsky's Silesian estate in 1811, Beethoven reportedly "improvised on the organ for half an hour to everyone's astonishment." Kerst, II, 196.

9. William G. Niederland, "Early Auditory Experiences, Beating Fantasies, and Primal Scene," *Psychoanalytic Study of the Child* 13 (1958): 498.

10. Niederland, p. 501.

11. Niederland, p. 474.

12. W. J. Wasielewski, *Ludwig van Beethoven* (Berlin, 1888), I, 33.

13. Heinz Kohut and Siegmund Levarie, "On the Enjoyment of Listening to Music," *Psychoanalytic Quarterly* 19 (1950): 68–69.

14. Anderson, I, 270, 67 (nos. 256, 54; italics mine).

15. See e.g. Knapp; Felix Deutsch, "The Choice of Organ in Organ Neuroses," *International Journal of Psycho-Analysis* 20 (1939): 252–262; Franz Alexander, *The Scope of Psychoanalysis* (New York, 1961), p. 345–358.

16. See Solomon, *Beethoven*, pp. 124–125.

17. Max Weber, *From Max Weber: Essays in Sociology*, ed. H. H. Gerth and C. Wright Mills (New York, 1958), p. 272.

18. Knapp, p. 191.

19. Anderson, I, 63 (no. 53, 1 July 1801).

20. Perhaps this is why, amid all the contradictory explanations that Beethoven offered to explain the origin of his deafness, the earliest one speculated on a connection to his bowels. "This infirmity is said to be caused by the condition of my belly," he wrote to Wegeler on 29 June 1801, and to Amenda two days later: "It is said to be due to the condition of my belly." Anderson, I, 59, 68 (nos. 51, 53).

21. Solomon, *Beethoven*, pp. 111–125.

22. Anderson, II, 1352.

23. Anderson, I, 64 (no. 204, 1 July 1801), trans. from Thayer-Forbes, p. 304 (revised).

24. Cited Nohl, *Brevier*, pp. 59–60, from Christoph Christian Sturm, *Betrachtungen über die Werke Gottes im Reiche der Natur* (Reutlingen, 1811); trans. as *Reflections on the Works of God in Nature and Providence* (Baltimore, 1822), p. 290.

25. Sandor Ferenczi, *Further Contributions to the Theory and Technique of Psycho-Analysis* (New York, 1960), 81–82. In addition to describing his hearing as his "most vital part," Beethoven asked, in the Heiligenstadt Testament: "Ah, how could I possibly admit an infirmity in the *one sense* which ought to be more perfect in me than in others, a sense which I once possessed in the highest perfection." Anderson, III, 1351–1352, trans. from Thayer-Forbes, p. 304.

26. Anderson, I, 220 (no. 204, 28 March 1809).

27. Tagebuch, No. 137.

28. I owe this suggestion to Harry Slochower.

29. Tagebuch, Nos. 1, 88.

7. Thoughts on Biography

1. T. S. Eliot, *Selected Essays* (New York, 1950), p. 4.

2. Ernst Bloch, *Spuren* (Berlin, 1930), p. 158.

3. John Dewey, *Art as Experience* (New York, 1938), p. 82.

4. Charles-Augustin Sainte-Beuve, *Essays*, trans. Elizabeth Lee (London, n.d.), p. 230.

5. Freud, "The Poet and Day-Dreaming," *Collected Papers*, vol. 4 (New York, 1959), p. 180.

6. Harry Slochower, "Psychoanalysis and Creativity," in *Essays on Creativity*, ed. S. Rosner and L. E. Abt (Croton-on-Hudson, N.Y., 1974), p. 163. "Clinical analysis of creative artists suggests that the life experience

of the artist is sometimes only in a limited sense the source of his vision; that his power to imagine conflicts may by far transcend the range of his own experience." Ernst Kris, *Psychoanalytic Explorations in Art* (New York, 1953), p. 288.

7. Anderson, III, 1114 (no. 1270, 10 March 1824, to Bernhard Schotts Söhne). Translation revised.

8. Letter of February 1893, to Gisela Tolney-Witt, cited in H.-L. de La Grange, *Mahler*, vol. 1 (New York, 1973), p. 272.

9. K. R. Eissler, *Discourse on Hamlet and "Hamlet"* (New York, 1971), p. 196.

10. Nicholas Rowe, *Some Account of the Life of Mr. William Shakespeare* (London, 1709).

11. Anton Ehrenzweig, "The Hidden Order of Art," *British Journal of Aesthetics* 1 (1941): 126.

12. Anderson, I, 359 (no. 349, 19 February 1812, to Zmeskall).

13. Marx, *Capital*, vol. 1 (New York, 1947), p. 157.

14. György Lukács, "The Dialectic of Labor: Beyond Causality and Teleology," *Telos* 6 (1970): 166.

15. Marx W. Wartofsky, "Art as Humanizing Praxis," *Praxis* 1 (1975): 56.

16. René Wellek and Austin Warren, *Theory of Literature* (New York, 1956), p. 68.

17. Siegmund Levarie, "Biography of a Composer," *American Imago* 36 (1979): 322–323.

18. M. H. Abrams, *The Mirror and the Lamp: Romantic Theory and the Critical Tradition* (New York, 1953), p. 278.

19. Abrams, p. 275.

20. Mario Praz, *The Romantic Agony* (London, 1933; 2d rev. ed., 1970), p. 2.

8. The Creative Periods of Beethoven

1. Anon., "Ludwig van Beethoven," *Janus*, no. 2 (1818): 10, in Jean Boyer, *Le "romantisme" de Beethoven* (Paris, 1938), pp. 191–192; Johann Aloys Schlosser, *Ludwig van Beethoven: Eine Biographie* (Prague, 1828), pp. 80–84. Both the anonymous writer and Schlosser begin the second period with the Romance, op. 40, the third period with the Fifth Symphony, op. 60. François-Joseph Fétis, *Biographie universelle des musiciens*, vol. 2 (Brussels, 1837), pp. 109–112. See also Walter Petzet, "Erfahrungen beim Studium von Beethovens Klaviersonaten, *NBJ* 5 (1933): 84ff.

2. See Warren Dwight Allen, *Philosophies of Music History*, 2d ed. (New York, 1962), pp. 85–96, 110–114, 263–264.

3. Schindler-Moscheles.

4. In the third edition of his biography (1860), Schindler eliminated

some of the more obvious crudities of this chronology, hedging the question of the transition to the third period by including a number of the same works in both the second- and third-period listings. See Schindler-MacArdle.

5. *AMZ* 45 (1843): cols. 417, 433, 449, 465.

6. *Revue des Deux-Mondes,* 1 October 1850, in Wilhelm von Lenz, *Beethoven et ses trois styles* (Paris, 1909), p. 69.

7. Carl Czerny, "The Periods of Beethoven's Compositions," *Cocks's Musical Miscellany,* 2d ser., 1 (1853): 137ff; William S. Newman, in *JAMS* 20 (1967): 515, notes an earlier reference to the three styles in Czerny, *Pianoforte-Schule,* op. 500 (Vienna, 1842–1846?), IV, 26.

8. (Leipzig, 1852), pp. 339–340. Brendel saw the first period as dominated by Haydn, the second as representing the fully developed product of "a healthy nature," and the third as stemming from loneliness and subjectivity.

9. Lenz, p. 70. Cf. Adolf Sandberger, *Ausgewählte Aufsätze zur Musikgeschichte* (Munich, 1924), II, 43; *Notes,* 2d ser., 20 (1963): 461.

10. *M&L* 8 (1927): 269.

11. (Leipzig and Paris, 1857), pp. 102–109, 163–166.

12. See Nohl; George Grove, "Beethoven," in *Grove's Dictionary of Music and Musicians* (London and New York, 1879), I, 201–202; Hugo Riemann, *Catechism of Music History* (London and New York, 1892), p. 156; C. H. H. Parry, *The Evolution of the Art of Music* (London, 1893), pp. 254–256; Parry, *Style in Musical Art* (London, 1911), p. 255; Ernest Walker, *Beethoven* (New York, 1905), pp. 144–149; Hans Boettcher, *Beethoven als Liederkomponist* (Augsburg, 1928), pp. 29–31; Hans Gál, "Die Stileigentümlichkeiten des jungen Beethoven," *Studien zur Musikwissenschaft* 4 (1916): 58–59; W. H. Hadow, *Oxford History of Music,* vol. 5: *The Viennese Period* (London, 1931), pp. 279–280; Vincent d'Indy, *Beethoven* (Paris, 1911); Ernest Newman, "Wilhelm von Lenz," *M&L* 8 (April 1927): 268–272; Newman, "Beethoven: The Last Phase," in *Testament of Music* (London, 1962), pp. 241–242; D. F. Tovey, "Beethoven," in *Encyclopaedia Britannica,* 14th ed. (London and New York, 1929), III, 319–320; J. G. Prod'homme, *Les Sonates de Beethoven* (Paris, 1937), pp. 100–101, 224; Hugo Leichtentritt, *Music, History, and Ideas* (Cambridge, 1938), pp. 189–190; Eric Blom, *Beethoven's Piano Sonatas Discussed* (London, 1938), pp. 168–172; William McNaught, "Beethoven," in *Grove's Dictionary of Music and Musicians,* 5th ed., ed. Eric Blom (London, 1955), I, 539–540, 550; Joseph Kerman, *The Beethoven Quartets* (New York, 1967), pp. 55, 89–92; Martin Cooper, *Beethoven: The Last Decade* (London, 1970), pp. 8, 132–133. See also F. Niecks, "Beethoven's Sonatas and the Three Styles," *Zeitschrift der Internationalen Musikgesellschaft* 6 (1905): 421f; Jules Combarieu, *Histoire de la musique* (Paris, 1920), II, 594–595; J. F. Rogers, "The Three Beethovens," *MQ* 5 (1919): 505ff; Roderich von Mojsi-

sovics, "Die fünf Stile Beethovens," *Die Musik-Woche* 3. 10 (1935):1ff; Hans Mersmann, *Beethoven: Die Synthese der Stile* (Berlin, 1922); Walter Riezler, *Beethoven* (London, 1938), pp. 135–136, 217ff. I cannot locate an unpublished program note by D. W. MacArdle, "Beethoven and His Three Styles—Why?" mentioned in Ivan Mahaim, *Beethoven: naissance et renaissance des derniers quatuors* (Paris, 1964), II, 564.

13. Kerman, p. 89.

14. Charles Rosen, *The Classical Style* (New York, 1971), p. 389.

15. Letter of 2 December 1852, to Wilhelm von Lenz, in La Mara, ed., *Letters of Franz Liszt,* trans. Constance Bache (London, 1894), vol. I, p. 152.

16. William S. Newman, *A History of the Sonata Idea,* II (Chapel Hill, 1963), 505–537.

17. Nohl was the first to use a tripartite division which treated the Bonn period separately; he gave the second period as Vienna to 1814, the third as 1815–1827. Thayer proposed a four-period plan for the first edition of his Beethoven biography—Bonn, Vienna to 1800, 1800–1816 with a further subdivision at 1806, and the last years—but he did not adhere to this outline in the text, and it was omitted by all the posthumous editors. But see Thayer-Forbes, p. 1106.

18. Gustav Nottebohm, *Beethovens Studien* (Leipzig and Winterthur, 1873), pp. 21–43.

19. Blom, p. 168.

20. Theodor Frimmel, *BJ*, 1st ser., vol. 1 (1908), 58–62.

21. "The third period seems to be merely the full realization of impulses and the sublimation of technical procedures that had been subconscious controlling forces in Beethoven's musical nature from the beginning." Newman, "Beethoven: The Last Phase," p. 242. One might visualize a graph of Beethoven's creative productivity as a series of simultaneous wave-like movements of unequal force, breaking and receding, with newer currents gathering strength to create the basis of the emerging style period. This might account more adequately than the linear three-stage theory for contradictions within each period—the references backward, the anticipatory works, the uneven development, and the differing rates of maturation of simultaneously developing ideas.

22. See Willi Hess, *Beethoven* (Zürich, 1956), p. 46. See also Solomon, "Beethoven, Sonata, and Utopia," *Telos,* no. 9 (Fall, 1971):32–47.

23. Cited in K. R. Eissler, *Goethe: A Psychoanalytic Study* (Detroit, 1963), II, 1365.

24. Schiedermair, pp. 190–196.

25. Solomon, "Beethoven's Productivity at Bonn," *M&L* 53 (1972): 165–172.

26. Max Unger, "Kleine Beethoven-Studien," *NBJ* 8 (1938): 80.
27. Thayer-Forbes, pp. 237–238.
28. See Solomon, *Beethoven*, pp. 219–220.
29. *The New Grove Dictionary of Music & Musicians*, 6th ed. (London, 1980), II, 376–378.
30. Kerman, personal communication.

9. Beethoven's Creative Process: A Two-Part Invention

1. Shelley, *Literary and Philosophical Criticism*, ed John Shawcross (London, 1909), p. 153.
2. Schiller, *Briefe*, ed. F. Jonas (Leipzig, 1892–1896), VI, 262.
3. Thayer-Forbes, p. 620; Anderson, I, 454; II, 928. J. R. Schultz reported in 1824: "I also learnt that he never writes one note down, till he has formed a clear design for the whole piece." *Harmonicon* 2 (1824): 10. Karl Holz told Otto Jahn that Beethoven had completed portions of a Tenth Symphony "in his head" and had played them for Holz on the piano. Thayer-Deiters-Riemann, V, 333.
4. "Stages in the Composition of Beethoven's Piano Trio Op. 70, No. 1," *Proceedings of the Royal Musical Association*, 97 (1970–1971): 15.
5. *Allgemeine deutsche Musik-Zeitung* 7 (1880): 401–405, 413–417; *Hallelujah* 6. 21–22 (1885). The former was partially reprinted in *Allgemeine deutsche Musik-Zeitung* 12 (1885): 200–201; *The Musical Times* 35 (1894): 225–227, 305–307 (abridged).
6. Translation of the 1885 version after Sonneck, pp. 146–147. The 1885 version contains eight minor "revisions" of the 1880 paragraph: five words or phrases are omitted and three others are altered. There are numerous differences in other supposedly "verbatim" passages; the "daily memoranda" that Schlösser claimed to have consulted have not survived. *Allgemeine deutsche Musik-Zeitung* 7 (1880): 401.
7. Thayer-Deiters-Riemann, IV, 421n1.
8. Riezler, *Beethoven*, 9th ed. (Zurich, 1966), p. 94, trans. G. D. H. Pidcock, *Beethoven* (London, 1938), p. 91; Newman, *The Unconscious Beethoven* (New York, 1927), p. 146.
9. "An Unpublished Letter of Mozart," trans. J. R. Schultz, *Harmonicon*, 3 (1825): 198–200, with corrections.
10. *AMZ* 17, (1814–1815): 561–566.
11. See Otto Jahn, *W. A. Mozart* (Leipzig, 1856–1859), III, 496–497; O. E. Deutsch, "Spurious Mozart Letters," *MR* 24 (1964): 120–123. Contrary to Deutsch, the letter is not mentioned in G. N. Nissen, *Biographie W. A. Mozarts* (Leipzig, 1828), or in the first edition of Ludwig Nohl, *Mozarts Briefe* (Salzburg, 1865).

12. Edward Holmes, *The Life of Mozart* (London, 1845), p. 320. For Moscheles's denial, see Jahn, III, 497n3.

13. Jahn, III, 496–505.

14. William James, *Principles of Psychology* (New York, 1907), I, 255.

15. Nohl, *Mozarts Briefe*, 2d ed. (Leipzig, 1877); Deutsch, p. 122; *Mozart: Briefe und Aufzeichnungen*, ed. W. A. Bauer, O. E. Deutsch, and J. H. Eibl (Kassel, 1962–1975), VI, 674. See also Neal Zaslaw, review of *Mozart: Briefe und Aufzeichnungen* in *JAMS* 31 (1978): 370–372.

16. *Mozart*, III, 505.

17. Deutsch, p. 121.

18. See *Mozart-Bibliographie bis 1970*, ed. R. Angermüller and O. Schneider (*Mozart-Jahrbuch*, 1975), (Kassel, 1976), p. 242.

19. Rochlitz, "Analekten für Künstler, Kunstrichter, Kunstfreunde," *AMZ* 17 (1814–1815): 697–702, 713–717, 729–735, 745–750. For Rochlitz, see the biographical sketch by Dörffel in F. Rochlitz, *Für Freunde der Tonkunst*, 3rd ed. (Leipzig, 1868), pp. 321–343; *MGG*, XI, 390–393.

20. Novalis, *Gesammelte Werke*, ed. Carl Seelig (Zurich, 1945), pp. 247–248, quoted in René Wellek, *A History of Modern Criticism*, vol. 2 (New Haven & London, 1955), p. 85.

21. Goethe also referred to "innocent, somnambulatory production" in a conversation with Eckermann of 2 January 1824 and again in a conversation of 14 March 1830. For his enthusiastic response on reading the "Mozart" letter, see *Mozart: Briefe und Aufzeichnungen*, VI, 674.

22. Letter of 15 November 1831, in O. E. Deutsch, *Schubert: Memoirs by His Friends* (London, 1958), p. 156; see also pp. 146, 216, 226, 302.

23. Franz Xaver Niemetschek, *Life of Mozart* (London, 1956), pp. 62–63. The connection with Rochlitz's letter was noted by J. H. Eibl, "Ein Brief Mozarts über seine Schaffensweise," *Österreichische Musikzeitschrift* 35 (1980): 584–585.

24. E. T. A. Hoffmann, *Höchst zerstreute Gedanken*, in *Gesammelte Werke*, ed. Eduard Griesebach (Leipzig, 1900), I, 47.

25. Wilhelm Heinrich Wackenroder and Ludwig Tieck, *Outpourings of an Art-Loving Friar* (New York, 1975), p. 23.

26. Friedrich Schlegel, *Lessings Geist aus seinen Schriften* (Leipzig, 1804), I, 336–340, in Wellek, *A History of Modern Criticism*, II, 22, 350.

27. Aristotle, *Metaphysics*, VII.8 (1034a), see also VII.7 (1032a), VII.8 (1035a).

28. See Erwin Panofsky, *Idea: A Concept in Art Theory*, trans. Joseph J. S. Peake (New York, 1968), pp. 9–43 .

29. Porphyry, *Life of Plotinus*, in A. H. Armstrong, *Plotinus* (New York, 1962), pp. 45–46.

30. For the first sentence of his paragraph on Beethoven's creativity Schlösser may have turned to a passage of 16 December 1828 in Goethe's

Conversations with Eckermann: "I carried the ballad about with me for a long time before I set it down."

31. See Schindler-MacArdle, pp. 456–457; August von Klöber, in *AMZ*, n.s., 2 (1864): 324, repr. in Kerst, I, 236.

32. See Deutsch, *Schubert*, p. 331.

33. Jahn, I, xi; III, 161–163. To his credit, Rochlitz never attempted to print this account, though several of its details were used in his anecdotes. See e.g. *AMZ* 1 (1798–1799): 54.

34. Nissen, *Biographie W. A. Mozarts*, p. 687; Anhang, pp. 29–30. Constanze Mozart had also provided material to Rochlitz. *AMZ* 1 (1798–1799): 289–291, 854–856. However, she repeatedly expressed doubts about the authenticity of Rochlitz's anecdotes. *Mozart: Briefe und Aufzeichnungen*, IV, 267; VI, 492.

35. Anderson, I, 106. For Beethoven's bitter resentment of his reviews in *AMZ*, see Anderson, I, 53 (no. 48, 22 April 1801); I, 96 (no. 81, September 1803); I, 338 (no. 325, 9 October 1811, to B&H). In January 1825, his nephew, Karl, calmed the angry composer: "Rochlitz is not guilty for the article about the 'medal' in the *musikalischen Zeitung*," inasmuch as "he has not been editor for five years." Köhler-Herre-Beck, VII, 113.

36. Anderson, I, 339 (no. 325). Alan Tyson, personal communication, notes that Beethoven's letter contains a delightful veiled reference to the "Song of the Flea" from *Faust*, in which Beethoven hazards that the stinging gnat will meet the same fate as Goethe's "grosser Floh."

37. Anderson, III, 1236 (no. 1415); T. Frimmel, "Ein Konversationsheft Beethovens aus dem Jahre 1825," *BJ*, 1st ser., vol. 2 (1909), 166.

38. *AMZ* 23 (1820–1821): 539.

39. First published in Rochlitz, *Für ruhige Stunden* (Leipzig, 1828), repr. in *Für Freunde der Tonkunst* (Leipzig, 1824–1832), 3rd ed., ed. Dörffel (1868).

40. Thayer-Deiters-Riemann, IV, 282.

41. Ibid., IV, 281. See also MacArdle-Misch, p. 387; Anderson, II, 951n2.

42. *Harmonicon* 2 (1824): 10–11.

43. Another possible source is W. C. Müller, "Etwas über Beethoven," *AMZ* 29 (1826–1827): 345–354.

44. Thayer-Deiters-Riemann, IV, 287–288.

45. G. W. von Biedermann, *Goethe's Briefwechsel mit Friedrich Rochlitz* (Leipzig, 1887), pp. 258–264. See also Wilhelm Bode, *Die Tonkunst in Goethes Leben* (Berlin, 1912), II, 171n.

46. The letter, which Sieghard Brandenburg called to my attention, is in the Morgan Library, New York.

47. Schindler-MacArdle, p. 244.

48. Enraged at the prospect that his rival, Karl Holz, had Beethoven's written authorization to write his posthumous biography, Schindler fab-

ricated Beethoven's deathbed request that Rochlitz be engaged as biographer, an honor that Rochlitz declined. Schindler-MacArdle, pp. 31–33. See also Clemens Brenneis, "Das Fischhof-Manuskript. Zur Frühgeschichte der Beethoven-Biographik," *Zu Beethoven* I, pp. 95–101.

49. Anderson, I, 68 (no. 54).

50. Anderson, II, 689 (no. 788).

10. Beethoven and His Nephew: A Reappraisal

1. Anderson, II, 558 (no. 607, 6 February 1816, to Antonie Brentano).

2. Schindler-Moscheles, p. 117.

3. Schindler-MacArdle, p. 231; See also 315, where Schindler charges Beethoven with some responsibility for Karl's attempted suicide.

4. Ludwig Nohl, *Life of Beethoven* (London [1879]), p. 150.

5. Nohl, *Eine stille Liebe zu Beethoven*, 2d ed. (Leipzig, 1902), p. 138.

6. Thayer, III, 372; Thayer-Forbes, p. 635.

7. Thayer-Deiters-Riemann, IV, 93; Thayer-Krehbiel, II, 393; Thayer-Forbes, p. 697. It is not clear whether this passage was written by Thayer or by his posthumous editors, who maintained his high level of objectivity. Thayer-Krehbiel (II, 401) headed pages dealing with this subject: "A Mother's Struggle for Her Child," and noted: "Johanna van Beethoven is at least entitled to the same hearing at the bar of posterity that she received in the tribunals of her day." See also Thayer-Forbes, pp. 694, 700–701.

8. Ernest Newman, *The Unconscious Beethoven: An Essay in Musical Psychology* (London, 1927), p. 21.

9. Paul Bekker, *Beethoven* (Berlin & Leipzig, 1911), pp. 30, 57; Eng. trans. (London, 1932), pp. 31, 57.

10. J. W. N. Sullivan, *Beethoven: His Spiritual Development* (London, 1927), p. 204.

11. Walter Riezler, *Beethoven*, 9th ed. (Zurich, 1966), p. 53; Eng. trans. (London, 1938), p. 49.

12. Rolland, p. 475.

13. See also O. G. Sonneck, *Beethoven Letters in America* (New York, 1927), p. 147. For one-sided defenses of Beethoven's actions, see biographies by Richard Specht, Édouard Herriot, Emil Ludwig, André de Hevesy, Vincent d'Indy, Marion Scott, Theodor Frimmel, George Marek, Jean and Brigitte Massin, and Karl Schönewolf, as well as the entries in *MGG* (Joseph Schmidt-Görg) and *Grove's Dictionary*, 5th ed. (William McNaught).

14. (New York, 1954); (London, 1957); *Beethoven et sa famille* (Paris, 1955); *Ludwig van Beethoven und sein Neffe: Tragödie eines Genies* (Munich, 1964). See also R. and E. Sterba, "Beethoven and His Nephew," *International Journal of Psycho-Analysis* 33 (1952): 470–478.

15. Thayer-Forbes, p. 697.

16. "His purpose was pure and lofty, and his action prompted by both love and an ideal sense of moral obligation." Ibid.

17. Ludwig Misch, *Neue Beethoven-Studien und andere Themen* (Bonn, 1967), pp. 104–108; Nettl, letter to *M & L* 39 (1958): 326; Willy Hess, *Beethoven-Studien* (Bonn, 1972), pp. 225–231. Joseph Schmidt-Görg, "Entwicklung und Aufgaben der Beethoven-Forschung," in Erich Schenk, ed., *Beethoven-Symposion* (Vienna, 1971), p. 246, apparently includes the Sterbas' book in his reference to recent attempts at "sensational disclosures." See also Harry Goldschmidt, "Der späte Beethoven—Versuch einer Standortbestimmung," in H. A. Brockhaus and K. Niemann, ed., *Bericht über den internationalen Beethoven-Kongress* . . . (Berlin, 1971), pp. 44–45; Goldschmidt, *Um die unsterbliche Geliebte* (Leipzig, 1977), pp. 242–255.

18. Review by Peter J. Pirie, *MR* 38 (1957): 337–339.

19. *Notes*, 2d ser., 12 (1955): 448.

20. *M & L* 39 (1958): 175.

21. Martin Cooper, *Beethoven: The Last Decade, 1817–1827* (London, 1970), p. 33; see esp. pp. 29, 31, 46. The Appendix to Cooper, "Beethoven's Medical History," by Edward Larkin, takes a rather different view, opposing conjectural postmortem psychoanalytic reconstructions. This does not prevent him from attempting (p. 475) a clinical diagnosis ("Affective Disorder, or Manic-Depressive Disorder") of Beethoven's mental condition. See also Cooper, *Ideas and Music* (London, 1965), pp. 51–54. For an extreme adoption of the Sterbas' theses, see Alan Pryce-Jones, Introduction to reprint of Thayer-Krehbiel (London, 1960).

22. *Journal of the American Psychoanalytic Association* 8 (1960): 577.

23. *The Psychoanalytic Quarterly* 24 (1955): 454.

24. K. R. Eissler, *Talent and Genius* (New York, 1971), p. 20.

25. Eissler, *Goethe: A Psychoanalytic Study* (Detroit, 1963), II, 1313.

26. Ibid. For other reviews, see *International Journal of Psycho-Analysis* 37 (1956): 507–508; *American Journal of Psychiatry* 113 (1956): 36–40.

27. Despite a surface appearance of thoroughness, major bibliographical lacunae weaken the book's utility. Its documentation derives from a small nucleus of the literature. For biographical data, the authors made good use of Thayer-Deiters-Riemann, Thayer-Krehbiel, Wegeler-Ries, Breuning, Schindler-Moscheles, and Nohl. For the letters, the unannotated Kastner-Kapp was used almost exclusively. Schünemann's edition of the conversation books was exhaustively consulted, augmented by Prod'homme, *Cahiers de Conversation* (Paris, 1946). Reminiscences of contemporaries are cited from Kerst and Stephan Ley, *Beethoven, Sein Leben in Selbstzeugnissen, Briefen und Berichten* (Berlin, 1939). A handful of other works are cited in passing. The periodical literature is almost wholly ignored. The relevant works of Kalischer, Schiedermair, Prod'homme, Leitzmann, Pre-

linger, MacArdle, Chantavoine, Frimmel, Unger, Sonneck, Schmitz, Bekker, Riezler, and Sandberger were not consulted. Schindler (1860) is cited solely from an abridged version. The only previous book containing a psychoanalytical study of Beethoven—Max Graf, *Die innere Werkstatt des Musikers* (Stuttgart, 1910), trans. and rev. as *From Beethoven to Shostakovich* (New York, 1947)—is overlooked, though written by a member of Freud's inner circle. The Sterbas were evidently unfamiliar with two other works which briefly anticipate their main thesis that Beethoven's relationship to his nephew is that of the adoring mother: Alexandre Oulibicheff, *Beethoven, ses critiques et ses glossateurs* (Leipzig & Paris, 1857), p. 77; Fan S. Noli, *Beethoven and the French Revolution* (New York, 1947), p. 53.

28. Joseph Kerman, "An die ferne Geliebte," *BS* 1 (1973): 129.

29. Other details of interest include a close reading of several passages in the Immortal Beloved letter (pp. 104–105) and an elucidation of hitherto obscure references in letters to Zmeskall (p. 110) which lead to the possible conclusion (partially drawn by Cooper, though not by the Sterbas) that Beethoven engaged in congress with prostitutes through Zmeskall's mediation in the second decade of the nineteenth century.

30. The Sterbas' objectivity should have ended the widespread error that Johanna's 1811 arrest was for adultery rather than for a minor theft. Krehbiel mistranslated Thayer's "Veruntreuung" (III, 372) as "infidelity" (Thayer-Krehbiel, II, 331, 400); this error was perpetuated in Thayer-Forbes, p. 634, and repeated in Massin, *Beethoven, une documentation* (Paris, 1967), p. 288; Rolland, p. 475; George Marek, *Beethoven, Biography of a Genius* (New York, 1969), p. 495, the last on the recommendation of Joseph Schmidt-Görg. Another irrepressible myth is the assertion that Johanna took a lover during Caspar Carl's final illness and had an illegitimate child by him. See Cooper, p. 22.

31. Graf, *Die innere Werkstatt des Musikers*, passim.

32. Arnold Schmitz, *Beethoven* (Bonn, 1927), p. 48.

33. Nohl, *Beethoven nach den Schilderungen seiner Zeitgenossen* (Stuttgart, 1877), p. 166, Eng. trans., *Beethoven: Depicted by His Contemporaries* (London, 1880), pp. 220–221.

34. Breuning, p. 40.

35. Thayer-Deiters-Riemann, IV, 513–541; Nohl, *Eine stille Liebe zu Beethoven.*

36. Letter of 22 February 1819, to Bishop Sailer, in Adolf Sandberger, *Ausgewählte Aufsätze zur Musikgeschichte* (Munich, 1924), II, 255–256.

37. Sir John Russell, cited in Sonneck, pp. 114–115. Schindler, too, called Beethoven "the great child" (Schindler-MacArdle, p. 383), and Rust earlier described him as "very childlike" (Kerst, I, 123). See also Nohl, *Eine stille Liebe*, p. 125.

38. Frimmel, *Beethoven-Studien* (Munich & Leipzig, 1906), II, 119.

39. See, e.g. Wegeler-Ries, p. 95; Ignaz von Seyfried, ed., *Ludwig van Beethoven's Studien* (Vienna, 1832), App., pp. 11, 15; Eng. trans. (Leipzig, 1853), pp. 8, 11.

40. Fischhof Manuscript (DSB), fol. 3r; Thayer, I, 241; Thayer-Forbes, p. 232; Kerst, I, 125; Louis Spohr, *Autobiography* (London, 1865), I, 184–189; Kerst, I, 131–132.

41. Thayer-Deiters-Riemann, III, 448; Thayer-Forbes, p. 595.

42. Nohl, *Beethoven nach den Schilderungen*, p. 121; Eng. trans., p. 158.

43. Ibid., p. 118; Eng. trans., p. 154.

44. Frimmel, *Handbuch*, I, 233.

45. Thayer-Deiters-Riemann, IV, 163; Thayer-Forbes, p. 738.

46. Thayer, journal entry of 4 July 1860, in Krehbiel, *Music and Manners in the Classical Period* (Westminster, 1898), p. 210.

47. Kerst, II, 82.

48. Krehbiel, pp. 206–208; Thayer-Deiters-Riemann, IV, 224–225; Thayer-Forbes, pp. 777–778.

49. Thayer-Deiters-Riemann, V, 256; Thayer-Forbes, p. 967. Breuning (p. 64) reports that Karl "was ashamed to accompany [Beethoven] . . . because of his 'ridiculous appearance.' Beethoven told us about it, greatly hurt and disturbed."

50. Breuning, p. 74.

51. Nohl, *Beethoven nach den Schilderungen*, p. 141; Eng. trans., p. 185.

52. Schindler-Moscheles, pp. 17–18.

53. Schindler-MacArdle, p. 231.

54. Anderson, II, 636 (no. 710).

55. Anderson, II, 771 (no. 904).

56. Anderson, II, 759 (no. 894).

57. Anderson, II, 789 (no. 933).

58. See Leo Schrade, *Beethoven in France* (New Haven, 1942), passim; Wilhelm von Lenz, *Beethoven et ses trois styles*, rev. ed. (Paris, 1909), p. 69; Joseph de Marliave, *Beethoven's Quartets* (London, 1928), pp. 229–230.

59. Lombroso, *Genio e follia* (Milan, 1864); 5th rev. ed. *L'uomo di genio in rapporto alla psichiatria, alla storia ed all'estetica* (Turin, 1888); Eng. trans., *The Man of Genius* (London, 1891); Leo Tolstoy, *What Is Art?* (New York, 1962), pp. 197–198, 222, 248. Thomas Mann's view of late Beethoven, shaped by T. W. Adorno, is also in this line. See *Doktor Faustus* (1946), ch. 8; Wilhelm Lange-Eichbaum [pseud. Wilhelm Lange], *Genie, Irrsinn und Ruhm: Eine Pathographie des Genies*, 4th ed. rev. Wolfram Kurth (Munich & Basle, 1956), pp. 274–276, 498–499. See also Lange-Eichbaum, *The Problem of Genius* (New York, 1932), pp. 120, 146. J. F. Nisbet, *The In-*

sanity of Genius, 4th ed. (London, 1900), p. 167, judged that "the eccentricities of Beethoven bordered upon insanity."

60. Frimmel, *Handbuch*, I, 232–234, 235–237.

61. Newman, p. 54.

62. See Schindler-MacArdle, pp. 164–165; Thayer-Deiters-Riemann, III, 438–439; Thayer-Forbes, pp. 589–590.

63. Eissler, *Goethe*, II, 1375, 1391.

64. Ernst Kris, *Psychoanalytic Explorations in Art* (New York, 1952), p. 60.

65. Edward Glover, *Freud or Jung?* (London, 1950), pp. 185–186.

66. Eissler, "Psychopathology and Creativity," *American Imago* 24 (1967): 52.

67. "The minds that we admire as truly creative produced values that are greater than themselves . . . The artist is capable of creating what he himself can never be; perhaps what rests in him is a potentiality that cannot grow into something psychic and personal, but can be realized only through and within an objective medium." Eissler, *Discourse on Hamlet and "Hamlet"* (New York, 1971), pp. 460–461.

68. H. Hartmann, E. Kris, and R. Loewenstein, "Notes on the Theory of Aggression," in *Papers on Psychoanalytic Psychology* (New York, 1964), p. 77.

69. Richard Wagner, *Beethoven* (Leipzig, 1870); Eng. trans., Albert R. Parsons (New York, 1872), p. 62.

70. Anderson, II, 887 (no. 1016). The Sterbas apparently regard any criticism of established authority as indicative of a psychological defect.

71. Schindler-MacArdle, p. 50

72. Thayer-Deiters-Riemann, II, p. 519; Thayer-Forbes, p. 403.

73. Solomon, *Beethoven*, pp. 231–255.

11. Recherche de Josephine Deym

1. See Solomon, "New Light on Beethoven's Letter to an Unknown Woman," *MQ* 58 (1972): 572–587; Solomon, *Beethoven*, pp. 158–189; Solomon, "Antonie Brentano and Beethoven," *M&L* 58 (1977): 153–169.

2. Harry Goldschmidt, *Um die "Unsterbliche Geliebte"* (Leipzig, 1977); Marie-Elisabeth Tellenbach, *Beethoven und seine "unsterbliche Geliebte" Josephine Brunswick* (Zurich, 1983). These books substantially derive from Siegmund Kaznelson, *Beethovens ferne und unsterbliche Geliebte* (Zurich, 1954); Jean and Brigitte Massin, *Recherche de Beethoven* (Paris, 1970).

3. Goldschmidt, *Unsterbliche Geliebte*, p. 175.

4. Goldschmidt, *Unsterbliche Geliebte*, p. 176.

5. Goldschmidt tries to shift the burden of proof to those who wish to "exclude Josephine Brunsvik with real certainty." They are called upon to prove "that she could not have been either in Prague or in Karlsbad or a neighboring spa during the time in question." Goldschmidt, *Unsterbliche Geliebte*, p. 162.

6. Virginia Oakley Beahrs, "The Immortal Beloved Revisited," *The Beethoven Newsletter*, ed. William Meredith, vol. 1 (Summer 1986), p. 22.

7. Jean and Brigitte Massin, *Ludwig van Beethoven* (Paris, 1967), p. 243.

8. Tellenbach, p. 113.

9. Nachlass Deym. Goldschmidt (*Unsterbliche Geliebte*, p. 166) notes this draft letter but does not quote from it or give its date. I am grateful to Sieghard Brandenburg for suggesting that I pursue this letter and to Clemens Brenneis for providing me with a copy of it.

10. Nachlass Deym. Written from Ofen, Hungary. Communicated by Clemens Brenneis.

11. Goldschmidt, *Unsterbliche Geliebte*, p. 169.

12. Nachlass Deym, in Goldschmidt, *Unsterbliche Geliebte*, p. 163.

13. Sieghard Brandenburg, *Beethoven: Der Brief an die Unsterbliche Geliebte* (Bonn, 1986), p. 30; Kaznelson, p. 252; Goldschmidt, p. 233.

14. For Beethoven's asserted paternity, see Kaznelson, p. 274; Tellenbach, p. 194. But Goldschmidt (*Unsterbliche Geliebte*, pp. 162–163, 168–169) demonstrates that Kaznelson was mistaken about Stackelberg's absence from Vienna.

15. Goldschmidt, *Unsterbliche Geliebte*, p. 165.

16. Kaznelson, p. 252; Goldschmidt, *Unsterbliche Geliebte*, p. 233.

17. Tagebuch, No. 1.

18. Tellenbach, p. 122.

19. Fanny Giannatasio del Rio, diary entry of 16 September 1816, in Thayer-Deiters-Riemann, IV, 534; Thayer-Forbes, p. 646.

20. Anderson, I, 175 (no. 151, 20 September 1807). The phrase also occurs in a fragmentary copy in Countess Deym's hand of a letter possibly written by Beethoven in 1804 or 1805. See Anderson, I, 134 (no. 112).

21. Beahrs, pp. 17, 22–24; Harry Goldschmidt, "'Auf diese Art mit A geht alles zu Grunde': Eine umstrittene Tagebuchstelle in neuem Licht," typescript, 1986.

22. Harry Goldschmidt, "Beethoven in neuen Brunsvik-Briefen," *BJ*, 2d ser., vol. 9 (1977), p. 143; Goldschmidt, personal communication.

23. Tellenbach, pp. 194–195, facsimile on p. 113. With typical circularity Tellenbach (p. 194) identifies Beethoven as the addressee because, by its form and content, "it could only have been directed to him."

24. For an analysis of the difficulties of the Josephine Deym hypothesis, see Barry Cooper, review of Goldschmidt, *Um die "Unsterbliche Geliebte,"* in *M&L* 60 (1979): 463–464.

25. Anderson, I, 175, 177, 178–179 (nos. 151, 153, 154, 156).
26. George Marek, *Beethoven: Biography of a Genius* (New York, 1969), p. 260.
27. Marek, p. 259 (italics mine).
28. Marek, p. 259.
29. Marek, p. 244.
30. Anderson, I, 135 (no. 114, spring 1805).
31. Anderson, I, 134, 135, 136, 142, 178 (nos. 113, 114, 115, 125, 154).
32. Massin and Massin, *Recherche de Beethoven*, p. 140.
33. Goldschmidt, *Unsterbliche Geliebte*, p. 301.
34. Goldschmidt, *Unsterbliche Geliebte*, pp. 298–301, 316.
35. Tellenbach, pp. 226, 232, 256.

12. Antonie Brentano and Beethoven

1. Elsewhere I have presented documentary evidence that Antonie Brentano née von Birkenstock (1780–1869) was the probable recipient of Beethoven's much-discussed letter of 6–7 July 1812, which was written from Teplitz, a Bohemian spa, to an unidentified woman whom he called his "Immortal Beloved." See Solomon, "New Light on Beethoven's Letter to an Unknown Woman, " *MQ* 58 (1972): 572–587; Solomon, *Beethoven*, pp. 158–189. The unpublished correspondence is quoted, with permission, from DSB, Handschriftenabteilung/Literaturarchiv, Nachlass Savigny, and GM.
2. Bettina von Arnim, *Goethe's Correspondence with a Child* (Lowell, Mass., 1841), II, 275–276 (letter of 15 May 1810), translation amended.
3. Franz Gräffer, *Kleine Wiener Memoiren und Wiener Dosenstücke*, ed. Anton Schlossar and Gustav Gugitz (Munich, 1918), II, 137.
4. Letter of 12 November 1806, to Gunda and Karl von Savigny (DSB).
5. Maria Andrea Goldmann, *Im Schatten des Kaiserdomes. Frauenbilder* (Limburg, 1938), p. 75.
6. Goldmann, p. 79
7. Goldmann, p. 81.
8. Goldmann, p. 81. This entry appears to date from 1798, perhaps in connection with Antonie Brentano's marriage, for the next entry reads: "On the 28th of July 1798 I got married, and the wedding ceremony took place in St. Stephen's in Vienna, and I left one week thereafter for Frankfurt."
9. Bettina von Arnim, *Goethe's Correspondence with a Child*, I, 28; *Goethes Briefwechsel mit Antonie Brentano, 1814–1821*, ed. Rudolf Jung (Weimar, 1896), p. 4.
10. Letter of 11 March 1798 (DSB). The entire correspondence file is in DSB.
11. The first is reprinted in *Goethes Briefwechsel mit Antonie Bren-*

tano, pp. 5–12; the second in *Frankfurter Beiträge Arthur Rickel gewidmet*, ed. Hubert Schiel (Frankfurt, 1933), pp. 68–72. According to Schiel, who worked with the manuscripts at the Frankfurt Municipal Archive before their destruction during World War II, the conversation of 25 January 1866 was published by Jung "insofar as it concerned Goethe," and he himself published the conversation of 4 May 1865. Schiel's version aims to be a diplomatic transcription, while Jung's is apparently in part a paraphrase, with the narrative altered—except for those passages pertaining to Goethe—from first to third person.

12. Antonie Brentano's children were Mathilde Josefe Maximiliane (3 July 1799–5 April 1800), Georg Franz Melchior (13 January 1801–1 March 1852), Maximiliane Euphrosyne Kunigunde (8 November 1802–1 September 1861), Josefa Ludovica (29 June 1804–2 February 1875), Francisca (Fanny) Elisabethe Magdalena (26 June 1806–16 October 1837), and Karl Josef (8 March 1813–18 May 1850).

13. Clemens Brentano, *Gesammelte Schriften* (Frankfurt, 1855), VIII, 110, 124 (letter of February 1800, undated letter [1804?]).

14. Wilhelm Schellberg and Friedrich Fuchs, ed., *Das unsterbliche Leben: Unbekannte Briefe von Clemens Brentano* (Jena, 1939), p. 299.

15. Letter of mid-April 1803, Schellberg and Fuchs, p. 300.

16. Letter of 23 April 1805, cited in *Briefwechsel zwischen Clemens Brentano und Sophie Mereau*, ed. Heinz Amelung, vol. 2 (Leipzig, 1908), p. 161.

17. Letter of 8 September 1799 (DSB).

18. Letter of 4 November 1803 (DSB).

19. Letter of 6 December 1799 (DSB).

20. Letter of 3 September 1803, to Gunda Brentano (DSB).

21. "The only thing that changes my monotony is my pregnancy," Antonie wrote. Letter of 13 April 1804, to Gunda (DSB).

22. Henry Crabb Robinson, *Diary, Reminiscences, and Correspondence*, vol. 1 (Boston, 1870), p. 55.

23. Letter of 1 September 1805, to Sophia Brentano, in Reinhold Steig, *Achim von Arnim und Clemens Brentano* (Stuttgart, 1894), p. 144.

24. Schellberg and Fuchs, p. 268.

25. Bettina von Arnim, *Werke und Briefe*, ed. Gustav Konrad (Frechen/Cologne, 1959–1961), V, 265.

26. Letter of 10 July 1806, to Clemens Brentano (DSB).

27. Letter of 3 October [no year], to Karl von Savigny (DSB).

28. Letter of 21 June 1808, to Gunda and Karl von Savigny (DSB).

29. Reinhold Steig, *Achim von Arnim und Bettina Brentano* (Stuttgart and Berlin, 1913), p. 161.

30. Goldmann, pp. 95–96; Undated letter, c.1807 or 1808.

31. Letter of 14 December 1808 (GM).

32. Letter of 21 November 1808 (GM).
33. Letter of 16 June 1809 (GM).
34. Letter of 28 July 1807 (DSB).
35. Letter of 10 January 1811, in *Gesammelte Schriften*, VIII, 163. See also Clemens Brentano's letter of 2 November 1810 to the brothers Grimm, in Reinhold Steig, *Clemens Brentano und die Brüder Grimm* (Stuttgart and Berlin, 1914), p. 136.
36. Letter of 26 January 1811, to Clemens Brentano (GM).
37. Letter of 9 January 1812 (GM).
38. Otto Jahn, "Ein Brief Beethovens," *Grenzboten: Zeitschrift für Politik und Literatur* 26. 2 (1867): 100–101.
39. Letter of 5 June 1811, to Merkel (GM).
40. Letter of 9 January 1812, to Clemens Brentano (GM).
41. Schindler-MacArdle, p. 259.
42. Thayer-Deiters-Riemann, III, 216.
43. Thayer-Deiters-Riemann, III, 216.
44. See Thayer-Deiters-Riemann, I, 506–508.
45. H. von Schrötter-Firnhaber, "Antonie Brentano," *Alt-Frankfurt* 3 (1930): 106.
46. Ludwig Nohl, *Neue Beethoven Briefe* (Stuttgart, 1867), p. 53. See also Solomon, "Antonie Brentano and Beethoven," *M&L* 58 (1977): 158n34.
47. Jahn, "Ein Brief Beethovens," pp. 100–101. For Beethoven's intercession with Archduke Rudolph, see Anderson, I, 328 (no. 316, 1811, to Ignaz von Baumeister). See also letter of 15 February 1811 from Archduke Rudolph to Baumeister: "Please speak with Frau von Brentano née Birkenstock about the two works which Beethoven praised." *BJ*, 1st ser., vol. 2 (1909), p. 321.
48. Letter of 26 January 1811, to Clemens Brentano (GM). Antonie's perception of Beethoven as an "immortal" may have some bearing on the origins of Beethoven's odd phrase, "my Immortal Beloved."
49. The autograph of "An die Geliebte" is in the BN, Paris.
50. Jahn, "Ein Brief Beethovens," p. 101. In a letter of 13 January 1854 to Wilhelm Speyer in Frankfurt (DSB), Jahn made discreet inquiry concerning Beethoven and Frau Brentano: "It would be splendid if you could entice from this excellent woman [Antonie Brentano's friend Marianne von Willemer] some additional information concerning Beethoven's connection with Frau von Brentano." Clemens Brenneis, who brought this letter to my attention, comments: "Unfortunately we learn nothing more from this concerning the relationship between Antonie and Beethoven; certainly, however, Jahn surely suspected more than he *knew* and shared with us."
51. Letter of 6 October 1812 (GM).
52. Tagebuch, No. 33.
53. Nohl, III, 13–14, 808n5.

54. Anderson, II, p. 531 (no. 570). Thayer notes the price—"ten louis d'or"—and follows it with an exclamation mark. Thayer-Deiters-Riemann, III, 520.

55. Anderson, II, 600 (no. 659, undated [1814?]). This loan appears to be the one that, according to Frau Brentano, Beethoven accepted "only after some time for use in extreme need." Nohl, III, 808n5.

56. Letter of 22 February 1819, in Adolf Sandberger, *Ausgewählte Aufsätze zur Musikgeschichte*, vol. 2 (Munich, 1924), pp. 254–256.

57. See Ulrike von Hase, "Joseph Stielers Bildnis Ludwig van Beethovens," *Musikforschung* 23 (1970): 445–449, reprinted in von Hase, *Joseph Stieler, 1781–1858: Sein Leben und sein Werk* (Munich, 1971), pp. 18–19.

58. *Katalog der mit der Beethoven-Feier zu Bonn am 11–15. Mai 1890* (Bonn, 1890), p. 20. The miniature was later given by Antonie Brentano to Edward Steinle; after his death it passed into the collection of Alexander Meyer Cohn. Its present whereabouts are not known. See also La Mara [Marie Lipsius], "Stieler's Beethoven-Bildniss," *Classisches und Romantisches aus der Tonwelt* (Leipzig, 1892), pp. 53–66; Köhler-Herre-Beck, II, 47, 50; Theodor Frimmel, *Beethoven im zeitgenössischen Bildnis* (Vienna, 1923), p. 34.

59. Anderson, III, 989 (no. 1125).

60. Anderson, III, 1014 (no. 1152).

61. Anderson, III, 1077–1078 (no. 1226). Hans-Werner Küthen deduced from several indications in the conversation books that the contact with Brentano may have survived into September 1823. See Küthen, "Quaerendo invenietis: Die Exegese eines Beethoven-Briefes," in Martin Bente, ed., *Musik-Edition-Interpretation: Gedenkschrift Günter Henle* (Munich, 1980), pp. 289–290.

62. Anderson, III, 1135 (no. 1302).

63. Anderson, II, 931–932 (no. 1062, 6 December 1821).

64. "The two sonatas in A flat and C minor are to be dedicated to Frau Brentano, née Edle von Birkenstock." Anderson, II, 983 (no. 1118). "The dedication of the C minor sonata is to be Antonie Brentano, née von Birkenstock." Anderson, III, 1003 (no. 1140).

65. Alan Tyson, *The Authentic English Editions of Beethoven* (London, 1963), p. 110, with title-page facsimile facing p. 112. See also Rolland, pp. 821–824.

66. Kinsky-Halm, pp. 224, 236, 351–352, 618. See also *BJ*, 2d ser., vol. 7 (1971), pp. 344–46 (nos. 748, 749, 752).

67. Köhler-Herre-Beck, III, 139. See also Beethoven's letter to Ries of 5 September 1823 in which he apologizes for failing to dedicate the Variations to Ries's wife. Anderson, III, 1086 (no. 1237). Indeed, a manuscript copy contains a draft dedication to Ries's wife.

68. Tagebuch, Nos. 123, 133, 139, 141.

69. Donald W. MacArdle, "The Brentano Family in Its Relations with Beethoven," *MR* 19 (1958): 10.

70. Anderson, III, 1014 (no. 1152)

71. Anderson, II, 667–668 (no. 758).

72. For her four narratives of this encounter, see Werner Vordtriede, "Bettina und Goethe in Teplitz," *Jahrbuch des Freien Deutschen Hochstifts, 1964* (Tübingen, 1964), pp. 343–365.

73. Letter of 2 August 1854, to Karl von Savigny (DSB).

74. Letter of 10 Hornung [February] 1798 (GM). Earlier this letter was mistakenly ascribed to Antonie Brentano herself. See Solomon, "Antonie Brentano and Beethoven," *M&L* 58 (1977) 165. I thank Renate Moering of GM for this new information.

75. Goldmann, p. 98. The passage is clearly derived from Goethe's novel *Elective Affinities* (1809), ch. 4.

76. The original letter is in the Beethoven-Archiv, Bonn.

77. Letter of 10 April [May] 1827 (BB).

78. All of these materials, which were preserved by Frau Brentano, are now in BB.

79. Goldmann, p. 100.

80. See Adolf Bach, *Aus Goethes Rheinischem Lebensraum: Menschen und Begebenheiten* (Neuss, 1968), pp. 418–428.

81. *Goethes Briefwechsel mit Antonie Brentano*, pp. 52–53. The allusion is to Dürer's "Hare," which Frau Brentano owned.

82. Johannes B. Diel, *Clemens Brentano: ein Lebensbild*, vol. 1 (Freiburg im Breisgau, 1877), p. 110n1.

83. Gertrud Gelderblom, "Antonie Brentano, Edle von Birkenstock," in *Festschrift Josef Stummvoll*, ed. Josef Mayerhofer and Walter Ritzer (Vienna, 1970), pp. 774–780.

84. Letter of 25 October 1820 (DSB).

85. Letter of 10 April 1821 (DSB).

86. Bettina von Arnim to Achim von Arnim, letter of October 1821, in Werner Vordtriede, ed., *Achim und Bettina in ihren Briefen: Briefwechsel Achim von Arnim und Bettina Brentano* (Frankfurt, 1961), I, 325; see also p. 354.

87. A. Niedermayer, *Frau Schöff: Johanna Antonie Brentano, ein Lebensbild* (Frankfurt, 1869), p. 12.

88. Letter of 15 July 1812, to Clemens Brentano (GM).

89. Bettina to Achim von Arnim, letters of 13 August 1824 and 1 September 1830, in *Achim und Bettina in ihren Briefen*, II 468, 893.

90. *Achim und Bettina in ihren Briefen*, I, 354.

91. *Achim und Bettina in ihren Briefen*, II, 477.

92. *Achim und Bettina in ihren Briefen*, II, 774.

93. Letter of 29 December 1845 (GM).

94. Letter of 1851, to Gunda von Savigny (DSB).

95. Letter of 21 April 1816 (GM).

96. Letter of 25 October 1820 (DSB).

97. Diel, *Clemens Brentano,* I, 110; Niedermayer, *Frau Schöff,* p. 6.

98. Undated letter [c. 1860] (DSB).

99. Letter of October 1862, to Edward von Steinle, in *Edward von Steinle's Briefwechsel mit seinen Freunden,* ed. Alphons Maria von Steinle, vol. 1 (Freiburg im Breisgau, 1897), p. 92.

100. Schrötter-Firnhaber, "Antonia Brentano," p. 105.

101. Alphons Maria von Steinle, in *Steinle's Briefwechsel,* I, 69.

13. Beethoven's *Magazin der Kunst*

1. Alexander Weinmann, *Die Wiener Verlagswerke von Franz Anton Hoffmeister,* Beiträge zur Geschichte des Alt-Wiener Musikverlages, Reihe 2, Folge 8 (Vienna, 1964), pp. 1–11. See also "Franz Anton Hoffmeister," by Weinmann, in *The New Grove Dictionary of Music and Musicians,* ed. Stanley Sadie (London, 1980), and *MGG.*

2. In Leipzig Hoffmeister published first editions of Beethoven's ops. 19–22, 39–42, 43 (overture only), 44, and 65, a later edition of op. 88, and his own arrangements of several works, including ops. 13, 20, and WoO 57. Richard S. Hill and Alan Tyson independently established that Hoffmeister's mid-December 1799 edition of op. 13 was actually the first edition. See Dorfmüller, pp. 209, 297–298.

3. Anderson, I, 42, 47, 50 (nos. 41, 44, 47; 15 December 1800, c. 15 January 1801, 22 April 1801).

4. Anderson, I, 73 (no. 57).

5. Anderson, I, 97–98 (no. 82, c. 18 September 1803).

6. Anderson, I, 18 (no. 12).

7. See Jacques Droz, *L'Allemagne et la Révolution française* (Paris, 1949), pp. 399–419; Denis Silagi, *Jakobiner in der Habsburger-Monarchie,* Wiener historische Studien, no. 6 (Vienna and Munich, 1962), pp. 45–49.

8. See H. C. Robbins Landon, *Mozart and the Masons: New Light on the Lodge "Crowned Hope"* (London, 1982), p. 66.

9. Richard Specht, *Beethoven As He Lived* (New York, 1933), p. 312.

10. Henri Brunschwig, *Enlightenment and Romanticism in Eighteenth Century Prussia* (Chicago and London, 1974), p. 185.

11. Anderson, I, 48 (no. 44, c.15 January 1801): "am 15ten (oder so was dergleichen) Jenner 1801." The letter was first published, with modernized spelling and punctuation, in C. G. S. Böhme, "Briefe von Beethoven," *Neue Zeitschrift für Musik* 6 (March 1837): 76. A diplomatic transcription, accompanied by a laid-in facsimile of the autograph, is in *L. van Beethoven:*

Seine an den Verlag von Hoffmeister und Kühnel, später C. F. Peters, Leipzig, gerichteten Briefe (Leipzig, 1927), pp. 10–12. The original reads: "nun wäre das saure Geschäft vollendet, ich nenne das So, weil ich wünschte dass es anders in der Welt sejn könnte, es sollte nur ein *Magazin der Kunst* in der Welt sejn, wo der Künstler seine Kunstwerke nur hinzugeben hätte, um zu nehmen, was er brauchte, so muss man noch ein halber Handelsmann dabej sejn, und wie findet man sich darin." The autograph, formerly in possession of C. F. Peters Verlag, has disappeared.

12. Louis Blanc, *Catéchisme des socialistes* (1849), rprt. in *Questions d'aujourd'hui et de demain*, vol. 5 (Paris, 1884), p. 216; Karl Marx, *Critique of the Gotha Programme*, ed. C. P. Dutt (New York, 1938), p. 10.

13. A significant exception is the perceptive note in Jean and Brigitte Massin, *Ludwig van Beethoven* (Paris, 1967), pp. 94–95. For other speculations, see Solomon, *Beethoven*, pp. 346–347; Jürgen Mainka, response to Solomon, "Beethoven's Class Position and Outlook," in *Bericht über den internationalen Beethoven-Kongress, Berlin 1977*, ed. Harry Goldschmidt, Karl-Heinz Köhler, and Konrad Niemann (Leipzig, 1978), p. 81.

14. See Constant Pierre, *Le Magazin de musique à l'usage des fêtes nationales et du Conservatoire* (Paris, 1895); Pierre, *Les Hymnes et chansons de la Révolution* (Paris, 1904), pp. v, 119–142.

15. Sir Thomas More, *Utopia*, trans. Ralph Robinson, Everyman's Library, p. 61. For similar systems of production and distribution see Tommaso Campanella, *Civitas solis* (1623); Vairas d'Alais, *Histoire des Sévarambes* (1677); François de la Mothe-Fénelon, *Les Aventures de Télémaque* (1699); Simon Berington, *Signior Gaudentio di Lucca* (1737).

16. Garcilaso de la Vega, *Royal Commentaries of the Incas and General History of Peru, Part One*, trans. Harold V. Livermore (Austin and London, 1966), pp. 255–256.

17. E.g. Leiden, 1715; Amsterdam, 1730; later eighteenth-century translations include Paris, 1776, 1780, 1789.

18. Garcilaso de la Vega, *Histoire des Yncas, Rois du Perou* (Amsterdam, 1737). The relevant passage contains the phrase, "il y avoit dans tout le Royaume trois sorte de Magazins" (p. 230).

19. The book was published anonymously, but its authorship was established by internal references to an earlier work by Morelly, *Naufrage des Isles flottantes, ou Basiliade* (1753). Despite the date on its title page, the *Code* actually appeared in late 1754; pirated editions followed in 1757 and 1760. For Morelly, see Richard N. Coe, "Le Philosophe Morelly: An Examination of the Political Philosophy of His Work," diss. University of Leeds, 1954; Coe, *Morelly: Ein Rationalist auf dem Wege zum Sozialismus*, Neue Beiträge zur Literaturwissenschaft, ed. Werner Krauss and Hans Mayer, vol. 13 (Berlin, 1961); Miriam B. Conant, "The Political and Social Ideas of

Morelly, with Emphasis on Early Imitators and Recent Critics," Ph.d. diss., Columbia University, 1962; Gilbert Chinard, intro. to Morelly, *Code de la nature* (Paris, 1950).

20. *Code de la nature,* ed. Chinard, pp. 286–287, trans. Fritzie P. Manuel in *The Enlightenment,* ed. Frank E. Manuel (Englewood Cliffs, N.J., 1965), p. 118.

21. Chinard, p. 291; Manuel, p. 119.

22. See Coe, "Le Philosophe Morelly," II, 839–841; Coe, *Morelly,* p. 350; Coe, "The Fortunes of the 'Code de la Nature' Between 1755 and 1848," *French Studies* 11 (1957): 117–118.

23. L'Abbé de Mably, *Collection complète des œuvres,* vol. 9 (Paris, 1794–1795), pp. 75–76.

24. Cited in Albert Mathiez, *Le Directoire* (Paris, 1934), p. 161.

25. Cited in Maurice Dommanget, ed., *Pages choisies de Babeuf* (Paris, 1935), pp. 210–211. For the influence of Morelly's ideas on Babeuf, see Coe, "La Théorie morellienne et la pratique babouviste," *Annales historiques de la Révolution française* 30 (1958): 38–50.

26. *Le Tribun du Peuple,* 2/35 (1795–1796), cited in Dommanget, p. 261. For the similarity between Beethoven's phrase and the two preceding quotations from Babeuf, see Massin and Massin, pp. 94–95.

27. Victor Advielle, *Histoire de Gracchus Babeuf et du babouvisme, d'après de nombreux documents inédits* (Paris, 1884), II, 58–59, trans. John Anthony Scott, *The Defense of Gracchus Babeuf* ([Andover, Mass., 1976]), p. 79. Lichtenberger wryly comments on Babeuf's demurral: "the only difference is that a chapter of moral philosophy had become a program of social revolution." André Lichtenberger, *Le Socialisme et la Révolution française* (Paris, 1899; rprt. Geneva, 1970), p. 221.

28. Advielle, II, 50, trans. Scott, pp. 68–69. This is apparently Babeuf's own formulation, attributed by him to Mably in error or, perhaps, for reasons of discretion. But it may also be Babeuf's free paraphrase and elaboration of a passage in Mably, *De la législation,* p. 84.

29. Separate publications: Amsterdam, 1776, 1777; Lausanne, 1777; Italian trans., 1797. Collected editions: London, 1789, with several rprts.; Toulouse, 1791, with several rprts,; Lyon, 1792; Paris, 1794–1795; Paris 1797.

30. Part four of the *Défense*—not containing the passages relative to this investigation—was printed in the court record: *Débats du procès instruit par la Haute-Cour de Justice contre Drouet, Baboeuf, et autres* (Paris, 1797), IV, 362–378. The complete *Défense* was first published in Advielle, II, 1–322. There are further references to the "Magazins" in the *Fragment d'un projet de décret économique,* probably written by Philippe Buonarotti and first published in his *Conspiration pour l'égalité dite de Babeuf* (Brussels, 1828), II, 305–319.

31. "Gracchus Baboeuf," *Frankreich im Jahre 1796: Aus den Briefen deutscher Männer in Paris*, III/9, 259–261; Fontanes, "Ueber die von Babeuf und die von Villeurnois und Brottier angezettelten Verschwörungen," *Frankreich im Jahre 1797*, IV/3, 319–334.

32. *Minerva: Ein Journal historischen und politischen Inhalts* (1796), II, 323–325, 562–566; III, 1–15, 102–134, 162–179, 291–324; IV, 120–130, 532–548; (1797), I, 515–532; III, 125–131, 179–182. See also Droz, p. 280; Walter Markov, "Babeuf, le babouvisme et les intellectuels allemands (1796–1797)," in *Babeuf et les problèmes du babouvisme: Colloque international de Stockholm, 21 août 1960* (Paris, 1963), pp. 188–193; Claude Mazauric, "Bilan des études sur l'histoire du mouvement et de l'idéologie babouviste," *Rivista storica del socialismo* 5 (1962):78.

33. There is no need to assume that Beethoven's exposure to French radical ideas must have come through his (in any event still unconfirmed) contacts with the personnel of the French Embassy at Vienna during General Bernadotte's brief ambassadorship for several months in early 1798. The representatives of the Directory were scarcely Babouvists. Bernadotte himself for reasons of discretion publicly proclaimed himself "a Republican both by principle and conviction" who would, "to the moment of my death, oppose all Royalists and enemies to the Directory." Letter of 6 September 1797 to editor of *Le Grondeur*, in Sir D. Plunket Barton, *Bernadotte: The First Phase, 1763–1799* (New York, 1914), p. 242. Yet he readily tailored his ideology to the advancement of his career, as demonstrated in his facile transition to monarch of Sweden and in his leadership of Sweden's armies against France in the decisive Battle of Leipzig of October 1813.

34. See e.g. Anderson, I, 9, 360; III, 1139 (nos. 6, 351, 1306; c. 26 October 1793, to Christian Gottlob Neefe; 28 February 1812, to Breitkopf & Härtel; 9 September 1824, to Hans Nägeli).

35. Anderson, III, 1165–1166, 1 January 1825 (no. 1343, to Karl Wilhelm Henning).

36. Beethoven's entire estate totaled 10,000 florins. By way of comparison, Carl Czerny, another Viennese bachelor composer, left 80,000 florins at his death. See *Berliner Musik Zeitung Echo* (1857), pp. 239–240. The contrast is striking, even though Czerny lived longer than Beethoven and had no nephew to support.

37. Anderson, III, 1110, (no. 1266, 25 February 1824).

38. Tagebuch, No. 100.

39. Anderson, I, 18 (no. 12). For the background of events alluded to by Beethoven, see Silagi, pp. 177–183; Ernst Wangermann, *From Joseph II to the Jacobin Trials*, Oxford Historical Series, ed. R. W. Southern et al., 2d ser. (London, 1959), pp. 133–187. The repression of political dissent had been so successful that by 1801 the Ministry of Police reported with satisfaction: "The French Revolution had first been depicted in such attractive colours

... that young men were swept off their feet in admiration of it ... If the welfare of the State at that time inexorably demanded ruthless measures to prevent the spread of the pernicious disease, the firm application of these measures has had the desired effect—so much so that since then no more revolutionary movement was to be perceived in any part of the Monarchy." Wangermann, p. 186.

40. Anderson, I, 43 (no. 41). See also Solomon, *Beethoven*, pp. 130–131, 136–137.

41. In *Lectures on the Philosophy of History*, Hegel noted: "France has a sense of reality, of accomplishment, because ideas there are translated more directly into action ... In Germany the same principle aroused the interest of consciousness but was developed in a theoretical manner." And in "Contribution to the Critique of Hegel's *Philosophy of Right:* Introduction," Marx bitterly observed that "the real life embryo of the German nation has grown so far only inside its *cranium*. The Germans have *thought* what other nations have *done*." The criticism of German "apathy" was widespread among German intellectuals during Beethoven's early manhood.

42. Anderson, I, 474, 445 (nos. 502, 462; c. autumn 1814, to Johann Nepomuk Kanka; 13 February 1814, to Franz Brunsvik).

43. Anderson, I, 58 (no. 51, 29 June 1801). More than a decade later, Beethoven continued to regret that he had "been compelled ... to set bounds to my inclination, nay, more, to the duty which I had imposed on myself, i.e., to work by means of my art for human beings in distress." Anderson, I, 474 (no. 502, c. autumn 1814, to Kanka).

44. Anderson, III, 1451 (App. I [6]).

45. Anderson, I, 6 (no. 4, 22 May 1793). The recipient was identified as Theodora Johanna Vocke (1749–1795) by Max Unger. See Joseph Schmidt-Görg, "Ein Schiller-Zitat Beethovens in neuer Sicht," in *Musik—Edition—Interpretation: Gedenkschrift Günter Henle*, ed. Martin Bente (Munich, 1980), pp. 423–426. Anderson, II, 822 (no. 955, 29 July 1819).

46. Tagebuch, No. 137; Anderson, III, 1223 (no. 1404, c. July 1825, to Karl van Beethoven). References to his audience as the "rabble" (*der Pöbel*) also occur in Beethoven's letters. See e.g. Anderson, I, 73 (no. 57, 8 April 1802, to Hoffmeister).

47. Tagebuch, No. 34.

48. Köhler-Herre-Beck, I, 252.

49. Jean-Jacques Rousseau, *Discourse on the Origin and Foundation of Inequality among Mankind*, in *The Social Contract and Discourse on the Origin ... of Inequality*, ed. Lester G. Crocker (New York, 1967), pp. 175, 211, 220.

50. "Analysis of the Doctrine of Babeuf," in Buonarroti, *Conspiration*, II, 137–150, trans. in Buonarotti, *Babeuf's Conspiracy for Equality* (Lon-

don, 1836), pp. 318–326; Anderson, I, 32 (no. 30, c. 1798, to Nikolaus Zmeskall).

51. Buonarroti, *Conspiration*, II, 132; Buonarroti, *Babeuf's Conspiracy*, p. 315; Advielle, II, 45; Scott, *The Defense of Gracchus Babeuf*, pp. 62, 92. In partial extenuation, Morelly described his system as one of *"inégalité harmonique"* and Babeuf's stated goal was *"l'égalité des jouissances."* See Albert Soboul, "Lumières, critique social et utopie," in *Histoire générale du socialisme*, ed. Jacques Droz, vol 1 (Paris, 1972), p. 133; Buonarroti, *Conspiration*, I, 213.

14. Beethoven and Schiller

1. Hans Vaihinger, "Zwei Quellenfunde zu Schillers philosophischer Entwicklung," *Kant-Studien* 10 (1905): 386–389; Gotthold Deile, *Freimaurer Lieder als Quellen zu Schillers Lied "An die Freude"* (Leipzig, 1907).

2. Körner wrote a second setting of the "Ode to Joy." See Karl Goedeke, ed., *Briefwechsel zwischen Schiller und Körner*, 2d ed. (Leipzig, 1878), I, 368 (letter of 23 April 1790).

3. For settings of "An die Freude," see Julius Blaschke, "Schillers Gedichte in der Musik," *Neue Zeitschrift für Musik* 72 (1905): 397–401. See also Franz Brandstaeter, *Schillers Lyrik im Verhältnisse zu ihrer musikalischen Behandlung* (Danzig, 1863). For settings of Schiller's dramas, see Albert Schäfer, *Historisches und systematisches Verzeichnis sämtlicher Tonwerke zu den Dramen Schillers, Goethes, Shakespeares, Kleists, und Körners* (Leipzig, 1886).

4. Thayer-Forbes, pp. 120–121 (letter of 26 January 1793). Beethoven's "Feuerfarb," op. 52, no. 2, is set to Sophie Mereau's text concerning the harmony of beauty and truth.

5. For Fischenich, see Max Braubach, *Die erste Bonner Universität und ihre Professoren* (Bonn, 1947), pp. 155–159, 199; Braubach, *Eine Jugendfreundin Beethovens: Babette Koch-Belderbusch und ihr Kreis* (Bonn, 1948), pp. 48–49.

6. Thayer-Forbes, p. 31. *Kabale und Liebe* also may have been performed. See Nohl, I, 136.

7. Hans Gerstinger, *Ludwig van Beethovens Stammbuch* (Bielefeld and Leipzig, 1927), pp. 17–18, 21. The entries are those of Klemmer, the widow Koch, and her son. The last also includes a quotation from Schiller's "Zürcher See."

8. Anderson, I, 6 (no. 4). The entry was in the album of Theodora Johanna Vocke.

9. Anderson, I, 27 (no. 21), trans. from Thayer-Forbes, p. 192. For two additional album leaves in Beethoven's handwriting containing verses from "An die Freude," see Nohl, *Brevier*, p. 105.

10. There is only a sparse literature on Beethoven's relationship to Schiller. The most thorough, though long outdated, study is A. C. Kalischer, *Beethoven und seine Zeitgenossen* (Berlin and Leipzig, c. 1908–1910), IV, 101–130. For the influence of Schiller's thought on Beethoven, see the standard works by Ludwig Schiedermair, Arnold Schmitz, Jean Boyer, Adolf Sandberger, and esp. Otto Baensch, *Aufbau und Sinn des Chorfinales in Beethovens neunter Symphonie* (Berlin and Leipzig, 1930), pp. 22–30. For Schiller and music in general, see Hans H. Knudsen, *Schiller und die Musik* (Greifswald, 1908); R. M. Longyear, *Schiller and Music* (Chapel Hill, N.C., 1966); *MGG*, XI, 1719–1720; Jürgen Mainka, "Schiller und die Musik: Eine Literaturübersicht," in *Wissenschaftliche Zeitschrift der Friedrich-Schiller-Universität Jena*, vol. 5, *Gesellschafts- und Sprachwissenschaftliche Reihe*, no. 1, pp. 217–219.

11. Andreas Streicher, *Schillers Flucht von Stuttgart und Aufenthalt in Mannheim* (Stuttgart, 1836), p. 215.

12. N II, 479; *Simrock Jahrbuch* 2 (1929):26 (letter of 13 September 1803).

13. Anderson, I, 18 (no. 12, 2 August 1794). The lieder were refused by Simrock. They were published as opus 52 in Vienna by Kunst- und Industrie-Comptoir in 1805. On another level, the large number of prior settings of "An die Freude" may have discouraged Beethoven from offering yet another straightforward setting for voice and piano. In view of the competition—which eventually included such well-known composers as Zelter, Rellstab, Zumsteeg, Romberg, Schobart, Winter, Kanne, and Gyrowetz—Beethoven would have had to offer something rather special.

14. Thomas Mann, *Last Essays* (New York, 1959), p. 64.

15. *Briefwechsel zwischen Schiller und Körner*, II, 356; trans. in Leonard Simpson, *Correspondence of Schiller with Körner* (London, 1849), III, 218.

16. *Briefwechsel*, II, 356, trans. p. 219.

17. *Briefwechsel*, II, 358–359, trans. p. 221 (letter of 21 October, 1800). Vaihinger attributes Schiller's disenchantment with the ode to its pre-Kantian character. *Kant-Studien* 10 (1905):387.

18. Thayer-Forbes, p. 472.

19. Anderson, I, 241–242 (no. 224, 8 August 1809). See also Anderson, I, 243 (no. 226, 19 September 1809, to B&H).

20. Leitzmann, II, 380. See also Eveline Bartlitz, ed., *Die Beethoven-Sammlung in der Musikabteilung der Deutschen Staatsbibliothek: Verzeichnis* (Berlin, 1970), pp. 211–212.

21. Anderson, I, 313 (no. 296, 10 February 1811). The quotation is from *The Maid of Orleans*, act 5, sc. 2. Beethoven also refers to Schiller's poem "Die Flüsse" in this letter.

22. Ignaz von Seyfried, *L. v. Beethovens Studien* (Vienna, 1832), App., p. 20. The quotation is from *The Maid of Orleans*, act 5, sc. 14.

23. Tagebuch, Nos. 111, 112, and 118.

24. Matthias Artaria wrote in a conversation book of 1825: "Have you read 'Ueber die Sendung Moses' by Schiller?" Köhler-Herre-Beck, VIII, 282.

25. Leitzmann, I, 319; Kerst, II, 184. Nevertheless, Beethoven did not respond to urgings that he set such works as *Fiesco* or "Burgschaft" to music. See Köhler-Herre-Beck, II, 323; Kerst, II, 76–77. For additional reminiscences by contemporaries, see Kerst, I, 206–207 (Anselm Hüttenbrenner); I, 278 (Braun von Braunthal); II, 62 (Johann R. Schultz); II, 76–77 (Ferdinand Leopold von Biedenfeld); Ludwig Spohr, *Autobiography* (London, 1865), I, 198–199 (Spohr); Ludwig Nohl, *Beethoven nach den Schilderungen seiner Zeitgenossen* (Stuttgart, 1877), p. 110 (Aloys Weissenbach). Not located is a reported reference by Johann Sporschil.

26. Köhler-Herre-Beck, II, 105; Prod'homme, *Cahiers de Conversation* (Paris, 1946), p. 428.

27. Köhler-Herre-Beck, IV, 47.

28. Köhler-Herre-Beck, II, 123.

29. Leitzmann, II, 382. One wonders if any other books in Beethoven's estate actually belonged to or were intended for his nephew.

30. In this period "the question of priorities, of sources and influences, is hopelessly entangled . . . [There existed] a community of thought and speculation which accounts for the wealth of crosscurrents and crossfertilization" among the leading German thinkers of the period. René Wellek, *A History of Modern Criticism*, vol. 1 (New Haven, 1955), p. 228.

31. Mann, p. 19.

32. Thayer-Forbes, p. 1046. Both men derived much gratification from popular approval. Schiller commented that "the assertion so commonly made that the public degrades art, is not well founded . . . [The people] derive the greatest pleasure from what is judicious and true." Schiller, "The Use of the Chorus in Tragedy." Beethoven, basking in the popularity that attended his *Wellington's Victory*, wrote: "One certainly writes nicer music when one writes for the public." Tagebuch, No. 16.

33. *The Robbers*, act 1, sc. 2. This and the following translations are from *Works of Friedrich Schiller*, ed. N. H. Dole (Boston, 1902).

34. Anderson, III, 1243 (no. 1423, August 1825).

35. Anderson, I, 32 (no. 30, 1798, to Zmeskall).

36. Schiller, Preface to *The Robbers*.

37. Schiller, "On the Sublime"; Anderson, I, 60 (no. 51, 29 June 1801, to Wegeler); Tagebuch, No. 26; *Iliad* 24:49.

38. Anderson, I, 68 (no. 54, 16 November 1801, to Wegeler); Schiller, "On the Sublime."

39. Schiller, "On the Pathetic."

40. Tagebuch, No. 136; Schiller, *Letters on the Aesthetic Education of Man* (1795), no. 25.

41. Schiller, "The Use of the Chorus in Tragedy."

42. See Thayer-Forbes, p. 888.

43. The only evidence to the contrary is several conversation-book references of 1825–1826 to general histories of aesthetics that include descriptions of Schiller's aesthetics. Baensch, p. 27. For evaluations of Schiller's aesthetics, see Wellek, I, 232–255; Georg Lukács, *Goethe and His Age* (New York, 1969), pp. 101–135; Herbert Marcuse, *Eros and Civilization* (New York, n.d.), pp. 164–176.

44. See esp. Schiller, *Letters on the Aesthetic Education of Man*, no. 9.

45. Schiller, *Naive and Sentimental Poetry:* "The Idyll."

46. Ibid.

47. For Beethoven and Schiller, see also Solomon, *Beethoven*, pp. 38–39, 309–314.

15. The Quest for Faith

1. Ludwig Nohl, *Eine stille Liebe zu Beethoven* (Leipzig, 1902), p. 63.

2. Contrary to Thayer's assumption of an earlier date, this took place between 1790 and 1792. See Joseph Schmidt-Görg, *Ein neuer Fund in dem Skizzenbüchern Beethovens: Die Lamentationen des Propheten Jeremias*, in *BJ*, 2d ser., vol. 3 (1959), pp. 107–110.

3. Schiedermair, p. 327.

4. Max Braubach, *Die erste Bonner Universität und ihre Professoren*, (Bonn, 1947), p. 110. For the religious character of the *Aufklärung*, see Ernst Cassirer, *Die Philosophie der Aufklärung* (Tübingen, 1932), ch. 4, trans. as *The Philosophy of the Enlightenment* (Princeton, 1951); Ernst Troeltsch, *Deismus* und *Aufklärung*, in *Gesammelte Schriften*, vol. 4 (Tübingen, 1925), pp. 370ff; for a contrary view, see Peter Gay, *The Enlightenment: An Interpretation*, vol. 1: *The Rise of Modern Paganism* (New York, 1966), pp. 347–351.

5. Adolf Bernhard Marx, *Ludwig van Beethoven, Leben und Schaffen*, vol. 1 (Berlin, 1863), p. 22n.

6. Anderson, I, 73 (no. 57).

7. Martin Cooper, *Beethoven, The Last Decade, 1817–1827* (London, 1970), p. 106.

8. Anderson, I, 60 (no. 51); I, 63 (no. 53).

9. Anderson, I, 60 (no. 51).

10. Anderson, III, 1353 (App. A).

11. Signs of this identification emerge in Beethoven's correspondence from time to time, as in "Thanks to my charming disciples and colleagues, I have drunk to the full a cup of bitter sorrow and have already won a crown of martyrdom in art." Anderson, I, 474 (no. 502).

12. For a valuable but incautious approach to this issue, see Ludwig

Schiedermair, *Die Gestaltung weltanschaulicher Ideen in der Vokalmusik Beethovens*, Veröffentlichungen des Beethoven-Hauses in Bonn, vol. 10 (Leipzig, 1934).

13. On a sheet originally in the Artaria Collection, presently on loan to the Department of Manuscripts, BL, from the heirs of Stefan Zweig. See Nohl, *Brevier*, p. 104; *Führer durch die Beethoven Zentenar-Ausstellung der Stadt Wien 1927* (Vienna, 1927), no. 529.

14. From a sketch leaf of September 1815, present location unknown. See *Katalog der mit der Beethoven-Feier zu Bonn am 11–15 Mai 1890 verbundenen Ausstellung . . .* (Bonn, 1890), no. 268.

15. Anderson, I, 250, 235 (nos. 232, 220).

16. Anderson, I, 192 (no. 169).

17. Christoph Christian Sturm, *Betrachtungen über die Werke Gottes im Reiche der Natur und der Vorsehung auf alle Tage des Jahres*, 2 vols. (Reutlingen, 1811). Beethoven's copy is in DSB, autogr. 40,2.

18. Schmitz, *Romantisch*, p. 91.

19. Beethoven reportedly called Jesus "nothing but a crucified Jew." Josef Blöchlinger, cited in Theodor von Frimmel, *Beethoven-Studien*, vol. 2 (Leipzig, 1905–1906), p. 117. A conversation with his nephew, Karl, implies that Beethoven "n'admettait la divinité de Jésus-Christ que comme un symbole ou comme un mystère et non pas comme un fait établi." Jean Chantavoine, *Musiciens et Poètes* (Paris, 1912), p. 66.

20. Kerst, II, 147–148, trans. Thayer-Forbes, p. 988.

21. Anton Schindler, *Biographie von Ludwig van Beethoven* (Münster, 1860), II, 28, trans. Schindler-MacArdle, p. 248.

22. Anderson, I, 197 (no. 175).

23. Tagebuch, No. 103 (1816).

24. Tagebuch, No. 138 (1817).

25. Charlotte Moscheles, ed., *The Life of Moscheles*, vol. 1 (London, 1873), p. 15.

26. Heinrich Heine, *Religion and Philosophy in Germany* (New York, 1959), p. 137.

27. Anderson, II, 923–924 (no. 1056); Köhler-Herre-Beck, ed., I, 352. For Beethoven and religion, see Schmitz, *Romantisch*, pp. 82–101; Cooper, pp. 105–119; Jean Boyer, *Le "romantisme" de Beethoven* (Paris, 1938), pp. 359–381; Rolland, pp. 667–749; Schmitz, *Zur Frage nach Beethovens Weltanschauung und ihrem musikalischen Ausdruck*, in Schmitz, ed., *Beethoven und die Gegenwart* (Berlin and Bonn, 1937), pp. 266–293; Schiedermair, pp. 327ff; Frimmel, *Handbuch*, I, 178–179; II, 61–62; Karl Weinmann, "Beethovens Verhältnis zur Religion," in *Beethoven-Zentenarfeier Wien . . . 1927: Internationaler musik-historischer Kongress* (Vienna, 1927), pp. 19–24.

28. Boyer, p. 380. Sailer was not a rationalist or an Enlightened thinker.

See Schmitz, *Zur Frage nach Beethovens Weltanschauung*, p. 273.

29. Tagebuch, No. 63a (1815).

30. Tagebuch, No. 160 (1818).

31. Tagebuch, No. 41 (1815).

32. Tagebuch, No. 93b (1816).

33. Tagebuch, No. 171. The passage is from Sturm, II, 565 (entry for 29 December).

34. Tagebuch, No. 73.

35. Tagebuch, No. 12 (1815). Beethoven copied the German translation by Johann Friedrich Kleuker, in Sir William Jones et al., *Abhandlungen über die Geschichte und Alterthümer, die Künste, Wissenschaften und Literatur Asiens*, vol. 3 (Riga, 1797), pp. 412–415.

36. Tagebuch, No. 64a (1815). *Bhagavad-Gita*, ch. 3, line 7.

37. Tagebuch, No. 94b (1816).

38. Anderson, II, 813 (no. 948).

39. Anderson, II, 578 (no. 633).

40. Tagebuch, No. 78 (1816).

41. Ludwig Feuerbach, *The Essence of Christianity* (New York, 1957), pp. 262–263.

42. Wegeler Collection, Coblenz; facs. in Stephan Ley, *Beethovens Leben in authentischen Bildern und Texten* (Berlin, 1925), p. 129; Robert Bory, *Ludwig van Beethoven: His Life and Work in Pictures* (London, 1966), p. 202. These inscriptions were known to most educated persons in Beethoven's time and even found their way into the ritual of Freemasonry. Beethoven copied them from Schiller, "Die Sendung Moses," *Thalia* 10 (1791): 17–18, which is a gloss, if not a plagiarism, of Voltaire, "Des Rites Egyptiens . . . ," *Oeuvres de Voltaire*, vol. 15, ed. M. Beuchot (Paris, 1829), pp. 102–106.

43. Sterba, p. 93; Solomon, *Beethoven*, pp. 156–157.

44. Ernst Cassirer, *Language and Myth* (New York, 1946), p. 77; Cassirer, *The Myth of the State* (New Haven and London, 1946), p. 92.

45. Actually the passage from *Exodus* may also be translated, "I shall be who I shall be," and this gives a futuristic, Messianic character to the Hebrew phrase as well. See Ernst Bloch, *Das Prinzip Hoffnung*, vol. 3 (Frankfurt am Main, 1959), p. 1475.

46. Cassirer, *Philosophy of the Enlightenment*, p. 165.

47. Tagebuch, No. 105b (1816). The entry is from Kant, *Allgemeine Naturgeschichte und Theorie des Himmels* (Zeitz, 1798), pp. 121–122.

48. Anderson, II, 920 (no. 1054). Cf. the Heiligenstadt Testament: "Oh when—oh when, Almighty God—shall I be able to hear and feel this echo again in the temple of Nature and in contact with humanity." Anderson, III, 1354.

49. Anderson, II, 922 (no. 1056).

50. N II, 163.

51. Köhler-Herre-Beck, I, 211.

52. See e.g. Anderson, I, 100 (no. 85); Tagebuch, No. 114 (citation from Pliny); Schünemann, III, 160.

53. N II, 375, 378; Dagmar Weise, ed., *Ein Skizzenbuch zur Pastoralsymphonie Op. 68 . . .*, vol. 1 (Bonn, 1961), p. 17; Thayer-Deiters-Riemann, V, 267, trans. Thayer-Forbes, p. 947.

16. Beethoven's Tagebuch

1. Dagmar von Busch-Weise, ed., "Beethovens Jugendtagebuch," *Studien zur Musikwissenschaft* 25 (1962): 68–88.

2. See, e.g., N II, 89, 132, 163, 319–320, 346, 353.

3. Berlin, DSB, autograph 35, 87a–c (calendars for 1819, 1822—not 1820, as Schindler wrote—and 1823).

4. Anderson, I, 131 (no. 110, spring 1805, to Josephine Deym).

5. Anderson, I, 246 (no. 228, 2 November 1809, to B & H), trans. revised.

6. Thayer, I, x.

7. Ibid.

8. According to the accession book of the manuscript collection (I, 71b) the *Stammbuch* was received on 11 March 1871: "Von Herrn Gust. Nottebohm in Wien gekauft um 20 fl. ö. Wo. Suppl. 2816." See Hans Gerstinger, *Beethovens Stammbuch* (Bielefeld and Leipzig, 1927), pp. 25–26; N I, 138–144; *AMZ*, 3rd ser., 6 (1871): 65–68, 266. There is no basis for the belief that Anton Gräffer's brother, Franz Gräffer, ever owned the *Stammbuch*. So far as is known, he had only a copy of Waldstein's entry, which he believed to be a letter rather than part of an album. For the provenance of the Heiligenstadt Testament, see Hedwig M. v. Asow, ed., *Ludwig van Beethoven, Heiligenstädter Testament* (Hamburg, 1952), pp. 7–13.

9. Charlotte Moscheles, ed., *Aus Moscheles' Leben* (Leipzig, 1872), I, 168, trans. as *The Life of Moscheles* (London, 1873), I, 181. The reference is to Johann Aloys Schlosser, *Ludwig van Beethoven's Biographie* (Prague, 1828).

10. Anton Gräffer was identified, and his role in the projected "Viennese biography" established, in Clemens Brenneis, "Zum Fischhof-Manuskript," *Bericht über den Internationalen Beethoven-Kongress, Berlin 1977*, ed. Harry Goldschmidt, Karl-Heinz Köhler, and Konrad Niemann (Leipzig, 1978), pp. 299–306; Brenneis, "Das Fischhof-Manuskript: Zur Frühgeschichte der Beethoven-Biographik," *Zu Beethoven* I, 90–116. See also Franz Gräffer and J. J. H. Czikann, ed., *Oesterreichische National-Encyklopädie*, vol. 6 (Vienna, 1837), p. 462; Georg Kinsky, "Zur Versteigerung von Beethovens musikalischem Nachlass," *NBJ* 6 (1936): 66–86; Douglas Johnson, "The Artaria Collection of Beethoven Manuscripts: A New Source," *BS*, I, 179–180. The

unpublished manuscript of Gräffer's autobiography is in the Wiener Stadt-und Landesbibliothek (Jc 138011, S. 43d); for extracts and further details, see the German edition of the Tagebuch (BB, 1988). It was Gräffer who introduced Rossini to Beethoven.

11. A copy of the announcement, published in the *Oesterreichische Beobachter*, is with the Fischhof manuscript (it also appeared in the *Wiener Sammler*). Clemens Brenneis has furnished me with a variant copy, lacking the final paragraph of the Fischhof copy. Further copies are in Berlin, DSB, autograph 47b. Hotschevar's "Nachricht an Ludwig van Beethovens Gönner, Freunde und Verehrer" (Report to Beethoven's patrons, friends, and admirers), with its promise that a "worthy biography" would soon be forthcoming, appeared in Bäuerle's *Theaterzeitung*, 6 October 1827, p. 492, partly reprinted in Thayer-Deiters-Riemann, V, 500. It too exists as a separate, variant offprint. Berlin, DSB, Jahn *Nachlass*.

12. For Fuch's copy, see Georg Kinsky, ed., *Manuskripte, Briefe, Dokumente von Scarlatti bis Stravinsky: Katalog der Musikautographen-Sammlung Louis Koch* (Stuttgart, 1953), p. 137. For Grasnick's, see Hans-Günter Klein, *Ludwig van Beethoven: Autographe und Abschriften: Katalog*, Staatsbibliothek Preussischer Kulturbesitz, Kataloge der Musikabteilung, ser. 1: Handschriften, vol. 2 (Berlin, 1975), p. 308. Fuchs also copied eighteen entries from Gräffer's copy: nos. 18, 25, 26, 27, 31, 35, 36, 39, 40, 43, 85, 98, 116, 135, 151, 153, 155–156, and 161.

13. See Dagmar Weise, ed., *Beethoven: Ein Skizzenbuch zur Pastoralsymphonie . . . Erster Teil* (Bonn, 1961), pp. 7–8; Alan Tyson, "A Reconstruction of the Pastoral Symphony Sketchbook," *BS*, I, 66, 88. The transfer of Gräffer's Beethoven collection to Gassner is confirmed by Aloys Fuchs. See Kinsky, p. 137. It is also confirmed by a letter from Gassner to Fuchs of 23 December 1842. See Brenneis, "Zum Fischhof-Manuskript," p. 301; Brenneis, "Das Fischhof-Manuskript," p. 101. According to Fuchs's letter to Schindler of 9 September 1852, Gräffer gave Gassner, who was related to him, "the whole package as a present." Martin Staehelin, "Aus der Welt der frühen Beethoven-'Forschung,'" *Musik-Edition-Interpretation: Gedenkschrift Günter Henle*, ed. Martin Bente (Munich, 1980), p. 440.

14. Letter of 4 November 1843 from Holz to Gassner, in Ludwig Nohl, ed., *Briefe Beethovens* (Stuttgart, 1865), p. 324. See also Kalischer-Shedlock, II, 438–439. Holz set a deadline of August 1844, which he subsequently extended. Thayer-Deiters-Riemann, V, 190.

15. See Martin Staehelin, "Die Beethoven-Materialien im Nachlass von Ludwig Nohl," *BJ*, 2d ser., vol. 10 (1983), pp. 201–219.

16. See Richard Schaal, "Fischhof, Joseph," *MGG*, vol. 4 (Kassel, 1955), cols. 276–277.

17. Eduard Hüffer, *Anton Felix Schindler* (Münster, 1909), pp. 20, 25.

18. Berlin, DSB, autograph 47a; Douglas Johnson, "The Artaria Col-

lection," p. 179; Fischhof, "Einige Gedanken über die Auffassung von Instrumentalkompositionen in Hinsicht des Zeitmasses, namentlich bei Beethoven'schen Werken," *Caecilia* 26 (1847): 94, quoted in Brenneis, "Das Fischhof-Manuskript," p. 92.

19. Brenneis, "Das Fischhof-Manuskript," pp. 103–108.

20. Ludwig Nohl, "Die Fischhofsche Handschrift: Ein Beitrag zu Beethoven's Leben," *Im neuen Reich* 9 (1879): 313–330. The article makes no reference to the Gräffer-Gassner copy.

21. Albert Leitzmann, ed., *Beethovens persönliche Aufzeichnungen* (Leipzig, n.d. [1918]), pp. 9–39, 49–59; Leitzmann, II, 241–266, 365–374.

22. Nohl, *Briefe Beethovens*, p. 325n.

23. Nohl, *Die Beethoven-Feier*, p. 52.

24. Nohl, III, 814n12. But Tagebuch material cited in vols. 1–2 derives from the Fischhof manuscript. See Nohl, II, 555.

25. Leitzmann, II, 385–386.

26. Clemens Brenneis, personal communication.

27. Nohl, *Die Beethoven-Feier*, p. 52.

28. Clemens Brenneis, "Das Fischhof-Manuskript in der Deutschen Staatsbibliothek," *Zu Beethoven* II, 86–87.

29. Thayer, I, ix; Brenneis, "Das Fischhof-Manuskript," p. 112n3.

Credits

I am grateful to the editors and publishers of the following publications for extending permission to reprint:

American Imago (Association for Applied Psychoanalysis and Wayne State University Press): "The Dreams of Beethoven" and "Thoughts on Beethoven's Deafness."

Beethoven Studies 2 (Oxford University Press): "Beethoven and His Nephew: A Reappraisal."

Beethoven Studies 3 (Cambridge University Press): "Beethoven's Tagebuch of 1812–1818."

Beethoven, Performers, and Critics, ed. Bruce Carr and Robert Winter (Wayne State University Press): "Beethoven and Schiller."

Beethoven-Jahrbuch (Beethovenhaus, Bonn): "Beethoven: The Quest for Faith."

Music & Letters (Oxford University Press): "Beethoven's Creative Process: A Two-Part Invention" and "Antonie Brentano and Beethoven."

Music Review: "The Creative Periods of Beethoven."

Musical Quarterly (New York: Macmillan, Inc.): "Beethoven's Birth Year" (vol. 56, 1970: 702–710) and "Beethoven: The Nobility Pretense" (vol. 61, 1975: 272–294). Reproduced by permission of the publisher.

Nineteenth Century Music (University of California Press): "Thoughts on Biography" (vol. 5, 1982: 268–276; © 1982 by The Regents of the University of California); "Beethoven's *Magazin der Kunst*" (vol. 7, 1984: 199–208; © 1984 by The Regents of the University of California); "Beethoven's Ninth Symphony: A Search for Order" (vol. 10, 1986: 3–23; © 1986 by The Regents of the University of California). All are reprinted by permission of the Regents.

"Beethoven's Ninth Symphony: A Search for Order" was presented in 1984 as the fourth annual Martin Bernstein Lecture at New York University, New York; an earlier draft was given in 1984 at Lewis Lockwood's seminar on Beethoven's symphonies at Harvard University.

354

"Thoughts on Biography" was presented in 1981 at the Colloquium on "Art and Biography" at Gross-Kochberg, German Democratic Republic.

"Beethoven's Creative Process: A Two-Part Invention" was presented in 1980 at the annual meeting of the American Musicological Society, Denver.

"Beethoven and Schiller" was presented in 1977 at the Detroit Beethoven Congress.

"The Quest for Faith" was presented in 1977 at the Beethoven Symposium in honor of William S. Newman at the University of North Carolina at Chapel Hill and Duke University.

"The Creative Periods of Beethoven" was presented in 1972 at the annual meeting of the American Musicological Society, Dallas.

Index of the
Tagebuch

This is an index to Beethoven's manuscript; the introduction and annotations to the Tagebuch are indexed in the General Index, page 363. Boldface figures refer to the numbering of the Tagebuch entries; a question mark before the entry number indicates an unconfirmed reference to the topic.

Index of
Compositions

Boldface figures refer to the numbering of the Tagebuch entries. For further details, see Index of the Tagebuch, page 356.

General
Index